C000137053

DOWN M_____
LANE

A PIECEMEAL HISTORY
OF BOSTON
AND THE SURROUNDING VILLAGES

BY

PAUL MOULD

First published in 2002

PUBLISHED BY
PAUL MOULD PUBLISHING

Copyright   Paul Mould   2002

All rights reserved. No part of this publication may be reproduced, stored in a retrieval system or transmitted in any form by any means, electronic, mechanical, recording, photocopying or otherwise without the prior permission of the publisher and copyright holder.

ISBN   0 9528708 5 1

PRINTED IN GREAT BRITAIN BY
THE CITY PRESS LEEDS LTD.

INTRODUCTION

This book is a compilation of the columns I have written in the local press over the last eight years. They have not been placed in any order, either chronologically or geographically.

To keep the number of pages to a reasonable level, they have not been divided into chapters or a new page started for each individual column, so you will often find yourself reading about one subject at the beginning of the page and something entirely different by the end of that page.

I apologise for this but there is an index to help you find more quickly references to people, places and events. I think you will find it is a book to dip into, when you have time to spare and hopefully you will find something of interest.

The first half of the book is based largely on my personal memories of growing up in Boston during and after the Second World War: schooling, sport, work and National Service. The second half concerns more the history of Boston and the surrounding villages, the local businesses and industries and the local celebrities and characters, who have been born in Boston or have had connections with the area.

I must also apologise for certain memories being repeated but I hope it does not spoil your reading. I have not included the town of Boston in the index, as it appears on almost every page.

I make no excuse for extolling the virtues of Boston, for as I say in the book: "I have yet to find a city, town or district, which in any way compares with Boston, either geographically, socially or, which becomes more important with passing years, climatically".
The index was prepared before the final proof, so some of the page numbers may have altered but the references will be found on either the preceding page or the following page.

I belong to Boston, dear old Boston town.
There's nothing the matter with Boston, for
It's worthy of its renown.
It's not just a question of friendly faces
Or even my family tree
But the more I see of other places
Here's where I want to be.

With apologies to
Harry Lauder and 'I belong to Glasgow'.

Front cover photograph by Alice Mowbray

"Dad's Army" on television featured the Home Guard and their rivalry with the A.R.P. but there were several more organisations, which did their part on the home front during the war. Initially the Home Guard were called Local Defense Volunteers.

There was also the Civil Defense, dressed in navy blue and the W.V.S., dressed in green and all these different bodies were controlled in an emergency by a supremo.

The man in charge in Boston in the early years of the war was Mr. Pulford, a well-respected and confident official but, unfortunately, when the bomb fell at the top of Liquorpond Street early one Monday morning, he failed to turn up to take charge of proceedings. His second-in-command took over, after an inevitable delay, and soon everyone was doing their appointed task.

A whole row of houses in Mariners Row had been demolished; chimney stacks dislodged over a wide area and windows blown in all down the street and there was several hours work, before the area was declared safe. Only then was it possible to look for Mr. Pulford.

He lodged with a lady in High Street, not far from the passage that had disappeared, when the bomb fell and, in common with most houses at that time, the toilet was outside. At the vital moment Mr. Pulford was using the toilet and the blast blew the door off, hit him on the head and concussed him. He was still there, when they found him.

In addition to all these organisations, each part of the town had it's own fire-watch. All able-bodied male residents, who did not belong to any other group, were placed on a roster and each night four were on duty. They split into two pairs and spend the night on top of the tallest buildings in the area. They were all issued with charts to help them recognise British and enemy aircraft, and during raids they watched for incendiary bombs and warned the fire service. Most of the fire watchers were middle-aged and had served in the First World War.

Almost everything was rationed during the war but the shortage that affected the children, of course, was sweets. The weekly ration per person was just 2 ozs; a small bar of chocolate or a small bag of toffees. In most families the children finished up with their parent's ration, but it was hard luck if your mother had a sweet tooth. Shopkeepers could not sell without taking the coupons, as they could only buy from the wholesaler or manufacturer the amount they had coupons to cover.

On the odd occasion, when a shop managed to obtain sweets off ration, the word spread quickly and a queue soon assembled. Dickinsons in George Street must have sold tons of liquorice wood to the children from Staniland school. This was an unusual supplement to the rations and today anyone would be deemed crazy to eat it, but in the prevailing conditions we were only too pleased to buy a handful and stuff it in our pockets; no need for a bag.

It looked like twigs off a tree but, when you chewed it, it turned yellow and tasted of liquorice. Small boys were walking down the streets chewing away just like the old fishermen with their Pigtail Twist tobacco.

Our mothers were more concerned with the meat rations. We were registered with Bob Creasey and he did his best to satisfy his customers, often producing a rabbit out of his cold room, not out of his hat, to provide us with a rabbit pie for Sunday dinner.

Unlike today chickens were a luxury; my uncle always brought us one for Christmas but that was the only time we saw one. Country folk fared better but even they had to have a licence to keep pigs, even if they just wanted one to fatten for themselves.

Clothing coupons were issued separately; they were not included in the ration book and there was an active black-market in these, as some people bought few clothes but everybody needed their meagre food rations.

Things that were not rationed were still scarce. Grocers received an allocation of tinned fruit two or three times a year, and they had a problem sharing a handful of tins between all their customers. The same applied to tinned fish and dried fruit was very difficult to buy. People had to save it throughout the year to be able to have a cake at Christmas.

Eggs were scarce but housewives became experts at making omelettes with egg powder but it was not ideal for Yorkshire puddings or pancakes.

On May 7th. 1945 a group of six German Generals and Admirals turned up unexpectedly at Field Marshall Montgomery's headquarters at Lüneberg Heath to surrender. Montgomery told them to return the next morning at 10 o'clock and he would be ready for them.

So it was that May 8th. 1945 became Victory in Europe Day. The official announcement was made by Winston Churchill at 3 p.m. and simultaneous announcements were made in Washington and Moscow. Later at 9 p.m. the King spoke to Britain and the Empire on the radio.

There was little time to organise official events, so celebrations were spontaneous. The May Fair was in the Market Place and the rides and sideshows must have broken all records that night. The festivities continued into the early hours then the revellers went home to the most peaceful night's sleep for six years. The May Fair was allowed to stay for an extra week.

It was a Tuesday and the country was given a two-days holiday, so everyone had time to recover from the celebrations. It was towards the end of the Easter holidays, so the schools were given an extra holiday later.

My brother and I were members of the 5th. Boston Scout Troup and Skip Lucas had taken most of the lads on the Sunday to camp at Huntingdon. Late on the evening of VE-DAY they took part in a hastily-arranged torchlight parade through the streets of Huntingdon.

I was not with them, however, as at the age of eleven I was already a bibliophile and I could not resist the opportunity to explore with my sister the bookshops up the Jews Hill at Lincoln, so I chose to visit relatives with my mother.

In the afternoon of VE-DAY we saw Gregory Peck in "The Keys Of The Kingdom" at the Ritz cinema and in the evening we joined a crowd of happy people singing and dancing in Portland Street.

Several parties were planned for the following week-end. There was one at the Sherwood Boys' Club in Field Street, run by Pop Norman. It was very popular with the youth of the day and music was provided by their own band: Bob Kitchen on piano, "Scorcher" Porcher on drums, "Mousie" Hall on double bass and Melvyn Franklin on piano accordion.

The landlord of the Vine public house in Broadfield Street had a flash of inspiration and made a sign in red, white and blue to put in his window, which read VinE

In 1941 there was much excitement in Boston, when Michael Powell and Emeric Pressburger came to shoot the film "One Of Our Aircraft Is Missing". Many scenes were filmed in the Skirbeck Quarter area and the Swing Bridge features in the climax.

Boston was chosen because the story concerned a bomber crew that came down in Holland and this part of Lincolnshire naturally resembled that country.

The crew were hidden by the Dutch resistance and finally made their way home.

The six airmen were played by Godfrey Tearle, Eric Portman, Hugh Williams, Bernard Miles, Hugh Burden and Emrys Jones. Googie Withers, Pamela Brown and Joyce Redman were three who helped them escape and Robert Helpman, the famous ballet dancer, was a German.

The film marked the debut of Peter Ustinov and must have whetted his appetite to go on not only to act in so many fine films, but also to direct eight films.

One Monday morning we were watching the filming of a scene, where the airman were climbing out of a window down a rope. One of the houses near Midgeley's shop had a round window, which served the purpose ideally.

Ten or twelve of us were in a group and we realised one of the film crew was watching us, then he came over and asked Jimmy Baker from Oxford Street, if he would like to be in the film.

They dressed him in Dutch clothes and clogs and he had to run across a cobbled courtyard, before a German soldier helped him on his way with a well-placed kick.

It was not until we saw the film much later that we realised he was taking a message to the English airman. Jimmy enjoyed his moment of glory and for years he had his leg pulled about being a film star.

1989; the year when Steve Davis last won the World Championship; the year when Daniel Day Lewis won an Oscar for "My Left Foot": it does not seem long ago, does it? However, in 1945 it seemed an eternity to look back to 1939, especially for a boy of eleven, who had had no conception of how everyone's life would change on "The day war broke out", as Robb Wilton termed it.

After September 3rd., several things suddenly disappeared: oranges, bananas, tinned fruit, tinned salmon and crab, railings from outside houses on the way to school and, of course, most of the young men and many of the young women.

Other things suddenly appeared: black-outs, blast walls, powdered egg, powdered milk, gift parcels from Canada, evacuees from London and, of course air-raid shelters.

The school playground shrunk, as air-raid shelters were built on all sides and they were numbered, so we all knew which shelter was allocated to which class. When the siren sounded, while we were at school, we were trained to remain calm and line up in twos outside the classroom and wait for the teacher to take us to our shelter.

In the evenings and week-ends and holidays, when the air-raid started to wail, everyone had a choice to either go to a shelter or remain in their own homes. Some homes had an Anderson shelter, which often doubled as a dining table but for the majority of families it meant diving under the kitchen table or down the cellar, if you had one.

In the early months of the war most people hurried to the shelters but, as time went by, and the German planes all passed over Boston on the way to more important targets, many became braver and chose to ignore the sirens. Once or twice in 1941 an odd plane still had some bombs left, as it returned home and dropped them on Boston, probably aiming at the docks or railway goods-yard. For quite a while after, the shelters were full and it would be about this time that my education broadened.

In the winter the raids seemed to occur in the evenings and the pubs emptied quickly and the camaraderie and beer were transferred to the shelters. The good-humoured banter and the colourful descriptions of Hitler, Goebels and Goering were music to my young ears, and one of the most enduring memories of the war years for me has always been the sight of two heavy ladies dancing up and down the aisle of the shelter with overflowing jugs of ale in their hands, singing "Bless 'em all".

Every class had at least one evacuee. They usually came from London but some came from other cities, Birmingham, Coventry or, in one case, from Hull. For a start the Boston children were amused by their accents and tried to mimic them, but they soon became accepted and the lad in our class was good at football and proved very popular.

Different accents were to be heard all over the town, as soldiers and airmen were billeted with anyone, who had a spare room. A good excuse was required, if you had an unused bedroom and refused to billet one or two serviceman. Most people were only too pleased to help and many life-long friendships blossomed as a result.

The soldiers were drilled in Liquorpond Street, practised trench warfare in the Lord Nelson field and shooting practice at the Kidstacks down the sea-bank. We watched the marching and played "war" in the trenches and in the holidays we went down to the Kidstacks looking for spent cartridges.

The airmen were collected by coaches and taken to East Kirkby and Coningsby, together with local tradesmen, who were busy building living quarters and runways as fast as possible.

The P.S.A. (Pleasant Sunday Afternoon) organised Bandstand Concerts in the Central Park and the forces joined in. Drill Sergeant Leathers was a favourite with the crowd, singing "The Donkey Serenade" and "Begin the Beguine".

On Sunday evenings there was often a concert at St. George's Hall in Stanbow Lane and the star turns here were Mary Mitchell singing "Where e'er you walk", Terry West singing "The Shrine of St. Cecilia" and Irene Blackamore dancing to "Oh! Salome".

Even the School holidays were affected by the war. The summer holidays were staggered. The first two weeks were taken early to enable children to help to pick the potato crop, and odd days were allowed for picking gooseberries, strawberries and raspberries.

There was a campaign for people to take "Holidays at Home", as petrol was scarce and travelling difficult, but for most people this made no difference, as very few had cars and many had never had a holiday.

Today with the power of television catch phrases become part of everyday conversation after a few weeks. Victor Meldrew's "I don't believe it" and Hyacinth Bucket's "The Bouquet Residence, the Lady of the House speaking" having joined Leslie Crowther's "Come on down" and Larry Grayson's "Shut that door" from a few years ago, and together with dozens of other examples can be heard regularly.

Radio had the same effect in the wartime. Every character in ITMA had their own catch phrase: "Can I do you now, sir"; "I don't mind if I do"; "After you Claude, no after you Cecil"; "I go…I come back". The children as well as the adults could be heard saying them. In those dark hours it seemed to make people closer. Every comedian had his own: Tommy Trinder, "YOU lucky people"; Arthur Askey "I thank you"; George Formby "Turned out nice again" and our own Arthur Lucan "On your way Mother Riley, on your way".

There were always queues, when a George Formby or Old Mother Riley film came to the cinemas and it was a nice feeling to know that Old Mother Riley's brother, Toby Towle, lived just up the road and we bought our fish and chips from his niece, Phyllis Vickers. You can image how proud I was, when at the age of eight I bought two pet rabbits from his sister, Mrs. Ladds, who lived in Rowell Row, now Wyberton Low Road.

Performances at the cinema were not continuous and the doors did not open until maybe twenty minutes before the start. Queues at the Odeon used to reach right to the car park at the back; at the Regal the queue for the stalls went down Bond Street, and for the circle along West Street past Day's Cash Stores. If it was raining, it was best to go to the New Theatre, because you could buy your ticket there and then queue inside.

The value of the cinema to the morale of the war-weary populace was recognised, and in 1942 for the first time cinemas were allowed to open on Sundays. It proved very popular and the queues started at 6 o'clock, although the programme commenced at 7.00. Two films were shown and usually they had been on the weekly circuit four or five years earlier.

The first film shown on a Sunday night at the Odeon was "The Rat" with Anton Walbrook, followed the next week by Gordon Harker and Alastair Sim in "Inspector Hornleigh", both of which were made in 1938.

Signposts were all taken down, when the war started, so the few people who had petrol for their cars and vans had to rely on their memory, when making a journey. Nothing was allowed to be displayed that would be of help to any enemy spies. The hoardings were either empty or displayed Government slogans such as Dig For Victory, Make Do and Mend, or Careless Talk Costs Lives, , or Be Like Dad, Keep Mum.

Towards the end of 1941 the workmen, who had been travelling by bus every day to Coningsby finished the job there, and most of them were flown to Iceland and spent the next four years building living quarters and runways near Reykiavik.

Bakers, Butchers, Grocers and Drapers nearly all had roundsmen to deliver their goods but, when the men-folk were called up, their place was taken by women. We were bakers and one of our vans was driven for several years by Queenie Pogson, who later married Ernie Hobart. They were allowed to drive without taking a test and as far as I know none were involved in an accident.

The airmen and soldiers who were billeted around the town were made very welcome, as most fathers, uncles and big brothers were somewhere overseas. As far as children were concerned they came in very useful for mending punctures, blowing up footballs and getting balls out of gutterings and spouts.

One airman, who was billeted with Mr. & Mrs. Fred Parker of Edwin Street, proved his value in a much more serious way. Their house overlooked onto the river bank and one evening at high tide five or six of us were playing near Gostelow's slip. Somehow Frankie Welberry fell in to the swollen river and was submerging for the third time, when Jock, the airman, who had seen it happen out of a bedroom window, rushed out, dived in and dragged him to safety. From that day one he was our particular hero.

Compared with some other towns and cities Boston did not suffer too many air-raids during the war. In the early years the German bombers headed for the industrial areas then in the latter stages, when they had lost most of their planes and they were sending over flying bombs, they did not risk wasting them in the North Sea, they timed them to stop and explode further inland.

The worst raid, as far as casualties were concerned, was the night a bomb fell at the top of James Street, which at the time had a narrow opening similar to Trinity Street. Eddy Loveley's shop stood on the corner and his two teenage daughters slept in a bedroom at the back over the bakehouse. The rest of the family survived but they were both killed.

A row of houses behind the shop was obliterated and the Royal George public house was badly damaged. In one of the houses a young mother and her three children were wiped out and their father was due home on leave. The irony was that Mrs. Harris and her family had just flitted from Edwin Street and he was coming home to see the new house.

Although many houses were flattened when the bomb fell on Liquorpond Street, I believe only one lady was killed; Mrs. Gee, whose grand-daughter, Maureen Hall, was in my class at Staniland School. My most vivid memory of that day was not the sight of the devastation nor the terrible noise, when the bomb actually fell, but it was the smell of soot as we went to school.

None of the houses in that part of Boston needed a chimney sweep for months, and in our own house the soot poured down into the grate and we all looked like Al Jolson.

In another raid a bomb fell on Holland Bros. at the junction of Wide Bargate and Tawney Street, where the Iceland Store now stands. It landed on the offices and, when two air-raid wardens, Mark Parkinson and Austin Davies, arrived at the scene, papers were tumbling out of the sky like a tick-o-tape reception in the streets of New York. There was a large crater in the middle of Tawney Street and Austin was investigating, when Mark shouted a hurried warning to tell him he was standing near a bomb.

The street was cordoned off and people were told to stay clear, until the Bomb Disposal Unit came and rendered it harmless.

Most families lost relatives, serving in the Armed Forces, and for them life was never the same again. Loved ones were reported missing in Italy or Africa and later in France or Burma, but it seemed particularly hard for those mothers and wives, who lost their sons and husbands, when the aircraft carriers, H.M.S. Exmouth and H.M.S. Ark Royal were sunk with nothing to mark their last resting place.

Men were killed closer to home also: the Home Guard trained with live ammunition and at Sibsey a hand grenade exploded too soon and Private Harness was killed and the unit Commander, Mr. Smith had his arm blown off.

The death, however, that affected me most happened in 1944 and had no connection with the war; it could have occurred anytime. I started at the Grammer School that year and I sat next to another ten year old with bright red hair called Gordon Butcher. One afternoon cycling home from school he fell of his bicycle at the top of Frampton Place under the back wheels of a coal lorry.

His empty desk the next day and the announcement by the Headmaster at assembly are memories that will never fade.

Earlier, while still at Staniland School, I had witnessed one of the most memorable fires in Boston's history and again it had nothing to do with the war.

Our classroom looked out onto Fydell Crescent and our attention was drawn by crackling noises outside and then flames rising high into the sky. Miss. Parker tried to maintain order but, when the fire engines arrived, she gave up the struggle and allowed us to watch the proceedings from the plentiful windows. Bedford's Mill was on fire.

For an hour or two we learned no tables or spelling but we did learn about the heroics of the firemen. The mill was far enough away from the school for us not to be evacuated; in fact it was probably thought that we were in the safest place.

I joined the 5th. Boston Scout Troup towards the end of the war, and one Sunday each month we went on Church Parade to either a local church or chapel. We used to assemble at our headquarters and march through the streets.

I could recognise the inside view of every centre of religion within five miles of Boston. The contrast was remarkable: one month we would be in a spartan, basically equipped chapel and the next month in an ornate church with sidesmen, servers and sometimes incense. The sincerity and reverence was just as great in both.

Our headquarters was an old building at the side of the river in South Street, just before Lincoln's seed warehouse, as you approached Fydell House. It is now a car-park and the warehouse has been transformed into the Sam Newsom Music Centre.

Our meetings were held upstairs and the sound of thirty or forty pairs of young feet rushing across the bare, wooden floorboards, as we lined up in patrols, must have been heard in the Market Place.

There were five or six patrols, each with seven or eight scouts, and all named after birds. My brother and I were in the Kingfisher Patrol and our colours, four pieces of cloth on our shoulders, were naturally Kingfisher blue. Some of you may remember the other patrols; I believe there was a Blackbird Patrol and a Curlew but my memories concern my own patrol.

Ray Issit was our patrol leader but he became Troop Leader, when Bill Westkin moved away and Ken Johnson was promoted. Two other unforgettable members of the Kingfishers were "Donkey" Warren and "Pud" Payton.

One patrol consisted almost entirely of the Mitchell brothers. Gordon was the leader, then there were two sets of twins, Tony and Terry, and Jack and Gerry, better known as "Buster".

Several times a year there were parades through the town and Skip Lucas tried to make sure we outsmarted and outmarched another Scout Troup, led by Skip Austin and the Sea Scouts, led by their Scoutmaster, Mr. Twiddy.

The parades were always led by either the Army Cadets or the Air Cadets, as they had bands and I believe the Boys Brigade also had a band. The Market Place was always crowded for these occasions and the "Stump" was always full.

The Reverend P. E. Mann, who held a post at St. Botolphs, was also a Scoutmaster and he often accompanied us, when we went on camp. His favourite camp-fire rendering was the Trek-Cart Song and Jacky Redmile, who went to live in what was then Southern Rhodesia, entertained us with parodies of songs, such as "There's a long, long trail a-winding".

Today scouts travel miles, even abroad, to camps and jamborees, but we had to be satisfied to go within marching distance. One year we were camping in a field not far from Kirton Church and for me it was a disaster.

The second thing to do when you set up camp, after raising the flag, was to dig the latrine. The scouts given this task did a good job, producing a hole big enough to last a month, but those detailed to find a strong piece of wood to sit on, did not do so well and I was the unfortunate, who happened to be on it, when it snapped.

I was just recovering from this mishap and had reached the point, where I was allowed back in the tent, when it was decided that we would play rounders. Our side was batting and I was waiting frustratingly at the back of the queue, when finally the lad in front of me had his turn.

He was the tallest and heaviest of us and he took an almighty swipe at the ball, missed it but continued his swing and hit me on the forehead. I never did have my turn; in fact I never knew how the game finished and, when I came round, I resembled someone out of a comic, with an egg-shaped bump above my left eye.

We all had nick-names: my brother was called "Fuzzy" because of his hair and, after that camp at Kirton, I was called "Shaver". At that time I was a little short-tongued and on our flag were the words "God Save The King". As we all assembled one night to take down the flag, I said the words but to the others it sounded like "God shave the King".

One Sunday in 1945 there was a fete at Frampton Hall, the home of Mr. Frank Dennis. For some reason our troop was asked to help prepare the grounds for the visitors, then we returned the day after the fete to restore the status quo. We must have done a good job, for we were invited back several times. In fact three of us went there every weekend that summer to help the butler with his more tedious tasks.

Although everything was scarce during the war, we always seemed to manage at school for text books, pencils and pen nibs. A few lucky children had fountain pens but most used wooden pens with replaceable nibs, and an ink monitor had to make sure that all the ink-wells were full every day.

One thing of which we had a plentiful supply at Staniland School was india rubbers. When the Regal cinema was built in, I believe 1938, the top surface of the floor in the foyer was made of rubber, and the off-cuts and all unused pieces were kindly given to the school. They were cut into small pieces and served as india rubbers for many years.

Staniland was a popular and successful school both for examination results and for sport, and with more children to accommodate an extra classroom was needed. This was provided by one class crossing over George Street every day to a room behind St. James Church.

The church, itself, was used on one occasion. The whole Junior school assembled there at the end of term one Christmas to say goodbye to Miss. Calthrop, one of the most loved and respected teachers in the school's history. She sang "In the deep mid-winter" and, as we came out of church, the girls were crying openly and the boys were trying to stifle their tears.

A smaller room over the vestry at St. James was used on a Saturday afternoon to give film shows for children. Rev. Johnny Jordan was both the M.C. and the projectionist, and before and after the show he played records on a gramophone. Today, if I hear Glenn Miller's recording of "Elmer's Tune", I recall those Saturday afternoons vividly.

Most of us had already been to a proper cinema in the morning. The Regal had the Hoodoo Club and the Odeon ran the Mickey Mouse Club. We all wore our badges and sang the Club songs, before the show. Then there was a cartoon; an episode of the current serial and finally a film, either a western or an adventure involving spies or pirates. The Flash Gordon serials were never as popular as The Three Mesketeers, which John Wayne made as "Stoney Brooks" throughout the Thirties, until achieving proper stardom with "Stagecoach" in 1939.

Our lives were shaped to a great extent by whatever film was showing that week. If it was Errol Flynn in "The Adventures of Robin Hood", the trees down the Polypads were stripped and we all had bows and quivers full of arrows on our backs. When Tyrone Power was in "The Mark of Zorro", we all had plasters on our knuckles through sword-fighting and all the sheds and coal-house doors suddenly had "Z"s all over them.

The Nelson Field was the scene of the battle, after we had seen "Bataan", Wake Island" or "Nine Men". The trenches became wider, as we dug lumps out of them to represent hand grenades and we defended the air-raid shelter to the last man.

A gang of us took part in a real-life adventure, which, in retrospect, was foolhardy to say the least. Our local barber was Bob Lewis and as his sons grew old enough they helped him in his shop. This tradition caused no problems, until it was Harry's turn. He was a rebel and objected to the restrictions on his leisure activities, so he ran away from home.

It was summer and his parents were not too worried at first, thinking he would come home, when he was wet or hungry but concern grew as the days went by. We knew where he was but he had sworn us to secrecy and for a week we kept him supplied with biscuits, cakes and pop and anything else we could sneak from our pantries.

He was hiding in a concrete observation post down the Sea Bank, near the Kidstacks and eventually some soldiers found him there fast asleep. He was returned to his parents and we could only image the scene, but afterwards he took his turn as a trainee barber. Our parents never did find out why we were reluctant to go to the barbers that summer, even when there was a heat-wave.

When I think of the crazy, dangerous things we did in the war years, it is a wonder any of us survived. Our mothers were worried about relatives overseas and stretching the rations but, if they had known of our exploits, they would have taken priority.

As the tide was rising, we used to crawl on the mud under the mussel stage down Skirbeck Quarter from one end to the other and never considered the danger. In the winter we used to improvise a game of ice hockey on a frozen pond, although we knew children had drowned there previously. We think children today do irresponsible things but they can be no worse than we were.

By 1944 we had become accustomed to the sight of American airman walking through the streets of Boston. They usually had gum in their pockets to please the children and nylons to please the young ladies. I was an avid collector of most things and soon added empty packets of Lucky Strike, Chesterfield, Camels and Phillip Morris to my collection; in fact the Camels packet usurped the green Black Cat as my favourite.

They were based at East Kirkby, so Boston was their nearest town, when they were off duty. They flew on bombing raids over Germany and did their best to relax and unwind in the Peacock and Royal, Rumpuncheon, Britannia and Mason's Arms, then later at the Gliderdrome.

One night, returning from a raid, one of their planes did not quite make it and came down in the Wash. An Air Sea Rescue unit, based at the Marine Hotel at Freiston Shore was called out, but all the crew were dead. For the next five weeks eight American ground crew airman lodged at the Marine, until they had recovered all the instruments and personal belongings from the wrecked plane.

Some of the bombing raids involved planes from several different airfields and they use to assemble over this area, before making a combined assault on the enemy. At 5.30 a.m. on 13th July, 1944 a Liberator took off from R.A.F. Marham in Norfolk in rain and heavy overcast conditions to take part in a raid on Saarbrucken.

There were nine in the crew. The pilot was N. J. Hunt, the co-pilot P. R. Roetzel, the bomber W. J. Hession, the engineer W. L. McKinzie, the radio operator H. C. Wilkinson, the nose gunner W. E. Caurington, the right waist gunner M. Osment, the left waist gunner D. L. McEwan and the tail gunner L. A. Jackson.

Although it was summer, soon after takeoff ice formed on the wings but it soon cleared and by 6.00 a.m. they joined planes from other airfields, assembling over Wrangle and Eastville.

At this point the ice re-appeared but worse this time; the propellers were covered with heavy ice and, in spite of Captain Hunt's efforts, the engines failed and the aircraft was out of control.

These details were given later by the sole survivor, D. L. McEwan, who attempted to leave the plane through the waist window but was caught half-in and half-out. He was semi-conscious from hitting his head on the side of the aircraft but was thrown clear, pulled his ripcord then lost consciousness.

By now it was 6.30 a.m. and he came round at 3.00 p.m. with two children looking at him and soon some members of the Home Guard arrived. He had dropped in a cornfield and his legs had doubled beneath him. It was feared that his back was broken but Dr. Bee from Wrangle arrived a little later and pronounced him just badly bruised and shaken. He learned later that all his mates had been killed.

The plane crashed on an uncultivated piece of land at Wangle Lowgrounds, which is now used for allotments, near the Black Bull, which is no longer in use. The tail fell off two miles nearer the sea and wreckage was scattered over a large area.

The body of the plane had made a hole 50' x 30' and thrown up a bank of earth 6' high. Mr. Joseph Johnson, the headmaster of Wrangle Common School lived in the School House, which was only three hundred yards away. He was deputy head warden for the village and had a telephone upstairs near his bed, so he rang control immediately and all the local roads were closed.

The Boston fire brigade arrived within twenty minutes and a R.A.F. fire tender with foam extinguishers. Ammunition was going off and the Police rang Mr. Johnson to confirm that the plane had been identified as from Marham and there were 12 500 lb. bombs on board. The firemen were warned not to go too close.

The immediate neighbourhood was evacuated and people warned to leave their doors and windows open to cause less damage, if the bombs exploded. The R.A.F. and Police were on guard everywhere but in those days no one thought of looting.

A report came through that a parachute had been spotted four miles away and a search party, comprised of Police, Home Guard and Civil Defense, was organised. As already stated the Home Guard found him in a cornfield.

The fire was eventually extinguished and people were allowed to return home but the two closest roads remained closed, until the Bomb Disposal Squad made all the bombs safe. This took five weeks and there were twelve men in the squad but they had to carefully dig down 20 ft. to reach some of the bombs.

Mr. Johnson instructed the children to hand in anything they found later near the scene of the crash, and amongst the collection was the radio operator's book and the identity plates for N. J. Hunt, the pilot and W. J. Hession the bomber.

Apart from Mr. Hudson, the Headmaster, all the teachers at Staniland School were ladies but, when I went to the Grammer School in 1944, I expected the staff to be all male. With all the young teachers in the forces, however, several ladies supplemented the older teachers, who for the most part had served their time in the First World War.

Mrs. Brough, the celebrated local artist, took first-year French; Mrs. Jakes was my first teacher for English Grammar and Mrs. Wilkinson replaced her husband as a Geography teacher. The youngest and most glamorous member of staff was Miss. Collins but I was not fortunate enough to have been taught by her, so I am not sure of her subject. Maybe someone can enlighten me.

All the male teachers were characters with their various idiosyncrasies and all past-pupils have their favourite anecdotes about each but, in spite of their eccentricities or perhaps because of them, most boys did well in their exams and all of them have a rich storehouse of happy memories.

"Doc" Morris was the Headmaster but he retired after my first year and was replaced by "Snag" Waddams, so my memories of him are mainly passed down from my brother. It appears he taught Religious Instruction himself and his wife taught Science. At morning assembly he often infused the boys with the following statement "The war is not yet over; we must put every ounce of strength into our efforts".

He came to Boston Grammar School direct from the Great War and, I believe, Sam Wray, the caretaker, had been his Batman and Mr. Burton, the groundsman at the Church Road Sportsfield had served under him as a Sergeant. Captain Morris had an artificial leg; a legacy of his war service.

The senior Maths teacher, "Binky" Border, was also Deputy Headmaster. He had been a Major in the First World War and was extremely frustrated, when he was told he was too old to take part in the Second World War.

"Froggy" Howes was the senior French teacher and was due for retirement, when the war started but, like Mr. Chips, he was persuaded to stay on. My most poignant memory of him was the time, when some first-formers were mocking the way he walked down the corridor. He had trouble with his legs and had to walk slowly.

"Binky" came up behind them and made them look even smaller than they were, when he told them that the man they were mocking was an Amateur International and in his younger days had played centre-forward for England.

"Froggy" had a nasal quality to his voice, which was perfect for sounding the French accents. Both he and "Binky" Border retired soon after the war.

"Snoddy" Deighton was the German teacher. His gown was always in shreds and he spent half of each period staring out of the window or into space; it was hard to tell which, but he must have done something right for German was my best subject and I finished with a distinction in my School Certificate.

From his nickname you would have thought that "Fritz" Wheeler was a German teacher but his subject was actually mathematics. He had an index finger missing and used to prod the boys with the stump and his voice was reminiscent of a Gestapo officer.

Several teachers had their own special aid to keep control. I never took Latin but I heard about Joe Gledhill's "Little Benjamin"' which I understood was a ruler. "Tilly" Turpin used an elastic band: he attacked from behind and flicked the back of your ear. He was the History master but he was also artistic: at the start of term he used to arrange the class by the colour of the boys' hair to create the best pattern. Like the other teachers, he kept perfect control and could reduce some pupils to tears, just by entering the room.

Only one teacher had trouble maintaining order: Mr. Ferguson, the Art Master, was too kind to be a teacher and he eventually left, after one boy was expelled for threatening him with a gun.

The two strictest disciplinarians were Bill Bastick (English) and "Tusker" Tonks (Maths). For different reasons both were red-faced and one day I was responsible for making Mr. Tonk's face even redder. With my friend Victor Emery I arrived back one lunchtime to find we could not enter the classroom because some other boys were holding the door. Like me, Vic was a well-built lad; he used to win the one mile swimming race down the Witham every year, and eventually we burst into the room.

We thought that we, in turn, would hold the door against the next boy to enter. So we did and we prevented him from entering for quite a while, until we realised all the desks were full and it gradually dawned on us that it was "Tusker" trying to get in. We tried to reach our desks but he charged in like an elephant and the air was blue, his bulging neck was red and our faces were white.

The Grammar School Master I knew best was Mr. Cox, the Geography teacher. He lived with his wife in a bungalow near the top of Tytton Lane East and we served them with bread. On Saturdays and in the holidays I went to their bungalow, while my father went to a house opposite.

They were the kindest, most considerable couple you could ever meet and I never liked to see boys mock him or play games on him, but I need not have worried: he was well capable of looking after himself.

His nickname was "Curious", as his favourite expression, when a pupil answered a question incorrectly was "curious, curious, I wouldn't have known". He was one of the elder teachers but was very fit and always wore running shoes.

The school quadrangle was split by four paths in the shape of the Cross of St. Andrew and, where they met in the centre, stood the weather hut, which housed the equipment for checking the temperature and measuring the rainfall etc. It was Mr. Cox's daily task to register the details and with his passion for being precise he was ideally suited to be the school meteorologist.

One morning, after a night of steady rain, some boys decided to play a joke on him and filled the rain container to the top, as only boys can. When Mr. Cox appeared to make his readings, he noticed more boys than usual observing, several with smirks on their face, so, without giving them the pleasure of hearing him utter even one "curious", he called one boy across, whom he correctly assessed to be the ringleader, and told him to take the container to the washroom and wash it well out.

Dr. Bernard Jackson was for many years the organist at St. Botolphs and he was also our music teacher. He had difficulty controlling the class, especially when he was playing the piano with his back to the boys.

Very few took music seriously and the half hour spent with "Jacko" was looked upon as a chance to relax and ease the tension of the more important periods. The music classroom was situated above the Masters' Common-room, as far away as possible from the rest of the school, so the wailing caused minimum nuisance.

His most amusing and challenging feature was the tufts of hair growing horizontally out of his ears. One day, while we were rendering "Nymphs and Shepherds Come Away" one daring lad could resist the challenge no longer. He crept behind Dr. Jackson, who as usual was engrossed in his work, and set fire to the hairs protruding from the left ear with a lighter and managed to regain his seat and put an innocent expression on his face, before "Jacko" turned round.

The consequences of his derring-do were that Dr. Jackson had to visit the barber to restore equilibrium by having the hairs removed from his right ear, and also that the piano was belatedly moved, so that no one could ever approach unnoticed.

When "Binky" Border retired, his place as Maths teacher was taken by Mr. McNeil, who to the boys soon became "McNab". The standard of mathematics soon deteriorated, not because he was a bad teacher, but because none of us could tell what he was saying.

Time and time again, when I talk to others of my year, we find we had good results in most subjects but most of us just scraped through on Maths.

"Titch" Collins took over the responsibility of Religious Instructions, after "Doc" Morris left and, with his past record as a missionary in Africa, he made the subject very interesting. He also taught German and proved to be a useful addition to the staff.

On the 8th June, 1946 every schoolchild received a letter from the King. It read: "Today, as we celebrate victory, I send this personal message to you and all other boys and girls at school. For you have shared in the hardships and dangers of a total war and you have shared no less in the triumph of the Allied Nations.

I know you will always feel proud to belong to a country, which was capable of such supreme effort; proud too of parents and elder brothers and sisters, who by their courage, endurance and enterprise brought victory. May these qualities be yours as you grow up and join in the common effort to establish among the nations of the world unity and peace". GEORGE REX.

The important dates of the war were listed on the back.

All organised sport was affected by the war: the Football League was postponed for the duration but we did have the local Schools League to maintain our interest. All the games were played on the Lord Nelson field and there were eight teams: Carlton Road, Kirton, Park Board, St. Botolphs, St. Nicholas, Shodfriars, Staniland and Tower Road.

The championship was usually fought out between Carlton Road, Staniland and Park Board, as these schools had more pupils to choose from. Staniland played in black and amber and I remember Kirton played in red and green shirts, but I am not sure about the others.

Mr. Hudson was an enthusiastic supporter of Staniland and Mr. Burton, his counter-part as Headmaster of Carlton Road, was just as avid a supporter of his team. They both used to patrol the sidelines, shouting encouragement.

Staniland were Champions for two consecutive years, largely due to their goalkeeper, George "Bunty" Stow, who allowed few shots to go past him. The whole team, though, were outstanding, including "Cocker" Harvey and Reg Wakefield and their simple method of scoring goals makes today's complicated formations and coaching systems look stupid.

They would not have dreamed of passing the ball across field; it went straight to the wingers, "Bowie" Barton and "Whippit" Bray, they took it to the by-line then centred for "Wokka" Revell to head it or fire it into the net.

Today pea viners harvest the crop and complete the process in the fields, working round the clock and moving from one farm to another during the night, but during the war it was done in the factories.

As with marbles and conkers, there was a pea season. As soon as the tractors appeared pulling trailers, loaded with pea plants destined for Willer & Rileys, we all practised the art of running alongside and jumping on the back of the trailer. Compared to this, catching a train moving out of a station was a doddle.

The less adventurous would pick up pods, dropped onto the road by the trailer-hoppers. The tractor drivers accepted the fact that their loads never arrived in tact, as one of the hazards of the job.

The road sweeper was kept busy clearing the gutters of empty pea vines for a few weeks but those peas, fresh out of the pregnant pods, tasted much sweeter than any I have had since.

I can not remember anyone coming to any harm from these escapades but there was little traffic on the roads then and the worst consequences was a scraped knee.

The sparsity of traffic made it quite an occasion, when an army convoy came through the town. The first vehicle was usually a jeep with an officer at the side of the driver. When we noticed this, we stood and counted how many vehicles were in the convoy. It was often as many as fifty or sixty.

They varied from heavy lorries to armoured vehicles and all were camouflaged. Sometimes we would think it had finished, then some stragglers would appear, as with the children following the pied piper. The last piece of the convoy was always another jeep with another officer riding shotgun.

When he had passed, we were able to resume our normal routine.

The necessity for these vehicles to keep within a reasonable distance of each other could have been the cause of a tragedy, that occurred one day on Spilsby Road. The girls were leaving the High School to go home for dinner and, as still happens today, Spilsby Road was suddenly covered with bicycles.

Unfortunately they spilled out of the school gates during a hiatus in a convoy and for some reason there was an accident. Olga Needham was run over and taken into Dennis Rickard's house and tragically she died.

With petrol so scarce many trades people turned to horses to make deliveries. Milk, bread and greengroceries were often purveyed this way and our coal was brought on a cart drawn by a horse, who knew the round better than the coalman.

Beer was brought to the pubs with horses pulling drays sometimes from as far as Spalding and carriers came into Boston regularly, bringing and taking goods from and to the villages.

The two horses I remember best pulled a cart for C. & C. Wrights, the ironmongers in High Street, opposite the Golden Lion. The cart was driven by Harry Dwyer, a kind, avuncular man, who was also landlord of the Robin Hood and he stabled the horses in an outbuilding in the pub yard that overlooked our garden.

Wednesday afternoons were special during the war years and, in deed, for several years after. For some schoolboys it was an exciting time and a chance to earn some money; for nervous ladies it was a time to stay indoors and avoid the main streets and for Harry Tooley it was his favourite time of the week.

Harry loved the sounds, the smells and the atmosphere of the cattle market and spent the day there every Wednesday with the glorious climax coming when the cows were driven through the town, down High Street to the cattle trucks in the Goods Yard in Skirbeck Quarter.

Harry was a welcome and very willing assistant to the drover, who was often a one-armed man and always wore a khaki coat. With his peaked cap in one hand and his coshing stick in the other Harry presented an awesome picture to the cows, who were experiencing a traumatic day in any case. He had no trouble keeping up with the pace, however fast they went.

The schoolboys were recruited by the drover to anticipate any trouble in advance and guard all roads, lanes, yards and passages ahead of the advancing drove. This they did by standing their ground and waving their arms, sticks or anything available to persuade the cows not to be diverted from their proper course.

After successfully arriving at the Goods Yard, the lads would hurry home with their reward jangling in their pockets but, in spite of the drover trying to press well-earned money onto him, Harry would not take anything. He had no interest whatsoever in money; to him it was just a nuisance.

Harry had been a Down's syndrome baby but none of us, who valued his company, thought of him as a Mongol, although he often amused us by touching the tip of his nose with his tongue. For all the years I knew him, he never aged. He must have been ten years older than most of us but he joined in all our activities.

Our games of football sometimes lasted three hours but Harry was still there at the end, although sometimes he had an enforced rest, when he folded up with 'stitch'. He seldom scored goals but he was a useful defender: when he connected with the ball, it was certainly cleared.

Although he spurned money, he never refused to eat. Whenever possible he timed his morning walk from his home in Edwin Street to coincide with the withdrawal from the oven of tea-cakes, to which he was particularly partial and which he ate appreciatively however hot. The men in the bakehouse knew it was in order to give him one daily, as he was always willing, if an extra pair of hands were needed.

He had no brothers or sisters but four cousins lived next door and he had many, many friends. When he walked up the street, everyone spoke to him and he knew most of them by name.

This column seems to have restirred memories for several people. Among those, who have found time to comment on their recollections are Ray Woods, a fellow pupil at Staniland School, Doreen Rushton, wife of the Corporal, with whom I rode pillion most weekends while in the R.A.F. and Hazel Rimington, retired Headmistress of Fishtoft School.

After writing about the 5th Boston Scout Troop, I received a call from Peter Blanchard, who reminded me he had been in the Kiwi patrol and Dick Gresswell, the Eastwood Road butcher, confirmed the rivalry between our troop and the Sea Scouts, of which he had been a member.

The Liberator bomber, which crashed at Wrangle Bank, was well remembered by Bernard Codd, the motor cycling star of the fifties, who was the last rider to win both the 350 c.c. and the 500 c.c. T.T. races on the Isle of Man the same day.

The crash woke him at 6.30 a.m. that morning and he went to see if anyone needed help but had to return home, when the ammunition started firing. He was with his sisters, Ena and Barbara, and, as they neared home, they noticed a parachute in their father's field.

They ran over and found the sole survivor, who was semi-conscious and asking for an American medic. Bernard confirmed that his legs were folded under him and they were frightened to move him, until Dr. Bee arrived.

The time though was only 8.00 a.m. and I stated he did not come round until 3.00 p.m. Still it was fifty years ago and he agrees I was right with the other details.

Now television rules so many lives it is hard to imagine how we spent our time fifty years ago. We participated in sport much more, instead of watching overpaid, under-talented idols, and those of us with a penchant for organisation set up clubs to provide somewhere for the others to go.

One such was Peter Luff, who lived down Woodville Road and ran the Meccano Club. His father was a train driver and his mother was prone to eulogise her son's qualities, much to Peter's embarrassment but who's to fault a mother for being proud. His club had many members and they spent numerous hours engrossed in the various activities Peter planned.

The only snag for my friends and I was the distance to travel, so we decided to establish our own club. We already had a 5 ft. snooker table in a loft over the garage, that now housed two bread vans but used to serve as a stable for the horses that preceded the vans.

We bought a second-hand full size table tennis table and rigged up an electric light then we were ready for business. We soon had thirty or forty members and our only problem was overcrowding. Once or twice some lad disappeared down the hole, which in the past had been used to drop feed to the horses, but no legs were broken.

We had to decide on a name for the club, as there were four of us: Peter Day, Noel Holgate, myself and Victor Emery, we came up with the Penopauvics. On second thought, however, we realised we might be mistaken for a Red Indian tribe, so we changed it to the Demons.

We arranged cricket and football matches against the Meccano Club in the appropriate seasons and honours were usually shared.

Peter Luff and I had a running joke through our years at the Grammar School that we would both become Members of Parliament and a few years ago I thought he had made it, when I read in the newspaper about a Tory M.P. called Peter Luff.

The last I heard of him was that he was in the Foreign Office, so it could have been possible but during the last election I saw the M.P. on television and it was not the Boston-born Peter Luff.

Of the other three demons only Noel Holgate remained in Boston; he retired a few years ago from his position as managing director of Hardy & Collins. Peter Day moved to the Midlands to work for De Havillands and Victor Emery took a post at the University of California. The last time I saw him he stopped over in Boston, en route to give a lecture tour in Russia.

Another school friend finished up in California: Peter Howes, whose father had a vegetable stall near Fosters in the market, which is still carried on by Peter's younger brother, Dick.

Peter was a jazz fanatic. His taste for traditional jazz was developed when bands like Freddy Randle and Mick Mulligan made regular visits to the Gliderdrome.

I once spent a week with him in London and every night we visited some jazz club, even finding Crooks Ferry Inn on the Sunday night. I often wondered if his love of jazz had anything to do with his settling in California.

A brief announcement in the Lincolnshire Standard informed me years ago that my friend had died in his thirties.

Masters at school always had problems, when there were too many Smiths in a class. They usually solved it by using initials but in my brothers form there were three J. Smiths, so it needed a second initial. They became Smith, J. B., Smith J .G. and Smith J. W. but to their friends they were Bill, Jeggy and Johnny.

Our class was not so rich with Smiths but even so another friend was always known by his initials instead of his proper name, Barry. His second name was Trevor and everyone knew him as Beatty (B.T.).

I was with him late one night, when he complained of terrific stomach pains and he was rushed to hospital with peritonitis, his appendix had burst. He became a teacher at a private school and sometimes visits Boston but I have always been out, when he has tried to see me, and the only time I saw him I was driving and he was going into Boots.

Pete Howes, Beatty Smith and myself were three members of a Brag school, that held regular sessions for a year or two. The other members were Curly Sharp, who has just retired from Allied Dunbar and John Clark, who is still making the headlines as a slow left arm bowler at cricket and is a past Town Champion at snooker.

In the years just after the war our Demon Sports Club grew and we arranged football matches with teams as far away as Winthorpe Olympic, who played on the Lincoln Road out of Skegness.

Our most important games, however, were those played against Wyberton Rangers, a team run by Bryn Johnson, Tommy Horn and Tony Farrow. They became our main rivals and our fixtures against them were just as important as a cup final.

In the summer we arranged cricket matches against the Sherwood Boys, who had a clubroom in Field Street. We played in the Central Park and both teams relied on a good fast bowler to take the wickets. We had Peter Day and they had John Tilling, both of whom went on to play for Boston C.C.

One match we played against them sticks in my mind, for during it I gained an unwarranted reputation for being a brilliant close fielder.

We had batted first and scored about 100, which would normally be enough to win but, after Peter Day had disposed of their first four batsmen, Frank Sargeant started hitting nearly every ball through mid-wicket to the boundary.

In desperation Peter asked me to field at short leg and like a fool I did. Sure enough Frank hit the next ball like a rocket straight at me. I had no time to avoid it and to save my teeth I put up my hands and caught it. I was an instant hero and we won the match but I never really enjoyed cricket afterwards, as they always expected me to field close in.

Frank became the Dean of Bradford, then the Bishop of Stockport and he is now Bishop at Lambeth, helping with the affairs of the Archbishop of Canterbury.

Our club finally broke up, when chasing girls became more interesting to most of our members than chasing a football. I still preferred the latter, so I progressed to running the Old Bostonian Youth team with Derek Whelbourn and Alan Woodthorpe.

There was a well organised Youth League in those days with Mr. Sewell, the Headmaster from Amber Hill School as Chairman and Derek Killick as Secretary. The meetings were held in Killick's barber's shop down Stanbow Lane.

For snooker and table tennis I joined the Mens' Own Club. Their clubroom was in Strait Bargate down a passage at the side of Liptons. The first flight of wooden stairs led to a room with two full size snooker tables and a 6' table between. A second flight brought you to the table tennis room with two tables.

The Mens' Own was run by Cyril Wright, Arthur Atkin and Pop Greenwood with Arthur's wife helping at busy times and when the men were playing in league matches. Billiards was the game then: there were two divisions in the Billiards League and only one in the Snooker League.

Cyril was one of the best billiard players in town; only his namesake, Jack Wright was better and Cyril also had the patience to teach the lads. The older players in the league today were nearly all taught by Cyril Wright: Bob Clark, John Clark, Brian Hooker, Fred Kirk all played in the league while quite young.

The Mens' Own always had six or seven Billiards teams and the No. 1 team contested the Championship most seasons with the I.B.C. Other clubs at that time were the Cons, above the New Theatre, British Rail, St. James, Waverley, above Broughs in High Street, U.S.C., behind Lloyds Banks and the Civil Defence.

Among the players who represented the Mens' Own were Dave Rushton, Ray Harley, Harold Renshaw, Johnny Frost, Bas Stopper and the Burt brothers.

When Boston played other towns at Table Tennis, the matches were played at the Mens' Own. For several seasons the team was Sid Harmon, Chelsea Howard and Ron Croft, then Terry Venters and Gordon Skinner came into the team and a little later Wendy Blades.

Table tennis was very popular then, as indeed it still is, but there were more people involved in their league than in the Billiards and Snooker combined. For some reason I did not play for the Mens' Own at table tennis; I played for the Young Conservatives on the top floor above the New Theatre.

I played with Peter Smith, who worked for Graves & Hobster, and Bernard Reed, who worked for Barclays Bank and later returned as manager.

Several ladies played in the league at that time. In fact we had an all ladies team at the Young Conservatives, consisting of Margaret Loveley, Violet Ashton and Eve Coles, and they were all good players.

During the war years St. Botolph's Youth Fellowship was a meeting place for the generation that were just too young to be called up. Rev. David Cartwright was in charge and their clubroom was in the shadow of the Stump on the corner of Wormgate and Fountain Lane; the premises now used as a wallpaper shop by Stanilands.

The long room downstairs housed a Billiard table and there were two table tennis tables upstairs. There were special club nights but during the school holidays there were usually several members present.

My sister Audrey and her life-long friend Doreen Bycroft were members, as were their eventual spouses, Johnny Colam and Dick Ryan, who for years was sports editor of the Lincolnshire Standard.

There were many members but this shortened list may bring back a few memories: Madge Smith, Lavinia Whalley, Rosemary Brown, Winsome Smith, Carol Chesman, Valerie Kinsey, Margaret Loveley, and the men: George and Peter Bell, Robin Midgeley, Maurice Dawson, Gordon Tait, Derek Holdsworth and Dick Westland.

Another male member later went to London and acted in various West End productions and can still be seen on the television, when films from the fifties, such as "The Battle of the River Plate", are shown. He was Johnny Britton.

They made their own amusement and one of their favourite pursuits was a game of "murder", for which the property was ideal, as it had several rooms and some attics on the top storey.

Before finding the murderer, the first object was to find the body and this was simplified during a game one night, when Doreen Bycroft fell through the ceiling from an attic and at least half the body was exposed.

In 1945 my cousin Leila Rastall joined the ranks of the G.I. Brides. Her wedding reception was held at our house, as at that time we lived at 65, High Street, which was a large rambling house that had at one time been a nurses' home.

It was next door to the Royal Oak, which in turn was aside the Lord Nelson and on our other side, nearer to Boston Motors, was Fred Herring, the cobbler. All four buildings were demolished, when the New Bridge was built.

The house was ideal for a reception, as there were several rooms all connected by long passageways and a large garden at the back with a huge pear tree. It was just before V.J. Day and similar weather to that we are now experiencing, so several guests were eating outdoors.

Leila married a pleasant U.S. airman named Lloyd Lewis, whose family ran a ten-pin bowling alley in a small town on the California coast. There were no bowling allies in this country then but we could imagine the place from seeing similar ones in films.

He had six friends with him and they were all tall and thin and most of them wore glasses, so it was hard to distinguish them but his best man stood out, as he had bright ginger hair and was called Red Horn.

Before the war Leila had worked at the County Hall, so she had plenty of friends in Boston, although she had spent the war first in the Land Army, then later in the WAAFs.

Lloyd was very friendly and, when he learned that I collected stamps, he introduced me to a friend of his, who had been wounded and now spent his time in a wheelchair in a home in Philadelphia. Paul Fulton was his name and we corresponded, until he died in 1950, and during that time he sent me hundreds of American Commemorative stamps and a giant stamp album. I sent him all the new issues of Great Britain but at that time they were very few; not like today, when there is a new issue nearly every month.

Lloyd and Leila went off to California and we heard from them regularly for a year or two, then we seemed to lose touch, until Leila contacted us about six years ago. She is now a widow and lives with her only son, who she calls Jimbo, further up the west coast of the United States at Gold Beach, Oregon.

They deal in antiques, mainly Mexican, and travel around the State Fairs in the summer and sell from a local shop in the winter. Quite an interesting life.

Every January Jimbo visits Mexico to replenish the stock but Leila worries until he returns, as there is danger from bandits. We hear nothing of this in our news; if Mexico is mentioned, all we hear is of illegal immigrants trying to enter the States over the Rio Grande.

One of the few things that was not rationed during the war was bread but this omission was rectified in 1946. Just as it was never realised that the Welfare State would lead to generations that expected to be looked after from the cradle to the grave, the consequences of bread rationing were also never thought through.

There were several pages in the ration books that had never been used and some genius in the Ministry of Food decided that they should play a part in bread rationing. They were all given different values with the result that it took the shopkeeper or roundsman twice as long to work out the coupons than it did to take the money.

Bakers were instructed to separate the various coupons, count them, put them in bags and wait until they were told where to send them. Months went by; the coupons accumulated but there was no word as to their eventual destination.

It had become apparent that an army would be needed to check the coupons and a huge building to accommodate them. In fact no coupons were ever sent anywhere and the bakers were left with a mountain of bags that they had to dispose of, when the fiasco was finally abandoned.

After fifty years it is easy to see the funny side of the situation and probably there are a few people, who remember bread ever being rationed but for me it had it's serious repercussions. It caused indirectly my grandmother's death and consequently my handicap of a weakened wrist that prevents me from taking a wheel off a car and once or twice has led to the embarrassment of asking someone half my size to help me.

My grandmother was turned seventy but had served in our baker's shop since 1904, and she had no intention of retiring. She coped well with everything, until she was faced with the task of working out how many coupons to take for three large whites, a small Hovis and a milk loaf.

Her mind rebelled; she admitted defeat; left the shop and from that point felt that her life was meaningless. She missed her regular routine and was soon ill in bed with her mind wandering to a happier past. She stopped eating and it became necessary for someone to sit with her. Mrs. Thompson from Pulvertoft Lane, a contemporary of grandmothers, relieved the family at mealtimes.

At this point I contrived to break my wrist. It was the summer holidays and we were playing football in the Nelson field. I fancied myself at that time as a goalkeeper and was throwing myself about determined that the ball would not pass. All went well, until a boy of eighteen, who worked on the railway, joined in the game, while on his way home. We were only twelve and he easily brushed past our defenders and let fly for the top corner from about eight yards. I managed to push it round the post but snapped my wrist back and they all crowded round me.

Dennis Robins, whose father was in the St. John Ambulance Service, told me it was broken, when I could not clench my fingers. I went home to break the news and was greeted by chaos. Aunt Amy, as we called Mrs. Thompson, had fallen asleep and grandmother had drunk some Zebo lead polish and the doctor had been fetched.

In the circumstances I never mentioned my wrist and it was two weeks later, after grandmother had died and been buried, before I told my parents.

It was a Monday and my father took me to Mr. Broomfield, a celebrated bone-setter from Alford, who held court in a room at the Red Lion at Spilsby every market day. He confirmed my wrist was fractured and it had mended itself, but the bone that should have been on the top had slipped to the side. If it were to be re-broken, he could not promise that it would make it any better.

With this news on top of the trauma he had experienced with losing his mother, after witnessing her rapid deterioration, my father felt sick and unable to drive. I felt much better, after Mr. Broomfield had snapped my tendons back into place and finally relieved my pain, so I led him into the bar of the Red Lion and, after drinking the only glass of whisky I ever saw him drink in his life, he recovered sufficiently to drive home.

Soon after the war, many years before Boston was twinned with Laval, a special friendship was forged with Bergen op Zoom, a Dutch town just north of the Belgium border. I still have the programme for the match, when they sent a football team to play Boston United.

Events were arranged in other sports between the two towns but after a year or two the connection seemed to be broken. Perhaps some reader could enlighten us as to how the link was made and why it did not last.

In 1946 Boston United played in the Midland League. After a five year football famine, the crowds flocked in and a four or five thousand gate was commonplace.

Several local players featured in the team: George Simmonds at centre half, the two wingers, Roy Houghton and Tommy Mitchum and Harry Sharp from Eastville at centre forward.

In those days there were inside forwards and wing halves and the only formation mentioned was the W formation. Players were allowed to use their skills and their individual flair was not destroyed by over-zealous, under-talented coaches.

If the wingers cut inside, the inside-forward automatically took their place on the wing and the whole pitch was used. Now for long periods all 20 outfield players occupy one third of the pitch near the centre circle, and if anyone dares to hit a long pass for the wingers or centre forward to run on to, he is considered old-fashioned.

Jock Bayne was a popular and reliable goalkeeper for many seasons and the full backs were Darwin and Trough, until the latter received a serious injury and Jack Duthoit took his place.

Every successful team had a good half back line and in that first post-war season Lock, Simmonds and Pate served Boston United very well. A high league position was welcome but the most important thing was that we finished above the local derby teams; Ransome & Marles and especially Grantham, who had Jock McCartney at centre forward.

In those seasons after the war many interesting players came and went. There was the Polish inside-forward Cieplinski, who was very fast. I remember one Saturday he ran into the goalpost and knocked himself out: they were square goalposts then, not the rounded ones they use today.

After George Simmonds retired, Roland Depear played centre half but he was soon transferred to Newport County. Other local players, who donned the United black and amber during those years were George Bell at left half and John Murray on the left wing.

Jack Stone came from Sheffield to play centre forward and stayed in Boston the rest of his life; later running the Station Hotel. He was an unusual centre forward; he scored most of his goals by dribbling through the defence: it was very rare for him to score from outside the penalty area.

Jack Duthoit was another, who settled in Boston and he remained life-long friends with Tony Freeman, who came to Boston at the same time as Jack to play on the right wing.

Tony now lives in Melton Mowbray.

Tommy Lowder also stayed in Boston, when his playing days were finally over but he gave sterling service to United for many, many years.

It was a great day for the town, when Don and Geoff Hazeldine came to join their ex Derby County colleagues, for it heralded Boston United's golden period, which culminated in the 1956 6-1 F.A. cup victory at the Baseball Ground.

I have the programme for Don Hazeldine's testimonial match, which was played on the 30th April, 1959. Boston won 6-4 against an All-Star X1 with Ray Middleton, the former United player-manager, in goal.

It was certainly an All-Star X1 for Billy Elliott, the international, was on the left wing and the great Len Shackleton was inside-right but the biggest star was centre forward....none other than Brian Clough.

Brian was then in the position that Matthew Le Tissier finds himself now. To quote from the programme notes: "we must all agree that it is remarkable how such a prolific goal-scorer can be overlooked for so long and so often".

Harold Kemps' painting of Bargate Green on VE Day and VJ Night must have brought memories flooding back to hundreds of Bostonians. On both occasions the crowds were colossal and he depicts this brilliantly.

The Moon Rocket, which was a focal point of the fair on the Green for many years, is instantly recognisable and the bunting recalls the decorations that appeared all over the town.

The bonfire on VJ Night was every bit as large as he painted it and a similar scene was repeated in towns and cities all over Great Britain.

There was a row of air-raid shelters on two sides of the Green and the more nimble and adventurous in the crowd climbed on top of these and joined in the singing and dancing. One sixty year old gentleman had been celebrating all day but still managed to ascend one of the shelters. While demonstrating the sailor's hornpipe to his younger companions, he fell off but, as often happens when a baby falls from a moving car, he suffered no ill effects, just bounced up and carried on dancing.

In 1950 the Young Conservatives used to reserve the two tennis courts at Burton House most Saturdays in the summer to stage a mixed doubles tournament. As there was always a surplus of ladies, Peter Smith, with whom I played table tennis in the winter, asked if I would help to redress the balance.

Dick Westland and Peter were the two males, whom the ladies hoped to be their partners, when the draw was made before the tournament. Dick was tall, which helped his service, and moved around the court both quickly and adroitly.

Over the next three summers I came to know him well and always enjoyed his company and we have remained friends ever since, although we only meet occasionally.

Our standard of tennis was not exceptional but we all enjoyed the contest and we sometimes attracted a few spectators.

Among the ladies were Violet Ashton, Margaret Smith, Nancy Allen, Barbara Taylor, Eve Coles, Denise Senior, Margaret Loveley, Taye Appleby, Beryl Ashley and sisters Margaret and Jocelyn Taylor.

Apart from Peter and Dick the men were Bernard Reed, Hugh Clancy, Bob Allen, Sid Lewis and Brian Manning. The Chairman of the Boston Young Conservatives at that time, Robin Midgeley, sometimes took part after some gentle persuasion.

As a climax the last tournament of each summer was played for the Midgeley Cup, which was donated by Robin's father, Councillor Bill Midgeley.

I believe it was won in 1950 by Peter Smith and Margaret Loveley, then in 1951 by Dick Westland and Eve Coles. In April, 1952 I started my National Service in the R.A.F. but by August I was stationed at Kirton-in-Lindsey and came home most weekends, so I was able to play in the tournaments.

That was the last year the Midgeley cup was played for, as Burton House changed hands and the tennis courts were taken up. My game had improved, as there was a tennis court just outside my block at Kirton-in-Lindsey and I enjoyed the game most mornings.

I was lucky in the draw for partners, as I was paired with Denise Senior, one of the more athletic ladies and we were the last winners of the Midgeley Cup.

The next summer we booked two courts in the Central Park but there was not the same enthusiasm and marriage had depleted our ranks, so the tournaments ceased.

Apart from a few friendly games about ten years later with Don Hazeldine that was the end of my tennis career.

After being deprived of sport for six years, people showed interest in every conceivable aspect of sport, when the war finally ended. All local teams enjoyed levels of support that had never been matched before, and have certainly never been matched since television gradually saturated our homes with coverage of every imaginable sport from all corners of the world.

When Boston Cricket Club played in the Central Park, there was a crowd all round the boundary and their presence lifted the players. The visiting teams always struggled to score, when Jack Harmon was bowling at one end and Reg Oughton at the other.

Boston's most successful team, however, was their water-polo team. For seven years from 1947 to 1954 they never lost a match. They won the Lincolnshire League and the Lincolnshire Knock-out Trophy every year.

Their hardest games were against Sleaford and R.A.F. Cranwell. Crowds of three or four hundred crowded into the old baths near the General Hospital for every home game, and three or four Blue Glider buses were filled for the away games.

The crowd was mixed but I was never sure if the female section was there to appreciate the standard of play or if the attraction was the seven hairy torsos and the well-developed biceps.

The all-conquering team was Ted Mableson in goal, George Brocklesby, Geoff Moulder, George and David Staniland, Harry Cowan and Alan Scotney. Over the years other members of the squad, who maintained success, were Charles Butler, Dick Gresswell and Vick Emery.

I started at the Boston Guardian in 1950 and joined a small but happy team. Apart from Mr. Skepper there was Hugh Clancy, chief reporter who later went to the Stamford Mercury, Ted Bray who passed over the hatched, matched and despatched to me, together with the whist drive winners, Lavinia Kirkby and Barbara Boggs. Charles Faulkner, the photographer, had a shop across West Street.

The Guardian used to be sold on a Wednesday and the Lincolnshire Standard on a Friday. There was a friendly rivalry but Hugh Clancy and George Bagley, who was then chief reporter at the Lincolnshire Standard, were the best of friends.

In 1938 my father was the President of the Boston and District Master Bakers, Millers and Confectioners. The next year Mr. Goodacre retired as secretary and father took his place and remained secretary for the next fifteen years.

Regular meetings were held and I helped by addressing the envelopes. The area covered extended as far as Spilsby and Skegness and there were 120 members at that time. The majority were bakers but there were four or five millers and about ten allied traders. If I were doing it today, I would only need eight envelopes at most.

In 1944 my father was elected to the National Association of Master Bakers and they held four meetings a year at the Trocadero in London. Their annual conference was in August and each year the week was spent at a different seaside town or a spa like Harrogate.

In 1947 my sister accompanied him to Great Yarmouth then in 1948 my brother and I went with him to Llandudno. We travelled in an old Vauxhall Cadet, which had been in mothballs during the war.

He had made friends with delegates from all over Britain but two in particular: a Mr. Bradley from Healing, near Grimsby and a Mr. Laud from Wellington in Shropshire. The three of them always stayed at the same hotel.

One year Mr. Bradley and Mr. Laud with their wives came to the Boston Bakers' Dinner, which was always held in the Louise Rooms at the White Hart Hotel. I believe George Truman from Sutterton was President that year and Coun. Mrs. Bertha Roe was Mayor with her daughter Mayoress.

Another Bakers' Dinner I recall readily was the year Bill Pannell from Norfolk Place was President and Coun. Midgeley was Mayor. Alderman Wrisdale from Wrangle was also a guest and their three wives were sisters.

After being involved in trade politics for twelve years, father became tired of the travelling it entailed and he was persuaded by Cyril Valentine to contest the Central Ward for the Liberals in the local elections in 1956.

He narrowly missed being elected but the next year he fought the South Ward, where he was known by virtually everyone, and won convincingly. He shared my view that local government ideally should not be concerned with politics, but we both had to admit that party backing was vital.

At that time Couns. Cyril and Emily Valentine had toned the art of canvassing to a fine degree. I joined the team of canvassers and had to admire the thoroughness shown by everyone. There was none of the tame house calling we experience today.

A team of four entered a street, two went down one side and two down the other and either the candidate or Cyril Valentine kept nipping across the road to give help, where it was needed.

Several streets were covered each night and when the canvassers returned to the committee rooms, they knew exactly which votes they could rely on, which were doubtful and which were a waste of time. Come election day no cars were wasted fetching in opponent's supporters.

The last hour or two in the committee rooms were hectic, as an army of helpers were dispatched to either cajole or shame reluctant citizens to make use of their vote, if the tellers had confirmed they had not already done so.

Then came the climax.... the count. After weeks of canvassing and the excitement of polling day, it can be an anti-climax but, if you win, you don't want the night to end.

The night father was successful there were two other councillors elected; Arthur Durrant and Alfred Adolf Goodson and all three served the town well. They were both Labour councillors but I know my father was sincere, when he congratulated them.

In the late fifties the Liberals had many triumphs in the local elections: Bruce Veal, Tom Balderston, Freddy Myatt and Ken Welberry were all elected, but the most dynamic Liberal councillor, unfortunately, left the town, just when his value to the community was being realised: that was Geoff Brooks.

With the Valentine's tuition all these councillors became adept at electioneering but the best two canvassers never stood themselves: they were Joe Cupper and George Twiddy.

Several years later, when father put up for the Holland County Council, we missed all this excitement, as he was the only candidate and was returned unopposed.

Just as today, fifty years ago anything that went wrong was blamed on the local council and anything that went right was quickly accepted, forgotten and went uncredited.

It has always been a thankless job to be a local councillor and it takes a special kind of person to undertake the task. They must be thick-skinned, public-spirited, confident and never disheartened by the lack of praise.

Very occasionally they may receive verbal or even written plaudits for some help given or some anomaly rectified, but such bouquets are rare.

This is why my father treasured a file of letters, which he accumulated during his fourteen years on the town council. He was just as pleased with a few scribbled lines from a pensioner, whose pavement had been repaired, as he was with a typewritten letter from Gerald Beaulah, expressing his appreciation when father helped to overturn a decision, which threatened his business.

There was not a week went by without some call for help from a disgruntled voter, who either came to the shop or approached father, while he was on his bread round. This partly was to blame for his soubriquet "The Midnight Baker".

To be honest his late finishing was more to do with helping customer's children with their homework or talking to their fathers about football.

The council officers always found dad accessible, which was a great help to them for they only saw most councillors at meetings. If Mr. Coley, needed a councillor's signature for any reason, he knew he could contact my father easily.

In the forties and fifties councillors willingly gave their time and experience without any reward or even expenses: there was no option of payment for attending meetings, as there is today.

If father had still been alive a few years ago, he would have been pleased to see Ernie Napier installed as Mayor of Boston, for Ernie was one of the lads that he used to encourage, when he served his mother with bread years ago.

Father declined when it was his turn to be Mayor, as mother was too ill to be Mayoress and my sister was living on the Isle of Wight.

As anyone who has read George Bagley's "Boston, It's Story and People" will know, there was a competition between Boston Grammar School and Kirton Grammar School as long ago as 1762, when Luke Hansard was sent to Kirton in preference to Boston.

This rivalry still existed in the early years of this century, when Kirton Grammar School under their Headmaster, Mr. Keal, were recording better examination results than Boston Grammar School.

Several boys cycled from Boston each day to attend Kirton Grammar School, including my father, Percy Handley, the builder's son and Arthur Leafe, who became a main-line engine driver and also landlord of the Golden Lion in High Street.

My father matriculated in his Cambridge examination, when he was fourteen and was waiting to go to university, when he enlisted in the Royal Flying Corps at the age of seventeen.

It was 1917 and he went to train as a navigator at Farnborough in Hampshire. At the end of the Great War he was in hospital and, when he returned home, he went into the family bakery business and never completed his education.

I believe he regretted this later in life and compensated by spending a lot of time and energy in first trade politics and later in local politics.

I have digressed as usual from the Second World War but this postscript will help me return. Mr. Clark from Woad Farm Road, who lived in a house near Kelsey Bridge during the war, told me that a German plane, a Junkers, crash-landed in a field down Pilley's Lane early in the war and the crew surrendered to the farmer.

He also reminded me of the occasion when a land-mine dropped in a field close to Rochford Tower but luckily caused little damage. Perhaps someone remembers either or both of these incidents.

All aspects of life were rekindled after the war, including amateur dramatics. The Boston Playgoers' Society soon staged productions at the Blenkin Memorial Hall.

They will have full details of the plays and casts but I believe one of the first was Goldsmith's "She Stoops To Conquer" and I remember seeing Sheridan's "The Rivals".

There was also a very active drama group at St. James Church in George Street. I remember more about their productions, as my sister, Audrey, was a member and I was often coerced into helping her learn her lines.

In 1950 she went with a group from St. James to see the passion play at Oberomergau and later they put on a passion play of their own. My lasting memory of that was the performance of Sidney Burgess as Judas Iscariot.

Another year their production was based on the Old Testament and my sister had to tolerate being tormented by my brother and I, when she told us she would be Eve. Any fears were soon evaporated, when she said Adam would be played by Dick Leafe, who recently retired as Verger at St. Botolphs, and even then was known by all as a perfect gentleman.

St. James's Hall used to be packed for their performances and many memorable productions were staged, none more so than "A Mirror To Elizabeth" with Margaret Ingram as Queen Elizabeth I.

Apart from those already mentioned there were numerous members of the drama group at that time, including Jessie Watling, Madge Smith, Doreen Bycroft, Jack Cole, Leslie Sutcliffe, Basil Heath, Fred Whelbourne and Ken Sharman. Ken's father was verger at St. James for many years and Ken succeeded him

Like most of those mentioned, Ken was also in the church choir together with his brother John, who moved to South Yorkshire and is the father of Helen Sharman, the first lady astronaut.

It was a retrograde step when St. James Church and Hall, which was only built in 1865, was pulled down in 1969 to make way for Sally Morland's supermarket.

It had been a focal point of my life: used for school classrooms while I was at Staniland school during the war; Saturday afternoon film shows; early morning communions on Sunday: playing Billiards and Snooker matches in the clubroom.

When I married, even the Wedding Reception was held in the Hall. It was Boxing Day, 1956 and it was a great success, thanks to my friend, Noel Holgate, another choirboy and server at St. James, who acted as M.C. and made sure everyone had a night to remember.

Noel used to play the cello in the Grammar School orchestra and later followed his uncle, Ernie Massingham, into the local dance band scene. Ernie played an electric guitar but Noel naturally played the double bass.

I think Noel played with his workmate at Hardy & Collins, Ken Woodthorpe, in the Tuxedoes but the personnel of the local bands changed over the years and I find it difficult to remember who played in which band.

One or other were at the Assembly Rooms on a Saturday and the Gliderdrome on a Wednesday. The big bands and jazz groups came to the Gliderdrome on a Saturday. Ted Heath with Lita Rosa, Dennis Lotis and Dickie Valentine; Oscar Rabin and his orchestra; Mick Mulligan and his Magnolia Players with George Melly and my particular favourite, Freddy Randall and his jazz band.

The first band after the war was Allam and Perkins, then came Gus Smalley's Gaiety and Jasper Sharpe's Embassy and the Tuxedoes. For certain numbers Noel used to abandon his double bass and sing, and by coincidence another boy from his form at the Grammar School sang with the Embassy, Eric Slinger.

I remember Ken Woodthorpe on trumpet, his brother Roy on trombone, Ken Johnson on saxophone and Tom Mashford on the drums. Charles Buttery played the piano with the Gaiety and Bob Kitchen with one of the others.

The overriding memory of those Saturday nights at the Assembly Rooms is when the Embassy were playing and towards the end of the evening someone always requested "Cherry Red and Apple Blossom White" with a trumpet solo by Alf Callow.

My sole experience of acting came while I was in the scouts. We put on a play at the Mission to Seamen near the dock gates. We all made sure our parents and family came to see us, as we were raising money for the troop.

I was padded up and my face blackened to appear as an elderly black maid and I spoke like Hattie McDaniel in "Gone With The Wind". As they went home my father asked my mother why I had not been in it after all. He never recognised me.

In 1944 every Saturday I helped to serve customers in our West Street café. I replaced my sister, who wanted to concentrate on preparing for her School Certificate examinations.

My mother had run the café in the thirties, before we three children had laid prior claim to her time and attention. Mrs. Wallace then was in charge for several years and she managed with one assistant during the week, but a reinforcement was necessary on a Saturday.

The menu was not elaborate: sardines on toast, beans on toast, toasted teacake or a selection of cakes were the main items and many people had just a cup of tea. The shop downstairs also sold bread, cakes and biscuits, so they were pleased with my young legs to run up and down stairs, when they were busy.

The property is now Priestley's fruit shop and before that the Cameo hairdressers, but during the war the shop was divided into two; we had one half and Mr. Gale had the other as a barber's shop. The café was above both shops.

I particularly liked clearing up after the customers, as the majority slipped a threepenny piece under the saucer and it financed by trips to the cinema. I rarely missed a programme at that time, and there were three cinemas with two of them changing their films in mid-week.

There were not so many cafes in those days and we were ideally situated next to the White Horse, which was a nerve-centre for carriers and shoppers coming into town on market days. Rail travellers with time to kill also made use of our café, as they walked down to the station.

The other side of Gale's barber's shop was Stanwells the butchers, which is now Ashton carpet shop. On the opposite side of West Street was Bullivants the chemists, who years later moved further down the street.

I was ten years old in 1944 and I had taken the examinations to go to the Grammar School but my name was not included in the list of scholarships and free places, so I was resigned to returning to Staniland School for another year, as I had another chance, when I was eleven.

Towards the end of August my parents received a letter to say I had been awarded a Parry scholarship and I would be starting at the Grammar School after all. After the initial panic, my mother organised my uniform and all the minor paraphernalia and, when the big day came, I was stood up the wall with the other new boys, fully equipped. We never found out if I had done well or if I had been next on the list, and lucky to be chosen for a scholarship that was only given occasionally from money left for that cause by the Thomas Parry Trust in 1875.

We thought it might provide a clue, if I were placed in the A form but we were still no wiser, because I was put in 3A2. I was always grateful for this afterwards, because the boys in 3A1 took Latin and we took German.

1944 was the last year parents could pay for their children to go to Grammar School and they changed the system of numbering classes the next year. Whereas forms 1 and 2 had been for the boys, whose parents had paid, and who started at the age of eight or nine, now everyone started in form 1.

In 1945 I found myself in 2A and together with about ten others, when the Latin period came round, we evacuated the classroom and joined the German class.

One repercussion of my sudden departure from Staniland School was the change in attitude of my former friends. Like most boys of that age I belonged to a gang and we had strict rules. We had recently expelled Roy "Inky" Barton from the gang and his only crime was that he had flitted from Pulvertoft Lane to Cheyney Street. We had all signed a type-written letter telling him of our decision.

So my fate was sealed as soon as they knew I was going to be a "Grammar School puppy dog". It sounds unimportant now and a few years later I was again friendly with them all, but at the time it was deadly serious to a ten year old and caused a few sleepless nights.

The gang consisted of Jacky Tebbs, Bob Marriott, Barry Barton and Ronny Thompson and together we controlled the Pulvertoft Lane – Edwin Street area, and the stretch of the river bank from Thompson's Slip to Gostelow's Slip. (A slip is an inlet in the bank, where the fishing smacks could be secured while they were repaired or painted).

The worst danger we faced was being doused with a bowl of water, if we made too much noise as we chased through the labyrinth of passages dissecting our domain.

When our class started at the Grammar School in 1944, there was no time wasted discussing how many there were in a class or bewailing the shortage of materials; the available staff did the best they could with what was there.

None of us suffered because of the prevalent conditions for, when we took our School Certificate in 1949, we achieved one of the best batch of results ever recorded. The quality of teaching is the most important factor and, in spite of what we said about them behind their backs, all the teachers were respected. How can children today respect teachers, who go to school dressed in T-shirts and jeans?

The first year the tallest boy in the class was Joe Lovelace: most of us were in short trousers but he already wore "long-uns". He hardly grew afterwards and when we left, he was the smallest.

Apart from Gordon Butcher, who was tragically killed in the first year, Joe was the first of our year to die. Since then Derek Marshall and Jim Sargent have been killed in car accidents, while Peter Howes and Ralph Mashford have also died.

The majority left Boston: at least three are abroad; Jim Ransom is in South Africa; Vick Emery is in New York and Mick Barnfield, whose father was headmaster at Kirton Holme School, emigrated with his family to Australia.

Those of us who stayed in Boston were in many cases tied to family businesses. John Cammack, the furniture shop; Ron Holmes, the shoe shop; Charles Wright, the millers; Philip Cooper and Michael Priestley, both produce merchants and Dick Parker, then undertakers, now boat builders.

Two others started their own business: Mick Andrews as a television engineer and he also helped his wife, Marjorie, in their Brothertoft Road shop and Alan Curtis, who has wholesaled clothes and household lines since Johnson's warehouse closed in Pump Square.

Robin Frost was the son of the Chief of Police and they left Boston somewhere round 1947 but he was soon replaced in the form of Geoff Hastead, the son of the Fire Chief.

I know others have stayed in the area, because I have read about them or seen their photographs in the Lincolnshire Standard. Stan Graves became a councillor; Tony Brown became a magistrate and I know Jack Sleight is still in the choir at St. Botolphs. When Austin Munks died, I read that Aubrey West was one of his workers, who had inherited the firm.

Noel Holgate retired as managing director of Hardy & Collins;   Derek Whelbourne still works for Johnsons Seeds;   Geoff Dunham has worked in the pharmacy department at Boots;   Eric Slinger used to help Jasper Sharp repairing false teeth and the last time I heard of John Harrison he was helping my brother-in-law with his book-keeping.

I know Alan Woodthorpe worked at Fogartys and Brian Redman at Rice, Waite & Marris, the solicitors. The last time I saw Don Smith he was managing Peter Taylor's garage at Skegness.

Don was the first in our form to show an interest in girls and used to entertain us with accounts of his amorous adventures. Later he encountered serious opposition from Rodney Newell, whose curly blond hair acted as a magnet and he upstaged Don by bringing photographic proof of his conquests.

Rodney married Lindis Perkins and she followed him to Australia to see their children, after they separated.

My close friend Peter Day went to work for De Havillands; Tony Jakes became an airline pilot; Peter Luff entered the foreign office and Barry Smith taught at a private school.

We all had nicknames at school and usually they were used as an alternative to our Christian names, but some were heard so regularly that they replaced the proper name. Try as I might, I cannot recall the real names of "Quack" Taylor, "Milky" Fox and, if I am still allowed to say it, "Darky" Whiteman.

There were many others I have neither seen or heard of since the day we left: Ray Blackburn, Maurice Choat, Geoff Cross, Ken Cross, Robin Everett, Ron Faulkner, Derrick Gosling, Tony Harrison, Bryn Johnson, Tim McKeen, Michael Penson, Jeff Thurlby and Brian Wrigley.

I can almost hear the form-master reading the register and it brings to mind the last scene in "Goodbye, Mr. Chips".

If I have forgotten any of my classmates, please do not be offended and I will be delighted to hear news of or better still hear from anyone I have mentioned.

It is hard to imagine now but in the wartime High Street was the busiest street in Boston. It was vibrant and property was much in demand; there were no empty shops then.

The four hundred yards between the goods yard and Fydell Crescent supported three bakers, three cobblers, two butchers, two barbers, two fish and chip shops, five grocers and, of course, four pubs.

Then there was Freddy Walker's bicycle shop. On Wednesdays and Saturdays it was one of the busiest places in town. People used to cycle from Wyberton, Frampton and Kirton and they all left their bikes at Walker's.

Freddy Walker was a little man and he looked even smaller, because he stooped as he walked or, I should say, ran: he was always in a hurry. He was ably assisted by Percy Jackson, who inherited the business when Mr. Walker died, and in the fifties and sixties many people thought Percy was Mr. Walker, because he always traded as Walker's.

They were very busy, as everybody relied on bicycles at that time. On market days a Mr. Norman was in charge of all the bikes left at Walker's, while their owners walked further into town.

They only paid a copper or two and they could shop with a free mind, knowing their cycles were in good hands and under cover. On a fine day there could be as many as a hundred cycles in Mr. Norman's care.

The yard at the side of the shop stretched right to the Nelson field, so there was plenty of room but I remember seeing cycles stored six deep.

Mr. Norman knew his clients, however, and the bikes nearest the wall always belonged to those who made a day of it and, if anyone had to be home for tea, their bikes were always handy.

I believe the money people paid for the service mainly went to pay Mr. Norman but Freddy knew what he was doing, because he was kept busy every market day repairing some of the bikes and, if anyone needed a new cycle, they naturally bought it from him.

Mr. Norman lived in a passage at the top of Liquorpond Street and, unfortunately his house was destroyed, when the bomb fell but luckily he was in a shelter.

Our shop was directly opposite Walker's and, instead of carrying bread and cakes from town, several women waited until they reclaimed their cycles then bought their supplies from us, so we benefited from Mr. Norman's hard work.

Quite a few of the cyclists, though, were on our bread-round anyway and had already had a delivery on the Friday.

Next door to Walkers was Wright's creamery and Mrs. Wright was turned seventy but still served customers, when her daughter was busy.

The milk was in churns and they ladled it into the customers' jugs. I often fetched our milk in a two pint jug and in the summer we always covered the jug, when we got home with a cloth with beads hanging down the side to keep the flies out.

On Wednesdays and Saturdays Mrs. Wright always made cream cheeses to coincide with the influx of villagers.

After the war when Mrs. Wright died, the shop was used by Arthur Braime to sell wet fish but during the war his father, Louis Braime, used to sell his fish together with shrimps and prawns from a tricycle, similar to those used to sell ice creams.

He cycled all round Boston and he was a colourful character with his fisherman's jersey and his ear-rings. There must be several readers, who remember him.

Fish was one of the few foods never rationed.

Next to the creamery was Percy White's fish and chip shop. It was Mrs. White, whose family had been fish fryers; Percy was actually a skilled french polisher but he was equally adept at frying fish and chips.

Their friendly rivals, Phyllis and Reg Vickers, were in exactly the same position. Reg was really a butcher but, when Mrs. Ladds, Phyllis's mother, retired from the shop, Reg helped his wife to carry it on and became a proficient fish fryer.

There were no organised queues in those days; you reached the counter as soon as you could and cursed your fate, if you chose to stand behind someone who wanted "a piece and a pennoth ten times". The counter at Vicker's shop was high and, when you reached the front, there was always the danger they would not see you.

The two shops fried on different nights but twice a week they both fried and a choice had to be made. After all these years, I will still not reveal which I favoured.

Fifty years ago our entry into the Nelson field was through the Chapel of Ease passage. We knew the name came from the building at one side of the passage but it always confused me that my parents referred to it as St. Aidan's Church.

It had stood empty and unused for twenty years and, after the railings were taken down at the start of the war, there was nothing to protect it from all and sundry.

It was not until I read George Bagley's "Boston: It's Story and People" that I found that St. Aidan's had been built around 1820 as a chapel of ease to the parish church. Presumably St. Botolph's must have been crowded at that time and it was felt necessary to relief it with a separate building.

Although it came under the jurisdiction of the Bishop of Lincoln, it was independent of the vicar of Boston and it was never licensed for marriages.

It was pulled down soon after the war and today there is only a small sign to show it was ever there.

The row of seven or eight houses on the other side of the passage survived longer but they too have gone now, but I remember them as happy homes with their share of lively children.

There were Mrs. Burgess, Mrs. Hall, Mrs. Homewood, Mrs. Stevens and Mrs. Judd at the bottom and a lady in her nineties, who I believe was called Mrs. Whitworth.

On the other side of High Street within one hundred yards of St. Aidan's Church was the Baptist Church. Built in 1937, it still stands and is still very much in use.

The caretakers, Albert and Lily Myers, lived in a house adjacent to the church but Reverend Piper lived further along High Street, next door to Mr. Crashley, a director of Graves & Hobster, the potato merchants.

Two hundred yards further up High Street, next door to Boston Motors, was the Salvation Army Citadel. Built in 1889, it is also still in use.

Opposite Boston Motors at one end of the Doughty Quay there was a Billiard Hall but this burnt down during the war. I believe it was an ordinary fire; not caused by incendiary bombs.

Next came William's newspaper shop and each year, as Christmas approached, I spent many a hour looking in their window, trying to decide which annual to ask for. My sister collected card games and we spent the long winter nights playing Lexicon, Kan-U-Go, Menu, Express, They're Off or another game from her extensive collection.

At Christmas she received yet another game and my brother and I usually finished up with a Nipper annual and a Pop annual and our father spent Boxing Day laughing at them.

After four or five houses, the next shop was George "Codger" Hall's, the glazier. He also sold paint and walked up the street with a white painter's apron tied around his waist. Whenever he passed a boy or girl, he made a noise like a cat, who had trapped his tail in a door, then carried on with a straight face, never turning round to enjoy their reactions.

Handley's the builders was opposite, next door to the Lord Nelson pub. Percy Handley drove a small lorry to deliver heavy materials to the various sites, but his workmen put their tools and smaller items on a hand-truck and pushed it to wherever they were working.

There were usually a bricklayer or carpenter and a labourer with each truck and about eight o'clock each morning four or five trucks left the yard. If anyone started working at Handley's when they left school, it was considered that they had landed a good job.

Mr. King and his wife lived in a house at the side of Mr. Hall's shop and his brother, Bill King lived with them. Bill was a fisherman and was a regular customer at my mother's shop for pigtail twist, which most fishermen at that time used to chew.

He was a very friendly man and, if I heard his voice in the shop, I always went through the curtain that separated it from our living room, because he fascinated me; he was cross-eyed.

Another facet of him baffled me, for he always wore thigh-boots, which were at least two sizes too big and his friends pulled his leg about it. Tragically there was to be a more serious outcome to his idiosyncrasy.

The fishing smacks never "went down", if a storm was threatening but sometimes they were surprised by an unexpected storm. On one such occasion the smack Bill worked on was caught out in the Wash and they were hurrying to pull their nets in, when Bill stumbled and fell over the side. His mate grabbed his legs to save him but all he had in his hands were Bill's oversized thigh-boots. His body was found a week later.

Each day as I walked to Staniland School during the war years I passed Herring's cobblers shop and I always looked at the miniature cobbler sat in the middle of his window, hammering on the sole of a shoe.

There were no electric wires attached to him and, if he had been clockwork, Mr. Herring would have spent most of his time winding him up and he looked too old to run on batteries. Yet I never passed that window without seeing his arm in continual motion. I never did find out how he worked, and I often wonder what happened to him.

My grandmother had a tin frog on her mantelpiece and, when you wound the key in his back, he tried to catch a fly that always stayed just beyond his reach. All the family remembers it but no one knows where it went.

It is particularly galling, when you see similar automatons on the Antique Road Show and some expert says they fetch fantastic prices in auctions.

Fred Herring, who lived at the shop, was helped by a brother, Sid, who lived down Woodville Road and was the father of identical twins. They were always busy, in spite of having two competitors within a short distance. Everyone had their boots and shoes soled and heeled several times in those days, before buying a new pair.

One of his competitors was Mr. Checkley. His shop was between Smith's coal yard and the Railway goods yard. He also could always been seen busy near his window and his wife, Maggie, served the customers to prevent him being disturbed.

The third cobbler was Percy James. His little shop was between the Baptist Church and Burrows & Marshall's grocery shop. His window was boarded up, except for a small square of glass in one corner near the door. On a dull day he supplemented the poor light with a gas mantle at the back of his shop.

He lived somewhere near Daisy Dale down Mount Bridge and walked to work every day. His workplace could have been mistaken for the Black Hole of Calcutta but he was never short of company.

Apart from customers, people popped in his door, which was never closed however cold, and spent a few minutes with him. His shop was the local Joke Exchange. He passed on all the latest jokes and collected others in return.

The two barber's shops at the south end of High Street were almost neighbours. Only White Horse Lane and Dalton's herbal shop separated them.

I know little of Brown's, as I never used the shop until much later, when my friend George Clark, who retired last year, became the resident barber. When young, I always had my hair cut at Bob Lewis's shop.

It is debatable whether I learned more at school or waiting for my turn at the barbers. There were usually three or four more mature customers, mainly fishermen, sat waiting and a lad with good ears could pick up several useful fragments of information at each visit. The secret was to stay quiet and hope they forgot you were there.

When Mrs. Clayton closed her sweet shop, there was a third Barbers opened. Len Simpson traded next door to Hardy & Collins for several years.

Between Percy James and Bob Lewis was Burrows & Marshall's grocery shop. They survived the longest of the five grocery shops. Jim Marshall went in the forces and Jim Burrows ran the shop through the war years.

When the war was over, they were one of the first shops to start making ice cream again. The other two were Smaller's in Wide Bargate and a shop down Tattershall Road. They were famous for their ice creams and, especially on a Sunday afternoon, there were queues outside their shop.

In the years when High Street flourished they employed two full-time staff, George Maddison and Fred Burgess, and all four were kept busy.

During the war the house next to W. H. Smith's coal yard in High Street was owned by Darbys, the memorial masons but soon after the war it became the offices of Hardy & Collins, and they extended it and built warehouses behind it and developed the site beyond recognition.

Over the years they diversified sensibly and had several strings to their bow but it was as crop sprayers that they grew most quickly. They specialised in aerial spraying and won contracts for working abroad. I remember Ken Woodthorpe and Tony Mills going to Sudan with pilots and engineers and staying for several weeks: a trip that was repeated several times.

In the fifties they employed many people, most of them my contemporaries or a little older and I was friendly with them all. In fact, when they arranged a football match with Parkinsons, the auto electricians, and found themselves a player short, Walt Ladds asked if I could play.

It was the last game of football I ever played and they shoved me on the left wing but I went out on a high note, cutting in a la Paul Merson and hitting the ball into the top right-hand corner. I forget who won but the score was something like 9-8.

Others who worked at Hardy & Collins were Roy Woodthorpe, Bob and Eric Kitchen, and Noel Holgate, who went on to become managing director.

After they were taken over by Newark Egg Packers and they in turn were taken over by Ross Foods, Walt Ladds stayed with Mr. Hardy and became his farm secretary.

Two employees, Dick Moore and Sam Larthwell lived in houses in Hardy & Collin's yard and "Mrs. Sam", as she was known by all the staff, cleaned the offices and made the tea. She looked after them like a mother hen.

She also kept an eye on her neighbour, Miss. Barwick, who lived in a little house between the yard and Mrs. Clayton's sweet shop. Over all the years I knew Miss. Barwick she always wore the same hat: a felt bonnet that had started life as red but had gradually faded until it finished as a dusky pink.

As she was leaving our shop one windy September day, a sudden gust dislodged her hat and I ran down the street to retrieve it. I was amazed how heavy it was and as I brought it back for her, I noticed she had countless layers of newspaper inside. I am not sure why it was there but, if a slate had fallen on her head as she went home, she would never have felt anything.

Miss. Thomas lived at 107, High Street. She was a refined, well-spoken lady, who lived to a good age and retained her decorum to the end. She never stooped but walked erect, as she, no doubt, had been trained to do as a young lady.

During the war her brother lived with her and he too was immaculate. He always wore leather leggings, and strode down the street as if he were walking the Yorkshire Moors. He died years before his sister and it was only after his death that I discovered he was quite famous.

I always thought he dressed too well to be a painter, as he was described by most people, and in fact he was Billy Thomas, the artist, whose paintings now change hands for hundreds of pounds.

Not many people will know that there used to be a brewery in High Street. It was at 101 and was owned by a family called Swinns. They also owned the Robin Hood.

This was years before the war, probably the 1920s. The Robin Hood is the only one of the four pubs left standing, which were in use at the start of the war. The Plough, The Royal Oak and the Lord Nelson were all pulled down, although they built a new Lord Nelson down Woodville Road.

Next door to our baker's shop, across the opening to Pulvertoft Lane, lived Harry Bullogh. He repaired false teeth when people broke them, and he was always busy, as he did a good job and did it quickly.

He never married and lived with his mother and aunt, Miss. Hawling. During the war the two old ladies used one of their front rooms to sell haberdashery and Harry mended the teeth upstairs.

His mother died first and he looked after his aunt for several years, until she also died, then, I'm afraid Harry went off the rails. He became an alcoholic and every time he had a customer the money went on drink instead of food. While our shop was open, we helped him survive with food that was past it's best (there were no sell-by dates at that time) and, when we closed in 1969, Jim Marshall took over the responsibility, until one day he found him dead on the floor with mice running over him.

When he looked in the cellar, it was full of empty bottles.

Ask anyone today who comes to mind when you mention the history of Boston and eighty percent will answer George Bagley, and the other twenty percent Harry Fountain but, if you had asked the same question fifty years ago, one hundred percent would have said Walter Whyers.

He was the undisputed authority on everything concerning Boston and was often called upon to settle arguments. He was a tailor by trade and his workshop was behind Scroxton's fruit shop in High Street, near Lunn's picture gallery.

He was a master cutter and made suits for many leading townsmen and the landed gentry. His son, Ben, was a dealer in butter and eggs and his premises were adjacent at the start of the war but later he traded from his home in Liquorpond Street.

Ben and his wife, Ivy, had been friends of my mother and father since the twenties, when they all four belonged to the Boston and District Motor Cycle Club.

Mother had no difficulty persuading me to fetch our weekly rations of butter and eggs, because "Aunt Ivy", as we called her, had a monkey in her garden and I used to love watching him.

I am grateful to the Rev. Robin Everett to take the time to write and bring me up to date with some of my school mates. Robin was not only in my class at the Grammar School he was also a co-member of the Fifth Boston Scout Troop and we were both born in January, 1934.

In fact for a time we were both in the Kingfisher patrol but he later became patrol leader of the Ravens and eventually Troop leader. He was Skip Lucas's right hand man for several years.

His sister, Mavis, was also a Guide leader and stayed with the movement most of her life but, when I phoned to thank him for his letter, he told me she died a few years ago.

He also explained that he spent twelve months in Montserrat, near Antigua, in the West Indies during 1986-87 and went back four years ago to help the islanders clear up after Hurricane Hugo. They are now threatened by a possible eruption of a volcano, that has been dormant for two hundred years.

Apart from providing the correct Christian names for some of our fellow pupils, Robin also mentioned some I had omitted. After his prompting, I now recall Gordon Barker and I remember Gary Gerson but I did not include him originally, as he was only with us for one year, but I remember well his red hair and freckles.

I am ashamed that I failed to mention Derek Simmonds, whose father George played centre half for Boston United and, even worse, I did not include Ron Ruskin and I had been talking to him only in August.

I used to watch Boston United with Ron just after the war and he often came home with me, because his parents were busy printing. We were two of a group of about eight lads, who were nearly thrown out of the Odeon one evening.

It would have been about 1950 and Ron was working with his father, Len, together with Chuck Elsam, who was also learning to become a printer. It was Chuck's laugh that started the trouble.

We had gone to see John Wayne in "The Fighting Kentuckian" but it was the second feature, "The Jones Family Down On The Farm", that set Chuck off laughing.

Every time Spring Byington as Mrs. Jones wanted Jed Prouty as Mr. Jones she opened the door and shouted Cy at the top of her voice. The cows, the sheep, the pigs and the horses all ran for cover and the family dog dived under the farmhouse.

This sequence tickled Chuck and it happened at least eight times during the film and each time his guffaws grew louder. His laughter was infectious and soon all eight of us were laughing uncontrollably. When the usherette asked us to be quiet, it only made us laugh all the more and it was not until Mr. Pearce, the manager, threatened to have us thrown out, that our merriment gradually subsided.

When the big film started, we were surprised to find Oliver Hardy in a John Wayne western and for a horrible moment it looked as if the cacophony would re-erupt but Ron managed to keep Chuck under control.

Robin Everett mentioned in his letter that Jim Wightman had moved to Grantham from the Grammar School but Dave McNaughton, a sub-editor at the Lincolnshire Standard, told me he knew Jim at Spalding Grammar School, and he went to university and qualified as a doctor. Later he became a General Practitioner at Grantham, so that would be when Robin met him again. Jim retired from his practice last year and now lives in a fine house just outside Grantham.

Since I started writing this column in May I have received numerous letters and phone calls, most of them complimentary. This week I received a long letter from Margaret Allgood, who left Boston in 1960 to live in Peterborough and has now settled in Rippingale, near Bourne.

Her mother, Mrs. Maddrell, sends her the Standard each week and she was kind enough to say she reads my column first, then Spectator, whose identity I suspected but now feel sure of, after reading Margaret's letter.

She was in my class at Staniland School but I remember her best from the Sunday afternoons I spent at my grandmother's house, 8, Station Street. At that time Mrs. Maddrell lived across the street from my grandmother, Mrs. Bob Blackamore, who was known to the neighbours as Aunt Louisa.

The Great Northern public house was on the corner of James Street, then came Margaret's house, then Cecil Brant's, whose younger daughter, Eileen, was Margaret's friend, then I think there was a Mrs. Polkinghorn.

My grandmother died in 1943, so I was only seven or eight and very shy. I should not imagine Margaret remembers me in Station Street, because as soon as either she or Eileen Brant came out to play, I retreated through the house and started playing on the Station Pad, a field at the back of the house.

Margaret names her other friends as Marjorie Revell, Meraney Craven, Violet Simpson and the twins, Eileen and Marlene Watts.

I wonder if she remembers any of these other girls from our class: Pad Ladds, Elaine Davey, Margaret Lacy, Cynthia Wright, Thelma Reed, Doreen Read, Alma Douse, Mary Robinson, Pamela Kinsey and Sylvia Fox.

I am pleased the Editor sent the letter to me unopened, for, if he had read it, I am afraid he may have asked her to take over the column. Her letter was so interesting and well written. For example, when she was writing about her early years, when she lived in Ransome Place, off London Road and attended St. Thomas's School.

"One very vivid memory I have of my early days at St. Thomas's School was when I was walking home after school along the bank and saw what I thought were German soldiers pacing up and down the swing bridge! I knew the war was on and, even though I was only maybe seven at the time, I thought that we had been invaded and I recall being very frightened and running back to school. I was not alone in my fear, others had done the same but we were all reassured that everything was fine; it was only a film crew making a feature film about the Dutch resistance, called "One of our Aircraft is Missing".

She also mentioned that during the war the Guildhall was used as a British Restaurant. "We were issued with discs which we presented to the lady with silver grey hair at the pay desk and then we sat down at long trestle tables and had wonderful dinners everyday".

The following passage reminded me of something that happened to my father and brother towards the end of the war. "Whilst I lived in Ransome Place or California Place, as it was known, our house backed onto the coal yard and railway, which was used for the trains to go from the dock, over the swing bridge, into the coal yard and back again. I was aware of the screeching, whining sound overhead and suddenly I was scooped up in safe arms, carried into the house and pushed under the stairs, as the German fighter, aiming for a train, machine gunned all around us. Afterwards, when we saw the bullet holes, we realised how lucky we had been".

My brother was always reluctant to leave his bed during an air-raid but during one of the last alerts two or three German planes seemed to stay over the town for quite a while. My father left the shelter to fetch my brother, thinking they might start bombing, and, as they were returning down High Street, one of the planes opened fire with cannon shells. They dived to the ground and in the morning the marks the shells had made could be seen in the wall of the house just above where they had lain.

Staniland School will celebrate it's centenary on the 18th January, 1996. The foundation stone for the original Staniland Board School was laid by the Chairman, Mr. R. W. Staniland on the 18th January, 1896.

The other members of the Board were: Mr. John Beaulah, J.P., vice chairman; Mr. Joseph Clarke, J.P., mayor; Mr. Joseph Cook, editor of Boston Guardian; Mr. Charles Newham Hunn; Rev. Father P. J. O'Donoghue, catholic priest, and Rev. J. Stephenson, M.A., vicar.

The school buildings in Fydell Crescent have gone but Staniland School still prospers in the new building in Peck Avenue.

The Education Act setting up the Boards had been passed in 1871 but twenty-five years passed before it was effective in Boston, and then in 1902 the School Boards were abolished and education became the concern of the County Council.

Staniland was always proud of it's academic and sporting success and, whenever I talk to a past pupil, it is not long before the honours board is mentioned. This was a record of all the children, who went from Staniland to either the High School or the Grammar School.

The honours board was on the wall in the Big Hall and it was the aim of us all to see our names added to the list. My sister and brother were already on it in 1944, so I was relieved, when I knew my name would also be there.

When my sister returned to Staniland to teach in 1952, the board was still in it's place but Mr. Hudson retired that year and soon after Mr. Morris took over as headmaster, he was told to send the board to County Hall and it was never seen again.

The politics of envy had arrived and no one was allowed to be a better scholar nor better at sport than anyone else. Anything that suggested that in the past anyone had done well was destroyed, in case it should make less successful scholars feel inferior.

The blinkered cretins never realised that the striving to do well improved the standards of everyone; they preferred to destroy all incentive and bring everybody down to the same level.

It has taken forty years to dispel these dangerous, depraved theories but, thank goodness, sanity has returned.

The teachers at Staniland during the war years were all brilliant. My first year in the big school was entrusted to Miss. Ruby Parker, later Mrs. Meadows. She laid a solid foundation for other teachers in future years to build on; the methods she instilled in her pupils served them well throughout their school years.

Mrs. Akehurst was handed the baton for the second year and she maintained the pace. She made learning interesting and whetted our appetites for more knowledge.

The honing was left to Mrs. Mauveley in the third year, the scholarship class. She was kindness personified but she kept perfect control of her class and most of the credit for any successes in the examinations was attributed rightfully to her.

Six boys and six girls out of her class in 1944 passed to go to the Grammar School and the High School. Only Park Board had a better record. The girls were: Margaret Lacey, Pat Ladds, Barbara Blackwell, Pamela Kinsey, Janet Troops and Janet Midgelow. The boys were: Peter Day, Victor Emery, Peter Luff, Gordon Butcher, Noel Holgate and myself. Dennis Robins joined us at the Grammar School a year or two later.

Each year two weeks before the Christmas holidays pillar-boxes appeared in the classrooms and we posted cards in it to all our friends. On the day we broke up the pillar-box was opened and the teacher handed the cards out. The most popular boy and the prettiest girl were kept busy walking up to receive their fan-mail.

Parents had little choice during the war years, when deciding what presents to buy their children but, if any of us had had the foresight to have kept them unused in their boxes, they would have been worth a fortune now.

Lead soldiers and cowboys and indians are very valuable now but we never dreamt then that they would ever be worth more than the few shillings our parents had paid. Train sets were the most cherished presents for boys and in good condition they fetch crazy prices now.

Children today must tire of hearing how their grandparents woke up on Christmas morning to find their stockings filled with an apple, an orange and a few nuts, but it was true, and they really did glean more enjoyment from them than it is possible to imagine in 1995.

All through the war and for years after the favourite meeting place for Grammar School boys and High School girls was Jimmy Ward's herbal store. When a tryst was being arranged, it was the first venue to come to mind.

His shop was only small but often over twenty people crammed inside with an overspill of another ten enjoying their drinks outside. At that time he traded next to the Co-op, opposite Cheers. Later he moved over to the north side, where his shop was larger but never so crowded as in his glory years.

Customers had a choice of Orange, Cherry, Blackcurrant, Sarsaparilla or, if either you had a cold or wanted to impress the girls of your manhood, you could order loudly a Hot Compo. The same boys, if they needed to slake their thirst after a football or cricket match, would prefer a sarsaparilla. My favourite was cold orange.

Jimmy's wife sometimes helped him or took over, whilst he had a meal and it was very rare you could go without seeing Jimmy's major-domo standing in his regular spot to the right of the bar. He was not actually a servant and did not work there, but he was always at hand to laugh at Jimmy's witticisms and join in the conversation occasionally, if only with a grunt, a guffaw or just a knowing grin.

His name was Ralph and, when he was not on "duty" in Jimmy's, he could be found in a house down Norfolk Place, across from Bill Pannell's bakers shop, where he lodged with a lovely, motherly lady called Mrs. Damms.

Dick Parkinson, who was an auctioneer with William H. Brown in Boston, before moving to Wisbech, mentioned Jimmy Ward in a welcome letter I received recently. He recalls in the cricket season calling at Jimmy's after nets and fielding practice and rolling the pitch with a horse-drawn roller, supervised by Joe Gledhill, to relax and revive with a hot sarsaparilla.

Dick also mentioned Mr. Burton, the groundsman at the old Grammar School sportsfield in Church Road, who regarded it as his field and looked after it accordingly. He paid particular attention to the cricket square and would mow the hallowed ground meticulously before a match on a Saturday.

Dick never knew whether he had Mr. Burton to thank or his girlfriend watching on a bench under the chestnut trees, when he gained his colours for taking 8 for 25.

Yvonne Himsworth phoned to thank me for remembering her grandfather, Walter Whyers and she told me he was responsible for the research, which discovered the correct site to place the memorial to the Pilgrim Fathers. Her parents were present at the official opening. Yvonne agrees with me that it makes no sense to move the memorial into Boston.

She informed me that their monkey was called Bimbo and reminded me that they also had a parrot, a fact that had slipped my memory.

Mr. G. Rayner of Lenton Way, Frampton wrote to say that he worked for Ben Whyers in 1936, making butter, grading eggs and delivering to shops on a three-wheeled cycle. He remembers seeing Walter Whyer's History of Boston books in the stock room.

Walter Ladds pointed out that I had made a faux pas, when I was talking about Reg Killick's butchers shop in High Street. It was Alf Lee, who worked for Reg and owned the shop eventually. Teddy Turner was the proprietor originally and Reg married his daughter, Madge, who used to sit in a kiosk inside the shop and take the money.

He also told me that Reg's parents were the owners of the fish and chip shop, before it was purchased by Kathleen and Percy White. Before the war apparently there had been another fish and chip shop further down High Street between The Plough and Skirbeck Quarter, run by Mr. Braime.

Frank Harness, who married Reg Killick's daughter, explained that Reg left the butchers shop to look after the farm, when Teddy Turner died.

Frank told me about a coincidence that happened, while Frank Sargeant was Bishop of Stockport. He had occasion to write to the head of the North Western Water Board to complain. When his complaint reached the appropriate office, the secretary asked the head of the Water Board how she should address the Bishop in the reply. He told her he would deal with it personally and started his letter: Dear Frank...

The head of the North West Water Board was none other than Graham Alexander, who had been a classmate and friend of Frank Sargeant years before at the Boston Grammar School.

Today we see such weird and fantastic characters on television that nothing surprises us in our everyday life. Someone walks down the street with green or pink hair and no one takes the slightest notice. The fun fairs no longer have side shows with geeks and fat ladies and men with two heads, because you can hire a video and see much stranger things anytime you fancy.

But during the war years the local eccentrics and notorieties caused great interest and helped to ease the tension temporarily.

For example, an elderly man dressed in short trousers riding a sports cycle round the streets of Boston would not raise an eyebrow today but, when Mr. Rimington Wells did just that fifty years ago, it was thought peculiar and for a while was the talk of the town. It was actually his hobby and kept him fit.

He was an optician and his shop was in West Street; the small shop later used by Howes and Davies, the tailors and now occupied by Barry Smith, selling carpets and blinds. He used to cycle throughout Lincolnshire and carried all sorts of equipment on his cycle.

He must have had other idiosyncrasies, because eventually he was taken away and spent his last years in a home. This was unusual at that time but now half the population end up in a home.

Another well-known character at that time was Sidney "What What" Richardson, who was also associated with a bicycle. In his case, however, he was seldom seen riding it; he nearly always pushed it round town.

He talked to himself incessantly and at regular intervals said quite loudly "what...what", hence his middle name. Children seeing him for the first time never knew whether to be amused or frightened, because he appeared to be holding a heated argument with himself.

My father told me he had been a brilliant scholar when young but had pressed himself too hard and his brain had snapped and left him in that condition.

He lived at Wyberton I believe and walked into town most days.

The person, for whom I felt most sorry, was a little old lady known to all children as Ginny Bottles. The only description of the conduct she had to endure sounds like a contradictory term; innocent cruelty. The column of boys and girls that followed her daily, shouting "Ginny Bottles" must have almost crazed her.

When she could stand it no longer, she turned and chased them and the air was blue. The excitement when she suddenly turned only encouraged them further, safe in the knowledge that she was too old to ever catch them.

How the constant baiting originated or why she was given that name I can only imagine but the bewhiskered old lady never had a moment's peace, until reaching the sanctuary of her home.

Another elderly lady excited pity, as she struggled through the streets on crutches with one leg always pointing forwards. I never knew her name but she had lost her foot and the stump was permanently wrapped in a towel.

If anyone entered into conversation with her during one of her many necessary pauses for rest, she would explain the cause of her predicament and tell them in no uncertain terms who she considered to be responsible.

Percy Stevens was known and liked throughout the town. He spread laughter and happiness wherever he went. He had a cleft palate which affected his voice but it never stopped him shouting a greeting to his many friends.

He worked for Percy Handley, the builder, but every Boxing Day he came in the morning to whitewash our bakehouse. It was the only day of the year, apart from Christmas Day, when it was not in use.

He had a unique way of passing on a joke or anecdote and every year he had my father doubled up with laughter and he, in turn, convulsed the rest of us later in the day.

I remember one year Percy had been on a trip to London to see the Crazy Gang at the Victoria Palace Theatre, and they had two hours after the show to go anywhere they liked to have a meal. Most of the passengers went to an adjacent restaurant but Percy and a friend looked for somewhere a little better and finished up at the Dorchester Hotel.

The menu was in French, so they asked the waiter to translate it for them but they did not fancy any of that "rubbish" and much to the amusement of the other diners they insisted on fish and chips. For years after we laughed about the day, when Percy Stevens had fish and chips at the Dorchester Hotel.

During the war years the Bath Gardens were used to train paratroopers with rope ladders between the trees and assimilated descents to practice landings. Then timber merchants were allowed to stock wood there and the resultant deterioration distressed those who remembered how beautiful it had been before the war.

They remembered the lovely trees, the landscaped parklands, the shady arbours and the numerous wooden shelters that suddenly appeared around a bend in the myriad walks.

Margaret Lee, born Margaret Cox, from Wheatley in Oxfordshire told as she remembered catching the ferry from the bottom of Pulvertoft Lane across to Skirbeck Road and walking to the Bath Gardens, where she spent many a happy hour.

Another of her childhood memories was hearing the siren of the Lizzie & Annie asking for the Swing Bridge to be swung to allow it access to the B.O.C.M. mill near the bottom of White Horse Lane.

The Lizzie & Annie was the largest boat to come up the river that far and it had to wait for a neap tide, so it only came three or four times a year and the children all ran to the bank-side to watch it's painstaking progress.

Margaret wrote to me in September, after I had mentioned the wedding of my cousin, Laila Rastall to an American airman. She had been in the same class as Laila at the High School and remembered her fondly and asked me to send her love.

Miles Cox, her father, was for many years in charge of the railway line on the dock and, after retiring, he looked after the library at the Stump. He always smoked a pipe and came to our shop for his Erinmore Flake. Mrs. Cox was a quiet, well-spoken lady and she also had a younger daughter, Mary, who now lives in Edinburgh.

Mrs. Cox was a sister of Mrs. Kemp, still very active, although in her nineties, the widow of Harold Kemp, who painted the scenes of Wide Bargate on V.E. and V.J. Days, the prints of which can still be obtained at Cammack's furniture shop.

When I mentioned the letter to my sister, she said she remembered Margaret Cox well, as she was Head Girl at the High School in 1942-43.

Mr. & Mrs. Cox lived in Oxford Street, next door to Mrs. Hardwick, a dressmaker, who worked from home, as her husband was an invalid and needed a wheelchair. He spent most of his time on Skirbeck Quarter, watching the fishing smacks preparing to "go down" or unloading their catch and he was able to wheel himself that short distance but, if he needed to go into town, his wife had to push him and he weighed at least sixteen stones and I doubt if she weighed seven.

In the next house lived "Tiny" Davies. I don't think she had ever been married and she was never referred to as Miss or Mrs.; everyone called her "Tiny". She was an expert at crochet work and took orders from customers.

She had a record of Edward VIII's abdication speech and delighted in playing it for anyone, who was interested.

In the first house on the left side of Oxford Street lived Mr. & Mrs. Clarke. For many years Mr. Clarke was employed by Currys each December to act as Santa Claus. He was ideal for the job, as he already had white whiskers and he was kindly by instinct. When I was a lad I was convinced that Santa Clause lived in Oxford Street.

Further down Oxford Street lived Eric and Eva Arnold. Eric worked on the railway and after the war became a councillor and eventually the Mayor, while Mrs. Arnold became a magistrate and lived to be a hundred, only dying last year.

There were some apple trees behind the last house on the left, which in the late summer became an irresistible temptation to some of the local children. They belonged to Mr. Keal, a milkman, whose wife gave piano lessons. Mrs. Keal also played the organ at several churches: for many years at Wrangle Church and I believe for some time at St. Nicholas Church.

The houses at the bottom of Oxford Street faced the river bank with their back yards opening onto the street. In one of those lived Mr. & Mrs. Brightwell with their daughter, Stella. Jack Brightwell was a sail maker and made canvass blinds for most of the shops in town. They served a dual purpose; being pulled out both when it was raining and also when the sun was damaging stock in the windows.

Mrs. Brightwell was a leading member of the W.V.S. for many years and Stella was a devotee of Old Time dancing. She always called in our shop for a bag of sweets to share with her fellow dancers.

As usual I have digressed, but to return to Margaret Cox; when she left the High School, she went to Oxford University and studied at Somerville College with a girl from Grantham called Margaret Roberts, who, as we all know, became Margaret Thatcher.

Some of my younger friends have enjoyed reading my reminiscences of the war years but they still ask "What was it really like? What happened when the war started? Did people panic or were things organised?"

The best way to answer these questions is to give the actual facts, so please excuse me if you find a surfeit of details an anathema.

Everyone was concerned and worried and in the first few months the biggest fear was that Hitler would use gas warfare, but there was definitely no panic.

Contingency plans had been made in advance and the Borough of Boston was part of the North Midlands Region, whose Commissioner was Lord Trent.

The Deputy Regional Commissioner was Principal H. A. S. Wortley and the County A.R.P. Controller was H. C. Marris. The Sub-Controller for Boston was Chief Constable Leonard Johnson.

A booklet was quickly published telling people what precautions to take and what to do in all emergencies. The price was 3d.

The expert knowledge of Sergeant J. R. Livock and Chief Fire Officer F. P. Carter assured the accuracy and soundness of the advice.

The booklet described the air raid warning as a fluctuating or warbling blast on electric sirens of two minutes duration and the "raiders past", which soon became known as the "all clear", as a two minute continual blast.

Seven sirens were placed around town. They were situated at the Municipal Buildings in West Street, Thompson's Mill in Spilsby Road, Fisher Clarks in Norfolk Street, Stinson's Garage down London Road, the Woodville Road pumping station, Witham Bank and the Dock.

In the event of a gas alarm wardens would use hand rattles and to cancel a gas warning they would use hand bells.

The advice on what action to take on hearing an air-raid was to stay indoors, if at home and, if in the street, go home where possible or to a public air raid shelter.

There were 46 public shelters in the Borough at the following sites: Bargate Green (6), Brown's Yard, behind the New Theatre (3), Shodfriars Hall (2), Buoy Yard (2), Bargate End (2), Norfolk Street (2), Thorold Street (2), Tawney Street (2, Soulby's Cellar (2), Market Place, near Lloyd's Bank, Burgess Pitt, Pump Square, Fydell Crescent, Pulvertoft Lane, Silver Street (Gratton's Yard), Wesleyan Church in Red Lion Street, General Hospital, Dolphin lane, Russell Square, Station Path, Bond Street (Malthouse), Carlton Road, Sleaford Road, Hospital Bridge, Bargate Bridge, Moulder's (Bargate), 36, Market Place, Morris's Cellar (Bridge Foot), Reynold's Cellar, Labour Club, Fydell House and 120 High Street.

If in a motor vehicle the advice was to stop at the first suitable place without blocking the highway, switch off headlights but leave on side and rear lights, leave vehicle unlocked but remove any valuables, park in open space away from buildings, if carrying petrol, explosives or anything dangerous or inflammable.

There were several horse-drawn vehicles in those days and they were not forgotten. The horses were to be unharnessed and tied by the halter lead not the reins to the rear of the vehicle, never to a lamp post or railings. The halter was to be fastened below the hub of the wheel and skid breaks or chains applied.

Everyone was issued with a respirator but they remained the property of the Government and there was a charge, if you either damaged or lost it. They were generally referred to as gas-masks and they were issued in a box but most people bought a canvass holder, that could be strung around the shoulder.

We were instructed to get used to them by wearing them regularly for a short time. At school we had lessons in taking them on and off as quickly as possible without damaging them.

The booklet advised them to be kept in a cool, dry, clean place; to be carried at all times; never exposed to strong light, heat, intense cold or moisture, and once a month they should be removed from the box and aired for twenty-four hours to restore the shape of the face piece.

Such was the fear of gas attacks at the start of the war that everyone obeyed these instructions conscientiously and you would no more leave the house without your gas-mask as you would without your trousers.

The all clear usually followed no more than a few hours after an air raid but it could be days after a gas raid, before it was safe to venture out, so people were advised to stock up a cellar or the ground floor room with the fewest windows with the following: food in tins, water in stone jars or bottles, torches, books, papers, wireless, table games, sanitary utensils, first-aid box and a respirator for each person.

Most of the advice given at the start of the war was common sense, but some of the details in taking precautions in the event of air raids and bombs falling were vital to save lives and prevent injuries.

Those not lucky enough to have brick blast-walls in front of their windows were advised to build walls of sandbags or boxes containing earth, sand or ashes outside their windows.

Window glass should be covered with cellophane or adhesive tape to avoid flying splinters caused by blast. It was a good idea to have an emergency frame made with wire netting and covered with a blanket and keep it at hand to replace any window that may be blown in.

Most of the bombs dropped were incendiaries and did not explode but merely burst into flames on impact. They were designed to penetrate ordinary roofs and rest between the roof and the ceiling or in the bedroom.

They would throw off white hot molten particles for about two minutes, then they would burn for fifteen minutes. In case one landed on your roof it was advisable to clear the space under the roof of all inflammable material and provide easy access, making sure that trap doors will move freely and a ladder is handy to reach it. A coat of thick lime-wash on the rafters would help to check the fire.

A good habit for all householders was to fill baths and buckets with water as soon as the alarm sounded, in case the mains were damaged in the raid and water was needed urgently. Most houses had at least one stirrup hand pump readily available.

While the possibility of gas attacks were prevalent, we all learned about the different gases.

Tear gases were harmless but they could be used to cause panic, as they were similar to the blister gases. The sore eyes soon recovered, after donning your respirator.

Nose gasses were worse, as the symptoms (headache, toothache, sneezing, sore throat and chest) were slow to clear, even when wearing your gas-mask but you must leave it on, until they abate, then go home, leave your clothes outside and drink plenty of liquids.

Lung gases were deadly but the gas-masks gave complete protection and they could be detected by the smell of chlorine and the coughing and choking effect.

Worst of all were the blister gases, for example mustard gas, as they gave no immediate symptoms but, although not deadly, they caused casualties and disorganised medical services. They could be vapour or liquid and in either form they caused blistering to the skin, so the gas-mask did not give full protection.

Mustard gas smelt of onions, garlic or horse-radish and the quicker-acting Lewisite gas smelt of geraniums. Their effect lasted much longer and anything contaminated by them should not be touched or even approached.

Any contaminated clothing should be placed in a sealed container and the authorities notified, then they would arrange for their removal and decontamination. Under no circumstances should anyone try to do this themselves.

All wardens carried bleach ointment and, if applied quickly, it would kill any liquid on your skin. If no ointment were readily available, you should mop off the liquid with a piece of rag, which should be burnt immediately, then wash the affected skin with soap and warm water and scrub firmly.

If the liquid entered your eye, you should wash thoroughly with warm water frequently and apply a drop or two of castor oil between the lids.

The recommendations concerning fire-fighting apply just the same today. Keep doors and windows closed, as a draught will make a fire larger: a closed door will confine a fire in one room for a considerable time.

If you are trapped in a burning building, you are safer in a room protected by a closed door than on a staircase or in a passage. Movement in a room on fire is safer, if you keep as close to the floor as possible. You will also see much better.

When moving across the floor or down stairs weakened by fire, keep close to the walls, where the rafters are strongest. Always come down stairs feet first.

If searching a burning building, always start at the top and work to the comparative safety of the lower floors. Never allow a person whose clothes are on fire to remain standing, as flames go upwards; lay them down and smother the flames with a coat or a carpet.

The exhibition of the history of Staniland School held at the Peck Avenue School on Wednesday the 14th February brought back many memories of the war years. In addition to group photographs of pupils and football teams there were many of the old classrooms and the exterior of the buildings; one showing the air-raid shelters in the playground.

Mrs. Ann Farmer is to be congratulated. She spent months collecting the photographs, letters, newspaper clippings and attendance records from former pupils and teachers, some now living miles away. She painstakingly mounted them on posters, which detailed the school's history from it's foundation on the 18th January, 1896, to the present day.

Mrs. Farmer was the school secretary for many years and it was obviously a labour of love, and she must have a very understanding husband to tolerate their home being taken over by the project.

All the hard work must have seemed worthwhile, when the exhibits proved to be so interesting to the many visitors.

It was a pleasure to meet some of my friends from fifty years ago at the exhibition. Ray Woods was just leaving and the first person I saw in the hall was Roy Barton, who was in Ward 9 at the top of Pilgrim Hospital the same time as me two years ago.

Another face I recognised from the past was Ruth Simpson, who with her two elder sisters was enjoying perusing the display. She told me her brother, Horace, now lived in Peterborough and was recovering well, after a heart bypass operation.

Their mother had a shop during the war at the corner of Blue Street and King Street, where the children of that area spent their "goody rations".

In those days, before the advent of supermarkets, there was a corner shop at the junction of any two streets. In fact there were five shops within one hundred yards of Staniland School.

Marshall's shop was on the corner of Liquorpond Street and King Street; Dickinson's, Walmsley's and Johnny Stow's were all in George Street and Clark's who made his own ice cream, was at the top of Broadfield Street.

Also half way down Queen Street Mrs. Elsam had a shop: her son Jack played for Boston United and his younger brother, Charley was a printer at Ruskins.

A little way up Liquorpond Street, opposite Johnson's fish and chip shop, was the "Little Wonder", the only off-licence I have ever seen with a sign outside, similar to a public house. Mrs. Bland kept it until she was well in her eighties and she sold sweets and a few groceries.

Her daughter, Mrs. Julian, lived next door to Johnsons and, when her mother died, she moved over the road and carried on at her mother's shop, till she in turn reached a good age. Her son, Tom, was for many years the scorer for Boston Cricket Club.

At the corner of Broadfield Street and Duke Street Mrs. Cartwright had a shop and behind it was Tom Sand's bakehouse. Tom had to go to the war and for five years my father combined his bread round with our own. When Tom came home he built his round up and soon moved to Argyle Street, where his son, Tony, still carries on the business.

There was another shop further down Duke Street, towards Locomotive Street, but I cannot remember the owner and I believe Mrs. Gardner ran a shop down Blue Street, towards Anwick Place.

Locomotive Street was an oddity: there was no access for its vehicles and the only way it could be reached by pedestrians was by a footbridge over the railway lines. There were several houses over the bridge and I remember one of the Nelson Field football fanatics, Neil Lockwood, lived in one. The whole street disappeared many years ago.

All these shops provided a living for their owners but not one of them exists today; all fell victim to the unrelentless march on the supermarkets.

Mr. Barkham, a retired sign-writer of Boston Road, Sutterton phoned to tell me that the German plane that crash-landed down Pilley's Lane during the war was actually shot down.

He was a member of the Home Guard gun crew that took the credit and they were proud of their success with the weapon that they maintained themselves.

Mr. Hughes of Dudley Close was right, when he corrected my spelling of Mr. Sidney Ritson's name and I thank him for telling us "Ginny Bottles" name: Louie Thorpe.

I remember Miss. Seth, the music teacher he mentioned. If I am thinking of the right lady, she stood only about four feet six inches high.

During the war years the biggest problem for shopkeepers was not to attract customers but to satisfy them. With most foods on ration and others in short supply many items were kept under the counter, and it was so easy to offend a casual customer if he saw you sell something to one of the regulars, then you had to tell him there was none for him.

The secret was to become a regular customer at as many shops as possible, but you had to register with a certain trader for foods such as meat, butter and eggs.

Coupons from your ration book could be spent anywhere and, if a shop was lucky enough to obtain a supply of oranges, customers converged on it from all over town and the shopkeeper marked the inside of the back page of the ration book.

The worst trouble arose from tinned fruit and tinned fish: there was a small allocation for shopkeepers about three times a year, and then they faced the impossible task of sharing maybe ten tins between forty or fifty loyal customers.

Cigarettes and tobacco were scarce during the war and for several years after. My job on a Monday evening was to help my mother ration the supplies we had received from Nicholson's amongst our regular customers.

We separated them into little piles under the counter and placed the piece of cardboard with the smoker's name on top. Most were allocated ten a day but some could not survive without twenty, and no doubt they had other piles in other shops.

Woodbines and Park Drive were then the most popular brands but Mr. Cyril Wright from the goods yard preferred Robins and Phil Smith "down the lane", as we always referred to Pulvertoft lane, would only smoke Player's Weights.

The more affluent customers smoked Player's Navy Cut, Senior Service or Gold Flake, and the elite or those who wanted to make an impression bought Piccadilly No. 1 or Churchman's.

The filter tip had not been invented, so ladies smoked Du Maurier or Craven A, both of which boasted cork tips. No one realised the danger of smoking at that time; in fact it was thought to be manly and advertisements proliferated. No self-respecting Hollywood hero would dream of making a film without smoking a packet or two.

Carreras must have thought that ordinary cigarettes caused some damage, as they advertised their Craven A with the slogan "Does not affect your throat". Their trade mark was a black cat; indeed before the war they actually sold a brand called Black Cat.

I collected most things, when I was a boy and I was particularly proud of my cigarette packet collection. Before the American packets became available later in the war, my favourites were Passing Cloud and Three Castles, and the one that made the other boys envious was a packet that had once contained twenty Kensitas with an extra little compartment that had housed "four for your friends".

Another prized packet was twice as long as the usual and had held ten Joysticks.

Most brands were sold in tens and twenties but Park Drive could be bought at one time in a packet with fifteen, and Woodbines were packed in fives but there was no top to the pack, more like the sweet cigarettes that children could buy.

These packets of five helped, when we were sharing out the weekly supply. By the end of the week most piles had been exhausted, unless someone was ill or holidaying, which was a rare occasion as the majority only had one week's holiday a year then.

Mrs. Kate Fletcher was one of our most regular customers. She relied on us for twenty Woodbines every day and we always put them by in fives, as she came four times a day, for she maintained that if she took twenty in the morning they would be gone by dinner time. She also enjoyed a quick chat with my mother and the walk up the lane gave her a short break from her chores.

On a Sunday we closed at lunchtime but she still relied on us to make her ration last the day, so she sent one of her grandchildren sometimes to the back door for her five Woodbines. This entailed my mother going through the kitchen, a short passage, then the living room into the shop.

One Sunday Michael Fletcher ran the errand and it was raining, so he followed my mother part of the way but stopped in the passage. She came hurrying back from the shop, pushed open the door and sent him flying.

There was a terrible thud, followed by a loud wailing. We all ran to see what had happened, expecting his face to be bleeding or maybe a bump on his forehead but, when mother asked him where it hurt him, he just repeated woefully through his sobs, "Me bum, me bum".

The only food that was never scarce during the war was vegetables. The slogan, Dig For Victory, was very successful: allotments abounded and many lawns were transformed almost overnight into vegetable gardens.

The rich soil in Lincolnshire and the Fens was used extensively to produce double crops and women and schoolchildren replaced the farm workers, who had gone to war.

Holidays were staggered in the summer, so children could help with the soft fruit picking and also with potatoes and harvesting.

Mr. Parsons, who had a farm in Tattershall Road, fetched ten or twelve of us from the top of Pulvertoft Lane every morning, while his potatoes needed picking. We took our lunch and he brought us back at four o'clock.

My lunch usually consisted of two tarts baked on a saucer, one filled with corned beef and potato and the other with bramley apples, with a bottle of dandelion and burdock to help them down.

His original contact with us was made through May Mawer, who bought potatoes and vegetables from him, and sold them at her back door and also from a large, deep barrow, which she pushed around the local streets.

Her perambulations inspired my brother to sing a parody of "Molly Malone", which ended: "She wheels her wheelbarrow; through streets broad and narrow: singing carrots and brussels alive alive-o".

Mr. Tebbs, her brother, lived next door to her down Pulvertoft Lane and he had allotments at the side of the railway behind the Goods Yard. She sold most of his produce and the carrots, parsnips, swede and turnips would have won prizes at any show. The leeks, cabbages and cauliflowers adorning her barrow were irresistible and tasted much better than any you could buy today. Remember, though, this was before the crops and land had been blighted by chemical sprays.

In the wartime the road beyond the level crossing at the bottom of Broadfield Street was always referred to as Green Lane; it is now known as Broadfield lane. There were few houses past Gosling's orchard but now there is Carver Road, Bradford Road, Francis Bernard Close and connections to Woodville Road through Staniland Road and Matthew Flinders Way.

Much of this land fifty years ago was used as allotments and you had to walk along the Forty Foot bank to gain access to Woodville Road or Hessle Drive. There was a field close to the bank, where a pack of cubs from Newark came to camp in the spring. Their leader was aunt to Ken Johnson, who lived at the fish and chip shop in Liquorpond Street., and each year he warned my father when the cubs were coming, so he could grease the special bread tins that were only used once a year.

They were twice as long as the ordinary tins used for steam bread; that is a flat loaf that is encased to prevent it rising and becoming crusty. They were ideal for cutting quickly to satisfy the appetites of thirty hungry cubs.

Many roads on the outskirts of the town were littered with allotments, and it was a common site to see men laden with garden tools and buckets making their way in the evenings and weekends to spend hours tending their vegetable patches, then returning home with their buckets full to share between family and friends.

Lasting friendships were forged on the allotments and they all had a shed to rest in and shelter from a sudden shower and, who knows, maybe there was a pack of cards hidden in a corner.

Families without gardens were encouraged to grow lettuce, mustard and cress, radishes and spring onions in boxes, barrels or even old tin baths. Packet seeds, sold in stores or grocery shops, had not then been established, so the seeds could only be obtained from seed merchants.

The southern corner of the Market Place was the nucleus for the seed companies: Sinclairs, Elsoms, Johnsons and Ingrams all had premises there, and the latter two had retail shops, from where you could buy your requirements to set up a salad garden.

Not many flower seeds were sold at that time, for as my father often reminded us: "You cannot eat flowers".

When the war started men between the age of 18 and 41 were called up, unless their job was considered to be too vital or, of course, if they did not pass the medical.

As the months passed and it became obvious that it was not going to be settled quickly, the reserved occupations were fewer and, especially after Dunkirk, the medical qualifications were relaxed.

So it was that the men in our bakehouse disappeared gradually, instead of being recruited at the same time.

Bill Conroy was the first to go. He was a fine, well-built young fellow and, when he joined the Navy, in my five year olds mind I figured that the war would soon be over now Hitler had Bill to contend with.

Bill's mother was a customer on our bread round and over the years another of her sons, Stan, and two of her daughters, Rene and Rita also worked for us: the girls in the shop. All four were good, conscientious workers.

Stan Motson was the next to go. He lived down Sidney Street and he helped to make the bread and morning goods like tea cakes and scones, then after dinner he was a roundsman, driving the blue Singer 8 van.

Stan was older, in his thirties, and he came back for a while after the war, before he moved to Carrs, where he stayed, until he retired. He had a very friendly, deep voice and I know he is remembered kindly by his nephew, John Motson, who will be commentating at the Cup Final again this year.

Stan never swore and he hated to hear others swear; he always substituted his own word "socker", when an exclamation was called for.

Apart from my father, Harold Hubbert was the only other, who was not conscripted. They had played their parts in the First World War.

He also came in the morning to make the bread, after my father had mixed the dough in the early hours, then after lunch and packing the brown Singer 8 with hot bread, buns and cakes, he would spend the next eight hours delivering around Frampton and Wyberton on Monday, Wednesday and Friday, and the Woodville Road – Fenside area on Tuesday, Thursday and Saturday.

His son, Garth, coincidentally has spent his working life, as his father did, down Pulvertoft Lane but in his case with J. Van Smirrens and the various firms that have succeeded them.

Several lads followed in quick succession; as soon as they learned the trade they turned eighteen and were called up. They were not with us long enough for their names to register but I believe Bernard Mallett was one.

Harry Fountain also worked in the bakehouse for a while but he was taken ill and became paralysed, and spent his life having to be pushed in an elongated wheelchair. Whenever I saw him, he always spoke and appeared cheerful, making the best of his cruel fate.

Arthur Sothon started working for us about this time and he was destined to stay with us, until we finished baking, giving years of loyal service. His health must have kept him out of the Forces and he spent all his time in the bakehouse. When the others started their rounds, Arthur would stay and bake the sponges, fancies and large cakes, such as madeira, coconut, seed, cherry and fruit cake.

He was an expert at making sponge rolls and kept alive our traditional fame for dough cakes, especially at Christmas, when customers came from as far as Old Leake to purchase them.

He also used to make ginger squares but we had to stop, when the yellow lines were put down in High Street, because then "there was no Parkin in High Street".

I received an interesting letter from Peter Leebetter, who now lives at Walton on Thames in Surrey. He tells me that before the war, about 1936, his weekly job on a Wednesday dinner time was to return my grandmother's washing to the shop in High Street from his grandmother, Sara Ward of 20, Duke Street. It appears my father took it to her every Monday morning. Peter's reward was 3d from his grandmother and a few jelly sweets in a bag from my grandmother.

He actually wrote to say I was mistaken, when I stated that Mrs. Cartwright's shop was on the corner of Broadfield Street and Duke Street. It was half way down Duke Street on the left and the shop further down was run by Mrs. Warrener. The Duke's Head, run by Bob & Gwen Julian, was on the corner.

50, High Street is the tall square building at the northern end of the Doughty Quay. At the start of the war it was used by Burton Altons as a warehouse and a hoist from the top storey loaded wholesale groceries onto their lorries to be distributed to shops throughout the south of Lincolnshire.

Their head office was in Nottingham and Mr. Atkinson managed the Boston branch. Later they moved to London Road and operated from premises at the top of Stells Lane.

We obtained the bulk of our requirements off them for many years, being served well by their representatives; firstly Jack West, then Roy Nichols and occasionally, when the others were holidaying by Mr. Atkinson's son Ray, who later replaced his father.

After they moved to London Road, 50, High Street was taken over by J. Van Smirren, the fish canners. When he started trading in Boston, I believe Jan Van Smirren had a factory down Wyberton West Road, or White Bridges, as most people referred to the area.

The Doughty Quay depot was very useful to them, as the smacks could land within a few yards and transport was curtailed. The same reasoning no doubt decided them to establish their much larger factory, which stretched from Edwin Street, though Pulvertoft Lane to the bottom of White Horse Lane.

They enjoyed a reputation as a supplier of high-class products, not just cockles, mussels and dressed crab but also delicacies for the most exacting epicure, such as rainbow trout.

Robert Van Smirren was instrumental in helping his parents to build the business and I appreciated his acquaintance and admired his attitude immensely. One day he would be attending an important meeting, maybe concerning the development of the Wash, and the next day you could see him helping to push a truck in the snow from Pulvertoft Lane to the Doughty Quay.

When the air raid shelter at the top of Pulvertoft Lane was pulled down after the war, Van Smirrens used the site and the derelict space next to it to build some garages and a factory unit to process the crabs.

If we ever had trouble with our vans, Robert would send his expert mechanic, Reg Wilcock across to help us back on the road.

When the girls in the factory had their tea brake, they crowded into our shop for ham and cheese rolls, sausage rolls, custards and cream puffs, and we were stood on our heads for ten minutes. The chaos was ended eventually, when one girl from each section came with a list, and gave us time to get them ready.

They also called in for sweets and cigarettes when they left work, and most of them had weekly accounts, which were always paid on Friday evening.

I wrote their names down so many times I will never forget them: Irene, Doreen and Margaret Warsop, Shirley and Marina Dawson, Rene Stier, Jean Clay, Alice Corcoran, Shirley Brinkley, Eileen Bell and her mother.... I could fill the page with their names.

One was always known as Aggie from the blowers. The blowers being I imagine, the part of the factory where the crabmeat was extracted from the claws. It was ages before I discovered her name was actually Aggie Doughty.

Another girl, who later came to live in Edwin Street after her marriage, was Gwen Rawson. She married Harry Ruck and encouraged him to become a Town & County Councillor; a task he has performed with credit for many years.

They remained our customers until their house unfortunately caught fire, and they had to move. Soon after they lived at the Assembly Rooms, when Harry was appointed caretaker.

Most of the workforce at Van Smirrens were female but one or two men were necessary to do the heavier duties and they usually stayed until retirement. Charley Buttram was a fixture for many years and John Bedryjchuk from the Ukraine, who I was sorry to see died recently, worked there until he was sixty-five.

A friend of mine, Les Woodman, was in charge of the retorts for some time but, after building his own house, he decided to start a building and repair business.

I had known Les since the days when I was one of the lads playing football with an old tennis ball in Trafalgar Place behind the Labour Exchange in West Street, and he came courting on his bicycle, dressed in his Air Cadet uniform with a bugle hung round his shoulder.

The uniform must have done the trick, because he married Beryl Aupin, who lived at Scott's fish and chip shop, opposite the top of James Street, and they have recently retired, living now down Wyberton Low Road.

In 1992 the following letter was sent to the Lincolnshire Standard from Don Knight, 76, Larkdown, Wantage, Oxon.: "1942 was the year I went to Boston. It was early January and I had been in the R.A.F. for one whole week. In mid-afternoon some 200 airmen arrived at Boston station, after a meandering train journey from Cardington in Bedfordshire. There being no R.A.F. camp in Boston, we were billeted on families around the town.

Two of us eventually found ourselves back at the station, having carried out kit-bags to addresses on a housing estate somewhere to the south-east of the town, only to discover our intended landladies had gone away.

It was dark, when we arrived back at the station but a good fairy in the shape of a R.A.F. corporal knew of an old lady, who sometimes took in airmen. So we met Mrs. Blackamore, another good fairy (if widowed grandmothers can be described as fairies), who took us in, warmed us, fed us and looked after us marvellously for the next couple of months.

Each day, including Sundays, we paraded outside a small chapel in memorable Liquorpond Street, where we were taught to march to and fro and in step. The chapel was used for lectures or other mysteries of R.A.F. life.

It was a cold, snowy winter and our lives seemed to be bounded by our billet in Station Street, Liquorpond Street and Boston Stump, when we went on Church parades. In the evenings we wrote home and polished our badges, buttons and brasses ready for the morrow. If there was any night life in Boston, it wasn't for us on two shillings a day, although that went much further than 10p does now.

Mrs. Blackamore's little house leaned, along with it's close neighbours, due to a bomb, which had demolished some nearby houses. As a result, our bedroom floor sloped from the door to the far corner, making night-time navigation very like being drunk. The beds had been levelled with blocks of wood and the door had been reshaped to fit the no-longer square frame. Nonetheless we lived happily with Mrs. Blackamore, who worked wonders with the rations she got for us.

I don't remember much about her family: she had a granddaughter, Thora, twentyish and I think a schoolteacher, who lived nearby and looked in quite often. There were also a married couple related to Mrs. Blackamore, who ran a cake shop close to the top end of Liquorpond Street. There we airmen took our morning tea-break, so they were a popular couple.

Nor do I recall much of Boston itself and I have not had cause to visit the area in all the years since the war. Perhaps it is time I took a nostalgic trip. I'll bet it might not be too easy trying to march two hundred airmen up and down Liquorpond Street these days".

After reading his letter in the paper, I phoned Mr. Knight and told him that Mrs. Blackamore was my grandmother and the popular couple at the cake shop were my mother and father. He was pleased to hear from me but sad to hear that my grandmother had died in 1943, after falling backwards down the stairs, and also that both my parents had died. My cousin Thora, he mentioned, had also died in Canada but she was not the schoolteacher; that was her sister Beryl, who now lives in Australia and spent the war years teaching at Amber Hill and later Leake Commonside.

I told him his letter must have amused Bostonians, who tried to imagine two hundred airmen marching up and down today's Liquorpond Street. The chapel he referred to is now used by W. Wells & Son, the tarpaulin manufacturers.

The damage to my grandmother's house was caused on the night in June, 1941, when the bomb fell at the top of James Street.

Both this bomb and the billeting of the R.A.F. personnel were mentioned in John Crabb's kind letter recently. I remember John but our paths never crossed, although we obviously have several mutual friends. Alan Woodthorpe, who worked at Fogartys, before he died, helped Derek Whelbourn and myself run the Old Boys Youth team at one time and he was the fastest winger I ever saw.

I remember John Taylor in the sixth form at the Grammar School, his friends called him Jit, from his initials. Although quite small, he had a very strong service and, as John said, he was an outstanding tennis player.

I was pleased to hear that Derrick Simmonds is fit and well and wish him all the best and I would like to assure John that I am working on the book and hope to have it finished by May.

Fortunately many of the preparations made at the start of the war never had to be implemented in Boston, but plans were made for any emergency. If there had ever been a real bad aid-raid with large numbers injured and others left without food and shelter due to destruction of or damage to their homes, temporary shelter would have been available at the Congregational Schoolroom in Red Lion Square and the Adult School in Liquorpond Street.

The local Public Assistance Committee were required by the Ministry of Health to prepare a scheme, known as the Prevention and Relief of Distress Scheme. A Relieving Officer was appointed to make sure that both establishments had a constant supply of iron rations, consisting of biscuits, chocolate, tinned soup, tea etc., and contingency plans to procure at short notice such perishable items as bread and cheese.

Facilities had to be organised for making tea and soup and hurricane lamps on hand for emergency lighting. Other buildings were provisionally earmarked for use, if necessary.

There was also an Emergency Hospital Scheme, which was administered jointly by the County Council's Public Health and Public Assistance Departments. The County Medical Officer dealt with the engagement of Doctors and Nurses, while the Public Assistance Officer organised the administration and obtained the equipment and supplies.

Boston General Hospital was Grade 1A, as it could perform all classes of work but Spalding Hospital was Grade 1B, because it was not so well equipped. Smaller establishments, such as the Isolation Hospital, Institutions or Convalescent Homes, were Grade 2 or 3.

The Ministry of Health supplied collapsible beds to be set up at any establishment, where there was insufficient accommodation at any time.

There were two First Aid Posts; one at Allan House in Carlton Road and one at Bargate, together with points at Stinson's Garage, London Road; the Municipal Buildings; the Mill Inn, Spilsby Road, the Unicorn Inn, Tattershall Road; Fenside Road and Boston Dock.

Dr. A. Eckford and Dr. S. Rendall were at the Allan House post with Mr. J. Laight L.D.S. as the anaesthetist, while Dr. R. C. Flower and Dr. G. R. Usmar were on duty at the Bargate post with Dr. D. MacTaggart as the anaesthetist.

There was also a mobile First Aid unit; a converted furniture van with a large amount of medical stores and equipment. If a major incident had occurred at a distance from the two posts, this mobile unit would have proceeded to the site and rendered medical and surgical attention to the injured.

Dr. A. C. Gee and Dr. M. J. Sheehan were attached to the mobile unit and there were two anaesthetists, Mr. Paul Moran and Mr. Williams, both Dental Surgeons.

Animals were not forgotten: there was a local office of the N.A.R.P.A.C. in High Street, whose secretary was Doris Kirk and the Chief Veterinary Officer was A. Anderson Walker M.R.C.V.S. from Grove Street.

At that time the Central Fire Station was in West Street, next to the Municipal Buildings and there were sub-stations at Bargate and Skirbeck. The Chief Officer was F. F. Carter, the Second Officer was H. W. Goodliff and the Engineers were W. H. Pestell and G. Jessup. There were only eight other full-time fireman but there were over a hundred in the Auxiliary Fire Brigade under Divisional Officer C. Crick.

The Borough Engineer, G. G. Cockrill and his assistant, C. R. Theobald were in charge of three Rescue Parties, two Decontamination Squads and two Road and Sewer Squads.

The Rescue Parties were also responsible for demolition of dangerous buildings and the Road and Sewer Squad were responsible to repair all damage underground apart from gas and electricity mains, which were undertaken by the appropriate public utility company.

The Leader of Rescue Party No. 1 was G. Newton, Rescue Party No. 2's Leader was J. Faunt and No. 3's was E. Hall. H. Hunter and A. Banks were the Leaders of the two Decontamination Squads and the Road and Sewer Squads Leaders were J. Croft and A. Twiddy.

The Air Raid Wardens covered ten separate areas: Railway Station, Central Park, Bargate End, Fydell Crescent, Skirbeck Road, Ingelow Avenue, Horncastle Road, Tower Road, Sleaford Road and St. Thomas's Church.

The Head Wardens for each area in the same order were: F. L. Oldham, H. W. Crampton, P. Rysdale, J. R. Stanwell, H. H. Morris, J. W. Addlesee, C. W. Rogers, T. H. Rickard, W. Hamer and A. Walker.

Each area had between twenty and thirty wardens, including several ladies.

The futility of war had been graphically expressed by Lewis Milestone in his film of Erich Maria Remarque's "All Quiet On The Western Front". Both he and the film deservedly won Oscars and Lew Ayres became a star in only his second film. The tragic ending, where the young German soldier is shot, while raising himself over the top of his trench to admire a butterfly, must have delivered the message to a whole generation.

There were other films with a similar theme. Ernest Hemingway's "A Farewell To Arms" made two years later in 1932 by Frank Borzage with Gary Cooper as an American soldier falling in love with an English nurse, Helen Haye, and surviving the hell of battle only to find the nurse had been killed by a bomb falling on her hospital. You would have thought war would have been confined to the history books: yet within twenty-one years the world was again at war.

Films about the First World War were still being made, when trouble resurfaced. In 1938 Edmund Goulding made "Dawn Patrol" with Errol Flynn and David Niven involved in dogfights over the English coasts, and two years later they were a reality.

Frank Borzage did his best to force the United States into the war with his 1940 film "The Mortal Storm", where two friends, Robert Young and James Stewart, become enemies, when Robert Young joins the Nazis. After sending his fiancée's father to a camp for Jews, Margaret Sullavan, his fiancée, is shot, while crossing the border with James Stewart in the Austrian Alps. Although popular the film did not achieve it's objective and we had to wait for Pearl Harbour.

In 1942 the morale of the country was lifted by Noel Coward's "In Which We Serve", based on the true story of Louis Mountbatten and the men of the torpedoed H.M.S. Kelly. Coward was so impressed by the director, David Lean, that he used him again in 1944 to make another inspiring film "This Happy Breed", telling this time about the experiences of a South London family during the blitz.

The Ealing Studio helped to make people feel better with "Nine Men", a film about a small patrol of English soldiers holding the Italians at bay in the Libyan desert. The same year, 1943, Fox made a similar film, "The Immortal Sergeant" with Henry Fonda and Thomas Mitchell but it is the British film that did best, although there were no stars.

After the United States joined the war, there was a succession of American films in 1943 about the war against Japan: "Bataan", Wake Island", "Guadacanal Diary" and many more. There was a marked difference between them and the less glamorous British film "The Way Ahead", which Carol Reed made with the Army Film Unit. David Niven and Stanley Holloway headed the cast, and the action took place in North Africa but it came over as a more realistic view of warfare.

Our own "One Of Our Aircraft Is Missing" was almost duplicated by the American made "Desperate Journey". This time the crew of a bomber shot down in Germany make their way home led by Errol Flynn and Ronald Reagan.

Ask anyone from my generation to name a film made in the wartime and there is a good chance they will say "Mrs. Miniver". Made by William Wyler in 1942 this film won seven Oscars, including best film and best actress, Greer Garson. Winston Churchill said it was worth many battleships in propaganda value and it was very popular in the United States, persuading millions to back the war effort.

Personally I prefer "Since You Went Away", made in 1944 by David O. Selzneck with his wife, Jennifer Jones, Claudette Colbert, Shirley Temple and Joseph Cotten. If anyone can watch the scene between Monty Woolley and his "son", Robert Walker without a lump in their throat, they are not human.

In 1944 Raoul Walsh stirred up a hornet's nest, when he made "Objective Burma" and made it appear that Errol Flynn had won the war in Burma on his own. It was withdrawn in this country after a week and not shown again until 1952, as there were complaints of anti-British bias.

An unusual and disturbing film was made in 1944 in which Skip Homeier was a Nazi youth, who went to live with his uncle, Fredric March, in America, when he was orphaned, and he caused problems with the local Jewish families; it was "Tomorrow The World".

Fredric March featured again in 1946 in "The Best Years Of Our Lives", which matched "Mrs. Miniver" by winning seven Oscars. It told of three soldiers, who found it difficult to resume their small-town lives after the war. It was made by William Wyler again but as before I preferred a film with an almost identical theme, "Till The End Of Time", starring Robert Mitchum and Dorothy McGuire.

Lewis Milestone, who started it all in 1930, made two good war films much later: "A Walk In The Sun" in 1946 and "The Halls Of Montezuma" in 1950.

In 1939 my mother had a sweet and cigarette shop to run, three young children to keep in order and, if either of the girls at the café in West Street were ill or on holiday, she also helped out there. On top of all this she hurt her leg in the playground at Staniland school, while taking my brother to keep an appointment, so it became necessary to employ a girl to help both in the shop and with our upbringing.

The first person to take on this mammoth task was Nellie Venters. I was too young to remember much about her but my mother always spoke highly of her, and my sister confirms that she was a great help, especially when mother developed varicose ulcers on her leg and had to rest.

I believe Nellie left to be married and her successor was Mary Wilkinson. I remember Mary better; she was very kind and again mother could safely leave us in her hands, knowing everything would be alright. Mother Nature intervened however, and she met and married George Heppenstall, who worked further up High Street for Walkers, the ironmongers.

The third brave recruit lived within walking distance; Dorothy Sewell's parents had a house half way down Pulvertoft Lane and her father worked on the railway. My memories of the time Dorothy looked after us are much clearer. If my mother was out and Dorothy was in charge, she took delight in teaching us harmless little songs, which to us seemed naughty and daring. For example: "I was under it, I was under it; I was underneath the sofa all the time; He put his arms around my sister, and the dirty devil kissed her; I was underneath the sofa all the time".

We inadvertently let mother hear us singing one of her songs one day and she was told to curb her ambitions to turn us into juvenile Music Hall entertainers. In spite of this, Dorothy and mother remained the best of friends, when Cupid in time scored another direct hit, we were sorry to lose her. She went to live in Nottingham, after she married but always called for a word with my mother, when she came home to see her parents. Each time she came home it caused excitement down Pulvertoft Lane, for she married well, and in those days it was unusual to see full length fur coats, except on the pictures.

After Dorothy came May Smalley but she did not stay long enough to make much of an impression but I recall her as being tall, thin and quiet, especially so, after Dorothy.

Janet Stephens came next. She lived with her mother in Mountain's Passage, down Sleaford Road. Apart from the Saturday morning Mickey Mouse Club programme and Bank Holiday visits to the cinema with my parents, my first ordinary trip to the pictures was with Janet. She volunteered to take me to the Regal to see George Formby in "Much Too Shy", and in doing so triggered off my interest in comedians but I was impressed just as much with Jimmy Clitheroe as with George Formby, probably because of his voice.

Janet stayed with us longer than any of the others and we saw her more in later years also, because she called in our shop regularly, after her marriage, when she lived down Park Road. She married Charley Drury, whom many will remember both as a popular local footballer and also for turning out on several occasions for Boston United.

Soon after Janet left we moved into the bigger shop at 110, High Street and combined the sweets and cigarettes with the bakery business, because my grandmother was too ill to manage. The first girl I remember there was Rene Conroy, who was a great help to my mother, in spite of suffering with a bad back.

Molly Lenton came soon afterwards and she was full of fun, reminding you of the Doris Day song, "Everywhere you go, sunshine follows you". Her mother had a fish and chip shop in Norfolk Place and her sister, Mavis Braime, was both a customer and a friend. I was sorry to see that Mrs. Lenton died last week at the age of 94.

Like several others Muriel Blackburn was conscripted from the bread round: her mother was a customer and she came straight from leaving school. Her elder sister married Clarence Atterby and served Boston well as Mayoress. Although young, Muriel was soon courting Tony Watson and he became a regular visitor to the shop. She was very efficient and very friendly with the customers and we missed her, when she married Tony but we never lost touch, as they in turn became customers on the bread round. Tony worked for several years in Van Smirrens office and later he was secretary of the Conservative Club. We still see each other on odd occasions at the Conservative Club.

Rene Conroy's younger sister, Rita had been with us for some time, when I joined the R.A.F. for my National Service. By this time we were also selling groceries and she managed very well for the two years I was away.

Conscription for men between the ages of eighteen and forty-one started immediately in September, 1939, and for women in 1941. After the war National Service was introduced in 1947 and the forces were boosted by 150,000 men each year.

It finished in 1962 and, like thousands of others, I do not think it is a coincidence that the crime rate starting rising about the same time. One of the benefits of National Service was that it provided an outlet for aggressive feelings, yet at the same time it curbed the criminal instincts experienced by many at that age.

On the 28th April, 1952 my time came to serve my country. Most of my friends were already part of the way through their two years, so I was offered plenty of advice. "Choose the R.A.F., because they always put you as near home as possible to save on travel warrants". "Don't go for a commission; Pilot Officers are given all the worst jobs. It is better to be one of the "boys"; you'll have a better time". "Put your name down for every camp team and every course you can go on; they can be a good skive". I must admit all this advice was very sound.

My medical had produced no problems and I discovered my former classmate, Charles Wright, from Old Leake was to report to R.A.F. Padgate on the same day. His father kindly arranged to pick me up outside our shop in High Street and we caught a train at Spalding station.

The week we spent at Padgate, during which we were kitted out, made to visit the barber and had our initial interviews, did not prepare us for our next camp. We were posted to R.A.F. Hednesford in Staffordshire to do our recruit training. It had the reputation of being the worst camp in the R.A.F. It was situated on a hill and the scenery was lovely, when it was fine, but, while we were there, it was nearly always raining. The conveniences had been allowed to deteriorate, because the camp was scheduled to be pulled down within the next year or two.

There were no plugs in the baths, no locks on the doors and holes in the walls between each cubicle. There was never any paper in the toilets and no hot water for washing and shaving.

We arrived there on Wednesday the 7th May and, according to letters I sent home to my mother, we were shoved around like pigs from one corporal to another, made to run backwards and forwards over an air-raid shelter for half an hour, then, immediately after receiving our first jabs, we had to carry our rifle and full kit for a mile. Later we discovered that these "corporals" had only been in the R.A.F. a few months themselves and gloried in putting raw recruits through the same treatment they had endured. Every night we were kept busy blancoing our webbing, bullying up our boots, ironing our clothes and buffing up our brasses before lights-out, so there was no time to slip out to the NAAFI, let alone find the camp cinema.

Apart from Charles there were two lads from Long Sutton in our flight, Wal and Roger, and I made friends with a boy from London called Laurie, who was two years older than most of us, as he had been deferred. We were in Hut 220, No. 3 Flight, B Squadron, No. 1 Wing and R.A.F. Hednesford was No. 11 School of Recruit Training. Corporal Evans was in charge of the hut and on the parade ground he was a little Hitler but at night in the billet he was quite decent.

Training was split into four sections: square-bashing, P.T., fieldcraft and lectures. The lectures were everyone's favourite section, as they gave you time to recapture your breath from the other three. The worst experience was in the gas hut, where you could not put your gas masks on, until you were inside; it certainly trained you to waste no time transferring it from the box onto you face.

When it was raining we were drilled in a large hangar. Away from the officers' eyes some of the drill instructors succumbed to their more basic feelings and they did not actually grow horns but they could be very cruel. Sergeant Cadwalladre was the worst: one day he insisted we were not trying and as a punishment he made us run around the hangar lifting our knees. He would not let us stop, even when it was obvious we were all exhausted and Corporal Evans pleaded with him on our behalf. When he finally gave the order to revert to ordinary pace, one boy kept running round like a horse trotting. At first we thought he was being funny but it became obvious he could not stop and he was taken to sick quarters. We never saw him again but heard later that he was discharged on medical grounds.

When Capt. Haslam left the army and came to teach English at the Boston Grammar School, he soon organised a Combined Cadet Force and luckily I was persuaded to join. We practised shooting at the Drill Hall and I somehow received my marksman's badge, which helped me to gain my Cert. A.

I did not appreciate the significance of this, until I had survived my first two weeks of square bashing at R.A.F. Hednesford. We were asked if any of us had the A.T.C. Certificate A and eight out of the flight of one hundred and fifty had but only two of us actually could produce them. It was more luck than foresight that determined I should have taken it with me. The other boy was Jim Lacey from Bedford, whose father by coincidence was also a baker.

We were both upflighted and missed three week's training but we lost touch with our friends. I moved to Hut 182 in No. 5 Flight and, although we used the same NAAFI, I only saw Chuck Wright, Wal and Roger from Long Sutton and Laurie from London on odd occasions, as we were kept busy trying to catch up with our new flight.

They had already taken their trade tests, had their interviews and the second part of their inoculations, so we had all this to arrange quickly. In spite of this, I managed to go to Stafford on the Saturday night and saw Alec Guinness and Petula Clark in "The Card".

The next weekend was Whitsun and we left the camp on the Friday evening and had to be back by 1.30 p.m. on the Tuesday. It was my first experience of hitch-hiking and I was a novice; during the next two years I became an expert but that first time I found myself in Nottingham at midnight. Instead of waiting there I was dropped off on the ring road and decided to walk through Nottingham, because I knew I wanted to be near Trent Bridge.

What I did not realise was that it took a lot longer to walk through Nottingham than it did through Boston, and at 1.00 a.m. I was still in the city centre and feeling tired. A policeman noticed me walking slowly and accused me of being drunk. I assured him he was mistaken and in fact I was more in desperate need of a drink, and he advised me where I wanted to be to have a chance of a lift to Trent Bridge.

Once there I soon found a lorry that took me as far as Sleaford but by then it was 3.00 a.m. and there was no traffic on the road. Knowing my father always mixed the dough about that time, I phoned home and he fetched me.

Before I enjoyed my weekend, I made sure of a lift back to camp. Peter Smith at Graves & Hobster arranged for one of their drivers, Billy Yarnold, who at that time lived in a caravan in the yard of the Ship in London Road, to take me to Walsall. I arrived there in the early hours of Tuesday morning and had plenty of time to hitch back to camp through Cannock Chase.

From a long list of trades you have to make five choices in order of preference and my five were: Clerk Organisation, Messing Clerk, Clerk Provisioning, Storeman and Cook. I had a good idea of the duties of a Clerk Org., for that was the trade of my friend, Noel Holgate, who had been at R.A.F. Spittalgate for over a year, so I was pleased, when I heard I had been given my first choice.

Jim Lacey and I were unfortunate enough to have our 75 jabs, the second and larger part of the inoculations, the day before we went to the rifle range. Jim, however, reported sick and spent the day in bed but, apart from my left arm being stiff and swollen, I felt alright and joined the others at the range. As I waited my turn, I witnessed three lads score 85 out of 85 and the Sergeant told us that we stood a good chance of beating the previous record for the best flight on the station. I hardly knew the others, as we had only been upflighted the week before, and I was dreading being the cause of their not breaking the record. I was one of the last six to shoot and I was very relieved to score 78 out of 85, good enough to be a marksman and help to set a new record. That night the atmosphere in the billet was much more friendly and we all sang along to the tannoy, as we stitched our badges of crossed rifles on our arms.

To celebrate we were all allowed to go into Birmingham on the Thursday and we had three good meals, went to the cinema in the afternoon and to crown a memorable day five of the more adventurous of us took a 28/- box at the Theatre Royal to see the D'Oyle Carte Opera Company perform "Patience"; my first experience of Gilbert & Sullivan.

The pass-out parade that marked the end of my training at R.A.F. Hednesford took place on the 18th June, 1952, but I missed it. Every boy in Hut 182 had the flu during the previous two weeks but I waited until the day before the parade, then reported sick with a high temperature and was admitted to sick quarters. I was afraid that I might have to wait and take part in the next pass-out but, when I was released, I was sent home for 48 hours and told to report to my new posting at R.A.F. Kirton-in-Lindsey.

All my friends, who preceded me into the R.A.F. had been posted to camps in Lincolnshire, so I was expecting to be stationed not far from Boston. Some were nearer: Cranwell, Digby, Spittalgate or Scampton, but Kirton-in-Lindsey was only fifty miles away and I was lucky, because it was a small camp and it made selection for the representative teams that much easier.

When I had reported to Padgate on the 28th April, I weighed 14 stones, now just seven weeks later, I weighed 12 stone. I was as fit as I have ever been, when I reported to the guardroom at R.A.F. Kirton-in-Lindsey that Monday morning. With a smile on his face the M.P. Corporal told me to take my pack to Block 41 and gave me directions then added, as I was walking away, "If you lose your way, just ask for the Waafery".

Block 41 was in the far corner of the camp with the main road on one side and two tennis courts on the other. It was mid morning and I did not have to report to the S.H.Q, until after dinner, so I took my time and noted the lay-out of the camp. The Station Headquarters were on one side of the parade ground and the flag was on the other; the Stores and Motor Pool were to the right and the signals building to the left.

Beyond the Stores were three hangers, hiding the aircraft, which I had noticed as I approached the camp. The airfield was littered with Tiger Moths around the perimeter.

I entered Block 41 cautiously, remembering the smile on the Corporal's face, I walked down the corridor, past the ablutions, to the far room and slowly opened the door and I could not believe my eyes.

The first face I saw, breaking into a broad smile as he recognised me, was that of Bas Stopper, a friend I regularly played snooker and table tennis against at the Mens' Own Club in Boston. He was sat on his locker, swinging his legs, talking to two other lads but he jumped down and offered to help me with my kit.

It was a real coincidence, because he said he was the only Bostonian on the camp and he was only there at that moment, as he was a batman and had been on duty in the Officers' mess late the night before. He explained that Room 1 was used by the batmen and I wanted to be in Room 4 with the other clerks. That was the room I had walked past, when I entered the block. As he helped me back, I asked him why it was called the Waafery and he explained that before R.A.F. Kirton-in-Lindsey became the School of Initial Training for Pilots and Navigators, there had been a lot of WAAFS on the camp and Block 41 was their billet. There was, however, not a single WAAF on the camp now.

After dinner I reported to the Progress section in the S.H.Q. and Flight Sergeant Breed went through my duties with me. I was to be the Documentation Clerk and keep all the documents up to day for every trainee pilot and navigator on the camp.

There was a new intake every four weeks and their training lasted twelve week, so at any time there were three flights on the station; one just starting, one half way through their course and one preparing for their final tests. My main task was to help the new intake to complete their forms on arrival and, considering that the majority had been to university or public schools, it was surprising how many panicked, when faced with seven or eight forms to complete in about an hour. Forms have the power to make even the best minds go blank.

While I was there, several interesting people took the course, before moving on to other stations and more modern aircraft to fly and navigate. I was responsible for making sure their documents followed them to the right destination.

The son of Frank Whittle, who invented the jet engine, went through on one of the intakes and several Middle East and Indian princes, but in the twenty-one months I was there only one person wrote Boston on the form for his place of birth and that was Gerald Hopper.

My first few weeks at R.A.F. Kirton-in-Lindsey were made more enjoyable, because Bas Stopper was already there. With his mates, Johnny Jessop, Brian Hooker and Gordon Skinner, he spent much of his time over the previous four years, as I had, at the Mens' Own Club, down the passage at the side of Lipton's in Narrow Bargate.

On market days Bas used to help his elder brother on a vegetable stall in friendly rivalry with another of his friends, Johnny Frost, who helped on his parent's stall.

Bas was about eighteen months older than me, so, soon after I arrived, he became demob-happy and starting marking off the days on his calendar in anticipation of his return to Civvy Street.

I soon made friends with most of the lads in Room 4, the majority of whom worked in the Station Headquarters and some in the offices out on the Wings. Only two worked with me in the Progress Station but one of these, Norman Bray, proved to be very helpful to me, as he lived in Cherry Willingham and he was one of the few airmen to run a car. It was a Heath Robinson job, that he had put together himself from three or four other cars but it served his purpose, and I was pleased to accept a lift into Lincoln on the Saturdays, when neither of us were on duty. There was no M.O.T. at that time.

Norman was training to be a Methodist minister, before being called up, so it was not long before he was known to us all as "The Vicar of Bray". He had a deep resonant voice, that was ideal for delivering sermons.

The other clerk in our office was Rocky Stone from Bristol. He had blond curly hair and looked a little like Danny Kaye; maybe that explained his frequent mad half-hours, when he entertained the rest of us by rushing round the billet from bed to bed and locker to locker, imitating a monkey. Even in the office, if the sergeant and corporal were away, he would swing from one filing cabinet to another.

There were five in our office and the Progress officer had the next office along the corridor, opposite the Orderly Room. He had to sign every letter, before it left our section and the task of collecting them for his signature often fell to me. His name was Flight Lieutenant Gunnell and, when he discovered that I came from Boston, he told me his wife had close relatives in Boston and they often travelled to see them at special times.

He offered to give me a lift home, whenever possible and twice he dropped me right outside our shop. Both he and his wife were very friendly and they had a young son, so there was plenty of room in his car. When he noticed my father was a baker, he plotted with me to surprise his wife with an iced cake for the Christmas of 1952. My father baked her a cake to his special brides cake recipe, iced it all over and decorated it with a Santa, a robin and a "Merry Christmas", and on Sunday the 14th December, I ventured back to camp with the cake safely packed by my mother into a fancy box.

I used to catch a bus outside the post office at 7.30 p.m. every Sunday and it took two hours to reach Lincoln, going through Gypsy Bridge, Coningsby and Woodhall Spa, stopping every five minutes and eventually arriving at Thorpe Bridge, allowing me ten minutes to change to another bus, taking the low road from Lincoln to Gainsborough.

After a busy weekend, I usually had a nap on the bus but that week I made sure I kept awake and guarded the box from any mishap. At Kirton-in-Lindsey I had to climb the hill to the camp, and I was careful to keep the box level and not bang it up a wall or hedge. I was pleased when I heard the "Blue Tango" drifting from the tannoy in Block 41 at 10.45 p.m., because I had completed my journey with the cake undamaged.

Most of the officers lived in the married quarters but Flight Lieutenant Gunnell had a caravan and that is where I delivered the cake on the Monday morning. Both his wife and his young son were surprised and delighted.

Earlier that year, towards the end of October our camp played a "derby" game of football against R.A.F. Hemswell, which was just six miles up the road, nearer to Lincoln. At half time we were winning 1-0 but they equalised early in the second half and it looked like being a draw, then in the last minute their centre forward broke away and he sent a pile-driver past our goalkeeper, who had no chance. Their centre forward was Fred Trueman.

Everyone knows what a brilliant bowler he was but few realise he was quite useful at football; in fact at that time he played several games for Lincoln City reserves. I never saw him perform for R.A.F. Hemswell's cricket team, for he was demobbed shortly after that football match.

Soon after I settled to the routine in the Progress Section at R.A.F. Kirton-in-Lindsey, the corporal, who organised most of the work, although Flight Sergeant Breed took the credit for a well-run office, was posted and we all wondered who would take his place.

Someone heard it was to be a corporal, who had just returned from two years at R.A.F. Bulawayo in Southern Rhodesia, as it was known then. They did not know his name but, when he walked through the door, I did: it was Jack Rushton from Boston, who was engaged to Doreen Goodliff, who lived with her mother down Pulvertoft Lane within a hundred yards of our shop.

The happy coincidence meant that Norman Bray had another passenger for his home-made station wagon as far as Lincoln each weekend. Jack soon realised it would be up to him to maintain the efficient handling of the heavy workload, because Flight Sergeant Breed, whom Jack soon started referring to as "Happy", because of Noel Coward's famous film "This Happy Breed", was influenced by the fact that he would soon be leaving the Royal Air Force.

Flight Lieutenant Gunnell was fully aware of the position and I am sure credit was given, where it was due, but unfortunately, he too moved on from Kirton-in-Lindsey. His place was taken by Pilot Officer Knight, whom I believe was just on National Service, although some signed on for an extra year. He did not seem like an officer; more like one of the boys but he did not carry the same clout as a Flight Lieutenant, when it came to addressing the senior officers.

When "Happy" Breed went, instead of Jack being promoted, another Sergeant was posted in. Sergeant Panton was even worse, because, whereas Flight Sergeant Breed had shown little interest, Sergeant Panton was just not capable of running the office. He had a drink problem, and a broad Scottish accent, and between them these two facts made it nearly impossible for us to converse with him.

I had an embarrassing experience one night, while I was on Guard Duty. At regular intervals two of us had to patrol the camp during the night, and while we were checking the married quarters, there were sounds of a heated argument coming from one of the houses. As we approached a woman ran out of the house in her nightdress and said her husband had gone mad, and she was frightened for her three children.

We said we would fetch the M.P.s but she entreated us to go into the house straight away or it might be too late. The woman's accent made me suspicious and, sure enough, when we anxiously entered the house, there was Sergeant Panton swaying and swearing in the middle of the living room with three small children huddled crying in a corner.

When he saw us, he quietened down and sat at a table with his head resting on his arms, and started sobbing. After a while his wife came back into the house and put the children back to bed. We could not stay long, because we had to cover the whole camp within an hour but, when we left them, he seemed to have fallen asleep.

I persuaded the other lad not to say anything, when we returned to the guardroom, and the next day in the office Sergeant Panton acted as if nothing had happened. I never found out if he realised I was one of his nocturnal visitors or, if indeed he remembered anything about it, but eventually some of his neighbours must have complained or maybe some other lads on Guard Duty reported a similar disturbance, because Sergeant Panton was posted away much earlier than usual.

This time Jack Rushton was made up to Sergeant and officially took control of the Progress Station.

Jack had not been on the camp long, when Norman Bray's jalopy gave up the ghost and he replaced it with a motorised bicycle. For a week or two we hitch-hiked into Lincoln as well as from Lincoln to Boston, but Jack was not a very patient hitch-hiker. Every time a vehicle passed us without stopping he commented "I hope your back wheels fall off", but retracted it as we ran up the road, if they changed their mind.

His patience ran out after a few weeks, and he bought a motor cycle and so began the most hair-raising experience of my life. With my heart in my mouth each week I used to ride pillion, clinging to his back and trying to make sure my body was leaning at the exact angle of his. We used to reach Boston in one hour fifteen minutes most weeks, and to accomplish this feat he used to use the steep, narrow streets descending from Lincoln Castle as a short cut.

We both survived for him to be the groom and for me to be a groomsman at the Baptist Church in High Street, when he married Doreen Goodliff, shortly before I was demobbed.

Both Peter Smith from Graves & Hobsters and Bernard Reed, who used to be the manager at Barclays Bank, assured me that they missed my services in their table tennis team at the Young Conservatives, after I joined the R.A.F. but I think it was the packet of Granola biscuits I always took with me that they missed more, because Brian Manning was a quite adequate replacement.

The experience I had gained however, over the years I played with them stood me in good stead, while I was in Kirton-in-Lindsey. With only three players in the camp team, I never thought I would gain a place, but there were only two other lads who had played in a league, so I was lucky. They both played in the Burnley league, although Jack Hill actually lived in Nelson. He was tall and thin and had a good reach, which he used to great advantage to play an all-out attacking game.

Dave Greenfield was just the opposite: his game was defensive and he wore his opponents down, returning everything in spite of his pen-holder grip. They were both account clerks and also lived in Room 4 of Block 41, so we were able to nip off for practise, as soon as we had finished our chores in the evening.

The others working in the S.H.Q. were envious, when we often finished early to travel to other camps to play evening matches in the R.A.F. Eastern Stations league. When we were drawn against teams further afield in the Group knock-out competition, we sometimes set-off in the morning.

In a letter I sent home on the 23rd October, 1952 I was pleased to tell my mother I had won all three games against R.A.F. Moreton Hall, and we scraped through to the semi-finals by winning 5 - 4. The news was not so good on the 11th December, for the previous day we had been at R.A.F. Patringham, on the Yorkshire coast, near Withernsea and we lost 3-6.

We must have played in the afternoon, because we stopped at Hull on the return journey and saw the first house of a variety show at the Palace Theatre, where the top of the bill was Jack Jackson, whose Saturday night radio show started the whole idea of disc jockeys in this country.

Unfortunately I never managed to be selected for the camp football team, but the S.H.Q. team won the inter-section league that first year. It appears the Officers team had won the previous year and our first game was against them. Two new arrivals helped us to win 5-0 and we never lost a match all winter.

Ron Underwood played centre-half, although he was not particularly tall, but he had been a trialist with Derby County and, when he jumped, he seemed to stay in the air, as if he was on a ladder and the opposing forwards never saw the ball.

Our best player though was Alec Orr. He worked with me in the Progress Section and he had played for two years in the Scottish League. He was an amateur, however, because he played at Hampden Park for Queens Park, which was an amateur team. He played as an inside-forward but today he would have been called a midfielder, because he controlled the game pretty much as Paul Gasgoine or Jan Molby does. We passed the ball to him, whenever possible and he never ran, he just strolled past defenders and, after he had attracted three or four round him, he just pushed the ball in front of one of us, not to our feet like the modern players seem to do, and the lucky recipient only had the goalkeeper to beat.

I was the left back but even I sometimes took advantage of the gaps he created to score a goal or two. One of the reasons I moved to the left wing, after the regular winger was demobbed and we had a surplus of defenders.

As Christmas approached in 1952, I made plans with my family and with my friend, Mick Clayton, and we all anticipated a full and varied holiday but everything altered, when the names were posted on the camp notice board for the fire picquet to stay on camp. There were eight names and mine was the last. If it had been Duty Clerk or T.V. Orderly, I would have been allowed to swap with one of the Scottish lads, who wanted to stay on camp and go home for hogmanay, but you were not allowed to swap, when your turn for fire picquet came round.

The disappointment, however, soon disappeared, for the whole camp changed at Christmas; it was more like a holiday camp. The tradition in the R.A.F. is for the Officers to serve the men with their Christmas dinner, and the Commanding Officer and the Station Adjutant set the example for the other Officers by sharing out the plentiful portions of turkey and York ham with roast and creamed potatoes, brussels and peas, followed by Christmas pudding and brandy sauce. I still have the printed menu, signed on the back by all on duty that Christmas.

On Friday the 13th February, 1953 all weekend passes were cancelled at R.A.F. Kirton-in-Lindsey, because we were all put on stand-by in case the expected high tides breached the sea defences. As we all know, that Saturday the sea broke through all down the Lincolnshire coast, and there was widespread damage and many were killed.

We were called out at 6.00 a.m. on the Sunday morning and taken to Great Coates, just north of Grimsby. All morning we filled sand-bags on the side of the road about three hundred yards from the sea-bank. Scibbans-Kemp biscuit factory was the nearest building.

In the afternoon we moved up to the bank to rebuild the defences. There was no proper roadway, just a narrow track at the side of a field and all the bad weather had turned it almost into a bog. There were tall hedges along the field and a dog-leg half way along the path, so it was impossible for a driver to see if another vehicle was coming towards him.

If they had met in the middle, it would have been chaos, for there was no point where they could pass, and the whole operation would have been stopped.

To ensure that a constant supply of sand-bags reached the bank, it was necessary for someone to be positioned at the bend and someone else at the entrance to the field to control the traffic. Alec Orr and myself were entrusted with this important duty, and we spent the afternoon waving a red flag at each other and neither of us could understand the unkind comments of the other lads, when at 5.30 p.m. it was considered that the job had been completed satisfactorily, and they staggered back to the lorries that returned us to camp. As we told them, someone had to do it.

That day there were fifty of us from R.A.F. Kirton-in-Lindsey and another fifty from R.A.F. Finningley, near Doncaster, plus a few soldiers and about a hundred civilians. The new bank held at the next high tide, so it was all worthwhile.

The R.A.F. station at North Coates, south of Grimsby was flooded and for a few weeks some of the lads from there came to our camp.

In retrospect April 1st, was a bad date to plan a demob party, but there was really no alternative, as we were all due to go home for Easter the following day, Maundy Thursday. Previously I had found an excuse to miss demob parties but this time it was for Alan Marshall from Leeds, and during the nine months I had spent in Block 41 I had come to know and like him well.

To me any kind of beer has always tasted like vinegar, so this was one of the few occasions that I forced myself to drink it in any quantity. Alan was in the signals section and most of his mates were in the room opposite ours: there were nine of us and the only other clerk was Derek Goodall. Derek came from Grimesthorpe, near Barnsley and I've often wondered, if he was the same Derek Goodall, who years later was the director of Calendar on Yorkshire Television.

There was a pub on the top road not far from the camp, but it was decided to go to The First And Last at the bottom of the hill, for the others assured me that the beer was better there. We had a good night and everyone bought a round except Alan, so that amounted to eight pints I drank, for they would not let anyone have halves.

My argument about going to the other pub made more sense to them, when we started back to camp, for it was much easier walking down the hill than it was coming up the hill, with eight pints inside us.

Roger Payne from Leicester was also on his first demob party but, whereas with me it made heavy footing, it made Roger light-headed. Half way up the hill we realised Roger was missing; then we heard a terrible crash and he ran out of the yard of a house the rest of us had already passed. For some reason, known only to himself, he had swung a dustbin lid over his head and it had flown through a window, when he let it go.

The owner of the house phoned the camp and, when we eventually reached the guardroom, the M.P.s were waiting for us and we thought that was the end of our Easter leave, but Roger admitted he was the culprit and the rest of us were excused.

152

We had good reason to be pleased that we gave Alan a last night in the R.A.F. to remember, because three months later Brian Greenwood, his closest friend, who also lived in Leeds, came back to camp from a week-end pass and told us that Alan Marshall had suffered a heart attack and he was dead.

My letter home dated the 12th March, 1953 had a 2¹/₂d stamp, bearing the King's head but the next letter, dated the 26th March, 1953, had the Queen's head on the stamp. One fact I had forgotten, until I read the second letter, was that Queen Mary, the Queen Mother at the time, died just before the Coronation.

In the first letter I had been pleased to tell my mother that I had passed my second trade test, and she had to prepare for the following weekend to change my sleeve badges from L.A.C. to S.A.C. but I would not be receiving any extra pay, until I had finished a year's service on the 28th April. I should not have taken the test so soon but Jack Rushton was to go on an advanced training course at Hereford for eight weeks and, if I were a S.A.C., I could run the office in his absence.

It appears that there was an outbreak of smallpox in the Todmorden, Bacup, Oldham area towards the end of March that year, and Jack Hill, who was on leave at the time, was not allowed to return to camp, so I replaced him as captain of the table tennis team, when we played at R.A.F. Swinderby.

The second year of my National Service followed the same pattern: plenty of sport and managing to get home most weekends. Alternate weeks during the winter, I watched Lincoln City, before finishing my journey in the evening. I still have all the programmes and some of the scores would cause headlines today. They were in the second division then and one week they won 8-1 against Blackburn Rovers. Those were the glory days of Graver, Garvie, Whittle, Finch and Troops; before Andy Graver was sold for a record fee to Leicester, and years before he came to Boston United.

After Christmas, 1953, I became seriously demob-happy; counting the days until April 27th. To help time pass, I put my name down for a Business Administration course run by the Committee of Education in H.M. Forces at Hull University.

The course opened at 3.15 p.m. on my birthday, 25th January, so I was able to travel directly from Kirton-in-Lindsey and I had a companion, because Norman Bray had also been accepted. It closed at 11.15 a.m. on Saturday 30th January, so we had a full week in Hull.

We lodged together with a Mrs. Dowling at 11, Outlands Road, Cottingham, just outside the city, but we were not far away from the University. All week I hoped to see my close friend, Victor Emery, as I knew he was at Hull University, but most of our lectures were held in the Arts Block and he was studying for a Science degree.

There were about twenty of us on the course and we made visits to several factories during the week: Spillers, Smith & Nephew, Metal Box and Reckitt & Colmans. I was most interested later in the latter, as the founder, Isaac Reckitt traded at the Maud Foster Mill down Willoughby Road in Boston, until he was 41 in 1833. When he was 27, he had built the mill with his brother, Thomas and they had traded in flour, grain and cereals but they hit difficulties, after buying a steam engine to manufacture cement and grind bones.

Isaac moved to Nottingham in 1833 and was in business as a corn factor, but Thomas became insolvent in 1935 and the mill was sold. I discovered that Isaac had moved on to Hull in 1840 and bought a starch works, which was only moderately successful until it received a Bronze Medal at the 1851 exhibition, after which there was a period of rapid growth and it became a national business.

Black lead was added to their range in 1852 and Paris Blue in 1873, then they linked with J. & J. Colman of Norwich in 1938 to form Reckitt & Colman, who manufacture also Brasso, Silvo, Harpic, Karpol, Windolene, Dettol, Disprin, Steradent and Bathjoys. At Norwich they produced Colman's mustard and semolina, Robinson's barley water and squash, Farmers' Glory and Three Bears Oats, then at Peterborough Gale's honey and Farrow's canned vegetables and fruits.

Their factory in Hull had seven or eight storeys and a different product came from each storey. The bags of blue were made on the ground floor and the whole huge room was covered in blue; the walls, the ceiling and the floor; the girls all wore masks.

When we went home on the Saturday, our heads were reeling, after lectures on Trade Unions, Industrial Relations, Sales Organisations, Advertising, Money & Banking, Stocks & Shares, Export Problems, Promotions, Business Accounts and Management.

In March I escaped from the office for another week; taking part in the Group Table Tennis trials at Chigwell, which was then in Essex. Ray Nicholson from Sheffield had taken Jack Hill's place and we were both knocked out by the Wednesday, but we spent the rest of the week at the Union Jack Club in London, as our warrants covered us until then.

Genealogy is becoming more popular, as people have more time to spend on leisure and, on retirement, instead of just marking time, waiting for death, the majority now enjoy life and find new interests.

From the evidence of many letters from far and near, written by descendants trying to trace their ancestors, a growing number of people are fascinated by the history and activities of their forefathers.

I must admit some strange and interesting facts can be discovered. For example my great, great grandfather was Saint Paul. No, please do not send for the men in white coats; let me explain.

He was born in 1811 and his Christian name was Saint, while his surname was Paul, hence Saint Paul. He had two children; William, born in 1843 and Elizabeth, born in 1848. On their birth certificates their surname was shown as St. Paul.

William St. Paul married in 1865 and his wife, Jane, had seven children, the fifth of which, Louisa, was my grandmother, born in 1877. In her "front room", as the lounge was always called, she had a photograph of her mother, Jane St. Paul, on the wall above the piano, and my mother explained to me that she chose my name in her memory.

So it is pure coincidence that the 25th January, my birthday, commemorates the conversion of Saul of Tarsus on the road to Damascus, when he became the real Saint Paul.

Louisa married my grandfather, Robert Blackamore, on the 22nd January, 1898, and they lived first in James Street, then at 10b, Station Street and finally at 8, Station Street.

The Blackamore family tree has been traced as far as the early sixteenth century, when John and Agnes Blackamore, living at Thorpe on the Nottinghamshire, Lincolnshire border had five children, the eldest, John, being born in 1555.

That John married Amabilia and six more generations followed (a third John, two Matthews and three Williams), all living in the Elston-East Stoke area, before James Blackamore was born at Long Bennington in 1802. According to the census he was a pig jobber, which I believe today would be described as a pig dealer, and in 1849 he moved to Boston.

His wife, Mary, had seven children, including twin girls and James also had twin sisters, so there is a long-standing tradition of twins in the family.

James, unfortunately, lived only four years in Boston but, when he died in 1853, his third son, John, settled here and married Elizabeth Brocklesby in 1857. She had eleven children; first a son, John , then twin girls and finished, nineteen years later, with twin boys in 1879, the year her husband died.

What the records do not tell you is how your ancestors died; it could have been in battle or by accident or illness but, whatever the cause in that case, it is easy to imagine the plight of a widow left with twin babies and three more children under five.

Large families were common in the nineteenth century but less than half survived infancy, as the ten-year census returns testify.

Elizabeth's eldest son, John, married Sarah Ann Tredenick in 1878 and my grandfather, Robert Blackamore was born the next year. I am indebted to Ian Blackamore, the son of my cousin, Owen, for all this information and the tradition still persists, for Owen had a twin sister, Olga, and Owen, himself had twin sons, while his eldest son, Richard, went one better, when his wife had triplets.

So on my mother's side my claim to belong to Boston stretches to 1549 through my grandfather and to 1811 through my grandmother.

Just when the connection started between the Blackamore family and Boston dock, I do not know, but Robert Blackamore was foreman on the coal hoist and both his sons worked with him, and later my cousin, Owen was a docker and there have been many more.

My grandfather weighed over twenty stones but he was never fat; he had a huge chest and strong arms and legs. If there was any trouble in the Station Street-Lincoln Lane area, the cry was "Send for Bob Blackamore". Mother used to tell us of the time, when a man was beating his wife outside the Duke of York public house. Grandfather was eating his Sunday lunch, when they fetched him but he abandoned his meal and hurried to the woman's aid. He lifted the man off the ground and was advising him not to re-offend, when the woman picked herself up and started hitting my grandfather, shouting "Leave my husband alone!" He never interfered again between man and wife.

My father was born in Kettering but came to Boston in 1904, when his parents bought the bakery at 110, High Street from a Mr. Baxter. At one time the property had belonged to a Co-operative Society.

My grandfather's father, John Mould, was a builder in Oundle and his eldest son, George was also a builder. George and my grandfather, James, married two sisters, Agnes and Catherine Mary Fox. Agnes and George moved to Sutterton and George built many houses in the area, before becoming landlord of the New Inn. He had a distinctive way of finishing the brickwork, before putting on the roof and I can still pick out several houses he built almost a hundred years ago. For example, he built the house at Reed's Point, nearest the main road.

When George heard that Mr. Baxter' shop was for sale, he persuaded my grandfather to move to Boston and, no doubt, my grandmother was pleased to be near her sister. The business became known as the Electric Bakery, because it was the first to use electricity to run the machines: the ovens, however, were oil-fired with a small flame-thrower directed through a side-opening.

Grandmother served in the shop, while grandfather made the bread and cakes and a roundsman delivered daily with a horse and cart. Doughcakes were a speciality and people from Skirbeck Road used the ferry at the bottom of Pulvertoft Lane to buy them.

When my father was nine, he cycled every morning to Kirton Grammar School, which at that time rivalled Boston Grammar School for academic achievements. Several boys went from Boston but his regular companions were Percy Handley and Arthur Leafe. The headmaster, Mr. Keal, had assembled a first-class staff and at the age of fourteen father passed the Cambridge Senior Examination in ten subjects, and a pass at that time was equivalent to a credit in the 1940s or an A today.

He was studying for an entrance examination into the Civil Service in 1916, when conscription started, and the man in the bakehouse and the roundsman were called up for the army, so he left school to help my grandfather with the business. It was only intended to be temporary, but in 1917 he volunteered to join the Royal Flying Corps. He went to Farnborough in Hampshire to train as a navigator and, when Armistice Day came on the 11th November, 1918, he was in Skegness hospital.

The depletion of a whole male generation and his awareness of the futility of the past four years warfare made the continuance of his education less meaningful, so he returned to the business, although Mr. Keal was insistent that he should still enter the Civil Service.

He persuaded his father to retire the horse and the stable became a garage for a motor van with hard tyres. I have a photograph of it taken at the first call in Oxford Street in 1920. That same year James William Mould was President of the Boston and District Master Bakers' Association; he bought the two houses next to the shop, 106 and 108 High Street to add to four terraced cottages down Warsap's Yard, which he had purchased in 1912.

Warsap's Yard was a passage between the bakery shop at 110 and Mrs. Lunnington's sweet shop at 108, High Street. As the tiny houses became vacant granddad had them demolished and laid a garden in the space. Mr. Ash, an inventor, occupied the last one, until 1930, when it was made into an extra garage.

Trade was increasing, the round was growing, everything seemed salubrious and father bought an Ariel motor cycle, joined the Boston Motor Cycle Club and started to enjoy life, but in 1922 everything altered.

My grandfather had a slight heart attack and the doctor told him to take things more easily, and he did. He never worked again: he was 53 years old and he died in 1955 at the age of 86, but he had virtually retired and spent most of his time in his garden.

To his credit he changed the business to J. W. Mould & Son and interfered little, when father made changes, the first of which saw the solid-tyre van replaced by two new Singer vans, bought from Harry Crampton at Edward White's Garage in Wide Bargate. Father himself, drove the blue van and Harold Hubbert drove the brown van, and between them they developed the bread-round covering Wyberton, Frampton, White Bridges and on alternate days Revesby Avenue, Woodville Road, Fenside, Tattershall Road, Freiston Road and Mount Bridge.

Every day from 1922 for the next forty years father went to the bakehouse to chute the flour and mix the dough at 3.00 a.m. and delivered bread and cakes hot from the oven from lunchtime until late at night, fitting in two meals somewhere along the way. In all that time I never heard him complain either of his unfinished education or of his father's unnecessary early retirement.

In 1932 my cousin Annie came over from Canada. Her father, Thomas Mould, was my grandfather's eldest brother and he emigrated to Canada around 1890. He emulated his father as a builder and built the first brick house in Toronto, and was honoured by having the street named after him: their address was 49, Mould Avenue.

He married before he left England and his cousin, John, emigrated at the same time with his wife, and their son became the Lord Mayor of Toronto.

Annie had a brother, John, but neither of them married, so that branch of the family ceased, after they both died, although Thomas's cousin's family flourished and there are several Moulds now in Toronto and Manitoba. One of them, Jean Mould, a jeweller, visited me in 1973, when she was with her relatives at Orton Longueville, near Peterborough.

When she crossed the Atlantic in a liner in 1932, cousin Annie was very much alive. I have photographs taken aboard ship and she stands head and shoulders above the other ladies and as tall as any man. It was two years before I was born, so I only have the photographs and my parents reminiscences to rely on, but she must have stood over six feet and weighed over sixteen stones.

She stayed for a month, so father had plenty of opportunities to use his Brownie camera, as he transported his cousin to Oundle and Sheffield to visit other relatives. Most of the snaps, however, were taken at Sutterton, while she was with her aunt Agnes and uncle George at the New Inn. She dwarfs my mother, who stands next to her on several of them, holding my brother, who was a babe in arms, with my three year old sister standing in front.

She never made the trip again, but father always wrote to tell her our news two or three times a year and, when he was too ill to continue, I succeeded him and maintained the flow of letters, until Annie died on the 7th March, 1980.

Almost a year after Annie returned to Canada my brother, Jim, was seriously ill. It started with a cold and his glands became swollen but they did not respond to treatment and Dr. Pilcher was very concerned, when they turned septic.

After consulting with his partners, he decided to operate. Most operations at that time were done in the patient's home, and two of them performed the operation to clear the poison from the glands in the back of his neck. The poison, however, reassembled and he could not eat and had trouble drinking.

They repeated the operations three times but each time his condition was just as bad, in a few days he became so weak that prayers were said for him in churches and chapels throughout Boston.

The doctors did not think he would survive another operation but Dr. Pilcher's son had just joined the practice and he suggested that they tried drilling holes through his eardrums and inserting a cord through the back of his neck, which they could use to clear the glands without having to operate every time.

The elder doctors said it would do no good and it was not advisable to put Jim through more pain, but my parents asked young Doctor Pilcher to try, as it was his last chance. My father had to help during the operation, because the others did not agree that it should be done. Thankfully it was a success; the cord was used to clear his glands and gradually he began to eat again and gain strength.

From that day my mother regarded young Doctor Pilcher as a saint and thanked him in her prayers every night, but this was just one example of his innovative methods, which endeared him to many in Boston. He was referred to all as young Doctor Pilcher, even when he was old enough to retire.

The recent report of a Grimsby fishing boat finding a large wartime mine in it's nets recalled the occasion during the war, when George "Growdy" Revell brought a mine up from the Wash in his nets.

He had already survived an explosion, when he was skipper on one of Beaulah's boats and the forecastle blew up, while it was berthed not far from the Town Bridge. He also skippered smacks for Stringers, Lovelaces and Gostelows, and I am not sure which was involved in the episode concerning the mine.

Most of the smacks that navigate daily down the Witham to the Cut End have a crew of three, but during the war many had to manage with the skipper and one other, and that day Growdy had just one man with him.

The two men found the mine when they drew their nets in, and decided to bring it back to Boston, where they knew there were many Royal Navy personnel, who would be able to deal with it. The trip back that day seemed to be much longer than normal, and they were relieved when they finally reached home safely and reported the mine.

Growdy lived in White Horse Lane, where his wife had been brought up at the Granger public house near the river. Her maiden name was Butler-Brewster.

He had not far to go home from the boat and he was just starting his meal, when they fetched him and told him to return out to sea with the mine on the same tide. He protested vehemently but to no avail, and they had to endure another perilous journey with their unwanted cargo, before the Royal Navy exploded it in the Wash.

These details were related to me by his daughter, Edie, who now lives down Norfolk Place but remembers me as a small boy, who used to pass her house when she lived at 5, White Horse Lane, to play near the old graveyard with Jack and Fred Brackenbury.

She married John Thomas Cater in 1939, when he had already served three years in the Royal Navy, and he was killed in February, 1944 on the tanker L.S.T. 421. She was left with two children, Janet and John.

She well remembers the morning, when the bomb fell at the top of Liquorpond Street. I have asked many people the name of the passage, which was obliterated in that raid but she was the first to tell me. Her sister, Grace Yarnell, lived there next door to Mr. Norman, who minded the cycles left each market day at Freddie Walkers. It was called Mariner's Row.

She reminded me that a row of five houses were left in a dangerous state in Bedford Place after the bomb fell and they were not demolished immediately. The house at the entrance of the Lord Nelson field, where Mr. Maltby, the fisherman lived was saved but these houses down one side of Bedford Place, which is now the site of the Doctor's new surgery, all came down.

While they were awaiting demolition, a notice was placed outside warning of the danger and telling people to keep out. One day she was walking past on her way home, when the ceiling of one of the houses fell in and a boy came running out. She had been saving her clothing coupons for over a year to buy a new coat and she was wearing it for the first time. She had bought it from Maurices on the Bridge Foot and it was red with a black collar and the pockets trimmed with black.

She was very proud of it but, when the boy shouted that his mate was under all the rubble, she forgot about her coat and with no one else about, she ran in the house and pulled the bricks and rubbish off the boy as fast as she could.

She lifted him out and carried him across the road to Doctor Pilchers, then carried on home without leaving her name. Her beautiful coat was ruined but the boy was saved. She often wonders if that boy is still alive and if he remembers anything about his narrow escape.

When she married her second husband, her name reverted to Revell, for he was Alec Revell but, unfortunately, he also died about fifteen years ago.

Coincidentally, when I was talking recently to Mr. Green at the Borough of Boston Rates Department, he told me he was born in White Horse Lane in 1939 and my column often brings back memories for him.

His father came through the war safely, only to be killed in a road crash in 1947, driving a lorry for Frank Thompson. He remembers getting into trouble once, when he went to Roger Tuddenham's scrap yard and exchanged his school cap for a funeral hat and went to school in it.

Last week I received not just one but three letters from my cousin in Gold Beach, Oregon, U.S.A. Before she became a G.I. bride, she attended the Boston High School and worked at the County Hall as Leila Rastall. Her letters usually run to four pages and update me on conditions in America today, and contain her impressions of the shortcomings of their government. She is no threat to Alastair Cooke but I always find them very interesting.

All three, however, this time were full of her wartime experiences, after she left the Land Army, when she was old enough to join the A.T.S. She trained at Harrogate in 1943 and did well enough in the tests to become one of the first batch of OWLS (Operators, Wireless and Line).

She was posted to Strathpeffer in the Highlands and was soon an expert in Morse code, sending and receiving messages, taking a wireless apart and putting it back together again.

Strathpeffer was a base also for the Norwegian Army in exile and twenty Norwegian commandos lived in the hotel across the street from Leila's hotel. They shared a canteen run by the Church of Scotland with the A.T.S. girls using one long table in the bare wooden hut, and the Norwegians the only other table.

Most of the commandos were over six feet tall but one, Hjalmar Karl, was only 5' 10" and seemed small amongst the others but he spoke the best English. Before the war he had signed on for merchant vessels and learned a different language every year.

The only refreshment available was weak coffee and the girls always had the cups to wash afterwards, then they chatted at their table, while the Norwegians stuck to their own table. One day Hjalmar crossed over and stood listening first to one girl then another, and finally asked Leila if she would sit at their table and talk to them and listen and correct their English. He explained that they liked her voice best and of course they would pay her. She agreed and said she would charge them one cup of coffee a night.

After that she spent her nights off duty helping them improve their English but their accent always betrayed their nationality. Seeing a salmon jump in a stream, they would say, "saarmon yump".

The path to the canteen was a rough narrow uphill track, covered with loose pebbles, which made a lot of noise as you walked, but one night, as Leila was returning to her hotel, a drunken Canadian lumberjack rushed at her out of the hedgerow and she stood frozen to the ground, but before he could touch her, there was a blood-curling roar and the would-be assailant bounded over the fields, as if the devil were after him.

When the tall Norwegian returned, he said that one of them followed her home every night, because, although most of the Canadians were gentlemen, like the Norwegians, they were always worried for her safety. She could not understand how she never saw or heard them and she almost felt sorry for the German sentries, when these commandos crept up behind them.

They often disappeared for a few weeks, when they went on a raid and they entrusted their prized gramophone and 50 records to Leila, until they returned and each time some never came back. She admired them tremendously and, as she says, few people realise the price those men paid.

One officer, Dagfinn Haugland, led a raid back to Norway and the Germans retaliated by rounding up every member in his family; parents, grandparents, brothers, sisters, aunts, uncles, even a sister-in-law, who had given birth the day before. She and her baby were dragged out of bed and the whole family were shot, then the farmhouse was set on fire. The German intelligence had made a terrible mistake, however, for the family murdered belonged to Nils Haugland, another officer, who was in a Convalescent Home at the time.

The poor fellow was demented, when he heard the news and went berserk, until an old Scottish doctor called on his experience of the First World War to calm him.

Crown Prince Olaf, who succeeded his father, King Haakon VII on September 21st 1957, came to Strathpeffer to hand out seven silver badges to Norwegian heroes. The insignia was a wreath with a H crossed by a 7 in the centre to represent the King. The Crown Prince presented six badges, then gave the commandos the seventh to award it as they chose. Leila was both flattered and astonished, when the men awarded the seventh badge to her, and today it is her most prized possession.

In 1944 my cousin, Leila Rastall, was one of six A.T.S. girls who passed an advanced course and was given two weeks leave, before being posted to an unknown destination. She was sorry to leave her Norwegian friends at Strathpeffer but anticipated with relish the thought of spending the rest of the winter in Cornwall or Devon, for she overheard an officer as they boarded the train in Inverness, say that they were going to the West Country.

After just two days at home, however, a telegram arrived telling her to report within a week to a holding camp at Cambridge. She was reunited with her five friends and the next day transport arrived to take them to Ormsby St. Mary, a few miles from Great Yarmouth. So much for the West Country but preferable to the Highlands.

They were given an old house next to the church to live in, which was quite comfortable, after they scrubbed and cleaned all the rooms. Opposite was a large estate owned by the heir to a brewery, who had lost both legs at Dunkirk and subsequently donated the estate to the army.

The officers of 76 division lived in the big house but the signals hut was set apart in the woods. Four miles south were the Sherwood Foresters and four miles north was the 4th East Lancs. regiment. The Foresters were a boisterous bunch but the East Lancs. had a reputation for being sobersides, and there was rivalry between them.

There was great rejoicing one day, because the Foresters had shot down an enemy plane, and someone was coming from Headquarters in Norwich to commend the gun crew. The visit was never made, however, and nothing more was heard of the incident. It turned out that the plane came over on the night of the Regimental dinner and the only people sober were three cooks. They manned the guns and shot down the German plane; something the proper gunners had never managed.

If the truth had come out, everyone would have been in trouble and there would have been embarrassment for the Foresters, so it was all swept under the carpet.

On another occasion the Sherwood Foresters did receive proper recognition for the capture of a German spy. A young Lieutenant arrived, saying he had been sent from the War Office to inspect the coastal defences. His papers and permits were in order but an old sergeant, who was detailed to accompany him felt uneasy, and thought something was wrong.

The Lieutenant said he had been at Division Headquarters the previous night and was moving on to the East Lancs. Brigade the next day. The sergeant asked him if he had met Colonel White at Headquarters and the Lieutenant said that he had spoken to him in the mess, and remarked on his having only one eye.

The sergeant immediately went to the Commandant and told him the Lieutenant was a German spy, a fact which was corroborated by a signal to Headquarters. The German Intelligence was very good; the Lieutenant was very well versed in every detail but, unfortunately for him, the sergeant was a personal friend of Colonel White and had received a letter from him that morning from Aldershot, where he had gone on a three week course, so he could not have been at Norwich the previous night.

A German reconnaissance plane often flew over the village early in the morning, so low that the pilot could give the girls a mock salute, as they went on duty. The soldiers assured the girls that "Recce" planes did not carry guns, only cameras, so they did not worry and returned the salute.

One morning Leila was walking past a house in the village with a broad dense hedge, a good six feet high, when she heard a plane and, before she could turn to salute, a shell hit the pavement behind her. The next second she was lying face down in a beautiful bed of flowers: she had jumped the hedge in one bound without a run-up. That jump would have won a medal at the Olympic Games but no one witnessed it, except the German pilot, so Leila just picked herself up, went out through the garden gate and went on duty.

Before Leila arrived at Ormsby St. Mary, the Division Headquarters had been at Great Yarmouth, but one Friday morning someone decided that there should be a full dress parade at 10.00 a.m. outside the hotel on the front which the army occupied. At precisely 10. a.m. the German planes came and shot and bombed the whole parade. Obviously a German spy had been more successful that time.

In 1943 when my cousin Leila Rastall completed her A.T.S. training as an OWL (Operators, Wireless and Line) at Strathpeffer in the Scottish Highlands, she was driven with five more girls to Inverness to commence a train journey that would take them all the way to Cornwall.

They were all due to a week's leave however before completing the journey, but they would be together as far as Kings Cross, where they would then go their separate ways. One of the girls, Barbara lived at Whittlesey and it seemed silly that they could not leave the train at Peterborough, but all the travel warrants were made out from Kings Cross to the various home towns.

It was midnight, when they boarded the train at Inverness. It was the type with a corridor running the entire length of each carriage, and each compartment had seats for twelve people.

Leila sat with her back to the engine next to the corridor and three of her friends sat on the same seat, with Barbara and one other sat opposite near the window. It was a slow train with frequent stops, before they joined the express at Edinburgh and at one stop three airmen got on and entered their compartment.

They were friendly and explained they were with the Air Sea Rescue at Nigg and they entertained the girls with renditions of "Dangerous Dan McGrew" and "The Face on the Bar-Room Floor". Eventually they all slept and Leila awoke to a lovely summer's day with the sun shining on green fields and trees, and she thought they should soon be pulling into Waverley Station.

It was Friday, 13th July and, as she checked the time, Leila thought it was not the best day to make a long journey. Because of her job and the electricity involved Leila could not wear a wrist-watch, so she had a pocket watch, which she kept in her bag wrapped in a handkerchief. She noted it was exactly ten o'clock and as she was replacing her watch, she became aware of a little red-haired girl standing in front of her. She had not heard the sliding doors but she must have come in while Leila was looking in her handbag.

The little girl had a freckled face and she was dressed in a blue tweed coat with a blue tam-o-shanter and a wool scarf, all good quality, as were her shoes and socks; she looked out of place travelling on a troop train alone.

Leila was about to ask her where her parents were and why she had entered their compartment, when the little girl spoke "My name is Saundra McCrindle, I'm ten years old, my sister, Heather, is in the army at Yarmouth and you are going to see her".

Leila laughed and explained to the little Scottish girl that because she was in the army, it did not mean she would be seeing her sister, but Saundra persisted, "Heather is a telephone operator in Yarmouth; do you not know where it is?"

Leila assured her that she knew Yarmouth but she would be going to Cornwall, the other side of the country. She asked the little girl to sit near her but Saundra remained standing, and they talked for half an hour. She talked of her school, her teachers, her favourite lessons but she always returned to her sister, "Heather has another ladder in her stockings but she will soon have enough darns to get a new pair".

She had just asserted for the tenth time that "You are going to see her", when she left as suddenly as she had arrived, and again Leila never heard the door open.

Leila turned to Nancy, who was sat next to her, and asked her if she saw where the little girl had gone but Nancy had not seen her. Indeed none of the others had seen the little girl, but Barbara said she had seen Leila talking to herself and thought it was odd. The airmen had been sleeping but, waking to such a weird conversation, they spent the remainder of the trip to Edinburgh sat in the corridor.

The strange episode was shoved to the back of her mind when Leila started her leave, but after the week her orders were changed and she was told to report to Cambridge instead of going to Cornwall. The next morning a driver arrived to transport her to her new posting....Yarmouth.

In conversation with the driver Leila learned that Yarmouth had been bombed at exactly 10 o'clock on Friday, 13th July and there had been many casualties, as some idiot had arranged a full dress parade outside the hotel, used as headquarters for the group, and somehow the Germans knew about it.

The driver stopped at a little cemetery, where some of the casualties had been buried and Leila knew what she would find. Sure enough one of the temporary wooden crosses bore the name HEATHER McCRINDLE.

The other week, when I called at the Lincolnshire Aviation Heritage Centre at East Kirkby, I introduced myself to the gentleman welcoming visitors at the door to the shop and café and, while I waited to see Mr. Panton, I discovered he remembered my father very well, and his wife was a regular reader of this column.

It was Harry Ely, who used to be a baker at the Mill at Old Bolingbroke, and we spent a pleasant ten minutes recalling the days when every village had a baker. He listed them all in the Spilsby area and my mind went back to my schooldays, when I used to address the postcards that my father sent out when there was to be a meeting of the Boston & District Master Bakers, Millers & Associated Trades.

Most of them were just names to me but later I met several, especially those who came to the Bakers' Dinner as President for that year, and took their place of honour at the top table: Joe Wildman from East Keal, James Picker from Wainfleet St. Marys, George Trueman from Sutterton, Charles Wright from Old Leake.

The area included both Spilsby and Skegness and with the millers and allied traders father as secretary always posted 120 postcards: today I imagine 10 would be ample.

To revive a few memories here are some of the village bakers from fifty years ago: Sibsey, Mrs. Capps and Mrs. Wells, Butterwick, Ted Sands, who later went to Sutterton and was baking down Horncastle Road, when he died while on duty as a Special Constable at a polling station one election day; Mr. Vinter bought his business at Butterwick, Leake Commonside, Fred Borrill and George Howsam, Eastville, Mr. Chapman, Wrangle, Reeson & Borrill, Kirton, Percy Jessop, Swineshead, Mr. Smith and Mr. West.

Modens were one of the Spilsby bakers and there used to be a School of Cookery at Skegness, but Sid Hanson of Skegness became the biggest baker in the area, when he bought out several others, before selling out himself to Mother's Pride.

Recently lists of various tradesmen in the town have proved to be of interest, so here is my list of Boston bakers, prior to the advent of sliced bread: John Loveley and Dowlmans in the Market Place, "Dada" Harrison down Dolphin lane, George Pape in Pump Square, "Bungy" Newton in Narrow Bargate, Mr. Gray round the corner near the old Lincolnshire Standard offices, Shepherds and Harold Panton also in Wide Bargate, Jim Sizer in Freiston Road, Mr. Barrand at Mount Bridge, Mr. Goodacre in West Street, later Mr. Vere, then Mr. Nesbitt, Eddie Loveley at the top of James Street, George Young at the corner of Tower Street and Station Street, Bert Meeds in Frampton Place, Mr. Lammie in Carlton Road and his brother in Argyle Street, Stan Bell in Tattershall Road, Bill Pannell down Norfolk Place, Mr. King down Chapel Row, Mrs. Leafe at the corner of George Street and Liquorpond Street, Tom Sands in Duke Street, Charlie Borrill at Newton's Corner down London Road and finally Alf Johnson, Aubrey Fox and Freddy Mould within one hundred yards of each other in High Street.

I have a terrible feeling I have forgotten somebody but no doubt I will soon find out.

Once sliced bread was introduced, all shops started selling bread and one by one the bakers disappeared but the few, who remain, cater for those of us, who still appreciate proper bread, which has been fully baked and allowed the optimum time in the prover. Sliced bread is obviously never well-baked or the blades would need replacing too often, and chemicals are added to keep it fresher longer. If you sop stale sliced bread for the birds, you will find it transmutates into a horrible viscous substance that bears no resemblance whatsoever to proper bread.

I would like to thank Lyn Naylor of Clarke Court, Wyberton for contacting me when she found some interesting newspaper cuttings, and a copy of the Boston Independent, dated Saturday, November 25th 1905.

The cuttings had been saved by her father, Harry Pierrepont, who was born in Sheffield but settled in Boston, and had the misfortune to be blinded just three months before V.E. Day, when he was 32.

After the war the family lived in George Street, next door to Frosts, who had a vegetable stall on the market, but they were flooded out in 1948 and St. Dunstans were instrumental in their moving to Kingsway. Harry worked on the switchboard at British Rail and, as I walked to the Grammar School each morning I passed Lyn walking with her cycle, accompanying her father to the station.

To their eternal credit the town of Boston bought Harry Pierrepont the first guide dog seen in the town. He called it Boy and it became a regular feature for many people, seeing Boy walk Harry to work and home again every day. Before he retired Harry had three guide dogs but Boy was always his favourite.

My cousin Bruce was born on January 10th 1929 and died at the age of twelve in 1941. He had sugar diabetes and, although insulin was then available, there was no National Health Service and little was known about stabilising the condition by one's diet.

After his death Aunt Ruby tried several jobs, finishing at the Woodlands at Kirton, especially to pay Dr. Usmar for the treatment in a vain attempt to prolong his short life.

He had three older sisters but his father Bart Rastall died in 1932, when Bruce was three, because he contracted Typhoid Fever from his job as a milkman. His sisters remembered how he suffered before he died, and how they first realised he had diabetes, when he drank a full bucket of water.

There are still friends, who remember Bruce, and I spoke to one recently, Ron Sharp, who was a member of the same gang in those years just before the war. Many people will remember Ron from the years he had a shop in Field Street and sold fruit and vegetables from his cart, driven by "Tommy", the most popular horse in Boston.

In the thirties his parents moved to Boston from Swineshead and bought a shop in Lincoln Lane, selling vegetables on one side and sweets on the other. After his father died, his mother remarried and the shop was known as Peacocks.

My brother and I sometimes visited Bruce, and we were co-opted into his gang to swell their numbers for the continuous conflict with the Williamson's gang. Mrs. Williamson also ran a shop; hers was further up Lincoln Lane, near the Duke of York and she had several sons and her daughters were also very active members of their gang.

The battleground was mainly that part of Lincoln lane near the old Fire Station, Mountain's slaughter house and the houses that my mother always referred to as "the Nine Row".

I remembered the names of some of Bruce's gang, Benny Ashton and Ron Beecham, but Ron Sharp filled in the missing names, Les Cook and Alan "Chucky" Read. They all attended Staniland School, except Bruce, who maintained the family tradition and went to St. Botolph's School.

Ron told me that they all wished to go to Bruce's funeral, which was to be at 12. 15 at the cemetery, and at that time the only entrance was in Horncastle Road. They were not allowed to leave school early, so at twelve o'clock the five lads burst out of Staniland School and rushed through town to reach the cemetery by 12. 15 p.m.

By coincidence James Follows from Hull has recently sent the Lincolnshire Standard an interesting letter detailing much of this part of town, including George White's various sales sites, and I should think he will remember Bruce and his sisters, because they lived next door to the New Sales Hall.

Balding Court, which he mentioned was near Mrs. Williamson's' shop and I believe Ron Beecham's parents lived there. I wonder if Fred Oliver, the bookie, was related to "Bingy" Oliver, a name often mentioned by Aunty Ruby.

Mr. Follow's mother was landlady of the Victoria Inn, central point of our battlefield. There were two other public houses in Rosegarth Street; the Hop Pole and the Stag and Pheasant on the corner of Pinfold Lane.

There was also the Blue Lion opposite Whittle's shoe lace factory, on the corner of Lincoln Lane and Stanbow Lane. Then a row of shops, as you walked to St. George's Hall and the White Hart. Ron Sharp listed them all; King's Cycle Shop, Walden's sweet shop, Holme's creamery and Killick's barber's shop among others.

Before the end of the war, Ron Sharp had joined the Royal Navy and was posted to the School of Signals at H.M.S. Arthur at Skegness, which was the wartime alias for Billy Butlin's first ever holiday camp. The young trainees used to be billeted four to a chalet.

Apart from Ron I have not seen any other members of Bruce's gang since he died, but Ron Beecham's sister, June, lived in Oxford Street after she married Ken Taylor, and she was a customer in our High Street shop.

I believe Bobby Williamson, the leader of the rival gang, also joined the Royal Navy, but one of his brothers came to live in High Street next door to Percy White's fish and chip shop, and his wife was also one of our customers.

I can still remember the feeling of fear and apprehension, when with my brother I had to brave the journey from Bruce's house in Rosegarth Street to my grandmother's house in Station Street, which meant passing through enemy territory.

I am pleased that this column stirs up so many memories for some readers. Mr. S. Scales of Butterwick was attending Staniland School in 1930/31, and remembers an occasion, when he and some friends arranged a game of football near the Broadfield Street Railway crossing after dinner one day. There was an area of about fifty yards where it was safe to play, without the danger of breaking any windows and calling down the wrath of the neighbourhood.

Afternoon school started at 2.00 p.m., and they had time to reach the playground after the bell rang to call everybody inside. He bolted his dinner down and was running out of his back yard, when his father asked him why he was in a hurry. On being told of the football game, his father made him change from his shoes which he had snobbed only that week, into his old boots, which were in the cupboard under the stairs. Snobbed was the term used then locally for resoling boots or shoes.

He changed quickly into his boots and was soon at the "pitch", where they selected two teams, four a-side, and immediately transformed themselves into Arsenal and Aston Villa. It had been raining that morning and on one side of the road a big puddle had formed and naturally the ball was attracted to it, as if it covered a huge magnet and, to avoid "hand ball", the boys dribbled it out onto dry land.

Lost in the fervour of the contest, no one heard the bell and a shout of "They've gone in!" brought them back to earth, and sixteen saturated feet ran hell for leather up Broadfield Street, across Liquorpond Street into George Street and Staniland playground. It was all to no avail and those sixteen feet were soon stood outside the headmaster's room awaiting punishment.

The headmaster found it unusual that there should be eight boys, who all forgot the time, but he had something that he was sure would help them remember in future, and they all received two strokes on each hand from his "old faithful" and they reported to their classrooms with stinging fingers.

The rest of the class watched spellbound, waiting to witness the inevitable caning for interrupting the class as well as being late, when further punishment was spared by the headmaster entering the room and he told the teacher that atonement had already been made.

An official looking man came in with the headmaster, and together with the teacher they conferred in a corner of the classroom for a few minutes, then the teacher told the whole class to place their feet in the gangway, so that the stranger could inspect their footwear. They spent about ten seconds at each pair of feet but, when they reached Scales, they told him to take off his boots and asked him why his socks were so wet. He explained that it had been raining, when he went home for dinner and, when asked, he told them his father was out of work.

He told the man he was called Stan Scales and, after nothing more was heard for several days, both he and his classmates forgot about the incident.

Some weeks later, however, a letter arrived in a green envelope addressed to Stan's father and he was told to report to the Police Station, with his son Stanley on Friday evening for the purpose of obtaining a pair of Police boots, which would be paid for out of money collected by the Police, when people paid fines.

Stanley's mother was most upset at the idea of her Stanley receiving Police boots, which she considered to be charity, and she said that the Police always stamped them inside with PB, so that they benefited the child and could not be sold by the parents. This would not have happened, if Stan had not changed into his old boots to play football. Mr. Scales settled the argument by pointing out that it was his name on the form and that was that.

It was bitter cold and frosty on the Friday night when they reported with about twenty others to the Police Station, and followed a sergeant to Bozeats in Church Street, where an assistant sorted out the right size, then retired with them into a small room and hammered hob nails into the sole, until there was room for no more. When Stan went to school in his Police boots on the Monday morning, it sounded like a horse clomping along the pavement.

"Mother would have told us", "Granddad would have remembered him", "If only Aunt Annie were still alive, we could ask her"; if you have not already said similar things, you can be sure you will sometime in the future.

We do not fully appreciate our elderly relatives, until they are gone and it is too late. We should all spend more time talking to them and, even more important, listening to them. They have all had experiences and learned lessons during their lives, that, if wise, you can benefit from and, if you find they tend to repeat their favourite anecdotes, a sensible question from you will prompt them to delve further into their memory.

I recently mentioned my grandfather's brother, George Blackamore, in my column and his daughter, Hilda Tebbs, phoned me and I arranged to visit her at her home in Windsor Bank, where she had lived all her life. Her son, Brian "Inky" Tebbs, is about the same age as myself and I played football against him in our younger days. I remember him as a good and fair player, who was popular both with his own team and their opponents.

I anticipated with relish the opportunity of discovering facts I had often regretted not discussing with my parents, who were both thirty-four, when I was born, so had already experienced almost half of their lives.

Hilda did not disappoint me, for, although eight years younger than my mother, they spent much time together and she was one of my mother's bridesmaids, when she married on the 23rd October, 1926. At that time cousins were much closer and they were more like sisters.

I had a copy of my parent's wedding photograph with me and she pointed out herself and identified the other adult bridesmaid as Ruby Allewell, mother's friend, and the two young bridesmaids as Nelly Blackamore, my Uncle Ernie's daughter, and Beryl Rastall, my Aunt Ruby's daughter.

She told me that, when my parents opened their café in West Street in 1928, she helped my mother serve the customers and later, when the birth of my sister was imminent, she managed the café, until she herself married.

Earlier, before my mother married, they worked together at White Tompkins, who had a factory under the archway down Tattershall Road in Witham Town. They sold packet peas and jelly crystals; an unusual combination. They later moved to the factory at the top of Spayne Road, which later still became Hursts.

Hilda showed me a prized photograph she had of their workmates at White Tompkins and, when I turned it over, I read all the names I had heard my mother mention over and over again: Ruth Manning, Ada Yeatman, Gladys Wortley.

Several of them I recognised myself: Kate Gunby, who became Mrs. Creek and lived near my mother in Station Street; Dinx Lewis, Victor Emery's aunt, who married Mr. Bembridge and lived in Edwin Street, retiring eventually as forewoman at Willer & Rileys. Then there was my mother's friend, Ivy Massingham, who married Cliff Holgate from Yorkshire and worked for several years with her sister, Ada, at the Lindis Tea Rooms above the Midland Bank and also the Louise Rooms at the White Hart. She, of course, was the mother of my friend Noel Holgate, and I had many opportunities to discover at first hand the kindness and genuine qualities that mother must have encountered as her friend.

There were only two men on the photograph and I recognised one as Gordon Upsall's father, who lived in King Street, not far from the Holgates. Hilda called him Billy Upsall and she said he married one of the girls, Bertha Mableson. Before she could point her out, I said it was the girl seated just in front of him, for I remember well Gordon's mother, who always walked at a brisk pace.

One of the girls, I think it was Gladys Wortley, had married Tommy Mitcham, who shared the left wing position for Boston United after the war with Ken Cooper, and another, Jenny Parvin, the sister of my Aunt Nellie, married Fred Bohn, whose parents were German. I had heard my mother talk about Fred Bohn, because his sister, Mrs. Stevens, lived in Chapel Passage, opposite our shop in High Street.

I thought I remembered my mother saying she had also worked at Dring's canning factory, so I asked Hilda where that used to be and she said down Norfolk Street.

One outstanding memory of her childhood was watching someone place a flag at the extreme top of the Stump at 11.00 a.m. on the 11th November, 1918, when she was ten years old.

The mysterious disappearance of the trawler "Gaul" has been in the news again recently, because the graves of three men, who could have been members of the crew have been discovered in Russia. In 1921 two trawlers, the "Bostonian" and the "Lindsey" left Boston and they were lost at sea: it was thought that they must have hit mines from the First World war but no trace of either was ever found.

They belonged to the Boston Deep Sea Fishing Company, whose chairman, Fred Parkes, had started the business when he was only seventeen, and had six trawlers before he was twenty. My mother often used to talk about him and said what a shame it was, that he left Boston and moved his fleet to Fleetwood, where it became the country's biggest fishing fleet. Boston could have rivalled Grimsby and Hull but she was pleased he never changed the name of his company. Eventually he became Sir Fred Parkes, when he was knighted for his public services.

He left Boston, after an unfortunate sequence of events, which started in 1922, when the S.S. Lockwood sank in the river and stopped ships reaching the docks for five months. Salvage experts could not move it, so Fred Parkes agreed to try, if Boston Corporation covered his expenses.

He also failed and it was finally moved by the Royal Navy but, when he asked for £12,000 to reimburse him for his efforts, the council, of which he was a member, refused. The matter was settled in court, but the whole episode left such a sour taste in his mouth, that he was determined to leave the town of his birth. Over the years this must have cost Boston millions; just to save £12,000 in 1922.

If only the Corporation had stopped to think about "The Pied Piper Of Hamlin", Boston could have benefited from seventy years of being the country's major trawler port.

My mother's cousin, Hilda Tebbs, told me how the whole town was in mourning, when the "Bostonian" and the "Lindsey" disappeared. Her friend, Rose Timby, who lived in Stanbow Lane, lost both her husband and her son, Billy.

Until she told me, I had no idea that my grandmother's brother, William St. Paul was also lost at sea: he was on the ship with Lord Kitchener, when it was torpedoed during the Great War.

Another interesting story she told me concerned by grandfather, Bob Blackamore. He was foreman on the coal hoist at the dock, and part of his job involved taking coal down to the Cut End to ships, which were too big to navigate the river.

Towards the end of the war in 1918 an exchange of prisoners was arranged on a troopship in the Wash, and the family discovered that one of the British troops was his nephew, Bill Blackamore, who had lost a leg. His pregnant wife was not allowed to see him, although he would be on a train in Boston station for a while, so my grandfather said he would take him a letter, chocolate and cigarettes, when he took the coal out to the troopship.

Two sisters had married two brothers, so Bill Blackamore's father, Charles, was granddad's brother but his mother, Ellen, was also my grandmother's sister, so the families were extra close.

My grandfather persuaded the officer in charge of the exchange to let him search through the British prisoners, while the coal was being loaded, as he had a son amongst them: even then he only received a grudging permission.

As he passed between the soldiers, many with arms and legs missing, he heard a shout "Well! I'll be blowed". It's Uncle Bob". He hurried over to his nephew, hoping the officer had not noticed, and quickly whispered, "Shut up, you fool, I'm your father".

I asked a few weeks ago, if anyone remembered "Bingy" Oliver, and it appears that he was quite a character. Apart from being a bookie's runner, he was also an amateur boxing promoter, specialising in junior tournaments.

People would cry shame today, but he arranged boxing bouts between boys as young as five. Hilda Tebbs remembers her young brother winning a pot teddy bear as the victor in one of "Bingy" Oliver's promotions and he could have been no older, because he died of diphtheria, when he was five and a half. Hilda's son, Brian, still has that pot teddy bear today.

I lost one of my main sources of encouragement, when my good friend, Dick Parkinson, died recently. He was two years ahead of me at the Grammar School but I always heard of his heroics on the football field in winter, and the cricket pitch in summer, because my brother, Jim, was in his class.

He was a prolific scorer of spectacular goals and well earned his nickname, Dead-shot Dick. In the summer he was a very useful fast bowler and gained his cricket colours by taking 8 for 25 one day on the Church Road pitch, which, since he had been a young lad living in the area, he had watched Mr. Burton, the groundsman, prepare many a time.

His family later moved to Woodville Road and, as those of you have read my book will know, it was on the Woodville Road playing field that I spent many evenings playing "thrasher" with my brother, Ken Johnson, Dick and his friend Johnny Smith.

Although Dick lived at Leverington, just outside Wisbech, he received the Boston edition of the Lincolnshire Standard regularly from his father-in-law, Cyril Keightley. On four separate occasions Dick was kind enough to write to say how interesting he had found my column, and each time he related memories of his own, which I in turn appreciated. He always signed off with some encouraging remark: "Keep writing, it's all good stuff", or "Congratulations on your article". It is surprising what a boost such words can be, when you are not sure how your efforts are being received.

In a letter he wrote in April he tells of a cycling holiday he planned with Johnny Taylor, who used to live in Tower Street. They hired a tandem from Mr. Rooke, who had a fruit shop in West Street, opposite the Labour Exchange. (His son Brian, was also in Dick's class).

They cycled down to Torquay, where they had arranged to meet Peter Kitchen and a friend of his, who lived near him at Sutterton, outside the G.P.O. Peter lived at the Angel Inn and he was Head Boy at the Grammar School, when I left in 1950.

Travelling over Exmoor, they reached Minehead and Weston-Super-Mare. They had an old primus stove set in a biscuit tin with a hinged side. Dick had several photographs recording the holiday and he remembered they cycled 120 miles on the last day, to reach home.

When I mentioned that I missed three week's square-bashing in the R.A.F., because I was fortunate enough to have my Cert A with me, Dick sent me a copy of his Cert A, which states at the front that "This certificate should be produced by the holder, when he reports to the Primary Training Centre", so it was not luck after all; I was just obeying instructions.

I would not fancy trying to pass for my Cert A today. On the back it stated that the cadet named had shown a satisfactory standard of proficiency in Drill, Rifle Training, Map Reading and Fieldcraft. Not only that I must have passed the Physical Efficiency Tests lists: 100 yards sprint, standing long jump, running high jump, running vault, 1 mile run, 1 hour walk, 15 ft. rope climbing, abdominal strength, heaving strength and swimming. It must be easier to be accepted for Gladiators.

He also sent me photographs of the first camp the Boston Grammar School Combined Cadet Force attended at Fingeringhoe in 1950. I had just left to start working at the Boston Guardian, so I missed it.

Dick was the Company Sergeant Major, and one photograph shows him on the Sunday March Past just behind Captain Dowson and in line with Sergeant John Tilling. In the second rank is Peter Jordan and Brian Wrigley, and further back I can pick out Graham Elkington and Phillip Green.

Fingeringhoe was in Essex, near Colchester and there were several lines of tents with contingents from many schools, but Boston Grammar School shone at Reveille, because they had the best bugler, Michael Mitchell from London Road, who played in the Salvation Army band. Unfortunately Michael was killed a few years later, when his motor cycle crashed one evening into a stationary car.

Another photograph is of Dick and John Tilling in combat dress with two others, Brian Drinkall and, I think, Michael Kirk.

Coincidentally Dick was back at Fingeringhoe nine months later; he was commissioned during his National Service and was posted there as Ranger Officer, retraining "Z" reservists during the Egyptian crisis.

One of his recollections I did share was the delivery of the first .303 rifles for the C.C.F. They were covered in thick grease and we sat in the Fives Court in the Grammar School yard, until the grease was all off.

When a few weeks ago, I listed the bakers I remembered from fifty years ago, I expected some response, but not the number of letters and phone calls, which ensued. The first letter came from Bill Collishaw, who detailed no less than thirteen I had missed. Henderson in Bargate, Smith & Peacock in Wormgate, Skinner in Freiston, Neal in Butterwick and Martins in Butterwick, Johnson at Leverton and "Baggy" Ablard at Leverton and six at Swineshead; Houlder, Miller, Cecil Smith, Len Smith and two Wests. Some of these I recall but others I believe must have traded more than fifty years ago.

I had remembered two others myself, Billy Altoft from Red Lion Street and Frank Borrill from Skirbeck Road, both of whom had been President of the Boston and District Master Bakers and Millers Association. Then, when I met Ray Loveley, he reminded me of several more.

He started with Frank Borrill and added two more Barrands, one in Station Street and one in Bargate, and he said there was another shop in Dolphin Lane besides Harrisons. I believe he said Martins but I had my cue in my hand instead of my pen, so I did not write them down. "Dadda" Harrison's son Ray, by the way, was a professional footballer and played centre forward for Burnley, when they were in the First Division.

Ray Loveley was still at school fifty years ago, so it was his father, Eddie, who was included in my original list, but Ray carried on the family business and he is now one of a handful, who provide proper bread for the local epicures. He has recently been in Pilgrim Hospital, after a heart attack, but I was pleased to hear he is back home.

I had to apologise to the wife of Mr. Pape's grandson, when she phoned after reading my column. I inadvertently referred to the owner of the shop at the entrance to Pump Square as George, when for years the initials above the window were clearly A.H. and his name was Arthur. Before our conversation, I had not realised that Mr. Pape's grandson was the Mr. Pape, who was a director of H. H. Adkins, the building contractors.

The letter which gave me most pleasure and satisfaction came from 84 year old Mrs. B. A. Vinter of Great Gonerby near Grantham. She professed to being a regular reader of my column and had been tempted on occasion to write, but was finally incited to do so when on the 12th September I mentioned that her husband, Reg Vinter, bought the business at Butterwick from Ted Sands.

It appears that they already had a bakery in New York and, when her husband died just two years later, she carried the two businesses on, employing four men and another woman. After another two years, however, Mrs. Vinter sold out and bought a shop and Post Office at Belchford, near Horncastle.

The passage in her letter, that I shall always treasure, referred to my father: "Your father came every Monday to our bakehouse, bringing the week's supply of yeast. He was a gentleman and, when I lost my husband, was a great help to me. I shall always remember him with great respect". Such unsolicited compliments mean much more than official letters thanking my father for his years of service to the community, and I know he would have valued her sincere remarks.

Mrs. Vinter bought her flour from Spillers, and the representative informed her that she and Mrs. Parrott of Mablethorpe were the only two lady bakers on Spiller's books.

She finished her letter with an account of her experience with bread rationing, after the war, which corroborated my own memories of the ridiculous scheme, which was indirectly responsible for my grandmother's death.

The assistant head of the Ministry of Food Boston office went to Butterwick Village Hall once a fortnight with orange juice for the baby clinic. Each time he called at Mrs. Vinter's shop and bought bread and cakes without offering any coupons. At that time Mr. & Mrs. Vinter were sitting up at night counting and separating the pile of coupons taken each day; there were some whole coupons, some half and some quarter, so it was quite a job.

Reg Vinter asked the official one week what happened when the coupons arrived at their office, did they count them or weigh them? He said he could not answer that but his advice was not to bother counting anymore but just to guess at it, so after that they went to bed much earlier.

I was pleased to see Chris Woods had returned from America and was playing again in the Premier Division, this time for Southampton. I believe records will show he kept more clean sheets for England than any other goalkeeper in proportion with games played, and his international career would have lasted longer but for injury.

He was not, however, the first international goalkeeper from this area and I am not referring to Ray Clemence, who came from Skegness. Boston produced a goalkeeper, who played for England in 1951 or 1952.

This boy went to the Boston Grammar School but showed no interest in football during his first two years, and I was surprised one Saturday to see him in goal for Wyberton Rangers, when our Demon Sports Club played them on their pitch down the Swineshead Ramper. He played well that day and even then he showed skill in cutting down the angle, when danger threatened.

By 1948 Mr. P. M. Fox had taken charge of Wyberton Rangers and he fired them with ambition to try for honours over a wider area. I had known Mr. Fox for some years, as he also was on the committee of the Boston Youth League, and the 5th. Boston Scout Troop used to go to camp each year on the back of his lorry.

He entered Wyberton Rangers in the Burrell Cup that year: this was organised by Mr. Houghton, father of the international footballer, Eric Houghton, who played many years as outside left for Aston Villa. His cousin, Roy, played outside right for Boston United.

Robin Everett, who is now Rector of Ibstock and Heather in Leicestershire, played in defence for Wyberton Rangers and he told me how they reached the final which was played before a crowd of 2,000.

They won and were thrilled to be presented the cup and their medals by no other than Tommy Lawton, who had just been signed, together with centre-half Leon Leuty, for Notts County. The £20,000 paid for Tommy Lawton was at that time a new record. As you will have seen, this greatest ever centre-forward died recently.

He was so impressed with Wyberton Rangers, that a match was arranged to be played on the Notts County ground against a team of Nottingham lads. It was billed as "Notts City Boys" against "Boston Boys" and thereafter the team always played under that name.

The match was played straight after Notts. County's Third Division game against Millwall and, Robin said, almost the whole of the 30,000 stayed to watch. Many of today's footballers have never played in front of such a large crowd. Gordon Upsall was an inside forward that day and he impressed several scouts but it was the goalkeeper, who was launched on the road to fame.

In those days England had an Amateur International team and for several years he was their automatic choice as goalkeeper. It made sporting headlines in all the daily papers when he signed for Aston Villa, but remained an amateur, as he intended to go to university at Cambridge, where he captained the football team.

He played many games for Aston Villa in the First Division and, if he had wished, he could have turned professional and, who knows, maybe played for England in full internationals. His name was Mick Pinner.

I was pleased to receive a letter from another of my Grammar School classmates, Derek Fox. It appears on leaving school he worked for William Sinclair & Son, the seed firm and listed amongst his colleagues Janet Troops, who was in my class at Staniland School, and my brother Jim. Others working in their office in 1949 were Len Day, George Wilson, Roy Woodthorpe and May Powell.

Derek said, that after two years National Service in the Royal Air Force, he joined Lloyd's bank and stayed with them, until retiring in 1993 at the Northampton branch.

He still lives in Northampton and, until recently, his cousin Tom Redman lived just up the road, but Tom has moved to the Newcastle-upon-Tyne area, where his son lives.

Derek has two brothers; Geoff, who also went to the Grammar School but three years before us, and Ken, who was a keen athlete locally and won many cross-country races in the early fifties.

We have all heard it said: "I don't like living in Boston; there is nothing to do; it is dead". The fault lies not with the town but with the individual. Anyone with that attitude would probably say the same wherever they lived.

It was just the same fifty years ago. I did not agree with such sentiments then, and I certainly do not agree with them now. For the size of the town Boston is blessed with a plethora of clubs and associations in sport, entertainment and culture. From angling to weight-training, from the Jazz Club to the Operatic Society, from the Archaeology Society to the Poetry Group, taking in such diverse interests as Martial Arts, Rambling and Family History, all are catered for in Boston.

Whatever your age there is no excuse for being bored in Boston. The same applied when I was a pupil at the Boston Grammar School; the biggest problem was finding time to fit in all the commitments, after precedence had been given to homework.

A typical week at that time would have appeared in my diary something like this:

Monday: played for the Boston Grammar School second team in the Chess League.

The Grammar School had two teams in the local league, which was comprised of approximately ten teams, who played all the matches in the clubroom above Blindell's shoe shop in the Market Place, next door to the Gas showrooms, which are now occupied by the Nationwide Building Society.

All the other teams were adults but we always gave them a good game and occasionally won, but usually finished near the bottom of the league.

Tuesday: attended Confirmation class in the Cotton Chapel at the Stump.

The weekly hour-long classes prepared us for our Confirmation Service, which was conducted by the Bishop of Lincoln in the Cotton Chapel. We had to learn the Creed, the Lord's Prayer and the Ten Commandments and be able to answer questions contained in the short Catechism.

Wednesday: played Mens' Own 5 in the Boston & District Snooker League.

Billiards was the dominant game at that time with two divisions, and only one division in the snooker league. The Mens' Own Club behind Liptons in Narrow Bargate provided nearly half the teams with others from the Indoor Bowling Club, St. James, Conservative Club, which was above the New Theatre, Waverley Club, above Broughs in High Street, British Rail, Civil Defence and the United Social Club (Bus Club) in Church Street, now Robinson's chemist shop.

Our team consisted of all schoolboys, and we had been taught the rudiments of the game by Cyril Wright and Arthur Atkins, who both preferred Billiards but instilled a love of snooker into a whole generation of Boston boys.

I never dreamed that fifty years later I would be the secretary of the League and write the reports of the matches each week.

Thursday: attended dancing classes at St. Christopher's.

Mr. Varcoe, who lived in Sunningdale Drive, was in charge of St. Christopher's Church, and the dancing classes held there were the cheapest method for my generation to be introduced to the intricacies of tripping the light fantastic. Our initial efforts, however, resembled more the approach of hippopotami to a water hole.

Later, when our pocket money allowed, we advanced to the much more sophisticated classes given by Ann Wagstaff in Bridge Street.

Friday: went to the Jazz Club in Red Lion Street.

At that time the Jazz Club was very popular. Local enthusiasts such as John Padley, Barry Eastick and Ivan Jessop created a rabid interest in Traditional Jazz and Dixieland, and occasionally they tempted a star player to appear.

In 1949 I spent a week in London with my friend, Peter Howes, and we went to a different jazz club each night, including Ronnie Scotts and Crooks Ferry Inn.

Saturday: watched Boston United in the afternoon; went to the Gliderdrome.

Boston United played in the Midland League at that time and there were local derbies with Grantham, Wisbech, Peterborough, Gainsborough and Ransom & Marles from Newark. When I was old enough to play for the Old Boys, Boston United lost a supporter but the gates used to average 4 to 5 thousand.

The Gliderdrome used to be crowded on a Saturday night and all the top bands came: Ted Heath, Oscar Rabin with singers like Dennis Lotis, Lita Rosa, Ronnie Carroll and Eve Boswell, but our favourites were always Freddy Randall or Mick Mulligan and his Magnolia players, jazz outfits.

Recently I attended a ceremony in the Boston cemetery, at which the ashes of Mrs. Ivy Leafe were laid to rest beside the grave of her husband, Arthur, who had been a classmate of my father at Kirton Grammar School in 1912.

Ivy Leafe was the landlady of the Golden Lion in High Street for thirty-five years, until she moved to Melton Mowbray in the sixties, where she served on the committee of the Melton Mencap Charity and helped to raise funds for many years.

She is still remembered by her many friends and customers in Boston, and the service was conducted by her nephew, Dick Leafe, who retired as verger at St. Botolphs a few years ago.

Dick was a member of the Old Bostonians football team, when I started playing for them in 1949, while I was still at the Grammar School. There was a shortage of full backs, who could use their left foot, so I found myself playing in the second team with players five or ten years older than myself.

Dick was the centre half but in earlier years he had played centre forward for the first team. His progress was stunted for quite a while, when he developed rheumatic fever and complications caused him to lay quiet in bed for over a year.

No matter, however, for which team he played or in which position Dick always gave his all and encouraged his team-mates to do likewise.

For an hour after the ceremony we recalled our former team-mates, some of whom, Cliff Brant, Dick Lincoln , Wilf Lowe, have died. Wilf was captain, when I was promoted to the first team, because George Jessop was injured. The other members of the selection committee were Alf Stones and Eddy Grimoldby, with Alf Read as chairman.

Alf watched all the first team games, and he is on any photograph you may see of the Old Boys taken around that time. There was always someone talking to him about football in his little office in the front of Shodfriars Hall; yet he still found time to run his family's ship broking company. At that time they had not amalgamated with Sutcliffe & Co., whose office was a little further along South Street.

For the ten years after the war the Old Bostonians were one of the leading local teams, and they contested many finals on what was then the Shodfriars Lane ground against either Bicker or Fishtoft.

For several years Peter Newton was the goalkeeper and his brother, Alan was centre forward. When Peter broke his leg, Dick Massingham took over and kept goal brilliantly for many years: he was much smaller than Peter but seemed to have springs on his heels.

Peter Pearson was a dominant centre half and later his brother, Bob, also performed well in that position. I was playing the day Bob played his last game: he injured his knee and walked off the field with his leg sounding like the crocodile in "Peter Pan".

Ken Woodthorpe then took over at centre half and his brother Roy was right back. Wilf Lowe was in front of me at left half, Eddy Grimoldby at right half and the inside forwards were Alf Stones and Colin Simmons.

Alan Peck was usually on the right wing and Reg Allen on the left wing, but later both Frank Sargeant, Dick Leafe's brother-in-law, and Noel Holgate performed more than adequately on the left flank, and Derek Fletcher on the right.

My brother, Jim, was often at inside forward and also Roy Tomlinson, who later became a teacher at the Grammar School. When Laurie Veale came to teach at the Grammar School, he also played inside forward, where he had shone while at university.

For several seasons Brian Brooks was our centre forward and he was very fast, often scoring hat-tricks. As our thoughts turned to our opponents, both Dick Leafe and myself found that centre forwards dominated our memories: Tony Winn, Alan Chester, Bill Faunt, Brian Gedney, because of the numerous goals they scored.

Apart from players others come to mind. When we wanted a team photograph, we usually went to Joe Farum in Queen Street. He was actually a docker, but he was an enthusiastic amateur photographer and his front room was always full of photographs waiting to be collected.

Every Saturday tea-time there was a queue of local footballers in the passage at the side of Liptons in Narrow Bargate, for in the single house near the steps to the Mens' Own Club lived Mr. Parker, a member of the St. John Ambulance. He was better than any bonesetter and worked marvels on our joints and muscles. One Saturday I took my brother to him, his knee was swollen like a balloon. He worked on it for a hour, until he had dispersed all the fluid through his pores and he was able to go dancing that night.

On a photograph of two Singer delivery vans my father bought around 1930, the telephone number shown clearly on the side of the vans was Boston 742. So at that time the local phone numbers had only three digits.

It is possible that even earlier the first telephones in Boston had only two digits; there may be people still alive, who can verify this. Before and during the war very few private houses had phones; they were restricted largely to businesses.

By 1940 our number had become 2742 and I believe it was about 1970, when a 6 was added to the front, but by then the number had been transferred to my friend, Stan Sellers of Yellow Top Hosiery, who used 110, High Street for a while to develop his company, after our bakery and grocery shop closed in 1969 and before we sold it to Dominic Murphy, the antique upholsterer.

Yellow Top Hosiery still use the number, since they have grown and now have units on the Riverside Estate down Marsh Lane, but of course it is now 362742. It makes you wonder how many digits there will be in another sixty years.

The telephone helped to make the corner shop the centre point of the local community: most streets had a shop on the corner, until the supermarkets came in the sixties and signalled the demise of all but a few.

In the Pulvertoft Lane/Edwin Street/Oxford Street area our shop was the natural nucleus for all emergencies. Any illness or accident or catastrophe usually triggered a dash by someone, and we would break off serving a customer to rush into the room behind the shop to call a doctor, or in some cases a 999 call for the police or an ambulance.

The corner shopkeeper, because of these phone calls, often learned secrets and details of customers' health, which was not for public knowledge and, even when he heard others passing on false information or expressing wrong opinions, he had to discipline himself not to be tempted to divulge the truth.

Some emergencies could be dealt with without using the phone. If someone had fallen and no bones were broken, just brute force and ignorance required, I would desert the shop for a few minutes to administer aid. I became adept at restoring elderly ladies to their feet: some, like Miss. Hawling, with ease, because she weighed very little and it was no harder than picking up a doll, but others, like Mrs. Louth, who was paralysed and a dead weight, needed more strength and expertise.

Since 1517, when John Foxe was born in a house on the site of Martha's Vineyard, formerly the Rum Puncheon, Boston has a history of connections with important religious figures.

Foxe was ordained in 1550 by the Bishop of London, John Ridley, who later became one of the persecuted Protestants during the reign of Queen Mary, featured in Foxe's Book of Martyrs, which by 1600 was the most widely read book after the Bible.

John Cotton, who was ordained in Boston, Massachusetts in 1633, had been Vicar of Boston, Lincolnshire from 1612 to 1631, when his wife of eighteen years died from ague. They had no children, but when he married again in 1632, his second marriage produced six children, the first of which was born aboard the ship to America and was christened Seaborn, and later became the minister at Hampton, New Hampshire.

The chapel in St. Botolphs was restored by American Bostonians in 1856 and named after John Cotton, who was immortalised in a poem by H. W. Longfellow.

John Wesley first came to Boston in 1759 and preached outdoors down Walnut Tree Walk, which later became Liquorpond Street. Methodism was already established in the town, as Alexander Mather, a Wesley convert came two years earlier and before that in 1751 another of Wesley's preachers, Thomas Mitchell, had visited Boston.

In 1761 John Wesley again came to Boston and that time indoor meetings were held and he paid his final visit, when he was 77 and he climbed to the top of the Stump, whose steeple he supposed to be the highest tower in England.

From 1936 to 1939 Arthur Michael Ramsey served as lecturer at the Stump under Canon Cook, and history will probably describe him as the best loved and respected Archbishop of Canterbury of the century.

A place in history is also guaranteed for Reverend Dr. John Anthony Newton. He was born in Grantham but moved to Boston when two years old, and was baptised at the Centenary Methodist Church.

In 1981 he acceded to the highest position in Methodism, President of the Conference. He had replaced Revd. Lord Donald Soper in 1978 as the Superintendent Minister of the West London Mission.

Yet this was the lad my brother used to refer to as "Duff" Newton, when he came home from the Grammar School in 1942 and told us of his classmates. He was always the quietest boy in the class and showed no aptitude for sport, but always shone academically.

When I took my University of Cambridge School Certificate Examination in 1949, John Newton was Head Boy at Boston Grammar School. My classmate, Derek Fox, recently sent me a copy of the programme for the Speech Day, held on Friday the 16th December, 1949 and the name J. A. Newton is mentioned six times.

He won all three major prizes: the Parry Medal, the Ogle Divinity Prize and the Dennis Empire Prize; he also won the sixth form Art Prize, and he was one of nine who passed the Northern Universities Higher School Certificate Examination. The other eight were: P. Cammack, M. T. Kirk, J. C. Middlebrook, L. Musson, J. D. Periam, J. L. Taylor, J. W. C. Usher and P. Yarsley.

Most important of all he won a State Scholarship tenable at University College, Hull, where he read History. He spent a short time in supply teaching after graduating, but then went back to Hull to do research on Puritanism in the Diocese of York, under the guidance of Professor Geoffrey Dickens.

This gained him a Fellowship at the Institute of Historical Research in London. In 1955 he offered himself for the Methodist Ministry but, before he could commence his training, he was sent to Kent College, Canterbury as acting chaplain and teacher of History and Religious Education for one year.

He was then a post-graduate student for two years at Wesley House, Cambridge, followed by three years as a tutor to the Ministerial Training College at Richmond.

In 1961 he returned to Lincolnshire and met his wife, Rachel Giddings, while on the Louth Circuit. After three years, he moved to Stockton-on-Tees, then he was sent for one year to St. Paul's United College at Limaru in Kenya, before being appointed tutor in Church History at Didsbury College Bristol.

He has written biographies of Susanna Wesley and Bishop Edward King, a picture of whom can be found in his study, together with a bust of John Wesley and a print of Boston Stump. He is a regular contributor to Radio 4's "Today" programme and has represented the Methodist Ministry in several televised services.

When Ronnie Scott was found dead in his Chelsea flat on December the 23rd., every jazz lover in the country mourned, because his name had become synonymous with jazz during the last fifty years.

The Ronnie Scott Jazz Club in Soho was the Mecca for all jazz fanatics and every star performer in the world had appeared thee. The sixty-nine year old musician was loved and respected by all the greats, as well as millions of ordinary people, who visited his club when they went to London.

It may surprise you to know that, when he was eighteen, Ronnie Scott lived for a time in Boston. He was a member of the resident band at the Gliderdrome in 1945/46; Johnny Claes and his Claes-pigeons.

He was already a virtuoso on the tenor saxophone and, together with Freddy Crump on the drums, he was the main attraction. On the nights he was not performing at the Gliderdrome, he could be found in the Rugby Room at the Peacock & Royal joining in a session with local jazz players Bob Kitchen (piano), Malcolm "Mousey" Hall (double bass) and Johnny "Scorcher" Porcher (drums).

It is Johnny I have to thank for this information about Ronnie Scott, and he also pointed out that in my book I mentioned Melvyn Franklin was a member of their group, when they entertained at the Sherwood Boys Club down Field Street.

Melvyn did in fact play his piano accordion at the club but as a solo performer, it was actually Reg Howard, who played the "squeeze-box" with them. Reg, however was so impressed by Ronnie Scott, that he put his accordion to one side and switched to the tenor sax.

Horace Battram was another member of the local jazz fraternity, and he was instrumental in organising the sessions, as his brother-in-law, Bill Blake, was manager at the Peacock & Royal and he let them use the Rugby Room, which was in the rear away from the main building.

Ronnie Scott left Boston when the band split up. Johnny Claes enjoyed a bet on the horses and one week he placed the whole band's wages on a sure-thing that let him down, and that was the end of the Claes-pigeons.

Years later, around 1980, Ronnie Scott played at the Blackfriars Theatre, and Johnny and a few friends went back stage during the interval and recalled old times, with the result that Ronnie was late starting the second half of his show.

The Boston edition of the Lincolnshire Standard reaches all parts of the country. Through them reading this column, I have made contact with many of my classmates who started at the Grammar School in 1944: Robin Everett at Ibstock, Jim Wightman at Welby, Derek Simmons at Beverley, Tony Jakes at Farnham and Derek Fox at Northampton.

Now I can add the name of Geoff Cross at Broadstone in Dorset. Geoff visited his brother, Eric, who lives in Hessle Avenue over the Christmas holiday, and last week I spoke to him for the first time, since he left Boston to go to Durham university in 1951 along with Robin Everett and Barry Smith.

He was always a keen and active member of the Zion Methodist Church and entered the Methodist Ministry, after leaving university. He spent several years in Bristol, before training as a teacher and obtaining a post teaching in a college.

When he retired, he was the head of adult education in Salisbury, Wiltshire.

I also received a letter from Leigh-on-Sea, but this time the sender had been at the Grammar School between 1941-1946. He was John Chappell, whose parents had a butcher's shop in Spilsby Road.

On leaving school he worked for the Lincolnshire Standard, first at Boston then at Skegness, but in 1954 he left Lincolnshire and spent the rest of his career in Fleet Street.

His twin sister lives at Anton's Gowt and she recently sent him a copy of my book for his birthday, and he kindly wrote to say how much he had enjoyed reading it, and how many of the people I mentioned he remembered. Harold Bland, who opened the batting for Boston Cricket Club for many years, was a close neighbour; Derek Killick used to be his barber and, of course, he knew all the Grammar School masters.

During his time at the Lincolnshire Standard he met Mr. Pearce, the manager of the Odeon, and he still hears from his daughter, who lives close by in Essex.

We have all admired and marvelled at the multi-coloured, regimented display on view at the Burton Corner and Sibsey Road trial grounds of W. W. Johnson & Son Ltd., but also most of us realise that they are not primarily for our appreciation, but to ensure a continuous programme of both new and improved varieties of seeds for the future.

These sites are just part of the eighty acres of land that are used solely for breeding and research work.

William Wade Johnson founded the firm in 1820, five years after the Battle of Waterloo, and the last year of the sixty year reign of George III, who died both blind and insane.

He was born in Bucknall and, after a difference of opinion with his father, he came to Boston at the age of seventeen, became a market gardener and sold his produce on a stall in the market, which was held on Wednesdays and Saturdays, just as today. He used his best plants to produce seed, which also he sold on his stall.

The demand grew, as the quality of his seeds was acknowledged, and from that acorn the oak grew, which has become today the largest privately owned seed company in the country. Most British seed companies have lost control to Scandinavian or other European concerns, but Johnsons is run today by the family's fifth generation.

The first shop and warehouse were purchased in Bridge Street, and for sixty years until his death in 1880. William Wade Johnson held the reins, assisted by his son, Alfred, a very able botanist, who developed the breeding and selection programmes, which laid the foundations for today's numerous and improved strains.

Unfortunately, when he was sixty, Alfred died in 1899, leaving an eleven year old son, Alfred de Bouys Johnson, but his ill-health had made him anticipate such a contingency and four years earlier he had made the firm a limited company. It was decided to appoint a General Manager and Mr. E. J. Deal came from Suttons of Reading. Alfred de Bouys completed his education at Reading University, before joining the company, then in 1911 a new warehouse and cleaning plant was built in London Road.

The firm expanded into the wholesale and general seed trade, offering a complete range of flower, vegetable and grass seeds. Throughout the 1920s and 30s the company prospered and built up a profitable export trade with the United States and Commonwealth countries, including South Africa. Seeds from W. W. Johnson & Son Ltd., were exported to the U.S.A. on the maiden voyage of the Queen Mary.

Johnsons became internationally renowned and received awards for their seeds from the four corners of the world. The Second World War, however, brought an end to their export trade, for by the time it was possible to recommence deliveries the market had disappeared; the overseas countries had learned to grow their own.

Alfred de Bouys had named his son William Wade, after the founder, and it was he, who decided to re-enter the retail market to bolster the established wholesale side, which sells to food processors, agricultural merchants, landscape contractors and also packs for other seed companies. The 8,000 retail outlets that were soon established included garden centres, supermarkets, hardware stores, department stores and D.I.Y. stores.

Johnsons are also the country's leading supplier of grass seeds and, even before they achieved fame as the grower of the seed used for Wembley, they were responsible for the pitches at Arsenal, Nottingham Forest, Leeds and many more.

I used to pass their warehouse in South Square every day when I went to the Grammar School; it is now demolished but the London Road plant built in 1911 is still part of the company's headquarters.

It is noticeable that their workforce are both happy and loyal: almost everyone I know, who has worked for Johnsons, stay until retirement, unless death interferes. My mother's friend, Ivy Whyers and her son Peter, both worked in the office for many years; my neighbour, Frank Burt, retired from their packaging depot down Fen Road and my classmate, Derek Whelbourn, went there from school and is still there.

My friend Mick Clayton died very young but I believe his colleagues, Claude Blakey, Johnny Walker and "Otto", all remained until retirement at W. W. Johnson & Son Ltd.

The Nobel Prize in Physics was won in 1996 by David Lee and Robert Richardson of Cornell University and Douglas Osheroff of Stanford University for their discovery that the isotope, helium-3, can become superfluid at extremely low temperatures. Their discovery was made in 1972 but the pioneering experiments in this field were instigated by a paper, written in 1960 by Bostonian Victor Emery and Andrew Sessler, while they were both at the Lawrence Berkeley National Laboratory in California.

A liquid becomes superfluid in much the same way as a metal becomes superconducting: it means it flows without friction, and one of the effects is the ability to flow upwards, climbing the walls of a container.

One of the prize winners, David Lee, spent a year at the Brookhaven National Laboratory in 1966 on a sabbatical from Cornell University, and Victor had joined BNL in 1964, so Victor's influence was easy to trace. Victor, himself, has concentrated on the theory of high-temperature superconductivity, which has the potential to bring technology into everyday life, which is much more difficult very close to absolute zero temperatures.

Victor Emery was at Boston Grammar School from 1944 to 1951, before gaining his degree at Hull University, and he took his PhD in theoretical physics at the University of Manchester in 1957. Since then he has always worked at the forefront of important problems in nuclear or condensed-matter theory.

He went to the Lawrence Berkeley National Laboratory on a Harkness Fellowship, but returned to England in 1963 and carried on his work at the University of Birmingham. The following year he joined the Brookhaven National Laboratory Physics Department, and he has become one of the world's leading theorists in the study of phase transitions, where substances change between liquid, solid and gas.

He travels the world, speaking on high-temperature superconductors and his model for the electronic structure of the copper oxide planes is referred to world-wide as the "Emery model".

He received his tenure at Brookhaven in 1967 and was named Senior Physicist in 1972. He served as Associate Chairman from 1981 – 85.

There are 3,200 employees at Brookhaven, and each year just two are awarded with the Distinguished Research and Development Award, symbolised by an engraved memento and 5,000 dollars. Victor received this award in 1995, and in nominating him Peter Bond, the Chairman of the Physics Department, referred to him as a mainstay of the BNL Solid State Theory Group.

Increditable as it may seem, another local man, Graham Smith from Swineshead, received one of the Distinguished Research and Development Awards for 1996. Graham was granted his tenure at BNL only in 1994, so he has quickly made his mark in the Instrumentation Division.

Graham received his PhD in 1974 at Durham University, and developed his interests in physics at the University of Leicester from 1973 to 1982, before joining BNL in 1982.

His work in fundamental areas of gas detector performance has led to many applications now in full use, and he has contributed a dozen publications on new techniques in detectors.

The Head of the Instrumentation Division, Veljko Radeka, recommended Graham Smith for the award, because of his contribution to the research programme and the impact he had made at Brookhaven and elsewhere.

Graham went to Boston Grammar School from 1960 to 1967, before spending six years at Durham University, where he was following in the footsteps of his brother, Norman, who left the Grammar School in 1964 and gained his PhD at Durham in 1970.

Norman is a Chartered Patent Agent and a European Patent Attorney.

Their father, Colin, who lives in Westfield Drive, Swineshead, is also an Old Bostonian, but his spell at the Grammar School was a little earlier, 1925 – 30.

He has just cause to be proud of both his sons.

Pure chance and romance joined together to make Boston the town with the largest producer of labelling products and systems in Europe. In 1850 John Fisher, who covered London and the Eastern Counties as a traveller in buckram cloth and tailoring, met a widow in Boston and decided to set up business here.

In London he had met George Clark, a bookbinder's son, and told him of his invention of an untearable label made of cloth. The two men settled in Boston and their first premises were behind the house in Sleaford Road, then known as West Road, where John Fisher lived with the widow, now his wife.

John Fisher & Co., soon to become Fisher Clark & Co., started as tailors and label makers, but their labels, pieces of cloth folded over and fastened together with metal eyelets and strung, were so successful that by 1857 they employed 22 people. Their customers included Queen Victoria, Prince Albert, the Prince of Wales and the Duke of Cambridge, who all found many uses for their stronger cloth labels, including game tags. The company still supplies the Royal Family today.

Rapid expansion made it necessary in 1870 to move to the Corn Exchange Yard in the Market Place, later to become the New Theatre Yard, now the site of Marks & Spencer Limited. In 1876 John Fisher sold out to the younger George Clark for a reasonable price, and the company branched out into wax-making, producing bottle wax for wine merchants. Mrs. Clark and her three sons made the wax in a wooden shed fitted with two metal coppers at their home in Skirbeck, but later premises were taken in Grove Street.

George Clark unfortunately died at the age of 41, and by then his wife had four sons and four daughters, and the two eldest sons, George and Charles, carried on the business. They had to develop a hand press to produce a more modern product, when an American company introduced a much stronger and cheaper label. The new tag had a single thickness with a glued-on washer.

They continued with the wax-making and in 1881 they secured a contract with the Postmaster General. Both aspects of the company prospered, but in 1898 Charles died and his younger brother, Tom, joined the firm.

They purchased an American tag-making machine to replace the hand press process and, when the Diamond Tag Company began trading in London and advertised tags printed in two colours for the same price as single-coloured tags, they updated their machinery again to stay competitive.

Once again they outgrew their premises, and in 1903 they purchased a plot of land in Norfolk Street and erected a purpose built factory. The new factory had a staff of 26, which by 1938 had grown to 350 and by 1965 to over 1,000.

The youngest brother, Ernest, joined his brothers in the firm in 1914 and became Company Secretary. The business became a limited company in 1921. George's son. Vernon, came into the company in 1919; Tom's son, Stewart, in 1923 and Ernest's son, Basil, in 1928. George lived to be 93 and did not retire as Chairman until he was 88, being succeeded by his son, Vernon.

Fisher Clark were the first company in the country to make self-adhesive labels, and in 1934 an in-house engineering department was established to design and produce the purpose-built equipment used in the factory.

At the start of the Second World War the company handled a great deal of government work, including items for the Ministry of Defence and the Post Office. Boston was considered to be a possible invasion area, so Fisher Clark were requested to move to disused silk mills in Macclesfield.

At that time the staff numbered 450, and it took five weeks to move them and the special equipment from Boston to Macclesfield. The Boston factory was used by the armed forces while they were away, but they returned after just one year.

By 1956 the Norfolk Street factory covered an area of 100,000 square feet, and although tags were still important, new labelling products were being developed and produced. Many shapes and sizes of self-adhesive labels were manufactured plus a wide range of tickets and time-clock cards.

More land was purchased in 1957 in Horncastle Road, and by 1960 that too had reached 100,000 square feet in size. In 1960 Fisher Clark were purchased by a holding company, Norcross Limited, and in 1968 they were amalgamated with Tickopress Limited, another labelling company owned by Norcross Limited.

As I passed the Guild Hall, which then served as a British Restaurant, each day on my way to the Grammar School, one question puzzled me: if, as we learned in our History lessons, the Pilgrim Fathers sailed from Plymouth in 1620, how was it that some of them were imprisoned in the cells on the ground-floor of the Guild Hall here in Boston in 1607?

I never received a satisfactory answer to this question, until I read a book written and published by Canon A. M. Cook, while he was Sub dean of Lincoln Cathedral. He, himself, refers to the research undertaken by Walter Whyers, the famed local historian, who was an authority on the subject.

The Pilgrim Fathers are often referred to as Puritans but they were actually Separatists, believing that any group of like-minded believers had the right to form itself into an independent church.

There were several pockets of Separatists, especially in the Norwich area, and one developed around Gainsborough, where a group of free-churchmen gathered for worship at the manor house at Scrooby, the home of William Brewster.

The idea of a congressional migration to Holland, where non-conformists were welcome, gradually grew in the group, and homes and furnishings were sold to raise the money to arrange passage on a ship. A Dutch vessel was to be lying near the mouth of the Witham to pick up a congregation of fugitives.

On September the 15th 1607 an attempt was made to arrest William Brewster and another member of the group, Richard Jackson but they were nowhere to be found. They were in fact in Boston; the whole group had somehow travelled the sixty miles from Scrooby without being noticed. To make the journey by road at that time was almost impossible, for many women and children were included and the only accessible road into Boston was down the coastline, as the fens had not yet been drained.

Walter Whyers favoured the alternative that the whole congregation were concealed in a number of flat-bottomed boats, which passed under the High Bridge at Lincoln in the dark, then past the walls of Tattershall Castle and drifted through Boston to the mouth of the Witham. The tides then came up the river as far as Bardney and transport was easier on the water than the roads.

In any case, after completing the journey successfully, they found that the Dutch captain had treacherously informed the local authorities, and they were all arrested, treated roughly and the more prominent among them locked in the Guild Hall cells. It was a month later before a trial took place in the courtroom upstairs with sympathetic townsfolk watching from the wooden rails at the back.

Most of the party were dismissed and made their way home, but several of them now had no home to return to, and seven of those considered ringleaders were jailed in the old prison near St. Botolph's church and later bound over to appear at the York assizes on December 1st, 1607. Richard Jackson and William Brewster were each fined £20 for "disobedience in matters of religion".

Early in 1608 they made another attempt to reach Holland, but this time they went down the River Idle and the Trent, then round by the Humber to a creek near Immingham, where another Dutch vessel was awaiting them. They had to hurry aboard and sail quickly, as a posse of constables were approaching. There is another memorial to the Pilgrim Fathers at this creek near Immingham.

Amsterdam was very prosperous and some of the Scrooby pilgrims were tempted to settle there but Brewster, together with John Robinson and William Bradford applied to the authorities of Leyden for permission to settle there, and declared themselves members of the Christian Reformed Church. It was February, 1609 and of the one hundred declared members, twenty-five were from the original Scrooby group.

For a while life at Leyden seemed full of promise, but by 1617 the leaders of the new Church began to explore the possibility of a migration across the Atlantic. Brewster had set up a printing press and there was trouble over some of his productions, and John Robinson had criticised the Dutch Church for observing Christmas and Easter. The news came of the great profits made by a ship from Holland that had been trading for furs with the Red Indians from the island of Manhattan, and the successful plantation of Virginia decided them to embark on their great adventure.

The final decision of the members of the Christian Reformed Church to migrate across the Atlantic was taken, after John Wincob arrived at Leyden with encouraging information about the prospects of establishing a plantation in America. He was a member of a family living in Sutterton and was in the employ or "belonged to" the Countess of Lincoln. Later in 1645 he was one of twenty Lincolnshire commissioners appointed to raise a monthly levy of £2,800 towards the new Parliamentary army during the Civil War.

His news fired a group of the more fervent to return to England to raise finance. The Virginian Company could not help, as they were almost bankrupt but King James gave his approval and a private company was floated in London by Weston, an ironmonger in 1618 and several investors joined, anticipating quick and easy profits from fish and furs with no interest in the adventurers' religious beliefs.

A full year was wasted, while an argument was settled as to whom should own any houses built in the new colony, but the pilgrims insisted that they should possess their homes, free from any rents, rates or taxes, because they were risking their lives. The company finally agreed, and in the spring of 1620 they bought the MAYFLOWER, "an excellent ship of 180 tons".

They fitted her out, engaged an experienced captain and crew, provided necessary stores and she sailed to Southampton with a few extra men on board, who were willing to pay £10 and join in the great adventure.

The Leyden congregation, including some of the Scrooby Separatists, found the money for a smaller vessel, the SPEEDWELL, and the two ships left Southampton together one morning in July. Twice they ventured beyond Land's End and twice they had to return as far as Plymouth. Reluctantly on the third attempt they left the SPEEDWELL behind to be sold, and the MAYFLOWER sailed alone with as many passengers as it could hold. Only five of the Scrooby group were included: William Brewster and his wife; William Bradford, Mrs Carver, sister of John Robinson and Francis Cooke from Blyth. Altogether there were forty-four members from the Leyden church plus forty other adventurers, twenty-three servants and the crew.

The voyage began well but heavy gales delayed progress, and it was November the 11th before they arrived at the outer shores of Cape Cod. The pilgrims were sick, cold and anxious to get ashore but they had to wait, while they sailed round the headland into the calmer waters of the bay.

Not everyone survived the voyage, but there were forty-one names on the covenant, which they all signed to establish order in the new Plymouth colony. William Brewster, as the Ruling Elder, led the worship and William Bradford was elected governor in 1621, after the first governor died of sunstroke.

The first winter was very severe and many settlers died, but after the MAYFLOWER had returned to England, another ship, the FORTUNE arrived with thirty more pilgrims, some from Leyden, and in 1625 the ANNE brought another sixty, including two of Brewster's children.

William Brewster lived to be nearly eighty and by the time he died in 1643 the Plymouth colony was firmly established in North Virginia, thirty-six years after he had led his group from Scrooby across Lincolnshire to Boston.

Another Lincolnshire man had been instrumental in the foundation of Virginia a few years earlier. An expedition promoted by Sir Walter Raleigh in 1584 had named the land Virginia, and a further expedition in 1587 had ended in tragedy but, after the Virginia Company was formed in 1606, a pioneer fleet of three small ships sailed from the Thames in December with 105 settlers.

John Smith was one of the council leading this successful attempt. He had been born at Willoughby, baptised in Louth Church on January the 9th 1580 and, when his father died in 1596, he left home and was indentured with a merchant at King's Lynn. His adventures fighting for three years against the Spaniards and later against the Turks in central Europe taught him how to subdue the "wild savages" in Virginia.

One day, however, he was captured by the Indians, exhibited as a trophy and finally trussed up ready for a ceremonial execution, when Pocahontas, the daughter of the chief, saved him by falling across his body and claiming him for herself. He was allowed to return to Jamestown and resume the task of governing the settlers until 1609, when he was hurt in an explosion and sailed home to write books and maps, which encouraged others to settle in New England.

Have you ever wondered who suggested that the settlement of small wooden houses built on the northern bank of the Charles River in 1630 should be called Boston? His name was Thomas Dudley and he was the Deputy Governor of the Massachusetts Bay Company, which received it's charter from Charles I on March the 4th 1629.

The Governor was John Winthrop from Suffolk, who assembled a fleet of eleven vessels off the Isle of Wight at Cowes at Easter in 1630, and they reached Salem in the middle of July only to find that settlement short of food and not ready to welcome another thousand inhabitants.

Although without fresh water, they had to move along the coast to the mouth of the Charles River, where they were welcomed by William Blackstone, who had arrived in New England several years previously as an ordained priest of the Church of England, but now lived as a trapper and rode around on a tame white bull. He assured them there was a plentiful supply of fresh water in the Trimountain Hills and Boston was born.

Thomas Dudley was related to the Earl of Dudley, Queen Elizabeth's favourite, and he trained in a lawyer's office in Northampton, before commanding a company of a volunteer force in the service of Henry of Navarre. Later he became steward to the Lincoln estates and hired a dwelling in Boston, because, like many others, he was influenced by the preaching of John Cotton, the vicar of St. Botolph's, who became his close friend.

The seat of the Earl of Lincoln was at Sempringham and it was the centre for all those interested in the emigration to Massachusetts. Actually Thomas, the third Earl of Lincoln, had died in 1619 and it was his widow and family who lived in the large house that had once been Sempringham Abbey. The young fourth Earl, Theophilus, soon married Bridget, daughter of Lord Saye and Sele, and went to live at Tattershall Castle.

The eldest daughter, Lady Frances Clinton Fiennes, married John, the second son of Sir Ferdinando Gorges, the Governor of Plymouth in New England, who had a charter from the Council of New England to develop unoccupied territory along the coast of Maine.

The second daughter, Arbella, married a young and wealthy clergyman from Stamford, Isaac Johnson, who had been educated at Emmanuel College, Cambridge, where he had been a friend of William Blackstone. He was to meet his friend again in the new Boston but, unfortunately both he and Arbella died within a year of reaching America.

Susannah, the third daughter, became the third wife of John Humphrey and their eldest boy was baptised in St. Botolph's in May, 1627. He was also connected with New England, and his second wife had been Elizabeth Pelham, whose father was related to the first Governor, John Winthrop, and had land both in Sussex and the fen-country, near Boston. Her father was actually Lord of the Manor at Swineshead and there still exists a civil parish of Pelhams land.

So all three daughters sailed across to New England, but John Humphrey and Susannah returned in 1641 and later he was given the governorship of one of the West Indies.

By 1640 there were 20,000 colonists with 300, about sixty families, coming from Lincolnshire, almost entirely from Boston and Alford. Sixteen of these local men had university training, and nothing of any importance that occurred in the early life of the Massachusetts Bay colony happened without some of these men being involved.

They could all be traced back to the meetings at Sempringham, and most of them had been influenced by the preaching of John Cotton. Even before John Cotton came to Boston, during the trial of the Pilgrims in 1607, the town was considered to be proud of being Puritans and of showing sympathy to those imprisoned. The vicar at the time Rev. Wooll was officially reported for refusing to wear a surplice and, when he left in 1612, the Mayor and Council were determined to appoint a man of similar views to succeed him.

John Cotton had started at Trinity College, Cambridge, but moved to Emmanuel to become senior lecturer there, because of it's Puritan influence. His fame as a theologian spread, after he was appointed to follow Rev. Wooll and the pulpit he erected in our great church is still there today, and the bunch of ostrich feathers featured on every panel pays tribute to the memory of Henry, Prince of Wales, whose death in 1612 was a sad blow for the Puritans hopes, for he had refused to marry the Roman Catholic princess from France, who later became the wife of his brother, Charles I.

John Cotton was vicar of Boston from 1612 until 1633, when William Laud was elected Archbishop of Canterbury, and commenced the enforcement of a compulsory uniformity in church affairs. After spending some months at Sempringham, Cotton and his friend Hooker sailed to America on the GRIFFIN with a large Lincolnshire group, which included Atherton, Hough and Leverett from Boston and Edmund Quincey from Fishtoft.

Over the next three years other ships followed, all with Boston families aboard, but the last to sail in 1636 with eighty Boston emigrants under the leadership of Harrington Fiennes was stopped by pirates from Dunkirk, and it is not sure if they ever reached Massachusetts. As the Civil War drew near in 1640, the sailings stopped, but the population of New England had by then reached 20,000 with the majority living in or around Boston.

Before he had been in the country six weeks, John Cotton had established Thursday meetings in the first church in Boston, a little wooden building. He produced long sermons for Sundays and also wrote pamphlets, books and poems. He also drew up codes of civil laws, which were largely adopted. He received regular contributions from his old parish, here in Boston, Lincolnshire and documents concerning the properties he still possessed here.

When Oliver Cromwell sent captured Royalists as prisoners of war to be sold as slaves after the Battle of Dunbar, Cotton wrote to say that they would be treated the same as all servants that emigrated, and would be free after seven years.

Boston attracted many university graduates, ministers, lawyers and scholars, several with administrative experience, so it was no surprise that as early as 1635 steps were taken for the provision of a school. The following year plans were made for a college of further education, and one day in October a Court met to choose a board of overseers to erect a wooden building on a site across the River Charles, appropriately called Cambridge, and that was the birth of Harvard University. Of the original twelve overseers or fellows no less than five had connections with Boston, Lincolnshire: Winthrop, Dudley, Bellingham, Humphrey and Cotton.

John Harvard, who like Cotton had been to Emmanuel College, was so impressed with "the immense possibilities of this courageous venture for learning" that, when he died in 1638, he left his fortune to the new foundation, and the next year it was formally determined that the college should bear his name.

When the number of fellows was increased in 1642, three more "Boston men" were added to the board: Herbert Pelham, William Hibbins and the Rev. Samuel Whiting.

The plantations at Plymouth and Salem were absorbed into the governorship of Massachusetts, and for the first sixty years of it's history there were only seven governors, six of them coming from Lincolnshire.

John Winthrop was the first governor, followed by Thomas Dudley, who died at the age of 77 in 1653. Then for ten years Endicott was governor and Bellingham for the next eight. Richard Bellingham inherited estates at Brumby and Manton near Gainsborough, but in 1626 he bought a house and came to live in Boston. Two of his children lie in unmarked graves in Boston churchyard, because he did not believe in infant baptism. In 1628 he was elected Recorder and chosen as Member of Parliament.

John Leverett followed Bellingham as Governor from 1673 to 1678. He was the son of Alderman Thomas Leverett, who had sailed across with his friend John Cotton in 1633. Thomas Leverett had been a member of Boston town council in 1625, when the town had avoided paying ship-money, and he was one of a dozen citizens who refused to subscribe to an enforced loan two years later. Whiting, the Mayor and his deputy, Tilson were sent to Fleet prison but Leverett together with Hough, Westland, Coddington and the rest managed to brazen it out.

When John Leverett died in 1678, Simon Bradstreet was chosen to succeed him as Governor of Massachusetts, and he remained in the post until 1692 when he was nearly ninety. He had just married his second wife, when he became Governor but his first wife Anne, had lived in the colony for forty years and achieved fame as the first American woman to have a book printed. It was a book of verse, entitled "The Tenth Muse".

My first article appeared in the Boston edition of the Lincolnshire Standard on the 4th May, 1995, as part of a special feature to mark the fiftieth anniversary of V.E. Day. The editor asked me if I would like to write a few more, now, after 84 more, this last column will feature the 59th anniversary of the visit to Boston of Joseph Kennedy, who was then American Ambassador to Great Britain.

He came to officiate at the unveiling of the American Room at Fydell House on the 4th May, 1938. At the time he was popular in this country but forfeited that popularity when, at the start of the war he advised President Roosevelt not to become involved, as it was inevitable that Great Britain would be overrun quickly.

Canon Arthur Cook attended the ceremony that day, now on the 4th May, 1997 there will be another ceremony in the gardens at the back of Fydell House, and one of his poems will be inscribed on the plaque below the armillary. This time the unveiling will be performed by the Australian High Commissioner, Dr. Blewett. The ceremony has been organised to record the visit to Boston of HM Endeavour, the replica ship of that used by Captain James Cook.

While Vicar of Boston, Canon Cook founded the Preservation Trust and the present Chairman, John Cammack, together with the Mayor of Boston, will be host to the High Commissioner. John Cammack has raised a discussion paper that highlights the part played by Boston and local scholars and explorers in making English, rather than Spanish, the language that predominates a large part of the world.

By coincidence, I have detailed the importance of people from this area in settling the early colonies in New England in my last four articles, but he also shows that our part of Lincolnshire was just as predominant in developing Australasia.

Foremost was Joseph Banks, who lived at Revesby Abbey. He was a young botanist, when he sailed with Captain Cook on the first voyage of the Endeavour, during which they charted the coastline of New Zealand and became the first European vessel to land on the east coast of Australia. The site where they landed was named Botany Bay, because he was a botanist.

This was the same Joseph Banks, who was so influential in draining the fens north of Boston and making the land so fertile. He was unable to accompany James Cook on the second voyage, but he encouraged several others from the locality to make further expeditions.

There were Matthew Flinders and his brother, Samuel from Donington. Matthew Flinders was the first man to circumnavigate the whole coastline of Australia. Others were Robert Rollett, John Franklin, Robert Fowler and Joseph Gilbert, whose name was commemorated in the Gilbert & Ellis Islands.

George Bass was the first to realise that Tasmania was a separate island, and so the Bass Straits were named after him. All these were local men, influenced by Banks.

In his discussion paper John Cammack traces Boston's importance back even further: to John Foxe and his Book of Martyrs. It was second only to the Bible as the most-read book in the land at the time of Francis Drake, and it is said he read from it every day.

Over the last two years this column has helped to put me in touch with many school friends, and because of it I have made several new acquaintances: on both counts I am very grateful. I would like to take this opportunity to acknowledge some letters received recently from: John Chappell at Leigh-on-Sea, Jim Fellows from Hull, Frank Ward from Edinburgh and Alan Ashton from Bishop's Stortford.

An amazing coincidence occurred a few weeks ago. Joan Leafe, the wife of Dick Leafe, who retired as verger at the Stump a year or two ago, phoned me to say that her brother Frank Sargeant, the Bishop of Lambeth was trying to contact his school friend Basil Tinkler, and did I know his address. At the time I didn't but just three days later I received a letter from Basil, in which he said that his sister in Boston had sent him my book as a Christmas present, and he had enjoyed reading it. He and his wife, whom I remember from her High School days as Janet Caress, left Boston thirty years ago and now live in Pitminster, Somerset.

****

The library at Boston Stump was started in 1635. It is situated in an upper room over the south porch of St. Botolph's church, and it is there that an anonymous scholar in 1841 wrote his Book "Boston In Golden Times".

For some time he had been researching the story of the Saxon town that in the seventh century stood on the watery waste of fen, which later became the site for Boston. This ancient town was called Icanhoe or Yccan's holme. Yccan was the Saxon word for oxen and holme was an island in the fens. At that time large herds of half-wild cattle grazed on the rich grass of the fens.

The author even suggested that Boston could have derived it's name from these cattle, because the Latin for an ox is bos.

One summer evening in 1841 he was working in the twilight in the ancient chambered library, searching through the shelves for the one volume which would authenticate his book. He was the sole occupant of the entire church but his only thought was to find this rare and ancient book, which would tell him all he needed to know.

Suddenly he heard behind him the faintest of rustlings; he turned and was amazed to see a tall figure dressed in the frock and hood of a Franciscan friar, with a small silken skull cap on his shaven crown but with rich auburn curls reaching to his shoulders.

He knew immediately that he was in the presence of a being from another world, but he knew no fear and addressed his unearthly guest in Latin, and for a while they conversed quietly in this common tongue, which spanned the centuries.

They had not discussed the actual project that the author was researching, but the figure moved to the shelves and picked a volume from the numerous books and handed it to the scholar: the very volume he was seeking.

As a result the scholar decided to remain anonymous, but on the title page of his book the "ethereal author" is credited thus: "By Roger Quaint, Monk of the Order of St. Francis and formerly of the Grey Friary, South End, Boston".

Those of you who saw Judy Cammack on Yorkshire Television's 'Tonight' programme recently will know how convincing she was in presenting her version of the origin of the name 'Boston '.

The correct explanation was given first; that it was named after St. Botolph. The second was ludicrous and would have fooled nobody, as it was claimed that Boston, Lincolnshire was named after Boston, Massachusetts.

Judy was talking to the presenter, Simon LeFevre, outside the Britannia Inn and she explained to him that in about 60 AD the local tribe of Coritani joined forces with the Iceni tribe, led by the legendary Boadicea, in rising up against the Romans.

Boadicea fought with great ferocity and was much feared. The Roman soldiers referred to her crudely as a 'Bos' which is the Latin for 'Cow'. The Coritani adopted this insulting and derogatory term as a badge of pride, and named their settlement 'Bos-tune' out of respect of their great leader.

'Tune' was their name for town, so Bostune became BOSTON. Judy elaborated by stating that some experts think that the term 'bossy' comes from 'like Bos; that is like Boadicea.

She made it all sound perfectly logical but, as she above all knows almost every detail of the history of Boston, she obviously had her tongue in her cheek. As my knowledge of Boadicea, or Boadicaea, however is limited, for a brief moment I wondered if there was a grain of truth.

Then sanity returned, and I realised that no mention was made in the poems of Cowper and Tennyson about the Iceni ever joining forces with the Coritani and Boadicea, the wife of Prasutagus, King of the Iceni, only became the 'Warrior-Queen', after both she and her daughter had been wronged by the Romans. She poisoned herself in despair, after the Roman Governor defeated her troops.

In 1821 the population of Boston was three times that of Grimsby and larger than Lincoln.

Boston had 10,373 residents, while Lincoln's inhabitants numbered 9,983. Gainsborough, Louth, Stamford and Newark were all much smaller.

As all genealogists know, the first official census was taken in 1801, and at that time Boston had 1,252 inhabited houses and a population of 5,926, so the town had grown considerably in twenty years.

The main reason for this vigorous growth was that this was the time of the second great effort in fen drainage. The 1810 flood made it obvious that something had to be done. The flood was caused by a "stolen tide"; a combination of a high tide and a strong wind. Eighty-two local families lost everything and seventy more were seriously affected. As Pishey Thompson observed "In all probability, the sea banks giving way saved the town from almost entire destruction...".

The first drainage scheme had included the construction of the Grand Sluice and the improvement of the Witham between Lincoln and Boston, enabling the enclosure of the land along the entire west bank of the river, notably Holland Fen. The result had been a vast increase in cereal growing and more traffic to the port.

This second drainage scheme was a tremendous undertaking: 40,000 acres to the north of the town, comprising East, West and Wildmore Fens were to be drained, and in places they stood under two feet of water.

The young Scot, John Rennie, was entrusted with the mammoth task and the fourteen-mile-long Hob Hole Drain was excavated, and a network of internal drains converged upon this main drain. Water was directed, unfortunately from the Steeping river, hastening Wainfleet's decline as a port.

To prevent water from the Wolds flooding the new-drained area, catch-water drains were dug and they made their way into the river at the Maud Foster sluice. The Boston sluice to the Hob Hole Drain was opened in 1806, but the complete task was not completed until November, 1813.

True Bostonians must, like me, be annoyed, when they hear people who have left the town to live in other areas, say superiorly "I would never come back to live in Boston".

I have yet to find a city, town or district, which in any way compares with Boston, either geographically, socially or, which becomes more important with passing years, climatically.

Some local scribes do more harm than good by forever finding fault and highlighting petty anomalies, while disregarding the abundant good points of life in Boston. It is the easiest thing in the world to criticise, but time is better spent contributing to the countless clubs, associations and organisations, which exist for the good of the town.

Over the centuries much wiser and more famous men than they have extolled the virtues of Boston, it's church and the surrounding district.

As early as 1540 John Leland visited Botolphstowne on the river Lindis and wrote: "... and from a parish church the best and fairest of all Lincolnshire and served so with singing, as no parish in all England".

John Wesley came to Boston in 1759 and again in 1761, and described it as "not much smaller than Leeds but, in general, it is far better built".

The diarist John Byng, later Viscount Torrington, was in Boston in the election year of 1790 and during " a pleasant hour's walk before breakfast" he admired "the beauty, grandeur and loftiness of Boston church, a building of most wonderful workmanship". The market was plentiful and the country lasses, who came with poultry, eggs and their òther little commodities, were neatly dressed".

William Cobbett in 1830 was much impressed by the relative prosperity and high farming standards he found in this part of Lincolnshire. Between Boston and Holbeach he saw rich pastures and thousands of sheep "lying like fat hogs".

Over a hundred years earlier Daniel Defoe was also impressed by "the very rich land, which feeds prodigious numbers of large sheep and also oxen of the largest size.....from this part comes the greatest wool, known, as a distinction for it's credit, because of it's fineness, by the name of Lincolnshire wool." He described Boston as "full of good merchants and has a good store of foreign trade".

By 1910, however, it was the rich agricultural land that impressed H. Rider Haggard, who noted "It is a belt of light silty land lying between the fen and the marsh, which for this purpose (potato growing) is worth twice as much as any other variety of soil..... from Wrangle to Boston the road is lined with neat dwellings having good gardens and little crofts, I remember few districts, which have given me such an impression of general well being of their inhabitants".

There may be a few readers, who remember the "sailing packets", that used to bring country people into Boston on market days from such diverse places as Sibsey Northlands, Sleaford, Donington and Horncastle. They used to navigate drains, such as the Maud Foster and they were all timed to reach Boston at 9.00 a.m. and they all left again at 3.00 p.m.

It is hard to imagine now but for centuries Boston was virtually an island in the fens, and the roads were so poor that it was much easier to reach the town by water communication. The most important waterway was obviously the Witham, and in the seventeenth century Lincoln was classed as an important port. Records show that the mayor of Lincoln paid annual dues to the corporation of Boston for the passage of boats along the Witham and through Boston to the sea.

In 1850 the American author, Nathaniel Hawthorne, made a pilgrimage from Lincoln to "Old Boston" on a river steamer, and the trip took six and a half hours, because "it stopped to take up passengers and freight, not at regular landing places but anywhere along the green banks".

J. B. Priestley made a journey through England in the autumn of 1933 and wrote of his impressions in "English Journey". This was the year after Boston had been joined by Skirbeck to become "Greater Boston".

This was a part of his impression of this area: "It was market day in Boston. The square was filled with stalls and any remaining space in the centre of the town was occupied by either broad-faced beefy farmers and their men or enormous bullocks. If there were any marked signs of an agricultural depression in these parts, I missed them. My hotel was in the market square and it was so crowded with farmers and farm-hands, clamouring for beer, that it was not easy to get in at all... Never have I seen more broad red faces in a given cubic capacity. Two more farmers and another seed merchant and the hotel would have burst. If Boston is like this when agriculture is under a cloud, what is it like when farmers are making money? The very Stump must be splashed with beer and decorated with froth....

Boston is the market town of a district of large farms, of 500 acres or so, and these farms are on rich silty lands that are admirable for a great variety of crops. The very process that destroyed Boston's importance as a seaport, pushing it further and further inland, enriched the whole farming community.... I looked inside the church, which was empty of visitors, then I paid my sixpence and began to climb the tower... At last, aching and exhausted, I tottered out on to the tiny platform at the top, where a fiendishly cold wind was raging, making my eyes smart. Through a blur of protective tears, I stared down at the curiously Dutch landscape.

The little old town was huddled at my feet. It was plain to see from here how the centuries had quietly ruined the place as a seaport, for here was the river, which had once found the open sea here, now wandering several miles beyond the town, through green pastures, in search of the receding Wash".

"It was dusk and tea time when I found myself back in the square, where the stallholders were packing up their unsold tea-sets, linoleum squares, blankets and chocolate.... I went into a cinema café for tea". This would probably have been the Scala café.

During the war years when I was a pupil of Staniland School, our favourite walk at this time of the year was down the "Folypads". Our adventure started, when we went through the gates close to the level crossing in London Road.

For a while that path ran parallel with and adjacent to the railway line, and our "bird-nesting" did not start in earnest until we climbed over the stile into the first proper field.

We then split into two groups: one covering the hedges on the right, the other to the left with the intention to join together at the opposite end of the field. Invariably at the first excited cry of discovery a full-blooded charge across the field, dodging the cow-pats, reunited the groups prematurely and our avian expert identified the egg and, if anyone needed it for his collection, the egg was replaced with a marble to pacify the bird.

This procedure was repeated in each field but eventually we reached "Bowser's Park", which years later I came to realise was the extensive parkland surrounding Tytton Hall. This manor house was mentioned in William the Conqueror's Domesday Survey in 1086. The present building is probably the third or fourth on the site and was built with a moat in the late nineteenth century.

At this point we usually hurried, because we wanted to reach Wyberton Church and explore "the island" near the church, where we had once seen a snake. St. Leodegar's was a medieval church and our journey probably ended at Wybert's Castle, an old earthwork, where in the 1960s by courtesy of Mr. & Mrs. Reg Killick an archaeological dig revealed the presence of stone walls and domestic pottery.

Wybert was a contemporary of Alfred the Great and is said to have joined forces with the Sheriff of Lincoln and the Lord of Bourne to rout and slay three Danish kings at Threekingham: hence the name of the village. Wybert, however, died heroically in a subsequent battle, facing hopeless odds against Danes, seeking revenge.

The Domesday Survey of 1086 records the male population of Wyberton at 36 and that of Boston at 42. Boston grew, because it was selected as the best site for the Witham to be bridged, and eventually it's boundaries were extended to include Skirbeck Quarter, which at one time had formed part of Wyberton Hundred.

At the time of the first census in 1801 the population of Wyberton was still only 353, but it had fared better than the once extensive hamlet of Tytton, which by them was extinct.

We were not aware of these historical facts, when we made our spring excursions; all we knew was that it was the best place to go "bird-nesting".

When I was five, my ambition was to become old enough and brave enough to follow my father up the bakehouse steps and watch him "shoot the flour". It sounded very adventurous but the wooden ladder was very steep, and my nerve failed me half way up.

Eventually I achieved my own private "Everest" only to experience a great disappointment; my father climbed that ladder every night, simply to chute the flour from the loft into the revolving mixing machine down in the bakehouse.

I forgot my frustration by climbing the "mountain" of flour bags and jumping from one summit to another; I realised much later that the various piles separated the different qualities of flour, and the end pile was Canadian flour and was the whitest.

What I did not discover until recently was that years ago all flour was brown, and the first white loaf was baked in this area.

That explains the name of White Loaf Hall at Freiston, because it was there when it was a monastery, that a monk in order to produce a finer loaf sieved the flour through his socks to extract the roughage.

The Hall later became a prison but the old bread oven survived.

St. James's Church at Freiston is the remains of a priory founded in 1114 as a cell of Crowland Abbey. The font in the church has a beautiful wooden cover, which was made from oak and features elaborate tracery, said to be the work of an apprentice.

Legend has it that the carpenter had delegated the task to the apprentice but, when he saw what a good job he had done and how well it was appreciated, he flew into a jealous rage and murdered the young lad. The ghost of the apprentice is supposed to haunt one of the lanes in Freiston.

Most local people realise that from 1900 to 1936 people came from Yorkshire and the Midlands to stay at the Plummers and the Marine hotels at Freiston Shore, but how many know that horse races used to be held on the shore between Freiston and Butterwick.

When Hurst's warehouse in South Square was developed as luxury flats and called Haven Hall, it was fitting, as on that very site in 1245 John Gysor, the mayor of London had built Gysor's Hall. He had to pay a ground rent of a pair of boots and gilt spurs.

He was not the first London merchant to have a property in Boston; in fact it is recorded that one year the City's court of hustings was suspended, because so many of its members wished to travel to attend Boston's fair.

John of Gaunt, brother of Edward, the Black Prince and father of Henry IV, whose county seat was Bolingbroke Castle, also owned Gysor's Hall in 1372, and successfully petitioned to have the charges for weighing merchandise transferred to the building.

The Hall survived for six centuries, then in 1791 Thomas Fydell bought the premises from the corporation. His family had leased Gysor's Hall for many years and it was directly opposite the family home, but twenty years later he dismantled it and used some of the stonework in the ground floor of the large warehouse he built there.

He also owned the warehouse on the Packhouse Quay, known to my generation as Lincoln's warehouse, and now the Sam Newsom centre.

Thomas Fydell, the long-serving member of parliament for Boston, also owned the original White Hart, which stood where Bridge Street is now, and the Unicorn, which was at the side of the river, where the present White Hart stands. The family had developed their interest in the wine trade at Chepstow before moving to Boston.

During my Sunday afternoon walks around the market place in the early fifties, I often paused at the plaque on the wall of the Rum Puncheon, later to become Martha's Vineyard, and wondered what Boston was like, when John Foxe was born there in 1517.

It was a private house when he was born, but later it was turned into the Bell Inn. In the nineteenth century it was pulled down and the building as I knew it was built.

What I did not realise at the time was that "The Acts and Monuments of the English Martyrs", written by John Foxe, was the second widest read book, after the Bible, during the sixteenth century, and was the inspiration for John Bunyan to write "The Pilgrim's Progress".

Foxe died in 1587, and during the last twenty five years of his life he revised his work many times, and the final version published in 1583, contained over two and a half million words, much longer than the Bible.

Foxe's father died while John was a small boy and his widow remarried. Her second husband was Richard Melton, and before he was ten John went to live at Coningsby. There was no school at Coningsby however, so it is thought that John came back to Boston and lodged with probably an uncle, and by the time he was sixteen he had an impressive command of Latin grammar.

In 1534 he went to Brasenose College, Oxford, where he met his lifelong friend Alexander Nowell, later Dean of St. Paul's. After three years he gained his Bachelor of Arts degree, and while reading for his Master of Arts he became a Fellow of Magdalen College, where he remained for seven years. He became the college lecturer in logic and wrote Latin plays.

He lost his fellowship when he refused to accept catholic orders, and moved to London in 1547, soon after marrying Agnes Randall, the daughter of a citizen of Coventry.

He became a tutor to the children of the Earl of Surrey, who had been executed by Henry VIII. The eldest son, Thomas Howard, later became the fourth Duke of Norfolk, the premier nobleman of England.

While watching the millennium on television, I thought I had found a connection with Boston, when it was announced that the music chosen to be played at the dome in front of the Queen, during the last few minutes of the twentieth century was "A New Awakening" by John Taverner. I knew that in the middle of the sixteenth century John Taverner had been laid to rest beneath the "Stump" bell tower, and that he was one of the leading composers of church music of the Tudor era.

He was a clerk-fellow of Tattershall's College, and later master of the choristers at Cardinal Wolsey's new college at Oxford. He became treasurer of the Corpus Christi guild and spent the last eight years of his life in Boston.

Between 1538 and 1540 he acted as the local agent for Thomas Cromwell, the Keeper of the Privy Seal, Henry VIII's right-hand man. He reported to him on the four Boston friaries, lamenting their great poverty and stating that all their possessions had been sold and they were contemplating selling the lead off the roofs. They received help but were forbidden to sell the lead, and Cromwell ordered Taverner to organise the public burning in the market place of the huge crucifix, which had long hung beneath the chancel arch in the parish church as a symbolic gesture against papal idolatry.

My bubble was burst, when a friend told me that he thought I would find that the music played in the millennium dome had been written by a present-day musician, John Tavener, not Taverner.

There was, however, a local connection with the celebrations and this time there was no mistake. My friend, John Hayhurst, asked me to confirm that the Gilbert and Ellis Islands had been partially named after a man born in Wrangle. I explained that Joseph Gilbert of Wrangle had commanded "The Resolution", which together with "The Adventure" had taken part in Captain Cook's second voyage and the Gilbert Islands were indeed named after him.

While John was in the forces, he spent time on Christmas Island and became interested in the Gilbert and Ellis Islands. It shows there is a "Gilbertese" language with only thirteen letters and, when the island gained independence the Gilbert Islands became Kiribizi and the Ellis Islands became Tuvalu. Kiribizi is the nearest spelling to Gilbert in their language.

These islands were the first to start their celebrations, as they lie to the east of New Zealand; in fact the eastern-most island has now been named Millennium Island.

In 1856 Pishey Thompson in "The History and Antiquities of Boston" stated that the "new dreyne in Cowbrygge" was completed in 1569, but he could find no official record of why it received it's name.

Tradition asserted that Maud Foster was the owner of land through which the new cut passed, and one of the conditions she insisted upon, before giving her consent, was that it should bear her name.

Hence in 1819, when Norman and Smithson for the sum of twelve hundred pounds built the windmill for Thomas and Isaac Reckitt, it was called the Maud Foster Mill. It was built of brick' it has seven floors, five sails (four at the moment), and an ogee or onion cap. There are other five-sail windmills at Alford and Burgh-le-Marsh, and the famous eight-sail windmill at Heckington.

While the Reckitts owned the mill, they experimented with "Reckitts' Blue" and at one time the interior walls were painted with it. Just before being demobbed from the R.A.F. in 1954, I attended a course on business management at Hull University, and one of the many visits we made was to Reckitts, where the bottom floor of their huge factory was used for making "Reckitts' Blue" and everything was covered with it; the walls, the ceiling, even the girls. We were pleased to move on to the next floor, where they were producing "Disprin".

The mill was worked by members of the Reckitt family until 1835, when George Cook of Digby became the owner. Then over the years it was owned by Jonathan Dent, George Spurr, Elvin Jessop and Alfred Ostler.

In 1953 the generosity of the Reckitt family enabled the mill to be repaired and saved from the developers.

Once again in 1990 the mill was under threat from planners, who wanted to convert it into a domestic residence and fit dummy, fibre glass sails. Fortunately James Waterfield bought the windmill, restored it and it is now one of the few working mills in the county.

The mention of pirates usually brings to mind Captain Kidd, Jean Lafitte and Sir Henry Morgan, and we think of the Spanish Main and the West Indies, but there were also pirates operating off the coasts of Britain in the sixteenth century.

The rugged coasts of Cornwall and South West Wales were their main hunting grounds, but in the 1570s the Lincolnshire coast was also infested with pirates. Gilbert and Sullivan could just as well have written "The Buccaneers of Boston", instead of "The Pirates of Penzance".

There are records of pirates sheltering in the Deeps at the mouth of Boston Haven, and they discouraged honest merchants from using the port and seriously disrupted trade in the area.

Something had to be done, so a raid was made on the pirates and four men were captured. Anthony Kyme, the mayor at the time and Alexander Skinner, an important customer of the port, wrote to Lord Burghley at Greenwich asking for directions.

Lord Burghley thanked them heartily but said that any action must be taken by Sir Henry Clinton of Tattershall, Lincolnshire's vice-admiral.

When Sir Henry Clinton contacted the mayor, he stated that it was not a matter for the corporation to deal with, and he would send his officers and marshal to take the prisoners into his custody.

Sir Henry succeeded his father as second Earl of Lincoln in 1585, and he had a reputation for "temper, ostentation and miserliness", even James I considered him to be "not subject to any heavenly influence". Later in life he became mentally unbalanced.

It is rare for a town to provide two Lord Mayors of London, but for a village to have this honour it must be unique. Gosberton, however, has done so: Sir George Bolles of Cawood Hall in 1617 and Sir Thomas Boor Crosby of the Eaudyke in 1912.

In the Domesday Book the village is recorded as "Gosberkirk" and several hamlets are included in the parish: Clough, Risegate, Belnie, Westhorpe, Rigbolt and Cheal.

There used to be monasteries at Rigbolt and Monks Hall and in the 1300s land around the church at St. Peter and St. Paul was owned by the La Warre family. Cressy Hall was once a fine mansion with a moat and private chapel together with a huge heronry.

A gas house was built in Gosberton in 1856 at a cost of £1,500, and a gas lighter was employed to make a nightly round of the twenty lights. In 1872 local subscriptions raised £1,000 to build the public hall on land donated by Lord Brownlow.

Snowhill, the junction near "The Five Bells" was so called because of cottages that used to stand there, and they were all white washed. It is the former site of a workhouse.

The neighbouring village of Pinchbeck was the birthplace of Christopher Pinchbeck, who became a watchmaker in London and gave his name to the alloy of copper and zinc, which he introduced for the making of cheap jewellery.

The village pump has gone but the stocks remain, opposite "The Bull". Knight Street is named after the Ogle family, who were so honoured and Guildhall, another street, commemorates the site of the former Guildhall.

In earlier days an annual horse race was held in the village on the Sunday, nearest to the 22nd June, but these ceased in 1850.

Flax was grown extensively around Pinchbeck, and at one time the flax mill employed 100 people.

It is not realised by many that nearly ten per cent of the population of Boston migrated to America in the 1620s and 30s. No less than sixteen of these were graduates of Cambridge University, so it is not surprising that Bostonians were instrumental in founding the Free Latin School and eventually Harvard University.

Richard Bellingham, Thomas Dudley, John Cotton and John Humphrey, the brother-in-law of the Earl of Lincoln, were all amongst the twelve overseers of the college, and Dudley and Bellingham, together with John Winthrop formed an executive committee.

When the number of overseers was increased in 1642 Samuel Whiting, William Hibbins and Herbert Pelham were also appointed. Samuel Whiting had been rector of Skirbeck and his son, John, was one of the earliest graduates of Harvard. His grandson, also John, was the first lay President of Harvard in 1707.

Richard Bellingham was a major donor of the Latin School and later became Governor of the colony. Another Bostonian, William Coddington, was a major sponsor of the Latin School and he became Governor of Rhode Island.

Rev. Samuel Whiting was a pupil of Boston Grammar School and another who made the trip across the Atlantic, Rev. Thomas James, was Master at Boston Grammar School for one year, and had probably also been a pupil there.

Rev. William Murrell, who was baptised in Boston in 1592, joined an expedition to New England in 1623, accompanied by William Blackstone from Horncastle. Murrell soon returned to this country but Blackstone stayed to become a legend in the new Boston. He is celebrated as the first white inhabitant of Boston Common, and had land on the peninsular of Shawmut, where he lived as a hermit. He is remembered as an eccentric, who rode round his property on a large white bull.

Leverett Road in Boston, Lincolnshire was named after Thomas Leverett and Congress Street in Boston, Massachusetts was earlier called Leverett's Lane, after the same Thomas Leverett and his son, John.

Thomas Leverett was an alderman of the borough of Boston, who resigned in 1633 and sailed across the Atlantic on the "Griffin" with John Cotton and landed at Boston, Massachusetts on September 4th, 1633. He became the ruling elder of the First Church but John, his son, was to gain even higher honours.

John Leverett was born on July 7th 1616 and went over with his parents but returned to England in 1644, and was appointed captain in the regiment of Col. Rainsburrow. He soon sailed back however, and was made a lieutenant in the Ancient and Honourable Artillery Company of Massachusetts, in which he had already served as a sergeant. He was elected Commander of the Company in 1652.

He had distinguished himself in 1645 against the Narraganset Indians, and he had a military command under General Sedgwick in 1654 to expel the French from Penobscot. In 1662 he was granted 1,000 acres of land in consideration of his services to the colony and 500 more in 1671. He was chosen as major-general of the colony in 1663.

He spent most of his life in the service of the colony: he was deputy for Boston from 1651 to 1653 and again from 1663 to 1665; he was Speaker of the House in 1651 and in 1663 and 1664; from 1665 to 1670 he was chosen as an assistant from the House of Deputies; he was elected Deputy-Governor in 1671 and finally he was the Governor of Massachusetts from 1673 to 1678.

In August, 1676 King Charles II conferred the order of Knighthood upon him, for he had been in England for the Restoration, advocating the interest of the colony, and he must have influenced the King.

When John Leverett died on March 16th 1679, his funeral was splendid and was described as "not unlike that of royalty in England".

Like a housewife faced with sorting out a box-room or the cupboard under the stairs, I have procrastinated as long as possible, but the time has come to unravel Boston's role in the Civil War, in which most towns and cities changed hands at regular intervals.

The conflict started in 1642, when the royal standard was raised at Nottingham in May. The next month Willoughby of Parham began to raise a Lincolnshire militia for parliament, and had a poor reception at Lincoln, Caistor and Louth but was met at Boston by a hundred volunteers, well armed and trained.

When the King decided to garrison Boston, Lynn and other seaports, parliament declared it an illegal act. In July the King visited Lincoln to rally support, and he sent a royal command to Boston with Sir John Monson that there should be no further mustering or training of men contrary to his commands. When a dozen or so prominent royalists landed from Holland near Skegness, however, they and their trunks were seized and brought to Boston then sent by sea to London. It transpired that the men and the goods they brought from Holland were friends and possessions of Prince Rupert of the Rhine, the nephew and chief military commander of King Charles.

Lincolnshire's ardent royalist High Sheriff, Sir Edward Heron, in October searched the South Kelsey home of Sir Edward Ayscough M.P., and took the arms and ammunition seized to his home, Cressy Hall. They were intercepted near Surfleet however, by a force led by Sir Anthony Irby, who had raised a troop of dragoons for parliament. Heron was captured; brought under guard to Boston and then sent to London, where, on a charge of high treason, he was sent to the Tower of London. He was held there for two years, and Irby seized Cressy Hall and took all the money, plate and goods to cover the cost of the arrest.

Sir Anthony Irby was Boston's greatest landowner and richest resident. He captained the troop of dragoons with his step-brother Richard le Hunt second in command, and the ex-mayor, Thomas Welby, as the provost marshal. Richard le Hunt later commanded Cromwell's lifeguards and had his own regiment in Ireland.

Irby's dragoons were not ready to take part in the first major encounter of the war, the battle of Edgehill on the 23rd October. In the battle Lord Lindsey, who was in command of the royal army and navy, was killed together with his eldest son. A second son, Montague Bertie, shielded his father's body as he lay dying, and he succeeded to the title and estates. After the restoration of the monarchy, he became Lord High Chamberlain and also high steward of Boston.

To continue the clarification of Boston's role in the Civil war, Sir Anthony Irby's dragoons towards the end of 1642 went to Hull, to help to oppose the advance of the King's army under the command of his northern general, the Earl of Newcastle. Early in 1643 a regiment under Sir John Norris arrived in Boston to join the Parliamentary forces, intending to push the Cavalier army back to Scotland, but they were tied down in Lincolnshire, as the Royalists gained the ascendancy with Gainsborough surrendering without resistance and Belvoir Castle being captured. Grantham was also occupied but was released later.

On the 27th February, 1643 a strong detachment of parliament's field army attacked Newark unsuccessfully, but the Boston volunteers distinguished themselves by seizing a piece of enemy canon. By April the Cavaliers had taken Stamford and Peterborough and had reached Sleaford, threatening both Lincoln and Boston. Oliver Cromwell, the future Lord Protector, commanded a force, strengthened by troops from Boston and Norfolk, which marched on Crowland, which fell after a three day bombardment.

The Boston mayor's feast was abandoned on May Day and the £20 saved was used to buy two extra canons from Lynn, and they can be seen to this day in the Guildhall Museum.

In June the Royalist army marched towards Boston from Newark, plundering Sir William Armine's house at Osgodby and reaching Donington, where they captured a number of grazing horses that were en route to Cromwell, who was at that time in Nottinghamshire. Hearing that Willoughby of Parham was besieged at Gainsborough by the Earl of Newcastle, Cromwell went to his aid but found he was heavily outnumbered and retired hurriedly to Spalding, while Willoughby sought refuge in Lincoln.

He soon, however, decided to move to Boston, "a town of greater strength, more fidelity and better manned and fortified". The importance of Boston was realised by the Roundheads; as Willoughby stated "...truly this place of Boston is of that importance, if the enemy get it, he will have the sea by it and passage to Norfolk and Suffolk". Parliament agreed and 400 muskets were sent to Cromwell, who was "particularly and especially recommended to have an especial care of the safety and security of Boston".

The Royalist forces penetrated to within a mile of Swineshead and Boston seemed at their mercy, when in August Lord Lincoln's home at Tattershall, well stored with guns and ammunition, fell. The Earl of Newcastle sealed Boston off from the north by fortifying Wainfleet and garrisoning Bolingbroke Castle, but surprisingly he made no attempt to attack the town but withdrew into Yorkshire to continue the siege of Hull.

For much of the second half of 1643 Boston served as the headquarters for Willoughby of Parham, and as well as being the base for the infantry it also housed Cromwell's cavalry. The men bivouacked in the Stump and tethered their horses to rings driven into the nave pillars. They tore out nearly all the brasses, destroyed the font and smashed the stained glass windows and most of the statues.

On the 9th October the Roundheads marched out from Boston to lay siege on Bolingbroke Castle. Detachments were left at Stickney and Stickford to secure a line of retreat. A large contingent of Royalist horse and dragoons gathered from Newark , Lincoln and Gainsborough and arrived in the Horncastle area, where they grouped and marched towards Bolingbroke, but they were defeated at the Battle of Winceby.

The night before the battle Cromwell slept in Boston, it is thought at the Three Tuns Inn in Church Street. His mount was killed under him in the first charge but another horse was soon found for him. As a result of the battle the Earl of Manchester accepted for Parliament the surrender of Lincoln on the 20th October, and Gainsborough also fell on the 20th December. By the end of the year the only Royalist garrison left in Lincolnshire was in the Isle of Axholme.

As fortunes fluctuated during the remainder of the Civil War, Lincoln, Gainsborough and especially Crowland changed hands several times, but Boston always remained in Parliament's control. On the 2nd July, 1644 the Earl of Manchester took his regiment to join up with the Scottish army and they overwhelmed the main Royalist forces at the decisive Battle of Marston Moor.

King Charles I surrendered to the Scots, after the rout of his army at Naseby in June, 1645 and the Scottish Commissioners broke their journey in Boston, when they travelled to bargain with the parliamentary leaders over the King's life. The council minutes record a sum of £4-6s-4d spent at the Crown Inn on entertaining the Scottish Commissioners.

Their bargaining had only a limited success, as King Charles I was executed in January, 1649. As protection from an anticipated invasion from the dead monarch's son, Boston's arsenal was restocked and £100 was spent to erect a small fort on the river below the town.

When my cousin moved out of Boston to Butterwick, it puzzled me that his address was Pinchbeck Road, when Butterwick was nowhere near Pinchbeck, but I later discovered that the school was also referred to as Pinchbeck School.

You have to go back to the year of the Great Fire of London, 1666, to find that Anthony Pinchbeck gave money for a free school, but he laid down that the children should be instructed in "writing, arithmetic and the classics". It was one of the earliest such institutions in Lincolnshire.

The school was open to all the children of the manor or hundred of Butterwick, which extended into Freiston parish.

One hundred acres of meadow were recorded in the Domesday Book as Butterwick and the name implies the presence of a dairy farm. In 1086 there were 36 Danish sokemen recorded in Butterwick, a large number for one community.

In the early eighteenth century the local church, St. Andrew's, was rebuilt in fine red brick but the effect was spoilt in the next century by the addition of stone extensions.

A few miles away in Fishtoft the church commemorates St. Guthlac and a statuette of this monastic saint looks out from a niche high up on the west tower. The nave of this fine church features a beautifully carved Perpendicular screen.

The parish had a population of just 211 in 1851 but by 1931 it had reached 1,517 and today will be much higher.

The state of the fens in 1300 made it difficult to reach St. Guthlac's for much of the year, so it was necessary to have two subsidiary chapels: St. Michael's, which was known as the "Fenne Chapel", and St. Thomas the Martyr, named after Archbishop Thomas Becket, in Huntingfield Manor.

Basil Blackamore, the brother of my Butterwick cousin, Owen, who unfortunately died last year, has for several years been responsible for the flower arrangements in St. Guthlac's church.

Fifty years ago, just after the war, each spring some quarten tins were reached down from the top of the cupboard in our bakehouse, washed and well greased; ready for the annual visit from a pack of cubs from Newark. It was the only time they were used, for everyone bought bread in half-quarten loaves by that time: in fact what used to be a small loaf had become a large loaf and a new small size had been introduced.

The old quarten tins, however, were just the job for a pack of cubs, for the extra long steamed loaves provided numerous slices. The cub mistress was the sister of Mr. Johnson from the fish shop in Liquorpond Street, and their camp was pitched on the field at the bottom of Woodville Road, near the forty-foot drain, which is now Matthew Flinders Way.

This seems a roundabout way to talk about Matthew Flinders Way, but I thought it might bring back a few memories for those who lived in that area at the time.

A memorial in Donington Church commemorates the explorer who was the first to circumnavigate Australia, and is so regarded in that country, that the heads of all Australian states make an annual pilgrimage every March to Lincoln Cathedral and then to Donington Church, and have tea at Donington Hall.

In 1980 they paid for a stained glass window to be placed in Donington Church to his memory.

Considering his accomplishments, it is remarkable that Matthew Flinders died at the age of forty, and for six years he was held captive on the island of Mauritius.

Donington's other famous figure was Sir Thomas Cowley, who established a school in 1719, which became very popular and attracted pupils from a wide area. In fact in 1871 a team from the school was one of fifteen teams to enter the very first F.A. Cup competition.

They were drawn away to Queens Park the Glasgow team, and had to withdraw because of the distance, but the game was eventually played in 1972, as part of the F.A. Centenary Celebrations.

When I was a member of the 5th Boston Scouts in the 1940s, Skip Lucas was kindly allowed by Frank Dennis to hold a summer fete in his grounds at Frampton Hall. While preparing the fete and on subsequent weekends, when three of us returned to the Hall to "help" the gardener and butler, I noticed several rabbits on the buildings and railings.

I was reminded of this many years later, when my niece was christened at St. Mary's Church, Frampton, and there was another rabbit on the chandelier in the church. It appears that this chandelier was presented to the church by Coney Tunnard, the solicitor who had Frampton Hall built in 1725. The rabbits were a pun on his Christian name: probably the earliest use of a logo.

Also at Church End is Cotton Hall, a H-shaped house with a walled garden, which was built as early as 1689. It's first occupants were the Cotton family, commemorated in the Cotton Chapel in Boston Stump and no doubt related to John Cotton, who became Governor of Massachusetts.

Thomas Tunnard inherited Frampton Hall and his elder brother, John, built Frampton House on the west side of the village in 1792. The poor road conditions made it difficult to reach the village church, so St. Michael's Church was built in 1863.

Ralphs Lane, Frampton was named after Ralph Smith, the last person to be hung in chains in this area. He murdered a gentleman, named Gentle Sutton and a commemorative plate marks the site of the gibbet, where he was hung.

Frampton Marsh, a favourite resort when travelling was restricted to foot or cycle, is now a bird sanctuary. During our summer holidays our usual bike ride was down the Marsh for a swim or to collect samphire, but we never realised that somewhere on that road we crossed the Greenwich Meridian.

From about 1740 a building in the yard of the Red Lion inn, now the site of Woolworth's, was used by a company of comedians, who periodically performed in Boston.

By 1777 their visits had developed into a regular six week season every spring, and the corporation paid for a riverside granary to be converted for use by these touring players. They used the high corn warehouses for dressing rooms and the building held an audience of 500.

The company was run by William Robertson, and during the first season the box office receipts totalled £372-8s. The "theatre" was described by Pishey Thompson as "very neatly fitted up".

This arrangement continued until the 14th March, 1805, when the final curtain came down, because the corporation decided to sell the building. By then William's son, Thomas Shafto Robertson was in charge and he faced the problem of finding a new venue.

The corporation proposed building a new theatre adjoining the Grammar School, but the headmaster, John Banks, vigorously opposed the suggestion and the idea was abandoned. Instead a playhouse was erected in Red Lion Street with the announcement "this temple of Thespis will, in point of elegance and convenience, be equal to any similar building in the county".

It was opened on the 29th January, 1806 with a commodious pit and gallery, surrounded by a tier of boxes and upper boxes at each end of the gallery. According to Pishey Thompson it was "a plain, substantial building, with nothing attractive in its external appearance, but its internal arrangement was judicious and well adapted for scenic representations".

Most people know that Hansard is the official record of the proceedings of the House of Commons, but few realise that Luke Hansard, the printer who gave his name to this was a pupil at Kirton Grammar School.

Luke Hansard was born in 1752 and attended the school, while the headmaster was Thomas Bateman, who also became Vicar of Frampton.

Kirton Grammar School was founded in 1624 by Sir Thomas Middlecott and it's fortunes fluctuated over the years, but it's reputation was such at the turn of the century that many boys cycled daily from Boston to benefit from the excellent teaching staff, headed by Mr. Keal.

The school unfortunately closed in 1919 and became an agricultural institute under the control of Holland County Council, with an experimental farm of 100 acres.

Another famous name connected with the area was that of Dame Sarah Swift, who founded the Royal College of Nursing. She was born at Blossom Hall, Kirton Skeldyke and was Matron in Chief of all Red Cross Hospitals during the First World War. A scroll in appreciation of her work can be seen in the church of St. Peter and St. Paul in the centre of Kirton.

In the 1960s Kirton Town was famous for it's Brass Band, which one year reached the final stages of a national competition in London. The band was formed in 1870 and to mark Queen Victoria's Jubilee in 1897 it played in front of 1,600 people on the village green.

When William Dennis first walked into Kirton, it is said that he sat at the side of the road for a rest, where later a statue was erected in his memory. He built up a huge potato business, which supplied all the potatoes eaten at a dinner for the poor to mark King Edward VII's coronation. When William Denis lay dying in 1924, the street outside his home was covered with straw to deaden any noise.

The foundation stone of the Grand Sluice was laid by the Boston M.P. Charles Amcotts on the 26th March, 1764. After years of deliberation, a major flood in 1763 emphasised the necessity of a scheme for improving the drainage of the area between Boston and Chapel Hill.

The work was supervised by Langley Edwards, an engineer from King's Lynn, and it was he, who performed the official opening on the 3rd October, 1766 in the presence of 10,000 spectators.

Another scheme, also the implementation of a plan by Langley Edwards, provided for a new sluice on the spot, where the old Black Sluice formerly stood. The South Forty Foot was scoured and cleansed from Boston to Great Hale, a distance of eight miles. Before this was done, the whole of the land between Brothertoft and Boston was frequently flooded during the winter, and the road from Boston to Swineshead was often under water and impassable.

One result of the construction of the Grand Sluice was the first major extension to Boston since the middle ages. The Boston Port Act of 1766 made the Witham General Commissioners responsible for the non-tidal river, and the Boston Harbour Trust had control of the tidal reaches. If river vessels passed through the sluice to discharge their goods, they became libel to harbour dues, so a wharf and warehouse were built just above the Grand Sluice.

This spawned further development and "The Witham Tavern" was built on the wharf and houses built for the workers became Witham Town. Then followed a sail-loft, a rope-walk and a second public house, "The Case is Altered".

Already in 1764 George Ward had built the massive Barge Inn, when the old bridge over the Barditch had been widened. It was intended to serve people travelling down river and heading for the town centre.

When I was a boy, I heard the fishermen refer to the quay in High Street as the "Dooty" quay, and wondered if it should be spelt "Duty", but years later I found it was actually Doughty Quay.

Similarly, when I joined the 5th Boston Scout troop, I thought our old wooden headquarters was on Packhouse quay, when really it was on Packhorse Quay. This quay in the eighteen and nineteenth centuries was the main quay for the port of Boston.

Lincoln's Warehouse dominated the quay and I often paused on my journey to school to hold a shouted conversation with Dick Lincoln, as he looked out of the loading door in the middle of the top floor.

The first stage of this building was commenced in about 1766; a period when there was a great revival in the port's activities. It was probably built by Thomas Fydell, as he was the first occupier mentioned in the deeds.

The Fydells were merchants in wine and other goods and provided eleven mayors for Boston between 1698 and 1797. They built the nearby Fydell House in South Street and lived there until they left the district in the nineteenth century.

The completed building was shown in 1811 in John Rennie's "Plan of Boston Harbour", and by then it was referred to as "Mr. Wilford's Granary". Ship owner and general merchant, Edward Wilford was married to Thomas Fydell's niece.

T. H. Lincoln and Sons, seed growers, took the warehouse over in 1937. The outside appearance of the building was typical of Georgian architecture with it's neat rows of small windows and it's sober façade. There is a sheer drop almost directly into the river on the west side.

Inside the atmosphere was that of an earlier age; the offices had long high desks, and the warehousing areas were low and dark, and connected to each other and the outside world with shoots.

In 1975, the Architectural Heritage Year, a report was prepared by the Boston and District Junior Chamber of Commerce, in a response to a scheme by their national organisation. Three members, R. M. Rennoldson, R. J. Christian and G. T. Lee surveyed Lincoln's Warehouse, which was then up for sale, to make positive and practical proposals to give it a continued life as part of the heritage of the town.

Their report contained an assessment of the buildings structural condition, with recommendations and costings for giving it a useful life. Several possible uses were suggested but, because of the thickness of the warehouse's walls, the conversion to a music centre was considered to be the best proposal, so in May, 1978 the Sam Newsom Music Centre was opened with an Inaugural Festival that ran from May 4th to May 20th.

Before 1774 the churchyard of the Stump was separated from the Market Place by a row of buildings, which included the Ostrich Inn, the gaol and some shops. John Parrish, a former mayor, offered to give the old inn and the property he owned to improve the town centre, if the corporation donated the gaol and their two shops.

The functions of the gaol were transferred to the house of correction in Spain Lane in 1775 and the next year the old gaol was demolished. It had been known as "Little Ease" and had been in use since 1550. Its equipment included a pair of stocks, horse locks, thumb screws and branding irons to "burn persons in the hand".

The stocks had been used to punish prisoners already in gaol, if they were convicted of "swearing", cursing, debauchery, drunkenness or other misdemeanours".

The Spain Lane house of correction also had its own stocks and whipping post. On top of all this equipment the corporation had a "hurry cart", a vehicle to which offenders were fastened and hauled round town to the door of every alderman's home, where they were whipped at the cart-tail.

John Ayre, the mayor in 1778, declared the Spain Lane premises to be insecure, but they remained in use for a further forty years.

The part of the churchyard immediately behind the properties to be demolished was known as "Half Crown Hill", and was used for the burial of the poorer classes. So many interments had taken place there that the ground was level to the Ostrich windows.

The demolition of the buildings was not completed until 1781, and the fully exposed churchyard had railings erected and Thomas Thurlow, Bishop of Lincoln, consecrated the churchyard extension.

Much of the magic of local government disappeared, when the office of Town Clerk was replaced by that of Chief Administration Officer. At one time the Town Clerk was more important than the mayor, and was often a member of the borough council or indeed a former mayor.

Francis Thirkill, who was Town Clerk from 1784 to 1816, was a councillor for twenty-four years. When he resigned, his successor was Henry Rogers, a partner in the same legal firm, Thirkill Son and Rogers.

He was a nephew of Thomas Fydell and eventually lived in Fydell House, where his horses and carriage together with his numerous servants made him one of the leading gentlemen of the town, and he also became lord of the manor of Freiston and Butterwick.

While he was Town Clerk no minutes of the council meetings were kept, and he held the position until 1831. When he left Boston in 1844 for his retirement home at Stagenhoe Park in Hertfordshire, he presented the town with the original "Five Lamps".

The next incumbent was Buxton Kenrick, who held the office until 1856 and was responsible for some radical changes in administration, but left the town under a cloud. He was made bankrupt and outlawed and, relying on the charity of friends, went to live in Lyons. There he met a young lady, Miss Gray, who belonged to a respectable family. They moved to Italy and he joined Garibaldi's force, which was besieging Capua. Eventually, when he was 62 and she was 28, they made a suicide pact; filled their clothing with sand; laid down at the water's edge and they drowned in the Bay of Naples. It could almost be the synopsis for a Merchant/Ivory film.

John George Calthrop succeeded Kenrick but had to retire after six years in 1862 for health reasons, and his place was taken by his partner, Francis Thirkill White, who had been Mayor in 1853. He, however, was dismissed in 1880, because of professional negligence over the sealing of a lease, and Mayor George William Thomas resigned his office to become a candidate for Town Clerk, and he was duly appointed.

Pishey Thompson, whose History of Boston merits more references than any other local book, was born in 1785 and entered Boston Grammar School as a pupil in 1792, but his father died the next year and he was transferred to Wragby School. In 1797 he moved to Mr. Adam's school at Freiston and became the assistant master at that school.

For fourteen years from 1805 – 1819 he was a bank clerk, first at Sheath's bank then, after the failure of the bank, at Garfit and Claypon's as first clerk. He then emigrated to the United States and became a bookseller in Washington for fourteen years. When his business failed, he took the post of assistant to the Senate Committee on Post Office affairs and later cashier at the Patriotic Bank of Washington.

His health failed, and in 1841 he returned to England and spent nineteen months with relations, mainly in Boston. For the rest of his life he was a journalist working sometimes in the U.S.A. and sometimes in England.

He had written his first History of Boston in 1820 and, soon after he attended the Boston Grammar School Speech Day in June, 1855, he completed his much larger volume and the "History and Antiquities of Boston and Surrounding Villages" was published in 1856.

With his connections across the Atlantic, Pishey Thompson was ideally suited to help the vicar George Beatson Blenkin plan the restoration of what became the Cotton Chapel, by organising the American appeal for funds, which were collected by Hon. Edward Everett, whose wife was descended from John Cotton.

Thompson celebrated his seventy-second birthday as guest speaker at the June, 1857 Boston Grammar School Speech Day and spoke in strong terms against corporal punishment. He attributed his limited literary distinctions to the barbarous treatment he received at school.

He died on the 25th September, 1862 at the age of seventy-seven.

As one contributor to that excellent book "From The Romans To B&Q-A History Of Wyberton" explains, there was a woad industry in that village at one time as well as the better-remembered brickworks. Woad was grown to provide the indigo colouring that was used universally in dyeing materials.

In 1788, however, the main area locally for growing woad was the 1,000 acre estate between Brothertoft and Holland Fen. When Major John Cartwright, a former naval officer from Nottinghamshire took over Brothertoft Farm, his main crop was woad and he provided regular employment for nearly fifty families, and each year for harvesting "a multitude of migrant Irish labourers".

He erected what was probably the first permanent woad-crushing mill, worked by three teams of eight horses, and eight large drying houses. Arthur Young, secretary of the Board of Agriculture, very much admired his farming methods.

Jealousy festered over his employment of the Irishmen and it grew into a riot, but at Cartwright's suggestion a meeting was arranged at Boston, and it was agreed to form an association for the suppression of the riot and tranquillity was soon restored.

After this experience, Cartwright saw to it that his own workers were well housed: he provided a school for their children and pioneered a form of community health service, far in advance for its time. By 1803 there were ninety-one members of the friendly society he organised and sixty-one children in the school.

Woad continued to be cropped in and around Boston until 1932, when the last man in England to grow woad commercially, Walter Sydney Booth, ceased to do so on his Skirbeck farm. He had regularly grown about a hundred acres. His land was developed after World War 2 as the Woad Farm housing estate.

It always seemed odd to me that boys from as far as Old Leake and Wrangle came to Boston Grammar School, yet a boy who lived in Sibsey, had to go to Alford Grammar School. The reason of course, was that Sibsey was in Lindsey not Holland.

As a result I never knew anyone, who lived in Sibsey, until Bill Pannell moved from his shop and bakehouse in Norfolk Place to the Trader Mill, the six-sailed windmill which is still in perfect working order.

The mill derives the name from "the Trader", the local name for the Stonebridge drain, which was built at the beginning of the nineteenth century and on which barges carried farm produce and packets, drawn by horses, carried people to Boston market on Wednesdays and Saturdays.

The central part of St. Margaret's church in Sibsey is Norman, but it is thought that an earlier wooden Saxon structure stood on the site.

Arthur Towle, who later became famous as Arthur Lucan, the creator of Old Mother Riley was born in Sibsey in 1885.

Around that same time the local vicar's wife was Annie Besant, who was destined to become a celebrity, after moving to London. Her claim to fame was that she was one of the earliest active trade unionists.

She was a negotiator for the "Matchgirls" in their historical dispute with their employers, Bryant and May.

White's Directory of 1842 describes Sibsey as a thriving community and the same can be said today; I now know many people who live in the village, and every year more choose to move there.

The real pioneer of Boston's engineering industry was William Howden, who established his Phoenix Ironworks near the Grand Sluice in 1803. He had served his apprenticeship in Edinburgh and worked for John Rennie at Blackfriars, London, before moving to Boston. An example of his work can still be found in London Road, Skirbeck Quarter, where a casting made at his ironworks in 1805, the year of the Battle of Trafalgar, marks the site of the Crown and Anchor Tavern.

He produced the first Lincolnshire-built steam engine for driving a river packet-boat, which made its first journey to Lincoln in December, 1827. The "Celerity" was the first iron-built packet for use on the Witham, and it was launched from Howden's riverside works.

In 1830 he produced his first portable steam engine, mounted on a wheeled wooden chassis and pulled by horses from place to place. It was used to power a variety of farm equipment and for a good many years, before ending its working life, it drove a drainage scoop wheel.

When William Howden died, his foundry was continued by his son until 1859, when his partners William Wilkinson and Henry White took over. At that time the number of employees was fifty men and twenty boys. In 1868 Wilkinson left to run a foundry at Poole, Dorset and Wright continued the Boston business but on a reducing scale until 1880.

Boston had been outstripped in importance by Lincoln, Grantham and Gainsborough, probably because of the extra cost of bringing the raw materials here from the Midlands, and the fact that the Boston works lacked railway sidings.

Ask the average Bostonian what he knows about Lord Nelson and they will probably say that it is a public house in Woodville Road, formerly in High Street. He or she may be surprised to learn that Admiral Lord Nelson was a free burgess of the Borough of Boston.

The honorary freedom was granted to him on the 2nd August, 1805 together with his less famous naval colleague, Sir Richard Calder.

In a letter of acknowledgment Nelson noted the corporation's thanks "for my conduct during my late command, by which they are pleased to think great advantages to the country have been derived. I shall endeavour by my future conduct to preserve the good opinion which they are pleased to entertain of me".

A little over two months later the admiral was killed at Trafalgar and three Bostonians were serving on HMS Victory to witness his death. They were Able Seaman John Lewis, Able Seaman John Warrundale and Ordinary Seaman William Thompson.

Nelson would not have been at the Battle of Trafalgar but for another Boston man named Gunby. He was a member of Nelson's bodyguard at the Battle of Copenhagen, and he used his sword to ward off a blow aimed at the admiral by "a fierce Danish officer".

Gunby was a man of remarkable physique, standing 6'4" high, and he cut the Danish officer dead at Nelson's feet. The grateful admiral promoted him to coxswain and presented him with the dead man's sword and a walking stick carved in imitation of a four-stranded rope.

It is thought that these relics are still in the possession of Mr. Gunby's descendants: his son used to live at Mill Hill in Wide Bargate.

The opening of the playhouse in Red Lion Street in 1806 was celebrated by a mayoral party in the Red Lion, and the box-office business flourished for a few years, but by 1819 it had declined.

Thomas Shafto Robertson, who was connected with the Lincoln theatrical circuit for over fifty years, had twenty-two children, so he was never short of juvenile actors and they helped the receipts in the playhouse's first season to exceed £1,000.

The building was advertised for sale, however, in October, 1821: it was described as "Commodious and substantial", 80ft. long and 40ft. wide. No buyer was found, so it was intermittently used for theatrical purposes until finally sold and demolished in 1850.

During those years Boston was treated to occasional visits by stage celebrities of the period. No less a person than Edmund Kean, the Laurence Olivier of his day, visited the playhouse on several occasions.

He played Shylock opposite the famous Miss. Marinus and his appearance as Richard III was reported as "the role afforded full scope for the actor's versatile powers".

When towards the end of his career, he again starred in The Merchant Of Venice, the prices were doubled but the house was still crowded. William Charles Macready, who replaced him as the first actor of the English stage, was a pall-bearer at Kean's funeral. He also played in Boston in November, 1834.

The famous actress, Dame Madge Kendall, twice appeared in Boston, and it is said that her visits led to the formation of the Boston Amateur Dramatic Company, the forerunner of the present Boston Playgoers' Society.

Little mention is made these days of the Boston and Skirbeck Iron Works, that once flourished at Mount Bridge, and became a large employer of labour.

William Wedd Tuxford came from a family of millers and flour dealers, but he was already well established as an agricultural engineer, when he joined John Wilks in his water-boring operations. It was he, who built the large eight-sail mill at Mount Bridge but it was known locally as "Wilks' Mill".

During the 1820s he was experimenting with machinery for sifting and cleaning wheat and patented such a machine in 1830, from which evolved the first portable steam thrashing set. At the Great Exhibition of 1851 Tuxford took the second prize for portable engines, and one of his portables drove the machinery at the Paris Exhibition in 1834.

Other Boston exhibits at the Great Exhibition were E. Tonge's specimens of embossed gem-painting on glass, and T. Small's apparatus for restoring animation in persons apparently dead.

By this time Tuxford's products were being exported throughout the colonies, as far afield as Australia and the West Indies. The range of products broadened to include iron bridges and pile-driving equipment.

When William Wedd Tuxford died in 1871 at the age of 89, his son, Weston Tuxford, continued the business at the iron foundry, while his brothers, Wedd and William conducted the milling business from Shodfriars Hall. Weston, however, died suddenly in 1885 at a time of severe agricultural depression, and the iron works passed to Collett and Company, who withdrew after four years and the mill and buildings were sold to be pulled down and cleared away.

John Pocklington was the purchaser, and he used the bricks to build his home at Heckington and the mill cap and sails were transferred to Heckington Mill.

Which is Boston's oldest inhabited house? It is probably Burton Hall at the junction of Spilsby Road and Wainfleet Road, home to several generations of the Johnson family. It was probably the manor house known early in the seventeenth century as Barham House of Broken Cross, Boston Long Fenne-end.

William Wade Johnson in 1820 at the age of seventeen started up on his own account as a market gardener, and for several years sold his produce from a stall in Boston market. He always had an interest in botany and he developed his business as a seedsman and nurseryman, and remained at the helm of the business until his death in 1881.

His son, William, another able botanist, joined the business in 1854 and took over at his father's death, but shortly after he lost the use of his legs and was obliged to turn the business into a limited company. He was a Skirbeck churchwarden and a staunch Conservative.

He died in 1899 at the age of 59. As his son, Alfred de Buoys Johnson, was only eleven years old, Ernest James Deal came to Boston from Reading to become general manager of the company. His son, Arthur Leslie Deal succeeded him in control of the company.

A shop and warehouse had been acquired in W. W. Johnson's time in Bridge Street, and the giant warehouse and processing plant, which became part of the company's London Road headquarters, was built in 1911.

Under Richard Wade Johnson, the great-great-grandson of the founder, W. W. Johnson and Son Ltd., became Britain's biggest privately-owned seed company with a staff of almost 200.

At one time Boston contained five of Lincolnshire's nine feather bed manufacturers. The leading one was started by Timothy Anderson in Pen Street in 1826, and soon afterwards transferred to Bridge Street. The stench from the heat treatment of the feathers proved unpopular with his neighbours, and in 1842 he moved to premises down West Street.

Timothy Anderson died soon after the erection of his new well-built factory, and the business continued under Richard Naylor. In 1848, however, this new building was demolished to make way for a temporary railway passenger station.

The business then was carried on by Timothy Anderson's widow and his son, Charles, first operating from Petticoat Lane then from Cornhill Lane. Charles married Fanny Susannah, the daughter of High Street printer, William Bontoft, and she also helped in the feather business.

Charles was commodore of the Royal Boston Yacht Club and he owned a pleasure craft "Little Pet", and a fishing smack "The Greyhound". At that time regattas were held for small racing yachts in the Deeps. Unfortunately Charles died young in 1863 and his boats were sold at auction. He had been a sergeant-major in the Artillery Volunteers and he was accorded military honours at his burial.

It was Fanny's turn now to run the company with her son, Charles Francis, and in 1871 they moved to more extensive premises in Trinity Street. They were employing a hundred people, when in October, 1876 the factory was gutted by fire. The present factory with the swan on the front of the roof was built the next year, and it was described as the biggest feather factory in the country.

It was possibly too ambitious, for nine years later the company went into liquidation, but Charles Francis Anderson who had married Elizabeth Brown Wells, set up in his wife's name as E. B. Anderson & Company, trading first from Lawrence Lane then in 1894 taking over the lease of the Trinity Street factory. Within two years, however, this company also were in financial difficulties and, in spite of a merger with the London & Continental Feather Company, they ceased trading in 1899.

Edward Michael Fogarty, who had been the company's London secretary, now formed E. Fogarty & Company Ltd., and acquired the lease of the Trinity Street factory. He bought the factory in July, 1901. He lived with his wife, Flora in Sleaford Road and his brother-in-law, Horace Wildee, was the company's first secretary. The business prospered and was listed at the Birmingham Stock Exchange in 1926. A note of interest: the swan was replaced by a lighter version, after World War II bomb damage.

When Catherine Booth died in October, 1890, the title on her coffin plate was "The Mother of the Salvation Army". Her funeral was said to be the most memorable since that of the Duke of Wellington: fifty thousand mourners filed past her bier as she lay in state in Congress Hall, London.

At her funeral service in Olympia more than 36,000 passed through the turnstiles, and special trains and buses were run with a dense crowd lining the entire four mile route from the City to Stoke Newington Cemetery, where admission by ticket was restricted to 10,000.

This great lady's formative years were spent in Boston.

John Mumford, her father, was born in Boston but was working in Derbyshire, when Catherine, or Kate as he called her, was born in Ashbourne in January, 1829.

He returned to Boston in 1834 and lived in Liquorpond Street, where in 1840 he was making gigs, which he sold from fifteen to twenty guineas, and market cabs from ten pounds to twelve pounds.

He had been an ardent Methodist but, while away from Boston, after the death of three children in infancy, he had taken to drink. He became an active member of the temperance society however, on his return to Boston.

At the age of twelve Catherine supported her father and became the secretary of Boston's juvenile temperance society.

The family moved to Brixton in 1844, where Catherine met a dedicated young preacher from Nottingham called William Booth, and they were married in 1855.

Together they founded the Christian Mission in Whitechapel, which was the forerunner of the Salvation Army.

At one of the first public meetings she conducted Catherine Booth "had the exceptional happiness" of leading her father "back to the full enjoyment of God's favour".

This year is the sesquicentenary of the Holy Trinity Church, as it was consecrated in 1848. William Roy gave the site, valued at £600 and contributed largely to the £4,000 cost of erecting the church.

In 1834 he had returned from India, where he had been senior chaplain at Madras, to become the first resident rector for Skirbeck. He actually purchased the advowson from William Vollans in 1837.

During his nineteen years as rector he concentrated his energies on the Spilsby Road area, the most rapidly developing part of his extensive parish, rather than on St. Nicholas's Church. In 1840 he gave the master's house and organised the raising of £1,500 to build Trinity School.

When Derby town hall was destroyed by fire William Roy bought the bell, which had been presented to Derby corporation by Charles I, and gave it to Holy Trinity Church.

While he was preaching at Holy Trinity on Sunday 17th January, 1847, a messenger arrived to tell him his rectory home was on fire. He calmly announced the fact to his congregation and dismissed them and everyone left to render assistance, but the house was burnt down and he lost his valuable plate and Indian furniture.

The following year however, he had a much larger and more imposing rectory built in Skirbeck Road; the house which was used as an annex to Boston College and which has recently caused concern as an eyesore.

His son, Robert Evelyn Roy, succeeded him in 1853 and held the living until he died in 1902, but his circumstances were reduced, when the agricultural depression hit everyone and he moved to a modest riverbank dwelling, the former Neptune Inn, adjoining St. Nicholas's churchyard.

In spite of this he gave land in Fishtoft Road for the building of St Nicholas school, and in 1862 it was erected by subscription and it opened with 110 pupils.

When Holy Trinity became a separate ecclesiastical district in 1875, he concentrated more on Skirbeck Quarter, that part of his parish on the other side of the river. St. Thomas's school started in 1865 in the charity almshouses supported by Sir Thomas Middlecott, who had been Mayor of Boston in the seventeenth century.

The School in Wyberton low Road was built the next year for £368, and started with 65 children. In 1877 it was licensed for worship, as the people of Skirbeck Quarter found it difficult to attend St. Nicholas's church.

The residents decided to pay for a full-time curate and one of the first was Sydney Herbert Nobbs, a descendent of one of the Bounty mutineers. He ended his ministry as chaplain of Guernsey prison.

A temporary church was erected in London Road and, because of it's corrugated iron structure, it became known as the "Tin Tabernacle". In 1909 a young curate, Albert Lombardini, arrived from London and was given the task of raising £4,000 for a permanent church, and on the 3rd July, 1911 the foundation stone was laid by William Garfit's wife on the site given by Mayor George Jebb.

Edward Lee Hicks, Bishop of Lincoln consecrated St. Thomas's church on the 9th May, 1912.

When Skip Lucas was Scoutmaster of the 5th Boston Troup, we held regular parades on a Sunday morning to a place of worship: sometimes a church, sometimes a chapel. One of the buildings that impressed me most was the Centenary Chapel in Red Lion Street.

We expected churches to be spacious and ornate, but most of the chapels at the end of our march were more spartan and, if a hundred people attended, they would be packed to capacity. The Centenary Chapel however, could comfortably hold a thousand people and it had a large gallery.

I often wondered why it was called the Centenary Chapel. I had also heard it referred to as the Wesleyan Chapel, so I thought it was probably connected either with the birth or death of John Wesley.

"Tilly" Turpin, the history master at the Grammar School, had spoken of the visits John Wesley had made to Boston, when he preached in the open down Walnut Tree Walk, which later became Liquorpond Street.

I discovered eventually that the chapel was built in 1839, regarded in Wesleyan Methodism as the centenary year of the establishment of the first Methodist society.

The original building was destroyed by fire on the 29th June, 1909 in a five-hour blaze, that at that time was one of the worst experienced in Boston. The foundation stone of a new chapel was laid the following year, and it was opened on the 30th March, 1911.

I have seen a photograph of the First Centenary Chapel and it too looked large and impressive. I do not know if it would have held a thousand people, but on one occasion in 1904 it was packed to full to hear a sermon and lecture by Rev. Thomas Waugh on the subject of "Manliness".

Twelve years ago I attended a friend's wedding at the Centenary Chapel and I still marvelled at the attractive building, as I had, when I sat there in my short trousers, badge-bedecked shirt, woggle and neckerchief all those years before. The broad paths and well-kept lawns made a perfect background for the wedding photographs.

Because of his statue in the Church surrounds, most local people have heard of Herbert Ingram, the Boston butcher's son, who founded "The Illustrated London News" in 1842. Few, however, will realise that his friend, Mark Lemon, the editor of "Punch" for the first thirty years of its existence, also lived in Boston as a teenager.

He lived with his uncle, Thomas Collis, the hop and timber merchant, who was Mayor of Boston in 1839. Mark Lemon returned to Boston in 1856 to assist Ingram in his campaign to win a by-election as the Liberal candidate, and he helped him to romp home over the Conservative, W. H. Adams.

Lemon pointed out at one election meeting how Boston had changed since he had lived here with his uncle. Owing to the energy and liberality of Herbert Ingram, who had urged the necessary legislation, the few flickering oil lamps had given way to brilliant gas street lighting. Even more important the pump in Pump Square, which had once been the sole source of water, had been replaced by an extensive system of piped water.

Soon after winning the by-election, Herbert Ingram bought the Boston Guardian, which encompassed the Skegness Advertiser and the Lincolnshire Independent, and for the rest of its days it trumpeted the cause of Liberalism.

Because Ingram was so heavily involved with making "The Illustrated London News" the most successful publication in the country, he passed control over the Boston Guardian to his local political agent, Thomas Wright, a member of the old-established High Street ironmongers, C. & C. Wright.

Ingram was drowned with his eldest son, also called Herbert, in Lake Superior on the 8th September, 1860, when the steamboat, Lady Elgin, which he had boarded in Chicago the previous day, collided with the schooner, Augusta.

His monument, from laying the granite base to completing the erection, took just over one week from September 9th to the 15th in 1862. The first stone was laid by Mrs. Thomas of the Market Place and some coins and a piece of parchment were deposited beneath the stone.

The text on the parchment read: "This monument was erected by public subscription to the memory of Herbert Ingram Esq., M. P. for Boston, a native of the borough, proprietor of The London Illustrated News and various literary publications. Mr. Ingram embarked on board the steamboat Lady Elgin, which sailed from Chicago, North America, September 7th 1860 and came into collision with the schooner Augusta at 2.00 a.m. on the following morning. The Lady Elgin foundered immediately and Mr. Ingram and his eldest son, also named Herbert, was drowned in Lake Superior".

This tragic accident has been well recorded over the years, but twenty-eight years later Ingram's youngest son, Walter, who had only been four years old when his father died, was also killed in an accident, equally as tragic and even more horrific.

He was an officer in the Middlesex Yeomanry Cavalry and travelled extensively, being in Zululand during the campaign against Cetewayo. At the start of Lord Wolseley's expedition to relieve Khartoum, he ascended the Nile in his own steam-launch, joined the brigade of Sir Herbert Stewart in its march across the Bayunda Desert, was attached to Lord Beresford's naval corps and took an active part in the battles of Abu Klea and Metammeh.

Later he accompanied Sir Charles Wilson and Lord Charles Beresford in their adventurous trip up the river, passing the enemy's batteries and coming within sight of Khartoum. He was mentioned in Lord Wolseley's dispatches to the War Office and was rewarded with a medal.

In 1887 Walter Ingram was in Egypt and was responsible for unwinding the wrappings of a mummy, disregarding the warning that anyone, who did so, would die a violent death within three months, and his body would be scattered to the winds of heaven.

Within three months he went to Aden to Berbera on the east coast of Africa on a hunting expedition, and was killed by an elephant which had been wounded by one of the hunters. When an attempt was made to recover his body, only a thigh bone was found.

In 1842 Freiston Shore was a popular seaside resort, especially for the people of Boston, and William White wrote "At Freiston Shore are two good hotels, pleasantly situated near the sea bank with ample accommodation and warm and tepid baths". The Coach and Horses was run by Thomas Plummer and by 1856 it had become known as Plummer's Hotel.

The landlord of the other hotel, the Anchor, was William Hackney and that also had changed it's name by 1856; to the Marine Hotel. They were still known by these names and still popular locally for a night out during and just after the Second World War.

The Plummer's Hotel had a handsome Georgian front and extensive buildings at the rear. A long room at the side had boarded-up windows and there was a wooden footbridge to take bathing parties to the water, which in those days came right up to the bank.

The hotel was literally left high and dry, when a large expanse of saltmarsh was reclaimed, and it was no longer suitable for bathing.

In 1856 the Marine Hotel was managed by William Hare, and fishing boats used to be moored close by and they caught herring, sole and sprats, as well as shrimps and oysters.

An omnibus travelled daily from Boston in the summer in 1856, and more recently Sharps ran a service there on Wednesdays and Saturdays, which was taken over eventually by Hoggs.

During the Second World War Freiston Shore was considered to be a possible invasion point, and there was a 6-inch gun emplacement and several concrete bunkers near the two hotels, and a unit of the Air Sea Rescue were billeted at the Marine Hotel and Austin Davis, the incumbent landlord joined them as an active member.

They were called out regularly, as several aircraft of both the enemy and the allies crashed in the Wash or the river banks.

There are still people in Boston, who can recall pleasant evenings spent at the Marine Hotel with Austin serving at the bar and his wife, Ethel, playing the piano.

The penny post was introduced in 1840, but previously the minimum charge for a single sheet letter was four pence for a distance of fifteen miles. For many country districts, even after the flat-rate post came into operation, letters were not delivered to individual addresses but dropped at collection points; for example letters for Fishtoft Drove were left at a house in Cowbridge, and a flag was flown to indicate there was mail for collection.

Boston's bankers, merchants and principal traders petitioned the Postmaster-General in 1845 for a daily mail service to the town of London, and four years later, after the Lincolnshire railway "loop" line was opened, two posts arrived from the capital daily.

James Buck, a printer in Bargate, succeeded Robert E. Creasey as postmaster in 1854, and the office was transferred from Strait Bargate to premises opposite Shodfriars Hall. There was a staff of four and one man did the whole of the delivery but, when he retired in 1886, after thirty-two years, his staff numbered seventy.

In the year before he retired the premises of John Allen and Company, grocers in High Street, near the Bridge Foot, were bought and cleared and a new post office was built at a cost of £1,400. Shortly afterwards the foundations at the rear gave way and rebuilding became necessary at considerable cost.

The first sub-post office had been opened in London Road, Skirbeck Quarter in 1856, the same year as the first street letter-box was erected in High Street.

By the time George Richards replaced James Buck, the postal department opened from 7.00 a.m. to 9.00 p.m. on weekdays and from 7-10 a.m. on Sundays. Residents in Boston, Skirbeck and Skirbeck Quarter enjoyed four deliveries a day, the first at 7.00 a.m. and the last at 5.30 p.m.

Fourteen telegraph messengers on bicycles delivered 12,000 telegrams each week, and a telegraph office was opened on the dock to deal with port business. When W. Reynolds Leak took over as postmaster in 1899, the number of telegrams weekly had reached 15,000 but that was the peak, as telephones were gaining popularity.

In 1874 the East Lincolnshire Railway started work on a line linking Boston with Louth and Grimsby, and the same year the Great Northern Railway began it's line from York to London by building the "Lincolnshire loop" connecting Lincoln with Peterborough by way of Boston.

The East Lincolnshire Railway initially intended to site it's terminus at the riverside end of Pulvertoft Lane, but subsequently they agreed to share the use of the Great Northern Railway's bridge over the Witham and their station off West Street.

The Peterborough to Lincoln loop actually opened to the public on the 17th October, 1848 and bands and crowds turned out all along the line, but Boston delayed their celebrations until the 26th October and it was worth waiting for.

The demand for tickets for a lavish civic dinner was so great that it had to be moved from the Guildhall to the Red Lion Street theatre. The borough's two M.P.s were present but Mayor Noble presided, and the principal guests included the Earl of Yarborough and directors of the railway companies. The cost of the ticket, 8s. 6d included a free trip on the railway to see Grimsby's new docks under construction.

Six hundred members of the working classes had a grand tea party at the Guildhall, and 2,500 children were excused school and had a feast of tea and buns, followed by a lecture on the steam engine.

Church bells rang, guns were fired, shops closed and all business stopped but, unfortunately, it was not long before disappointment and disillusion hit Boston. Extensive locomotive headquarters had been built alongside Broadfield Lane, and the prospect was extra prosperity and prestige for the town but in December, 1852 it was announced that the headquarters were to be removed to Doncaster on the main line. This decision eventually resulted in the departure from Boston of 700 workmen and their families.

From 1848 to 1853 the headquarters of the Great Northern Railway were situated in Boston, but they were then moved to Doncaster, which was on the main line. The offices of the Chief Mechanical Engineer and Locomotive Works Manager were built beside Broadfield Lane to the west of the tracks.

For five years the G.N.R. became one of the main employers in the town but seven hundred jobs were lost, when the move was made to Doncaster. Two new streets provided accommodation for railway workers: King Street and Duke Street, named after the M.P. for Boston, Sir James Duke, who later became Lord Mayor of London. Later Locomotive Street was added beside the Locomotive Depot, but it could only be reached over a footbridge or for a vehicle by opening crossing gates facing each other diagonally.

After the station was opened in 1850, the adjacent area was also developed and Station Street was built across a field, and Irby Street and Tower Street were also laid out. It was originally intended to widen Lincoln Lane to the same width as the new Station Street, but that never happened.

After the headquarters were moved to Doncaster, the Broadfield Lane offices were used as the Depot for the company's lines in southern Lincolnshire. The Goods Shed, a permanent warehouse with office attached was built in Stell's Lane, and the Civil Engineer's Shop was erected close by for producing gates and huts. Later the Star and Garter pub was built next to the Goods Shed. Sleepers were made at the Hall Hills factory down Tattershall Road.

In 1886 the Civil Engineer's Shop was destroyed by fire and new offices and workshops were built in Sleaford Road, after Rope Walk Road was demolished. This was a large complex of buildings, including a Saw Mill, Blacksmiths' and Carpenters' Shops, Fitters' and Turnery Shop, a workmen's mess room and even a fire station with its own brigade. Today only the one building remains and it has recently been taken over by the Railway Social Club, after being the Besco Club for several years.

The inaugural trip from Boston to Barton-on-Humber on October the 27th, 1848 cost 13/6d for first class and 11/- for second class. For the first trip from Boston to London tickets cost for the return journey: 22/6d first class, 17/6d second class and 8/7¾d third class.

For over twenty years from 1964 two railway coaches stood on the 'hot box' siding behind the Sleaford Road signal box, until it was decided to sell the rails to raise money.

Orders came from Doncaster to cut up and burn the coaches, but a local railway enthusiast approached the local P.W.D. foreman and subsequently rang Doncaster, who put him in touch with the appropriate department at Derby.

One of the coaches was a Gresley with coil spring suspension, one of only ten that were built at Doncaster in 1922, with a corridor and three first-class and four third-class compartments. It became coach no. 2701 on the Great Northern Railway, and was involved in a bad crash at Retford soon after going into service. It escaped undamaged and continued in passenger traffic until 1958, when it was converted into a camping coach and was based at Mundesley-on-Sea in Norfolk.

While stood in Boston, it was used as a store vehicle for the Permanent Way Department, and the other coach which had been used on the Great Eastern Railway, was used as a canteen for the workers.

The local enthusiast arranged for the Gresley coach to be moved to the Plough Inn at Swineshead Bridge, and the Great Eastern coach was moved to Norfolk. The railings had to be removed, while A. P. Crane Hire lifted them off the bogies onto low-loaders.

The landlord of the Plough Inn had the roof made watertight, all the glass repaired, the bogies enamelled and the lettering on the coach renewed, and he planned to use it as an extra restaurant at the side of the inn but Boston Borough Council objected, quoting the Lincolnshire County Council that it would be a traffic hazard, although it was well away from the road; in fact it would have been close to the railway line.

On checking with the L.C.C. Highways Department, it was found that they had no objections, but the Boston Borough Council were determined to have the last word, and a lady travelled all the way from Bristol and ruled that the position of the coach was not environmentally suitable.

The coach was then sold to the landlord of the Stoneyford Lodge Hotel, near Heanor in Derbyshire, and eventually in 1994 it was purchased by the Severn Valley Railway for use on their heritage line. The November issue of the Heritage Railway magazine announced that the Lottery Fund had awarded the Severn Valley Railway, based at Kidderminster, £84,300 towards the cost of £157,807 for the planned restoration of the G.N.R corridor composite no. 2701, which, but for the intervention of a Boston railway enthusiast, would have been cut up and burnt in the 1980s.

"Rail 150", the celebrations of 150 years of rail in Boston, will be staged by the Boston Borough Council on Saturday and Sunday, the 12th and 13th September.

An engine hauling twenty-five ballast wagons had made the first crossing of the Sluice railway bridge on the 1st June, 1848: a remarkable achievement, as the construction of the bridge had not started until the 29th September, 1847.

June also saw the completion of the London Road level crossing and bridges over the South Forty Foot and Redstone Gowt. September 14th 1848 was actually the day, when a ballast train crossed the Maud Foster iron bridge for the first time.

The last section of the East Lincolnshire Railway from Firsby to Boston was completed on the 20th September, and the official opening was on October 2nd 1848. A temporary passenger station was provided initially, until the present station was opened in November, 1850.

There had been proposals to link Boston by rail to London and Nottingham as early as 1836 but, although the local ship owners had welcomed the prospect of the Nottingham line to bring coal and other produce to Boston more cheaply, they were against the London link, which would threaten their business.

A station was opened at Peterborough in 1845 and a goods conveyance service was laid on to Boston, which ran daily from March, 1847 to connect with London trains.

Numerous proposals were made in the next few years to connect Boston by rail with Lincoln or Cambridge, or even Wakefield. In June, 1846 two companies; the Great Northern and the East Lincolnshire, were granted permission to bring lines into Boston, and in July Ambergate were given approval to run a line linking Boston to Nottingham and it's coalfields via Grantham.

When this was announced, the town celebrated by lighting bonfires and ringing church bells. The directors of Ambergate included the Mayor of Boston, John Rawson, the Boston M.P., Sir James Duke and Herbert Ingram, who had just launched "The Illustrated London News".

On Saturday the 10th October, 1854 the people of Boston were all excited, and work continued throughout Friday night to complete the preparations for a very important visitor to Boston station, which had been opened in 1850.

Local tradesmen, Messrs. Storr, Sinclair and Huggins with their workmen put the finishing touches to the galleries, which had been erected at the station to accommodate the visitors, and the station was tastefully decorated with flags and festoons of laurel. At the entrance to the station a beautiful archway was constructed.

At dawn on the Saturday morning the Union Jack was displayed from the top of the Custom House, and another flag was fixed on the top of the tower of St. Botolph's. Merry and joyful peals were sounded from the church bells throughout the day.

About 2.00 p.m. the Mayor, the Town Clerk, the Corporation and the town clergy assembled on the inner platform and a crowd of well-dressed citizens, admitted by tickets, wended their way to the gates of the station. A scarlet cloth was laid from the buildings to the track side, and the Boston brass band took its place on the opposite platform.

At. 3.05 p.m. precisely a gun planted on the Witham Bank announced the arrival of the Royal Train, for the very important visitor was indeed Queen Victoria. She had made a visit to Grimsby and stopped at Boston on her journey back to London.

At least 10,000 spectators alongside the track and at the station cheered Her Majesty, while the band played the National Anthem as the Royal Train glided into the station. The Mayor stepped forward and, kneeling on a cushion, presented a Corporation address to the Queen, who approached the side of the carriage and graciously received the address, amidst the deafening cheers of the crowd. The previous year her eighth child, Leopold, had been born, but the Queen looked exceedingly well, and was smiling and cheerful as Prince Albert came to stand at her right hand side and the Princess Royal and the Prince of Wales to her left.

The Queen noticed a man on the platform selling newspapers and she beckoned to one of her suite, who bought two or three and handed them to the Queen. The Royal party remained standing, accepting the rapturous cheers of affectionate loyalty from the crowd for about six minutes, then they resumed their forward journey.

Three years later the Queen's ninth child, Beatrice, was born and in 1861 Prince Albert died and the Queen went into prolonged mourning, making such occasions as her visit to Boston a thing of the past. The Princess Royal, also named Victoria, married Frederick III of Germany and was the mother of Kaiser Wilhelm.

William Turner Simmonds holds the record for terms of office as Mayor of Boston: he completed five terms, the last in 1905. His father, John Cabourn Simmonds, had also been mayor in 1864.

It was John Cabourn Simmonds, who built the Britannia oil mill on Packhouse Quay in 1856. He lived at Fishtoft Manor and, after some early financial problems, his business flourished to such an extent that on Christmas Eve, 1870 operations were switched to the newly-built Skirbeck oil mills next to the Black Sluice pumping station in Skirbeck Quarter.

He was a keen businessman and, although he did not make close friends, he had the reputation of being straight in all his dealings. His seed-crushing and oil cake manufacturing business grew, because his customers knew that he did not have two prices for the same article, and he never took advantage of another man's weakness.

In 1873 his son, William Turner Simmonds, came home to assist in the management, and the constant growth in the following years made them one of Boston's biggest employers of labour.

William Turner Simmonds had served an engineering apprenticeship with the Great Northern Railway and worked overseas. Both he and his father became directors of the Boston and Midland Counties Railway, which at one time planned a rail link to Freiston Shore. They played a vital part in getting Boston dock built on its present site, rather than at the Shore.

The agricultural depression at the turn of the century reduced the call for cattle cake and Simmonds and Company, like many businesses at that time, ceased to trade in 1905.

On a point of interest, in 1903 William Turner Simmonds became managing owner of the Boston Autocar Company, which owned the first two cars registered in Holland county, DO 1 and DO 2.

On the 7th April, 1913 a man with no living relations died at Anderson's Hotel in the Market Place at Boston. His death went almost unnoticed; yet 43 years previously he was feted throughout the land, and his name was on the front page of every newspaper.

In 1870 Albert Harold Cawood had with two colleagues made the first ascent of the Matterhorn without guides. He was a prominent member of the Alpine Club, and had already achieved fame by making an unaided ascent of the Jungfrau with one companion.

He was born in York and led a very adventurous life. He spent a considerable time in India, Syria and at Mount Lebanon, before he lived for five years in Switzerland and then in Paris.

He went on a pilgrimage to Mecca, travelling in disguise but, after reaching the Red Sea, he was laid up with a fever and never completed the journey. At one time he was attached to the suite of the Maharaja Duleep Singh, who was granted the Elvedon estate in Suffolk by Queen Victoria, after he had been deposed from his Punjab throne in 1848.

Cawood came to Boston Grammar School as modern languages master in 1879, and proved to be a loyal and long-serving member of the staff. He had taught for some years at Rossall but he stayed twenty-six years at Boston Grammar School, and would have been happy to stay longer. He had a delightful habit of giving nicknames to the boys and made their French lessons enjoyable.

The first ever inspection of the school by H.M. Inspector of Secondary Schools took place in 1905, and they decided that the existing system for teaching French needed a thorough reform, and they urged the governors to make changes. As a result Cawood was given notice to leave at Christmas, but the governors saw fit to mark his long service with a pension of £30 a year.

The year after he died the governors agreed to a request by J. L. Burchnall, later to become a professor of mathematics, that on behalf of the Old Bostonian Club a brass to Cawood's memory should be erected in the school.

It reads: TO ALBERT HAROLD CAWOOD, TRAVELLER AND MOUNTAINEER, FOREIGN LANGUAGE MASTER IN THIS SCHOOL FROM 1880 – 1905, THE FRIEND OF ALL THE BOYS AND TO AN OLDER GENERATION THE BEST OF COMPANIONS AND STORY TELLERS. THIS TABLET IS ERECTED BY THE OLD BOSTONIAN CLUB, 1914.

Motorists entering Boston from the west are now greeted with the impressive view of the flats, crowned by the beautiful white swan that was Fogarty's feather factory, when I was a pupil at Staniland School. The demolition of the properties on the left at the top of Trinity Street and on the corner of the station approach in West Street has opened up this Victorian vista.

The former building on the site was destroyed by fire in 1876. F. S. Anderson & Company, one of five companies that at one time made feather beds in Boston, at the time of the fire employed a hundred people.

The rebuilding was completed the following year by Samuel Sherwin, who had been responsible for building the gasworks near the Grand Sluice, with bricks he made himself in an adjacent field. Sherwin also built many important buildings in the Victorian era: the Red Lion Street Congregational Church, Blenkin's vicarage, Thorn's cigar factory, the Main Ridge Drill Hall, Small's Market Place emporium, the cottage hospital, two banks and the Cross Keys hotel.

The new swan-surmounted building in Trinity Street was described as the biggest feather factory in the country, but nine years later the company went into liquidation. Edward Michael Fogarty acquired the lease of the building and actually bought it in July, 1901. He and his wife, Flora, lived in Sleaford Road and E. Fogarty & Company Ltd., went public, being listed at the Birmingham Stock Exchange in 1926.

When his health deteriorated, he retired to Bournemouth and died in 1935. C. B. (Bert) Fleet joined the company in 1927 and became the manager in 1933. He became managing director in 1950 and company chairman in 1964.

In 1896 the Trinity Street feather factory had been one of the first three locations to install a generating plant to provide electricity. The two others were Simmond's mill in London Road and Joseph Cook's 'Boston Guardian' office.

During the Second World War, because of bomb damage, the original swan was replaced by a lighter version.

On Christmas Day, 1877 a steamer, S.S. DANAE, owned by Mr. Joseph Robinson of North Shields, with a full cargo of wheat for London, sank in the North Sea, forty miles off the Horn Reef on the coast of Jutland.

Strong westerly gales caused heavy seas and the steamer was thrown on her port side and her cargo shifted. A barque was seen in the vicinity but failed to notice the signals of distress, but later a smack was sighted and responded to the signals.

It turned out to be the Smiling Morn of Hull and, after three hours of manoeuvring in the great gale, they managed to stand the smack on the lee quarter of the DANAE near the poop, where the nineteen members of the crew had finally launched a lifeboat, after three other boats had been smashed or washed away. With great difficulty all the crew were assisted onto the Smiling Morn and their lifeboat secured.

The smack abandoned its fishing voyage and returned to Hull with the nineteen seamen. They had just enough food for their five-man crew, but made it last for the five days it took to return to Hull with their nineteen guests. They did manage to beg some bread off another smack but they saw no other steamers.

On arrival at Hull the shipwrecked men were taken to the Sailor's Home, and on the evening of the 30th December they were returned to North Shields by the local agent of the Shipwrecked Mariners' Society.

The Victoria Cross was not inaugurated until 1881, but the five members of the Smiling Morn crew for their "considerable, exceptional and brave action" received a Medal Of Gallantry, which was first instituted in 1855 and which, where the recipient has risked his own life, reads on the obverse "Awarded by the Board Of Trade for Gallantry in Saving Life".

The medals were minted in either silver or bronze and the Master of the Smiling Morn, W. Brittain received a silver medal. The other four members of the crew received a bronze medal and £2 each. They were J. Barderson, Mate, T. Finn, seaman, F. H. Frith, deckhand and A. Stroud, cook. All Bostonians should be proud to know that seaman, Thomas Finn was from Boston and his grandson treasures the Medal of Gallantry, still in its presentation case.

In March, 1878 a ninety year-old man died in Boston, who had been a hero of the Napoleonic Wars, and had served his country in numerous famous battles.

James Brooks Brook had been born in the Yorkshire village of Orset in 1788, and he was seventeen when he enlisted in the army. He first saw action at the blockade of Macho in China in 1807, then in the Peninsular War he fought at Corunna in January, 1809; at the siege and capture of Badajos in April, 1812 and at the Battle of Vittoria in June, 1813.

On Easter Sunday, March 31st 1814 he took part in the Battle of Toulouse, then came Quatre Bras on June the 15th 1815 and two days later he was shot and wounded at the famous Battle of Waterloo.

On returning to service he was attached as a servant to Sir Robert Wilson at Paris and, together with Lieutenant Bruce and Lieutenant Hutchinson they helped in the escape of the Marquis Lavalette, who was under sentence to be shot. They were all captured however, and spent three months in a French prison. Lt. Hutchinson later became Lord Donoughmore and Lt. Bruce became Lord Cardigan, and achieved everlasting fame at the Battle of Balaclava.

In 1817, while servant to Captain Wright, Brook sailed to India and returned by an overland route through the deserts of Arabia and across the Red Sea, eventually landing at Portsmouth on his return home. In 1825 he took another trip to India, and the next year he was at the taking of Rangoon in the Burmese Empire. For this action he received a gold medal from Lord Combermere for "patience, perseverance and bravery, the best traits of a soldier".

In 1818 he had been promoted to colour sergeant but he blotted his copy book in 1828, when he was reduced to the ranks for a charge of drunkenness, while serving at St. Helena. He obtained his discharge on December 21st 1829 and chose of pension of £64, instead of 1s.7d a day, but the land granted to him in Canada never materialised.

He spent several more years travelling the world in the company of a celebrated naturalist, before settling in Boston and living quietly with his many memories.

Irate parents are not just a hazard peculiar to present-day teachers; as far back as 1878 schoolmasters were in danger from over-protective fathers, who thought their children had been treated too severely.

John Henry Wray, assistant master at the Wesleyan school was teaching arithmetic to a class of eight year olds, when he was called away for a few minutes. He set the class a sum to do while he was away, and turned the paper over on his desk and told them not to copy from it.

When he returned, he found that a little girl called Crick had obviously copied from his paper, and as a punishment he told her to stand on a chair and hold a slate high above her head, bearing the words: "I am a thief for stealing sums". After ten minutes he allowed her to get down and rejoin the class.

At 2.15 p.m. in the afternoon there was a knock at the door and, when Mr. Wray opened it he found William Crick, the girl's father stood there. He demanded to know why his little girl had been punished and called a liar, and threatened to black Mr. Wray's eyes. Mr. Crick, a blacksmith, aimed a punch at the teacher, who dodged and ran back through the school to the amusement of all the children, with Mr. Crick chasing him all the time declaring he would knock his teeth down his throat.

John Turner, the headmaster, witnessed the scene, and in spite of the father's violence he managed to calm him, and led him from the school to protect the children from the bad language he was using.

John Henry Wray charged William Crick with assault and using threatening behaviour, and the case was heard at the Boston Borough Police Court, where the magistrates were the Mayor, J. Thorns, with J. Maltby and T. Kitwood. After hearing all the evidence, the Mayor told Crick: "We shall bind you over to keep the peace towards Mr. Wray for six months in the sum of £20 in your own recognisance.

School Boards for Boston and Skirbeck were established in 1894, although the Education Act of 1870 had provided for their election by local ratepayers. The idea was that they should be formed in areas where there were insufficient schools for the poor, and reluctantly it was decided that, the local rival religious groups were unable to fund and maintain adequate school premises and facilities.

By 1896 three Board schools had been built: Park and Staniland in Boston and Tower Road in Skirbeck. All three have therefore celebrated their centenaries recently. Staniland school was named after R. W. Staniland, who was the first Chairman of the School Board.

These new schools replaced the Wesleyan schools, Boston East and West Infant schools, the St. James' Boys school and, in Skirbeck, the Holy Trinity school.

The borough's boundaries were extended to include the whole of Skirbeck Quarter and a part of Skirbeck on the 1st April, 1932, and "Greater Boston" was born. The census for 1931 gave the population of the old borough as 16,597, and the revised estimated figure for 1932 was 21,871.

The number of councillors was increased from eighteen to twenty-one, and the number of alderman from six to seven. The new authority took responsibility for all contracts, debts and liabilities of all the public elementary schools, with the result that the education rate for the residents of Skirbeck was reduced from 3s.4d to 2s.1d. The rate for residents of the old borough however, was only raised by an extra halfpenny.

It now became possible to employ a full-time school nurse and the North Holland dentist now spent half of his time in the borough, instead of just 40%.

On Sunday morning in August, 1894 a Boston pilot, named Hack, made the serious mistake of bringing the steamship Ethel up the River Witham one hour after the turn of the tide, instead of entering the dock on a rising tide.

With no water to support her, the ship broke in half near the bridge, and when the tide turned, water filled the vessel and, in spite of efforts to remove her, she sank down right below the water, preventing any passage along the river. All the trawlers that were out had to put in at Grimsby, and the Hamburg liners heading for Boston Dock went to King's Lynn. Five Danish and Norwegian bargues and several trawlers were left stranded in Boston Dock.

At 4.00 p.m. on the Monday work commenced to unload the cargo, and a large gang of men were set to work widening the river to permit the passage of trawlers and smacks. The men took advantage of the urgency to demand higher pay and, after a short strike, they were successful and settled for six shillings a tide. The pilot, Hack, was suspended.

Mr. Wheeler, the Borough Engineer, together with the Harbour Master and the Dock Master, made plans to refloat the Ethel, as soon as the spring tides made it possible. A supplementary deck was built between the main deck and the hold, placed upon strong baulks of timber braced to the ship's strings. About 500 watertight petroleum barrels were placed underneath this supplementary deck. The aft bulkheads of the engine room were fortunately found to be watertight, and they were pumped dry.

The biggest problem was to brace together the forward and aft bark of the vessel, but ten steel wire bridles were braced over the timber deck and strutted with heavy timbers. A sail cloth was placed around the centre of the ship, where the plates had buckled when the ship broke. A berth was dug on the adjoining marsh to accommodate the ship, if the attempt was unsuccessful.

A large number of people assembled at high tide on the Thursday, and with the aid of Corporation horses on the bank, the Ethel was refloated and went into her berth with little trouble. A steam launch was immediately sent into the Deeps with a message to any ships in waiting, that their way was clear and they could enter Boston Docks with the afternoon tide.

The recent forecast of the changes in the weather during the next century, and the possible dire consequences for the East Coast of England, will not boost the confidence of local property developers but, if we look back in history, we will see that Boston has grown and flourished in spite of the threat of floods since before the charter of incorporation was granted.

Writing about the terrible flood of 1543 Nicholas Robertson explained that the seadykes were so decayed that "through the default and insufficiency the town of Boston and more than seven miles compas about was in most peril of utter destruction and waste".

Just 28 years later another major flood caused tremendous damage down the east coast: many lives were lost, thousands of sheep perished, and among much local damage Skirbeck church was devastated. This was the famous flood of 1571, the subject of Jean Ingelow's renowned poem.

As a result in 1576 the borough appointed thirteen members "to be of assistance to the dykereeves in making the seadyke book and to allot every man to his part of the seadyke to be made and amended".

In the reign of Henry VIII the Court of Sewers was set up to co-ordinate the sea defences, and it was still in force on November 13th 1810, when a night of continuous rain and hurricane force winds, together with a swift evening tide 4 inches higher than any previously recorded, inundated Boston and tore several gaps in the sea banks.

An area of thirty miles between Wainfleet and Spalding was flooded, and the road from Boston to Fosdyke was impassable. The Court of Sewers sat in continuous session in Boston's Guildhall, but they ignored the advice of their engineer Mr. Rennie, and instead of raising and strengthening the banks, they just repaired the breaches.

In February, 1816, however, another exceptional high tide caused such alarm that they finally acted upon Mr. Rennie's advice, and raised the banks 2 feet above the level before the great flood of 1810.

In 1944, when with about sixty other apprehensive boys, I experienced my first day at the Boston Grammar School, we were all placed in "houses"; either Mustons, Parrys, Gannocks or Laughtons. I doubt if any of us gave a thought to the people, who had "left their footprints on the sands of time" or why they had been chosen.

If new names were chosen today; maybe Medlock, Spikings, Newton and Parkes; most of us would know why, but would the boys who will be starting at the Grammar School in September?

They also had four "houses" at the High School and my sister was in Ingelow House. Now this I could understand, because I had read "High Tide on the Coast of Lincolnshire", and I knew that Jean Ingelow was a famous poet that had been born in Boston.

In fact, when I made my daily journey, "trudging unwillingly to school", I passed the house where she was born, just before reaching my destination. The house survived, until the new Haven Bridge was built and for several years it was used by Hallmey's the wholesale confectioners.

Jean Ingelow was born there on the 17th March, 1820. When only six days old, she was baptised in St. Botolph's Church; the first child of William and Jean Ingelow. During the next eleven years they had three more daughters; Susanna, Sophie and Eliza, and three sons; William, George and Henry. Their nursery window overlooked the river, so Jean had first-hand experience of the vagaries of the tides.

Her grandfather had been a coal and coke merchant, which led him to owning several small trading ships, and ultimately moving into banking. By the time Jean was born, her father was in charge of the bank, but the export trade had diminished and Boston was still suffering the effects of the Napoleonic Wars and the Peninsular campaign. There had been a local disaster, when the sea had broken through the sea-banks at Leverton and Friskney in 1810. All these factors contributed to the family banking business collapsing in 1825.

For the next nine years the children were educated by their mother and her sister, Rebecca, then in 1834 the family moved to Ipswich, where the children were taught by a local clergyman. Jean began writing verse and with one of her brothers contributed to "Youth's Magazine".

Jean Ingelow was never married, but some of her early verse refers to an unhappy love affair and the courtship of a young girl by a sailor, who was lost at sea. Was she drawing on her experience or just using her imagination?

Her most famous poem was referring to the high tide of 1571, but the effect of the 1810 disaster on her family must always have stayed in her mind.

History shows how close a Bostonian came to being the first lady Poet-Laureate. When Alfred, Lord Tennyson died in 1892, a petition was sent to Queen Victoria from leading writers in the United States on behalf of Jean Ingelow's appointment to the vacant position. Queen Victoria, however, would not consider appointing a female poet.

Jean Ingelow wrote children's stories as well as poetry, but she was 43 before she had a book of poems published.

Tennyson was delighted when he read her second book, and when he met her by chance in a London street he exclaimed, "Miss. Ingelow, I do declare you do the trick better than I". Afterwards Tennyson not only admired her writings but liked her as a person, and John Ruskin spoke of her as one of the few people he had "ever truly loved". She also enjoyed the friendship of Christina Rossetti.

In all 30 editions of her poems were published, and they were read and loved by hundreds of people and ensured financial security for Jean and her family.

Jean died on the 20th July, 1897 and there was a glowing obituary notice in the Times the following day. She was buried beside her mother and father in West Brompton Cemetery. Her name lives on in Boston with Ingelow Avenue, the Ingelow Manor home for the elderly and the m.v. Jean Ingelow, Boston's river dredger.

There is also a letter in Boston's Guildhall Museum, which reads: "Miss. Ingelow presents her compliments to the Mayor of Boston and thanks him for giving her the opportunity of contributing to so interesting an object as the proposed chimes for the church. She has much pleasure in forwarding a donation of five pounds, which she hopes he will accept as a slight expression of the hearty interest she feels in her native place".

In 1986 Lyn Ellis, cancer victim and prolific fund raiser, became the first women to be awarded the honorary freedom of the Borough of Boston, followed later by Margaret Haworth. Earlier this year Jim Howes was similarly honoured and during the century ten others have received this accolade.

Six of them had earlier held the office of major: James Parkin Rowe, John Henry Mountain, Reuben Salter, Edward Arthur Bailey, Charles Henry Wing and Tom Kitwood. Two others were long-serving aldermen, who had not served as mayor: Arthur Lealand and Alfred Chester. The final two had brought dignity and honour to the ancient office of town clerk: Cyril Louis Hoffrock Griffiths and Robert William Staniland.

When the Boar War started late in 1899, the "Gallant Eight", rifle volunteers from well-known local families, marched off to join the 2nd battalion of the county regiment. One died on active service but the other seven were granted the honorary freedom of the borough on their return home.

One of these was Meaburn Staniland, the son of Robert William Staniland, but together with his brother, Geoffrey, he was killed in 1915 on the Western Front during the First World War, so he never knew that his father also received a honorary freedom in the 1920s, when he retired as town clerk. This was the only time a father and son both received this special honour.

Meaburn had been named after his M.P. grandfather, who was elected as the second member for Boston in 1865.

The idea for the Old Bostonian Club was first suggested by Rev. E. S. Roberts of Gonville and Caius College, Cambridge to the Headmaster, William White, but the actual genesis can be traced to a September evening at the home of a Mr. West in Surbiton, where Harry Palmer of Abingdon and another friend talked of old days shared at Boston Grammar School.

The outcome was a meeting of eighteen former pupils on the 20th April, 1900 at Anderton's Hotel, Fleet Street, London, where the club was founded. The host, Dr. A. Hopewell-Smith was secretary and the Chairman was C. V. Cook of Jermyn Street, London.

Within a year the membership was 170 and Dr. Hopewell-Smith remained as the London secretary until World War I brought the Club's proceedings to a halt, and Arthur Hill was the secretary in Boston.

The "Club" became the "Association" in the early 1930s, so on the 20th April, 2000 the Old Bostonian Association will celebrate its centenary. Several plans are being made to mark the occasion, the most important of which is the decision to place stained glass windows in the annex, which the Foundation has kindly consented can be used by the Old Bostonian Association as a museum.

On the 1st November, 1956 Lord Ancaster unveiled ten panels of stained glass in the bay window on the west side of the "Big School", which were dedicated in a ceremony by Canon Ellis. They illustrated various aspects of the school's history, and in one panel depicting the declaration of the Beast Mart, the Mayor, Town Clerk and Headmaster at that time can clearly be identified as W. A. Midgley, C. L. Hoffrock Griffiths and W. J. Ricketts.

The Field Street Mission has served several various purposes during the last century. Although a long way from St Botolph's, in the early 1900s it was a kind of parish hall, used for social events and a variety of functions. It had living rooms and bedrooms attached and was run by two sisters, Annie and Lottie Brand. Services were taken there by Curates or Readers.

In his memoirs the Revd. Stephen S. Thistlewood recalled looking forward always to going there with his sisters, for Annie and Lottie Brand were their maiden aunts. If there had been a recent social event, he wrote: "we would be regaled with left-over cakes and other delicacies". Their aunts also taught them card games and played charades.

Fast forward to the immediate post-war years and the Field Street Mission was then a popular venue for teenagers, as it was used in the 1940s and 1950s by Sherwood Youth Club. Socials, dances and sporting activities made it, apart from Jimmy Ward's the main meeting place for boys and girls and their cricket team played its matches in the Central Park. The club was run for many years by Mr. Norman.

Music was often provided by their own jazz group; Bob Kitchen on piano, Johnny Porcher on the drums and Malcolm Hall on double bass. Reg Howard used to play the piano accordion but, after watching Ronnie Scott at the Gliderdrome, he switched to the tenor sax.

In the late 1950s and the 1960s the Field Street Mission was used as the headquarters of the Boston Liberal Party. Those were the days, when the Liberals had a strong presence on the council and almost every by-election fell to them, as they had such a well organised band of canvassers.

Led by Cyril and Emmy Valentine, their numbers increased steadily. One by one Tom Balderston, Bruce Veal, Geoff Brooks, my father, Fred Mould and Fred Myatt gained seats, but it was not just those who joined the council, who were responsible for the success. There was a willing band of experienced canvassers always ready to help and they worked in pairs, and the star pair was George Twiddy and Joe Cupper.

I hate to think what they would say about the turn-out in elections today, for if it fell below 75% at that time, they would think they had failed.

One vote can often be very important, and the development of Boston, especially West Street, could have been so different if Mayor Simonds had used his casting vote for an alternative proposal on the 1st April, 1901.

Two proposals had each received ten votes from council members, sat round a table in the corporation rooms, which were reached by a badly lighted, ramshackle staircase in a building in the market place.

Plans had already been prepared for a new police station in Bank Street, but Mayor Simonds voted instead for plans for a new Municipal Buildings in West Street, to incorporate not only a police station but also a court house and a fire station.

The proposal was that 1,149 square yards should be purchased at £1 per square yard, and at a special council meeting fourteen days, later an amendment that a poll of the town be taken before such a large expenditure be undertaken, was defeated by thirteen votes to nine.

A public enquiry was held later that year by order of the Local Government Board, into the application by the corporation to borrow £20,000 for the scheme; after which a local man, James Rowell, was appointed architect and S. Sherwin & Son were appointed as the main contractors.

Edward VII was invited to perform the opening ceremony but, when he was unable to accept the invitation, Mayor Joseph Cooke presided at the official opening on Thursday the 16th June, 1904.

The new police station incorporated six cells, a drill yard for the use of the police and an exercise yard for the use of prisoners, and also the chief constable's residence. The court house and fire station had been included as planned, but the Municipal Buildings also housed extensive council offices, a council chamber and the mayor's parlour, the public library and reading room and the school of art.

The police station, the fire station and the pubic library have all since been relocated, but for many years West Street was the centre for much of the activity in the town.

April the 3rd 2001 was the centenary of the day when three Boston pilots were drowned in the Wash. Thomas Shepherd from Freiston Low Road with eight children, George Dawson of Tunnard Street with four children, and Thomas Finn of Horncastle Road with five children, sailed from the pilots' sloop in an open row-boar to pilot the Norwegian steam collier, "Harald" as far as the Lynn Deeps. They left on the morning tide and should have returned to their sloop on the same tide, but a strong westward squall sprang up and they were lost.

The s.s. Harald, the first boat of a new line of colliers running from Boston to the Elbe, was taken down the river by Upper Station pilot, J. W. Longstaff, who returned on the "Privateer". Three Lower Station pilots were necessary to take the row-boat to the ships, and the alarm was raised when the s.s. Southwood arrived in port the next morning without a pilot. W. Parker, the Pilot Superintendent immediately launched the "Olivette" to search for the missing men and sent a trap to Freiston Shore.

The bad news however, had spread through the streets of Boston the previous night, and the only people who could have known of the tragedy, were the crew of the steam tug, "Boston", who had seen the row-boat making for the sloop between 11.00 a.m. and 12.00 a.m., when the squall blew up. The body of George Dawson was found by William Garner and taken to Fosdyke Bridge, and at the inquest held there at the New Inn, Joseph Oldham, captain of the "Boston", said that they did not realise the pilots were in trouble, yet his crew said they were dead, when they returned to town.

When pressed Joseph Oldham said they could not have reached the pilots, because of the sand between them and he had to escort a boat up the river. The coroner remarked: "Didn't you think the lives of three men were more valuable than a boat?".

The biggest irony was, that as I have written previously in this column, Thomas Finn, when eighteen, had received a Medal of Gallantry for saving 19 lives at sea but, when his own life was lost, no one went to his assistance.

The bodies of Thomas Shepherd and Thomas Finn were washed ashore at Holbeach Marsh seven weeks later, and a jury returned a verdict that the deceased were accidentally drowned. The Mayor, Alderman Simmonds, held a public meeting at the Assembly Rooms, and opened a fund for the widows and families of the three pilots, and the St. Thomas Choral Society held a Benefit Concert at Shodfriars Hall, stage-managed by George Gale, to raise money for the fund.

Some fascinating glimpses of what life was like growing up in Boston a hundred years ago, can be found in the memoirs of Stephen S. Thistlewood, "A Son Of Boston Remembers". His father was a hairdresser and tobacconist and hanging on a wall in his shop was an old halberd, a long pike like weapon with an axe head, and also a casting of the town's coat of arms mounted on velvet and framed in oak. At one time he also had an aviary with canaries and other song-birds.

His shop was open from 8.00 a.m. to 7.00 p.m. in the week and to 9.00 p.m. on Saturdays. A shave cost a penny and a haircut tuppence. You could buy a packet of five Woodbines for a penny and an ounce of tobacco for three and a half pence. A bottle of whisky was three shillings and sixpence, and a two-piece flannel suit could be bought for thirty-five shillings. Most children received a Saturday penny each week, and the writer usually bought an orange for a halfpenny and a bag of broken biscuits for the other halfpenny. Biscuits were weighed out of big tins, and there were always broken pieces left when the tin was emptied.

Pleasures were of necessity simple; with just a few horses and traps and the odd bicycle on the roads, it was safe to play marbles in the gutter coming home from school, and the children played 'whip and top' on the pavement. The poor children, who often ran about without socks or shoes, would knock a nail through a tin lid, put a knotted string through the hole and run it along the street. Those a little better off would have a wooden hoop and a stick, and the luckiest children would have an iron hoop with stick attached.

In October conkers were the main sport and, as still happens today, boys sought out the biggest possible and seasoned them in the oven to try for a champion. Another favourite pastime for the tougher boys was to strike the pavement with their hob-nailed boots to see who could make the biggest spark.

In the school holidays the boys used to take a picnic down the sea bank, and sit on the platform of one of the wooden watch-towers, which were lit at night to mark the channel to help the pilots bringing boats up the river. As the tide was coming in, the boys would paddle in the warm mud.

As the children grew older, they were allowed to go to the Swimming Baths on South Terrace. Even then Boston had municipal swimming baths. Children were taken from school to the baths once a week and taught to swim. When the sun was on the deep end and they could see the bottom, they use to drop pennies in and dive for them. After a swim the children often walked and played in the pleasant Bath Gardens, which were adjacent.

I received a letter last month from Mrs. L. K. Chambers from Ampleforth in North Yorkshire. She had visited Boston in May to try to uncover more information about her great-grandfather, Freeman Baxter, who had been a baker at 110, High Street until 1904.

She had looked through the records at Boston Library and spoken to the present owner of the property, who had told her that my family had owned the bakery for many years. After returning home, she discovered my address and made contact.

It appears that Freeman Baxter was left with four children, when his first wife died in 1904 and he moved to London, where he remarried and had four more children. Mrs Chambers had traced all these children but what she did not know was if her great-grandfather had been a tenant or the owner of 110, High Street, and how soon after his wife's death, had he sold the property.

I was able to tell her that he was definitely the owner and he sold the property in 1904. It wasn't much, but she thanked me profusely, as she now knew when he actually moved to London and it would help her enquiries there.

I was sure of my facts, as I had listened to my grandfather's tale of how he moved to Boston in 1904 many, many times, when I was a child. My grandfather's brother George Mould, had settled in Sutterton earlier and was an established builder. Several of the houses he built are still inhabited; indeed they look quite modern and they have a distinctive feature: a course of bricks near the roof are of a lighter colour and have been laid upright, instead of flat. The house nearest to the main road at Reed's Point is a good example.

My grandfather, James Mould, was baking at Kettering, where there was a surfeit of bakers, and his brother George wrote to offer him his advice "You should come to Boston". Fortunately he took that advice and often said that he never regretted his decision.

When George Mould stopped building, he became landlord of the New Inn at Sutterton and the bakery my grandfather bought in 1904 prospered until High Street was ruined by the yellow lines, and closed in 1969.

In August, 1905 a young fireman from Hull, Charles Smarth, stole a steam launch on the River Witham at Boston, and after being caught, he was remanded in custody in the police cells, which were part of the new municipal buildings in West Street.

His tasks on his first day in custody was to clean out the cells, after which he was allowed to go out into the exercise yard. He seemed a quiet and obedient lad, so the constable in charge of him left him on his own for twenty minutes but, when he returned, he could find no trace of him.

Smarth had climbed a water spout, fifty feet high, and scrambled along the gutter at the top of the municipal buildings, crossed the roof at the end of the block and climbed down the exhaust pipe of the gas engine, used for driving the electric plant. He only had to then scale a low wall, separating the buildings from a brewer's yard, and he was free.

In spite of an extensive search by policeman on bicycles, and his description being circulated throughout the district by telephone and telegraph, Smarth reached Tattershall undetected and broke into the Post Office during the night and stole some postal orders and a bicycle.

He was spotted near Lincoln and Inspector Sparrow of the Boston Borough Force went to Lincoln, and was actually talking to Inspector Swaby and Sergeant Young of Lincoln, when Smarth cycled past them down Melville Street. They chased him along the Waterside North and trapped him, when, not knowing the district, he turned down Bridge Street, which was a cul-de-sac.

He still did not give up without a struggle, for on reaching the wall at the end of Bridge Street, he turned round and rode at full speed, trying to break through their hastily formed cordon of bicycles, but he was fetched off his machine and captured.

Later at Boston he was sentenced to six months imprisonment for stealing the launch, and at Lincoln Assizes he was sentenced to an additional three months with hard labour for the thefts he made during is escape.

The present town bridge was opened in 1913, and it replaced the first bridge in England of cast iron by John Rennie in 1809. Rennie also built the three footbridges over the Maud Foster Drain, the Vauxhall, Hospital Lane and Cowbridge footbridges.

Rennie's town bridge contained 208 tons of cast iron and an eighty-six foot single-span arch. It opened for carriage traffic on the 2nd May, 1809. The previous bridge had been wooden and had rested on a pier, whose foundations proved difficult to remove; in fact the last of the piles were not drawn up until ten years after the opening of Rennie's town bridge.

Certain buildings had to be removed before Rennie's bridge could be erected to provide sites for the abutments, and the whole scheme cost £24,000. £10,000 of this was raised by the corporation borrowing a hundred sums of £100 each, and agreeing to pay an annuity of £7 to each of the lenders' nominees, who were mainly children and grandchildren ranging in age from two to twenty-five. As a result by the end of the century the corporation had paid out £58,000, and there was still one surviving annuitant.

To protect the freemen of Boston from strangers coming to trade in the town, the corporation imposed tolls upon carts and wagons using the bridge, and also upon horses, cattle and sheep crossing over.

A public meeting held in June, 1828 called for the abolition of the tolls, which were considered illegal, but the corporation stood their ground until December, 1830, when the court ruled against them and the bridge tolls were abandoned.

It may surprise some people that the first council houses built locally were not provided by Boston Borough Council, but by Boston Rural District Council.

There were forty-four houses in all, and they were built at the start of the Great War in 1914. Eight parishes were involved but the largest numbers were situated in Kirton and Algarkirk; twelve each.

It was not until 1926 that Boston Borough Council built their first council houses and they were erected in Westfield Avenue. More were built on the same site in 1928 and also others in Sherwood Avenue.

By the time local government were reorganised in 1974 the combined authorities had over five thousand council houses.

The years immediately before the First World War were notable for other building projects. The railway bridge over the Forty Foot Drain in Skirbeck Quarter was built in 1911; the same year that Fosdyke Bridge was opened.

The Guildhall was also restored in 1911, thanks mainly to the generosity of Frank Harrison, the local timber merchant and magistrate. This building, that had been the venue for so much of Boston's history, was still used for public functions but was gradually developed as the borough museum. As several readers will remember, the former courtroom and council chamber were used during the Second World War as a British Restaurant.

In 1913 a new Rifle Drill Hall was built in Main Ridge, replacing the old Drill Hall in Artillery Row.

After the armistice was signed in 1918, the development of the town continued. The Central Park which had formerly been Oldrid's park, was opened in 1919 and a year later St. James's Hall in George Street was opened by the local Member of Parliament, W. S. Royce.

In June, 1918 a crowd of several thousand people assembled at Kirton station to welcome twenty-five year old Sergeant Harold Jackson, who had been awarded the Victoria Cross for showing extreme heroism in the face of heavy odds.

The village was decorated with flags; peals were rung on the bells of the Parish Church, and he was welcomed on the station platform by Alderman William Dennis J.P., Chairman of Kirton Parish Council. A procession marched through the village to the Grammar School field, passing cheering crowds.

On the platform erected in the field Alderman Dennis presented Sergeant Jackson with a £50 war bond, a gold watch and a purse containing £25. He commented "Your King and country are proud of you and your friends and the citizens of Kirton are especially proud and delighted to honour you".

Harold Jackson was born in Kirton and on leaving school he worked at Tunnard Brothers, farmers and potato merchants. In 1912 he left to work on the railway at first Nottingham then Wood Green, where he enlisted at the outbreak of war. He joined the East Yorkshire Regiment and was wounded twice, before receiving his medal. He had four brothers also serving, one of whom was awarded the DCM.

In September, 1918 Mrs. Ryall of Nottingham, the sister of Sergeant Jackson, received a letter from Lt. Col. G. East-King of the East Yorkshire Regiment: "I cannot tell you how sorry I am about the loss of your brother, Sergeant Harold Jackson VC, but I am sure that if he had to be killed he died in the manner he himself would have chosen".

"He and I, about 4.00 a.m. set out to find out the results of our attack and found the line rather in an unsettled state, so we patrolled out to get in touch with the enemy. When a few hundred yards from our line, an enemy machine gun opened fire and he was instantly killed. He was buried later quite near to where he fell, near Thiepval, and we have erected a wooden cross with the full particulars over his grave".

"I personally feel that I have lost a true comrade, as he always accompanied me everywhere and it was a great blow and loss to me, so I can deeply sympathise with you. We are very proud indeed of our VC and there is not a man, who does not feel that he has lost a soldier impossible to replace".

When the First World War ended, there was a general election held in December ,1918: known as the "khaki election". As a result of a Redistribution of Seats Bill, Boston ceased to be a parliamentary borough and combined with the old Spalding division to form the Holland-with-Boston constituency.

Ask ten of your friends, which party won the seat for this constituency at that election and you will be lucky, if one of them gives the right answer. It was the Labour party, and they won again in 1922 and for a third time in 1923. In each case the winning candidate was William Stapleton Royce, and to date he is the only Labour member to go to Westminster from this constituency.

Royce had unsuccessfully fought the Spalding seat as a Conservative and Unionist in two 1910 elections, and was president of the new constituency's Unionist Association. Whey they selected Major Ernest Arthur Belcher for their candidate, Royce was so upset that he defected to the Labour party. The local repercussions were manifold. Royce had been one of the founders of the Lincolnshire Standard, which, as a Tory organ, was to enjoy its first chance of sabre-rattling at election time. He was now a director and the chairman of its, board, Colonel Archibald G. Weigall, was the Conservative candidate for Horncastle.

Born into a poor Spalding family, Royce had made his fortune as a contractor in South Africa, after running away to work on the railways there. He had retired to Pinchbeck Hall, where he farmed extensively.

The enlarged constituency had some 40,000 electors, of whom over 22,000 voted. Royce had a 1,070 majority over Belcher, and polled more than eight times the number of votes cast for the Hon. Arthur George Villiers Peel, the Liberal candidate. He was returned again in a three-cornered contest in 1922, when the Conservatives were represented by Sir Henry Fairfax-Lucy Bt., barrister and former guardsman, and the Liberals by Ewan Andrew, son of the proprietor of Punch. Thirteen months later he was successful for a third time; this time in a straight fight with the Conservative challenger, Arthur Wellesley Dean.

Royce died on a London bus in June, 1924 on the day, when he was formally offered the governor generalship of Tasmania.

Hugh Dalton was Chancellor of The Exchequer in Clement Attlee's Labour government, after the Second World War. He was a lecturer in economics at London University, before the war started. He was the Labour candidate for Holland-with-Boston in the by-election, caused by the sudden death of William S. Royce in 1924.

His father was canon of St. George's Chapel, Windsor. Hugh Dalton had already conducted three unsuccessful election campaigns in the previous two years. His conservative challenger was Arthur Wellesley Dean, a prominent south Lincolnshire farmer, and the Liberals were represented by Richard Pattinson Winfrey, just down from Cambridge and newly qualified as a barrister. He was the youngest parliamentary candidate in the country.

At the by-election Dean won the seat for the Conservatives but Dalton ran him close. It proved that Royce had held the seat through three elections mainly because of his own popularity. After his fourth defeat, Dalton stated: "...my reaction is sheer weariness and anger. I am utterly sick of politics and I feel a fool to have come on this adventure".

Hugh Dalton's relations with the Tories during that election were quite good, but they were very strained with the Liberals. Winfrey's father had already been a M.P. and now as Sir Richard Winfrey he was managing director of the 'Guardian'. He and Lady Winfrey were very active in the campaign and, as Dalton later recalled: "It was put about that I had written an anti-religious book, which was used as a textbook in Communist Sunday schools".

At the next general election Dalton was replaced as the Labour candidate by George Rivers Blanco White, against whom Dean secured a much more convincing win. Blanco White's wife was Amber Reeves, a university lecturer and novelist, whom it has been revealed in recent years was romantically linked with H. G. Wells. Blanco White was later made the recorder of Croydon and was one of the most widely-quoted divorce commissioners.

The Boston house furnishers, Cammack & Sons, founded in 1919 by Mr. F. A. Cammack, is one of the few businesses in Lincolnshire which has survived and prospered during the last 79 years and four generations.

Francis Alfred Cammack learned the trade of cabinet making at Simpson's in Strait Bargate, and later at Small's Emporium in the Market Place. While serving in the Royal Naval Air Service during the First World War, he designed and built the earliest automatic bomb release rack.

After the war he set up business in Wide Bargate with his eldest son, Sidney, and his two younger sons, Frank and Kenneth, joined in due course after leaving school. In spite of the recession they moved in 1932 to the present building, which has four floors displaying high quality furnishing fabrics and furniture. It had the first lift in Boston and also the first oil-fired central heating system.

Mr. F. A. Cammack retired at the start of the Second World War and, after the three sons had all been called up for war service, the shop was managed by Mrs. Elsie Cammack.

On Good Friday, 1940 a bomb fell in front of the shop without exploding and came to rest 30 feet under the shop. The bomb disposal squad spent several days excavating the hole, digging out the bomb and rendering it harmless.

The three brothers continued to develop the business after the war, and it became a limited company in 1947. In the fifties John and Roger joined the company, representing the third generation.

Cammack & Son's display stand won the first prize at the very first Boston Trades Fair in 1959, and about the same time their Threadneedle Street premises were rebuilt to provide a pleasant and efficient workroom for carpets, curtain making and re-upholstery.

Today the tradition and courtesy and craftsmanship is carried on by the fourth generation; John's son, Richard and Roger's son, Tony.

There will be few people alive today, who remember the first bus service between Boston and Spalding. It started soon after the finish of the First World War, when the Progressive Company bought several double-deckers from the London General Omnibus Company and surprised the local people, who were expecting to see smaller buses similar to those coming in from the villages on market day.

They were made by AEC, who had first started production at Walthamstow in 1910, and they had solid tyres and open top decks and stairs. The company had provided a steady supply of these buses during the war for troop transport in Flanders.

The name PROGRESSIVE was painted on each side, but the initials LGOC were still on the radiators. When the company grew and extended it's service by adding a new route from Boston to Skegness, they increased their fleet with new single and double-deckers from Straker-Squires, a Bristol company.

These were all painted red and white and had a distinctive short bonnet, which was unusual in those days. The maker's 'S' monogram was prominent on every bonnet. The company also bought one Dennis single-decker, which was used for private outings: especially by the freemasons. This had a black roof, instead of the usual coloured finish.

Much excitement followed when the company bought a Federal bus, made in Detroit, because it had giant pneumatic tyres and was pumped up in public by an engine-driven tyre pump.

The Progressive Company lasted until the mid-twenties, then they were succeeded by W. T. Underwood Ltd., who in turn made way for United, a North Lincolnshire company, whose buses were all painted black and yellow.

In 1928 United were taken over by the Lincolnshire Road Car Company, but they had opposition for a few years from Smith's buses. Laurence Smith was a local man, who had worked for the Progressive Company and his first bus was used to take workers from Boston to the new sugar beet factory at Spalding.

Then he bought four Leyland buses and employed old Progressive drivers, and people could go from Boston to Skegness on his red and white buses for just one shilling. Unfortunately he was only in business for a few years.

In the early years of this century country people used to come to Boston on market day on carrier's carts. These large horse-drawn vehicles started out early in the morning, and also brought produce to the market; then in the evening it returned the shoppers to their villages with their purchases.

Their journeys always stopped and started from the cobbled yards of local inns like the Red Lion in Bargate and the White Horse in West Street. Numerous stops were made on the way for pick-ups and deliveries.

Around 1920 these carts began to be replaced by village buses, and the smell of petrol gradually ousted the smell of horse droppings. The majority of these vehicles had not begun life as buses but had been converted to meet the demand.

Several of them were Ford Model Ts, with a lengthened chassis and a chain drive to take the power from the original position of the rear axle to a new position further back. One, however, was built on a pre-1914 Sunbeam chassis and with it's squat bonnet and radiator it resembled a mobile greenhouse.

On most of them a box-like body was mounted on the chassis with the seats placed lengthwise, and a row of small windows with steps up to a door at the rear end. Often the bus body was lifted off with block and tackle after market day and detachable sides were fitted, so it could be used as a lorry for delivering cattle cake or farm produce.

One of the first proper buses in this area was acquired by H. H. Milsom of Coningsby: it was a solid-tyred, red-painted Daimler, built at Coventry, and it stayed in service for a good many years. The goods and produce were carried on a spacious rack on the roof.

As the buses became more numerous and longer, the inn yards were no longer practical, so new venues were needed to load and unload , and terminals developed at Russell Square for west and south-bound routes and further down Wide Bargate for north-bound vehicles. Cropley's Blue Glider buses and Hunts of Alford were two companies, who covered several routes out of Boston during my youth, and they still delivered parcels and goods in the 1950s as well as carrying passengers. When my father was the local agent for Standard Yeast, Hunts made weekly deliveries for him to village bakers like Wells and Mrs. Capps at Sibsey and Ted Sands at Butterwick.

341

Although the need for a girls' school had been discussed as early as 1872, it was not until the 19th January, 1921 that the Boston High School for Girls came into being. It's aim was to "give a sound liberal education on modern lines to fit girls for home life and for entrance to any of the careers open to women".

Allan House in Carlton Road had been the home of G. W. Thomas, the disgraced ex-mayor and town clerk, then later of William Bedford, the miller and draper; now it became the first home of the Boston High School.

The first headmistress was Frances Mary Knipe, who had taught at Putney for several years. She had a staff of seven other teachers and 112 girls on the first day. There was a shortage of both books and desks and for the first three weeks workmen were hammering in the classrooms. Gradually order was created out of chaos and by September, 1921 the number of pupils was increased to 180, when the old Pupil Teachers' Centre was taken over.

At this stage the girls were divided into three houses: two named after the private schools, Conway and Ingelow, and the other called Allan House. By January, 1922 the huts had been built to accommodate the extra pupils and there were now four new classrooms, a Science laboratory and an Assembly Hall.

The first issue of the school magazine appeared in July, 1924 but by then the headmistress had married the noted Lakeland painter, Bernard Eyre Walker, so she was obliged to resign. Her successor was Ethel Mary Ridley, who came from the County Secondary School at Kentish Town. She also held the post for just over three years, then had to relinquish it when she married Herbert Haycroft Morris, the headmaster of the Boston Grammar School.

The third headmistress was Ethel Strachan Henry, like Miss. Knipe from Putney. She had taken the post of the first headmistress at Spalding High School, which had also opened in 1921. She had resigned from Spalding High School in December, 1925 but spent a year on a world tour, studying educational systems in various countries.

She was to stay much longer and her nineteen-year headship was to see Boston High School for Girls move to it's present location in Spilsby Road.

It was decided as early as April, 1931 that new premises would have to be provided for the Boston High School for Girls, but the foundation stone for the Spilsby Road school was not laid until the 18th November, 1937.

Alderman J. W. Gleed, later Sir John Gleed, performed the ceremony, introduced by Alderman Tom Kitwood. The same two gentlemen were present at the official opening on the 9th May, 1939 but this time Gleed presided and Alderman Tom Kitwood performed the opening. He had just retired as chairman of the county education committee.

Miss. Ethel Strachan Henry, the headmistress, with her staff and the girls had suffered great discomfort for many years. The quarters at Allan House had been inadequate for a growing school, and the students could hardly be expected to give of their best, while using huts and even a storeroom as classrooms. Several girls, who attended Allan House in the thirties still live in Boston, and they will confirm that some of the girls who lived in, did quite a bit of learning in the bathroom.

Some of the classes were held in the Witham Marsh school, half a mile from the main school, which was not an ideal arrangement and must have wasted time for both teachers and pupils.

In spite of all these privations, the new school was greeted with mixed feelings. Scores of ratepayers regarded the Spilsby Road school as far too lavish, and in the issue of the Boston Guardian on the day after the official opening, one opinion was expressed that "the new High School need not have been quite so palatial". One wonders what the comments would have been concerning the recent addition to the school.

When Miss. Henry finally left in 1946, she was replaced by Miss. Esme Thomas and she in turn was succeeded by Miss. Mary Webb.

My mother's father, Robert Blackamore, was foreman on the coal hoist on Boston Dock. I was only four, when he died on the 1st November, 1938 but I have many memories from the stories concerning him that my mother used to tell us on long winter nights.

He weighed over twenty stone but never looked fat; he had a huge chest and strong arms and legs. People in the Station Street, James Street and Lincoln Lane area always said "fetch Bob Blackamore", if anyone needed help or if there was any trouble.

Our favourite tale was of one Sunday lunchtime, when someone ran to fetch him, because a man was hitting his wife outside the Duke of York public house. Granddad left his dinner on the table and hurried to the woman's aid.

He lifted the man off his wife and was telling him what he ought to do with him, when the woman picked herself up and started hitting my grandfather with her umbrella, shouting "Leave my husband alone, you bully". He never interfered again between man and wife, after that experience.

He was 59, when he died and he had been ill for over a year. They lifted his bed downstairs when he was taken ill, partly so his many friends could call and see him more easily and partly to help my grandmother, who was lame.

Their house at 8, Station Street was double-fronted, and every Sunday my mother took us there to tea. After the meal, while my grandfather lay in bed in one room, my cousin, Beryl Rastall, played the piano in the other front room and we all stood around the piano singing.

It must have taken two hours to go through our repertoire, which included "Harbour Lights", "Isle of Capri", "Ragtime Cowboy Joe", "Two Little Girls in Blue", "The Lights of Home", "When You Wore A Tulip", the complete score of "The Desert Song" and many, many others.

Granddad never complained, and if he did not feel too bad, he joined in with his favourite "Ole Faithfull". After he died, we still visited Grandmother every week but "Ole Faithfull" was omitted from the sing-song and it was some weeks, before we managed to sing with the same gusto.

There are some very interesting old photographs of Boston on the walls of the restaurant at Asda's Supermarket. The one to the left of the door to the Gentlemen's shows dockers working on the coal hoist at Boston Dock in the 1920s.

The heavily-built foreman standing on the extreme right was my grandfather, Robert Blackamore. At that time, it was regarded as a honour to work on the dock, and an even greater honour to work on the coal hoist. Nepotism played a big part in landing these prestigious jobs, but my grandfather would have used a different word.

Suffice it to say there were several Blackamore's in the coal hoist gang, and it was taken for granted that, if you were male and your name was Blackamore, you would eventually find yourself a member of this selective band.

My grandfather's eldest son, my Uncle Ernest, known to everyone as Blackie, worked with his father and, when his younger brother, Wilfred, was old enough, he too joined the coal hoist crew. It was strenuous work and unlike his father, brother, uncles and cousins Wilfred was not built like the others. His chest measurement would have been almost ten inches less and he was more suited to work in an office.

He was a brilliant artist, and both my sister and I have paintings of his that are admired regularly by visitors. He was certainly not cut out to work on Boston Dock, but he was determined to follow the family tradition.

He always did his share of the work, but it took its toll and he strained his heart and died at the age of 27, leaving his widow, Mary with a two-year old daughter, Barbara. During his short but happy life he brought pleasure to his family, and my mother used to tell us how he was always singing and his favourite song was Sigmund Romberg's "When I Grow Too Old To Dream". Years after he had died, if my mother heard that song, it always brought tears to her eyes.

My mother and father were married at Boston 'Stump' on August 23rd 1926. After my mother died in 1969, I found in an old biscuit tin the receipt for her wedding bouquet and flowers. It is fascinating to compare the prices she paid then with today's prices.

They were bought from G. Burr, Wholesale and Retail Florist and Fruiterer, 9, Market Place, Boston. There were three bouquets of pink roses at 12/6, two baskets at 6/- (no doubt for two young bridesmaids), four ladies sprays at 10d. and one gentleman's buttonhole at 6d., making a grand total of £2. 13.4d.

I also found a receipt for the Wedding Breakfast for 45 @ 3/- = £6. 15.0d. The caterers were W. F. Leafe & Son of George Street, Boston and, although they were confectioners, their invoice stated in one corner "Fresh Milk delivered daily to all parts of the town". 3/- per person was equivalent to 15p and today you would be lucky to be quoted £3 per person.

Together with these two bills mother had placed a postcard, dated the 18th August, 1926 with a photograph on the front of the George Hotel at Swaffham. The writing on the back was short and to the point, "Dear Sir, I shall be pleased to reserve you a double room for the 23rd inst. Yours faithfully, E. Wilson". I knew my parents had spent their honeymoon in Great Yarmouth but they obviously broke their journey to spend their wedding night in Swaffham.

Soon after they were married, father took a lease on 17a, West Street and they opened Mould's café, next door to Gale's barbers shop, and for fifteen years it was a popular venue for villagers coming to the White Horse with the carriers, or people who had time to kill on the way to the station to catch their trains.

A menu that has survived from 1938 shows that prices were still very reasonable then: a buttered teacake was 3d., a ham salad was 9d. and, if you felt really rich, you could have a salmon salad for a 1/-.

The recent report on the television news about an infant girl being turned away from a hospital in Leeds, and her parents being told than an operation would be pointless, but the parents persevered and the little girl underwent a successful operation in Newcastle, reminded me of a similar occasion here in Boston in 1932.

My brother, Jim, was taken ill shortly after his first birthday. The trouble started in his neck; his glands were swollen and they did not respond to the normal treatment. They became septic and it was impossible for him to eat and very difficult for him to even drink, so naturally he lost weight and his condition deteriorated.

Dr. Pilcher was his doctor, and he and his partners operated several times but to no avail. It reached the point, where congregations in churches and chapels all over town were asked to pray for him.

Dr. Pilcher's son had just joined the practice and he suggested drilling a hole in each ear drum, and placing a cord along the back of the neck to remove the poison from his glands, then they could prevent it reforming by using the cord instead of a further operation.

His father considered the idea impossible, and did not think it was fair to put my brother through more pain, when it was pointless. My parents, however, asked young Dr. Pilcher to try and, when none of his colleagues would help in the operation, my father helped him. It seems strange now but in those days before the National Health Service many operations were performed in people's houses. The operation was a great success and his condition gradually improved, until he could eat again.

This was one of the early examples of Dr. Richard Pilcher's innovative ideas, which endeared him to patients for many years. Mother realised that but for his intervention Jim would have died, and she sang his praises throughout her life and, like most Boston people, she still referred to him as young Dr. Pilcher even after he retired.

Jim still bears the scars at the back of his neck, and his pierced ear drums prevented him from serving his National Service, but his shaky start in life has not affected his enjoyment nor curtailed his sporting activities: he still spends two evenings every week playing badminton, and makes regular visits to the West End theatres from his home in Thaxted.

In most streets or neighbourhoods there is one person or one family, who cause general displeasure to their neighbours. Either they insist on having their radio or music centre on full blast, or they hold all-night parties without warning or they spread malicious gossip throughout the area.

These people are very fortunate that the ancient fenland custom of "ran-tanning" has gone out of fashion.

"Ran-tanning" was very effective, and one wonders if it would not be a good idea to re-introduce it today, but it would be considered illegal.

It appears that in earlier times, if a person incurred the wrath of his neighbours in this area, a crowd congregated near the house of the offender for several nights in succession, and made as much noise as possible.

They would beat drums or tins with sticks; boo, shout or sing at the top of their voices; play on home-made instruments and sometimes even burn an effigy of the pariah.

The last reported incidence of "ran tanning", this quaint custom that resembled mob law, occurred at Quadring Fen in February, 1928. A woman had been scandalising her neighbours and between thirty and forty people assembled around her house.

The noise swelled, until it attracted the attention of the police and upon their arrival the less committed members of the crowd dispersed, but 23 later appeared at Boston Sessions House.

Of these 5 swore they were not present and the cases against them was dismissed, but the others were fined five shillings each and ordered to pay witness' costs with seven days' imprisonment in default.

Charged with aiding and abetting the others by allowing them to be in his garden, one man was charged ten shillings, again with seven days in default.

Arthur Towle was born in Sibsey in 1885, but the family moved to Boston while he was still young. In 1899 at the age of fourteen he 'trod the boards' at Shodfriars Hall, which was then a theatre seating 650 people.

He changed his name to Arthur Lucan and worked his way up the Music Hall ladder, reaching the top as Old Mother Riley and her daughter, Kitty. Kitty McShane was, of course, his wife.

Their film career started in 1936, when Oswald Mitchell produced and directed a film, "Stars On Parade", especially to provide a showcase for Music Hall comedians. Top-liners like Robb Wilton, Jimmy James and Albert Whelan were in the cast, and brothers Syd and Max Harrison, but it was Lucan and McShane that became cinema stars.

Between 1937 and 1952 Arthur Lucan made fifteen films with Kitty McShane in them all, except the last, "Old Mother Riley Meets The Vampire", which co-starred Bela Lugosi and Dora Bryan. His films helped to keep people laughing and boosted morale during the war.

He remained a top of the bill Music Hall act, until he died on stage at the Tivoli Theatre, Hull and he was buried in the city. There is a bust of him in his Old Mother Riley outfit of shawl, and bonnet and laced up boots in the theatre at Hull, but here in Boston his home town, where members of his family still live, there is nothing to commemorate this famous comedian.

This will be rectified however, on the 24th June, when a Boston Preservation Trust Blue Plaque will be unveiled at Shodfriars Hall by his six-year-old great, great, granddaughter, Katie (Katharine Charlotte).

Arthur Lucan had one son, Donald, who was married three times. His first wife had one daughter, Marylyn; his second wife also had one daughter, Suzanne, and his third wife had two daughters, Katharine and Alison. Katie's mother, Margaret was the daughter of his first wife's child, Marylyn.

When I read that Ken Morley, alias Reg Hollingsworth, was coming to Boston on December 1st to officially open the new Harmony Music shop, and Laurence Brown told me that he would be signing copies of his historical novel, "Housecarl" at the shop that day, I wondered just where this shop could be. I knew Harmony Music were formerly trading in a shop beyond the Regal, and they were moving to the top end of West Street but, with the new cinema complex replacing all the empty Co-operative shops, I could not imagine just which property they were moving to. Unless....

Sure enough, when I took Mae West's advice and 'went west', I found they had moved to the same shop that my father had run as a café throughout the thirties and during the war. At that time the property consisted of two ground floor shops and a café over them both. We sold bread, cakes, biscuits etc., in one shop and Mr. Gale ran a gentleman's hairdressing business in the other. The steps in our shop led to a café, which was very popular with country folk, who came up to Boston either on the buses, which used Russell Square as a terminus, or others, who travelled up on Market days with the carriers, who used the White Horse yard. It was also the last chance for people going to the Railway station to have a cup of tea and a snack, unless they risked the station buffet.

I still have a copy of Mould's Café menu for 1938, and for a shilling customers had the choice of a salad with either salmon or ham and tongue. By the time I was old enough to help in the café on a Saturday in 1944, the war time shortages had made egg and beans on toast the star item on the menu. As the customers left, I hurried to clear the table and usually found a penny under one of the plates, but occasionally there was a nice shiny threepenny bit.

When the lease ran out, the property became the Cameo Ladies' Hairdressers for several years, then later Reg Priestley used it for a very successful fruit and vegetable business.

In the early 1950s there were two tennis courts at Burton House, and the Boston Young Conservatives held mixed doubles tournaments on Sundays during the summer. The standard of play was quite high and a draw was made for partners each time, so the same pairing could not dominate every tournament.

Some of the ladies were very strong players and we all hoped to be lucky enough to be drawn out with one of these. Among those attending regularly were Margaret Loveley, Violet Ashton, Eve Coles, Margaret Taylor and her sister, Jocelyn, Barbara Taylor, no relation, Nancy Allen, Taye Appleby, Denise Senior, Margaret Smith and Beryl Ashley.

Robin Midgeley was the President and played occasionally, but the regular men included Peter Smith, Bernard Reed, Bob Allen, Hugh Clancy, Brian Manning and Dick Westland.

Of these Dick, now the Revd. Richard Westland, is the only one with whom I have kept in contact over the years. In a recent conversation I discovered that at the start of the war Dick attended Boston Grammar School and lived in Kingsway, opposite the Woad Farm, from which the estate was named, after the war, when Boston Borough Council paid £10,000 for 36 acres.

From his bedroom window Dick sometimes watched German planes drop incendiary bombs, but one night in early 1942 he saw parachutes drifting down from an enemy plane. As they came lower, he could see in the moonlight that they were too small to support men but there were packages hanging from them.

On investigation he found that they contained thin newspapers, printed in German. Although he was learning German at the Grammar School, he could not translate all the paper and it puzzled him why they should drop them, if they could not be read. He came to the conclusion that the plane must have been running out of fuel and offloaded anything they could to lighten the load.

Dick still has a copy of the paper and years later his friend, Peter Kitchen, who taught German before he retired, translated it for him and he found it must have been intended for the Russian people, as it warned them that they were doomed, for Germany was going to overrun their country.

At 7.45 a.m. on Monday, 27th July, 1942 a bomb fell on Mariners Row, a passage off High Street in Boston, which was at the side of Brown's grocery shop and ran behind the houses at the top of Liquorpond Street.

If the German airman had waited twenty seconds, he would have hit the dock, as no doubt intended; if he had waited five seconds, I would not be writing this column now, as it would have landed on my father's shop at the top of Pulvertoft Lane.

As it happened, Mariners Row was obliterated and Mrs. Gee at No. 6 was killed. She lived alone but her granddaughter, Maureen Hall, often slept with her. Fortunately she was not there at the time.

At No. 5 lived Charles Barton with his wife and four children, George, Roy, Barbara and Ted. Mrs. Barton had been admitted to hospital a day or two before and the children had gone to their aunt in Pulvertoft Lane, but for this they would all have probably been killed.

In those dangerous times your fate could be decided by such happy or unhappy coincidences. Mrs. Harris and her three young children were not so lucky. They moved from Edwin Street to a house at the top of James Street just two weeks before a bomb fell on Loveley's bakehouse. Mr. Harris came home on leave to find his whole family wiped out.

I was reminded of these times, when I had a chat with Bas Teft, while waiting my turn at the diabetic clinic at the Pilgrim Hospital recently. Roy Barton was one of his friends that featured in our conversation, but Bas referred to him as 'the beacon', as we all had nicknames at the time. Other names that came under discussion, before I was interrupted by the doctor, were Jimmy 'Rabbit' Rivett, Brian 'The Hook' Hooker and Alan 'Wilf Mannion' Chester, who headed literally hundreds of goals during a long career in local football, with teams such as Unicorn and New Park Rangers. As Bas said, the ball in those days was heavy leather and the laces often left their mark on your forehead.

Most Bostonians will know that Boston is twinned with Laval in France, and of the exchange visits and sporting activities, and many older residents will remember that soon after the Second World War, before twinning was common, Boston has a similar arrangement with Bergen op Zoom in the Netherlands. I still have a copy of the programme, when Boston United played a Bergen op Zoom football team.

How many people, however, know of the connection between Boston and Orpington in Kent. Mention Orpington and the majority will think of the famous by-election and Eric Lubbock's success for the Liberals, but the people of Orpington had good reason to be grateful to Bostonians towards the end of the war.

German bombing raids became scarcer early in 1943, mainly because they had lost so many planes, but in 1943 and early 1945 the V1 flying bombs and the V2 rockets caused havoc around London and many inland cities. Boston and towns near the coast were not affected, as they were programmed to explode well inland and not wasted by falling in the sea.

Orpington was one area badly hit by these flying bombs and rockets, and Boston sent 400 Morrison shelters to Orpington and Greenwich. The inhabitants of Boston also played their part, as the Women's Institute organised a collection and over 1,400 household items were sent to be distributed among the bombed-out families of Orpington.

Boston did have one last taste of the Luftwaffe: on the 4th March, 1945 early in the morning a German plane flew low over the streets of Boston firing cannon shells at anybody moving. My father and brother were in High Street, hurrying to the shelter at the top of Pulvertoft Lane, and they swore they saw the pilot's eyes as they dived to the ground. When they were asked was there more than one plane, they replied in unison: "We did not stop to find out".

St. Michael's church at Coningsby is notable for several reasons: not just for its famous one-handed clock. The 16$\frac{1}{2}$ ft. painted dial is thought to be the largest of its kind in the world.

The church tower is also unusual, as it stands outside the church and has a beautiful arched carriageway underneath and an unglazed rose window on the west wall.

A reminder of a past tragedy is found at the apex of the south porch; a stone monkey. The story is that a monkey escaped from a travelling circus and snatched a baby, who was the heir to the Earl of Coningsby. While dodging his pursuers, the monkey dropped his prized trophy and the baby fell to its death. That was the end of the Coningsby line.

Inside St. Michael's is a Royal Air Force Chapel and behind the altar is a Dutch national flag. During the Second World War this flag was used by a Dutch lady Resistance worker to cover the bodies of three British airmen.

The Battle of Britain Memorial Flight is centred at R.A.F. Coningsby, manned by volunteer former fliers and it is open to the public from Monday to Friday.

Members of the R.A.F. join with the villagers at Christmas to organise tree lights in St. Michael's churchyard, and the Commanding Officer puts on a Christmas meal for the Senior Citizens of Coningsby and Tattershall.

A relic of the time, when the fens were still undrained, can be found on the corner of the building of the Lea Gate Inn. It is a bracket for a lantern, which helped to guide travellers over the treacherous fens. According to records there was at one time a toll bar at the Lea Gate Inn.

The magic of Christmas is stronger than the evil of wars. This has been proved time and time again. There is the famous occasion during the First World War, when on Christmas Day British and German forces forgot about their hostilities and came out of the trenches to play football against each other.

When the First World War started, the 2nd Battalion of the Lincolnshire Regiment was in Bermuda, but they soon found themselves at the front. Many famous poets fought and died in those muddy trenches; Rupert Brooke, Wilfred Owen and the Canadian, John McCrae, who wrote "In Flander's Fields".

Old Bostonian Godfrey Finn's uncle was in the 2nd Battalion of the Lincolnshire Regiment, and he was wounded and taken to Wimeleux, where the medical officer was John McCrae. Godfrey's uncle unfortunately died from his wounds and John McCrae died soon after from pneumonia. The words of "In Flander's Fields" are engraved at the gate to Wimeleux graveyard and, when Godfrey went over to France to see his uncle's grave, he found him buried close to the grave of John McCrae.

Godfrey's cousin, Eric Stray, joined the Royal Engineers in 1938 and, before the Second World War started, he had already spent months building water towers in the desert in North Africa. He later joined Colonel Orde Wingate's 'Chindits' and they were flown from Northern India and dropped behind the enemy lines in Burma.

The special feeling of Christmas was illustrated on Christmas Day, 1944. With no sign of the enemy they risked tuning in to Forces' Favourites on the B.B.C. and they heard a recording of church bells from before the war. Eric said to his mates "I recognise those bells; they belong to Boston Stump". His mates in unison said "Get away" or words to that effect. The voice of Jean Metcalfe, however, came on to say "That was the bells of St. Botolph's Church at Boston in Lincolnshire.

As Jim McDonald proved in "Coronation Street", if you ask anyone who has been in the forces to tell you his service number, he will rattle it off; especially the last three, which you had to shout out on pay parade. Similarly, if you ask anyone, who went to Boston Grammer School, which house they were in, they will immediately answer either Laughton's, Parry's, Muston's or Gannocks.

As I have suggested before, if you then ask them what they know about the man their house was named after, you usually receive a blank stare. In case you are ever asked, here are a few helpful facts.

Dealing with them in chronological order Robert of Muston comes first. In 1329 the Dean and Chapter of Lincoln "conferred the School of St. Botolph" on Robert of Muston. This does not tell those in Muston's much but gives a definite link with schooling.

Next comes William Gannocke: he was a freeman of Boston, who decided to move to Sibsey in the late sixteenth century. Boston had received it's Charter on the 1st June, 1545 and the first Mayor was Nicholas Robertson, who received an allowance of £55, as did subsequent Mayors. Any balance had to be handed over at the end of his year of office or he would be jailed until he had done so. The Mayor could be elected either on Lady Day, 25th March, or New Year's Day.

With such strict rules for the Mayor, it was no surprise that Freemen were also treated harshly and William Gannocke had to pay the messenger, who delivered notices of council meetings, in order to remain a freeman when he moved out of the Borough.

More is known of John Laughton, whose Charity School was founded in 1707. He had a small estate in Skirbeck Quarter and had come from Holbeach, where he was in charge of a Free school. Early classes of Laughton's Charity School were held in the Cotton Chapel in St. Botolph's Church, and later in the Old Church House in Wormgate. The aim of his school was "to teach so many of the poorest freemen's sons....to learn to read English, to write and to cast up accounts".

Finally we come to Thomas Parry. Much could be written about his political exploits, but suffice it to say that he was elected as the second member for Boston as a Liberal in 1865 but was accused of bribery by the other Liberal candidate, Meaburn Staniland, who was given the seat. One year later, however, Staniland resigned and Parry regained the seat.

Thomas Parry died in December, 1879 but his name lives on, as he left money for the Parry Gold Medal and the Parry Scholarship.

When a few weeks ago I flippantly suggested four more recent names to replace the four houses at Boston Grammar School, it created a ripple that resulted in an article on the front page of the Grammar Gazette, and a letter from the proof reader Mr. R. J. Abbott, the Latin master.

My suggestion that the pupils of today would recognise all four names was only half right, as they were au courant with Len Medlock and Barry Spikings but they were not familiar with the names of either Revd. Dr. John Anthony Newton or Sir Freddie Parkes.

John Newton started at the Grammar School in 1942. He was born in Grantham but moved to Boston at the age of two, and his mother had a grocery shop in Fenside Road. He read History at University College, Hull and offered for the Methodist Ministry in 1955. He filled several posts, including one at Limaru in Kenya in 1972/73 and he lectured at Nairobi University, then in 1981 he acceded to the highest position in Methodism, President of the Conference. He represented the Methodist Church in televised services and often was featured live on Radio 4's "Today" programme.

Sir Freddie Parkes had been to the Grammar School much earlier. During the twenties and thirties he built up a fleet of trawlers, and traded as Boston Deep Sea Fishing Company. He brought employment and prestige to the town but, unfortunately, the council at that time hindered rather than helped him, and finally in frustration he moved his company to Fleetwood, where his trawler fleet prospered and eventually he was knighted.

I discovered in a telephone conversation with Mr. Abbott, that he and Nigel Wainwright had the onerous task every year of sorting through the forms giving the academic and sporting details of his new pupils. It seems that, unless they have a father or older brother at the school, they are allocated to a house purely by chance in an effort to balance the houses.

He was surprised and fascinated to hear that in 1944 it was simply a matter of geography. If you lived in the centre of Boston, you were in Laughtons; if you lived to the south of Boston, starting at London Road, including Wyberton and Kirton, you were in Gannocks; if you lived to the west of Boston, starting I believe at Sleaford Road, you were in Mustons, and if you lived to the north of Boston, starting at Bargate Bridge, including Freiston, Fishtoft, Butterwick, Leverton, Old Leake and Wrangle, you were in Parrys.

While I attended the Grammar School, Laughtons dominated most sporting activities, especially swimming, as we were lucky to have the best two swimmers of our generation, Ken Johnson and Victor Emery.

I stood behind a man at a supermarket checkout last week and his trolley was full of countless loaves of sliced bread. I found myself wondering how many coupons he would have needed to have bought that quantity in 1946. Not that there would have been a supermarket then nor even sliced bread.

Many today will have forgotten or never known that bread was once rationed, and you needed your ration book when you bought a bread loaf. During the war meat, sugar, butter, lard, eggs, cheese, dried fruits and even clothes, using a separate book, were rationed and, when oranges appeared again after the war, the shopkeeper marked the back of your book but bread was never rationed.

One of the many reasons why Clement Attlee's Labour government only lasted one term was that some chinless wonder in Whitehall devised a crazy system to ration bread, using all the coupons in a ration book that had never been used for anything else. There were five or six differently lettered coupons involved and they were all given a different value. Buying a loaf became a long process, as the shopkeeper, after taking the money, had to fiddle with everybody's ration book to remove the correct coupons. Bakers' roundsmen took twice as long to complete their rounds.

When the scheme was first muted, the National Association of Master Bakers, Millers and Associated Trades called an emergency meeting of their executive committee at the Trocadero Restaurant in London, to point out to the Government that it was unnecessary and unworkable. My father and Mr. Bradley from Healing, near Grimsby were the two members of this committee representing Lincolnshire, and they came back from the meeting to tell local bakers that the N.A. had resolved to take no part in this ridiculous scheme.

On the Monday the rationing started therefore, the Boston and District Bakers, at that time numbering nearly a hundred, did not take coupons and on the Tuesday morning my father was very surprised to be told that the headline in the Daily Herald mentioned Boston and he was named in the article. The only other town mentioned, where coupons were not being taken was Wellington in Shropshire, represented by Mr. Laud, a friend of my father's. So much for solidarity.

Thousands of pounds were wasted sending forms to bakers to be filled in and returned at a later date with the coupons collected, but that later date never arrived, for they would have needed an army of clerks just to check them. Bakers throughout the country were left with sack loads of coupons in sheds and lofts: those we collected filled two-thirds of our coalhouse, until it was admitted that the whole scheme was a failure.

When I recently mentioned the circus animals parading down King Street from the railway goods sidings, it brought back memories to Frank Ward, who lived in Duke Street before the war but moved to Scotland in 1952, when he became a Customs and Excise Officer. He married a Scottish girl and still lives in Edinburgh, although he retired in 1990.

He also remembers pipe bands marching through the streets and the smell of the tar-boiler, as he watched the mouth-masked men spreading the aggregate. He recalled the milkman with churns balancing his bicycle, ladling out the milk into jugs; he used to watch for my father's bread van and sometimes received a jam tart, as his parents were good customers; he remembers steam lorries and the regular visits from the 'dilly' cart.

Both Frank and his father sang in the choir at St. James's Church in George Street, and he remembers once singing a duet with Irene Blackamore from King Street in the Blenkin Memorial Hall and the Mayor presenting them with half a crown each.

He attended Staniland School and he remembers, when he started at the Grammar School, cycling there on his first day with Ray Tinkler. Among his friends at school were Pip Sands and Roy Woodthorpe and it was Roy, who helped him scrape potatoes on an ancient machine, housed behind Sinclair's South Street warehouse. The Fighting Services Canteen was situated in Sinclair's premises and Frank's mother was a shift controller there.

At the weekend Frank often camped down Frampton Marsh and watched the Flying Fortresses, high in the sky, making their way to bombing raids on the continent; then at sunset it was the turn of the R.A.F's Lancasters, flying much lower and not yet grouped in formation.

Frank's mother and father both lived into their nineties, but his grandmother had not been so fortunate. She had lost her husband in 1902, as a result of an illness brought on by his service with the Lincolnshire Regiment overseas, mainly in India. She was left to bring up a family of five and worked exceedingly long hours, washing railwaymen's' clothes, making home-made wine and later, like many women in Boston, picking over huge packs of peas in her own home, discarding blackened and damaged ones and earning a pittance.

Boston was well served by cafes and restaurants before and during the Second World War. The waitresses in the Lindis Tea Rooms above the Midland Bank were dressed in black with white aprons and head pieces to match. In the Market Place there was Coney's Café, King's Café and the Scala Restaurant, and in Wide Bargate the Tudor Restaurant was popular.

Towards the end of the war or just after, a new establishment attracted a new type of customer, including boy scouts from the Fifth Boston troop, who called for 'stones on leather' (beans on toast) after the scout meeting.* It opened in a little shop at the bottom of Bridge Street but later moved to High Street and was always packed in the evenings.

About the same time the property on the corner of the Market Place and Strait Bargate, which had been used during the war for people to take their salvage, was transformed into the Cherry Corner Snack Bar, and became the number one meeting place for the younger generation. After seeing so many American films, where such places were the centre of activity, it seemed that Boston had joined the modern world.

Its success soon led to competitors opening similar snack bars: the Spick and Span in New Street and the Pop Shop in West Street. Even Woolworth's had a snack bar at the bottom of their shop for a few years.

All these alternative meeting places had an effect on the little shack that had been used throughout the war by schoolgirls and boys as a favourite rendezvous: Jimmy Ward's Herbal Store. Jimmy was still very busy and his regulars never deserted him, but now you could drink your sarsaparillas and compos in comparative comfort, instead of spilling half of it, when someone caught your elbow. At the height of his halcyon days there must have been thirty or forty chattering teenagers squashed into his trysting tabernacle.

* The singer, Donald Peers, was very popular at the time and they took their name from his most famous song and called it: 'The Shady Nook'.

Geoff Brooks was the youngest, most energetic and enterprising member of Boston Borough Council in the late 1950s, and it was a shame when he left Boston to live in Sussex. He recalled in a letter the years he spent at Boston Grammar School during the war.

He joined the Air Training Corps; 715 Squadron, which was based at the Grammar School. There was some rivalry with 141 Squadron, which consisted of other Boston boys who were keen to join the R.A.F., and their bugle and drum band was a cause of envy.

Apart from discipline and drill they learned the Morse Code, Aircraft Recognition (friend and foe) and air navigation, which involved being able to recognise the main stars, planets and constellations.

When they went to camp at R.A.F. or U.S.A.A.F. stations they learned a lot about the aircraft at that base and were taken up for flights. Geoff's greatest thrill was being allowed to take over the controls of a Lancaster bomber in the air. They were also allowed to use a Link Trainer, an early flight simulator.

They also attended weekend courses at R.A.F. Outstation, learning to fly a glider. They slept in a Nissan Hut and in the winter everyone wanted to sleep in the middle beds, as the single stove was in the centre of the room and it was freezing at each end. They learned to put together a Daglan; a light metal frame with a central skid instead of landing wheels, with an open seat on the skid and basic controls of a rudder bar and joystick. There was a large wing fixed to the frame and control wires to operate the rudder, elevators and ailerons.

The pilot was strapped into the seat and two cadets held the wing tips, as the glider was turned to face into the wind. The pilot had to learn to maintain the glider in balance on the skid by controlling the ailerons with the joystick, then the glider would be connected to a motor winch some distance away and pulled along. The speed was gradually increased each time, until fast enough to take off and the pilot was then able to practice landing on the skid.

The learning progressed, until they were higher in the air and doing more and more manoeuvres. It was a great experience and pleasure for lads aged from fourteen to eighteen. Geoff was one of the smaller and lighter lads and a minimum weight was needed to balance the aircraft, so, when it was his turn, he had to sit on a two stone sandbag.

My friend, Malcolm Hall, reminded me this week that, when Cherry Corner Snack Bar opened after the war, they introduced Boston to another American innovation ... the juke box.

Until then the only way to hear the latest record was to save your pocket money for a month, then take 5/4½d to Hildreds or Lingards and make sure you did not drop it on the way home. They were all 78s at that time but no one referred to them as such, until the E.P.s and L.P.s came much later.

You can imagine the excitement, when it became possible to go to Cherry Corner and immediately hear the latest records for just 3d. If you cared to invest a shilling, you could choose five records and enjoy a twenty minute session. This was before the days of Melody Maker and the top twenty, but the latest Dinah Shore or Perry Como were always available or, if like Malcolm, your taste was for the big bands you could listen to Harry James's 'Trumpet Blues' or Stan Kenton's 'Peanut Vendor' as often as you chose.

The post war teenagers are now today's senior citizens, and can often be heard expressing the opinion that music today is rubbish, and song lyrics now make little sense and are repetitive. They tend to forget some of the records that were popular in the late forties and early fifties: the crazy babbling of Danny Kaye, the mad rendering both with voices and various instruments by Spike Jones and his City Slickers of such tunes as 'Chloe'.

Some of my friends wasted good money buying a record by Red Ingle called 'Erutan Yob', which turned out to be 'Nature Boy', a popular song of the time, spelt backwards. Amy Camus, an American singer will not be remembered by many, but she decided to turn her name around and some people will recall Yma Sumac, who became famous as the multi-octaved singer, who had hits with such records as 'Virgin of the Sun Gods' and 'Wimoweh' many years before it was recorded by Karl Denver.

The photograph for May on the St. Botolph's calendar for 1998, which features each month a view of old Boston, brings back happy memories every morning, as it shows Strait Bargate as it was fifty years ago.

Looking south there is Weaver to Wearers, "Bungy" Newton's bakers shop, Kwick Dry Cleaners, Lipton's, Smith's Cleaning & Dyeing, Joan Burns dress shop, the Red Lion hotel, S. T. Hopper's, Mason's and Tebbutt's. There is a weighing machine outside the Red Lion hotel, which closed down in 1961, prior to Woolworth's moving from across the road.

Between Kwick cleaners and Lipton's is a passage, which I, together with many of my generation, walked down thousands of times. It led to the Mens' Own Club and that is where we became adept to varying degrees of Billiards, Snooker and Table Tennis.

Access was gained by climbing two flights of wooden steps at the bottom of the passage, and there were two full size Billiards tables with a smaller table between. At that time pool had not been introduced to this country; it was just a strange game sometimes seen in American films.

370

Snooker was frowned upon by some people and Billiards was THE game. There were two divisions in the local Billiards league and only one in the snooker league. We were lucky to be taught by two of the best Billiards players in Boston, Cyril Wright and Arthur Atkin. Cyril in particular was considered with Bill Sillman to be the next best to Jack Wright, who of course was recognised as one of the best in the country.

Between them Cyril and Arthur ran the club every evening, and in the daytime it was opened by Pop Greenwood or Arthur's wife. We spent most of our winter evenings at the club and it was always full during the holidays, even in summertime, often with six at a table playing crash, golf or shell-out.

The Mens' Own had seven or eight teams in the Billiards league but snooker was gaining popularity, and two Town Champions were spawned at the club: John Clark and Bob Clark.

A further flight of steps led to the table tennis room with two tables separated by a heavy curtain, and the Boston team often played their matches there. The team then was John Dyer, "Chelsea" Howard and Ron Croft with later Terry Venters and Wendy Blades.

During the past few years many of the old established sports and social clubs have closed down in Boston. Only last year the Besco club closed but fortunately it has become the new home of the British Rail club, who lost their previous clubroom on the station platform.

In 1999 Norprint Social Club was demolished, and all the societies and organisations that had used it for many years for their annual functions were left to scout around for alternative venues. A year or two before that the Boston & District Motor Cycle and Light Car Club had also closed.

As secretary of the local Billiards and Snooker League all these closures made life more difficult, especially towards the end of the season, when thirty-two tables are needed at the start of the Snooker Team Knock-out. We had already lost the use of the Pump Square Snooker Club tables in 1994, and earlier those at the Boston Health Services Club at the Conference Centre at Pilgrim Hospital; the Waveney Club above the Co-operative shop on the corner of Wyberton Low Road; the Indoor Bowling Club down Roseberry Avenue and the United Social (Bus) Club, who played in the former Chapel on the corner of Station Street and Tower Street.

Over the years several players ran teams from their private houses with various degrees of success: Geoff Ferguson had the White House Club at Fishtoft; Brian Hutson had Sanderstead down Horncastle Road; Tommy Horn ran the Fydell Street Antiques Club and they won the top division of the Snooker League in 1978/79, and Shane Gray's J.S.G. Club down Broadfield Lane headed the main division in 1987/88.

With Keal Coates having to close this season, no village teams remain north of Boston. Old Leake, who at one time had four teams no longer take part, and Stickney dropped out. South of Boston however, it is a different story: teams from Wyberton, Graves Park, Kirton Leisure Centre, Sutterton, Donington and Gosberton all play in our leagues.

When I first played in the league in 1948 the Conservative Club was then above the New Theatre Cinema; the Indoor Bowling Club was above Gratton's later moving down Threadneedle Street; the United Social Club was down Church Lane, where Robinson's chemist shop is now and there used to be clubs at St. James in George Street and the Waverley Club, above Brough's tailors shop in High Street.

From the records of past winners right back to 1913/14, there have been other clubs but I do not know the venues: Civil Defence, Gas Company, St. Botolphs, Beaulah Institute, British Legion, Seamans Institute and LNER, which obviously became British Rail.

Each part of Boston recalls distinct memories of their own. I can never walk past Fish Hill, the area immediately in front of the Assembly Rooms, without imagining I can hear the unique call of a newspaper seller, who graced that spot for many years.

I never knew his name, but every afternoon he did his paper round in record time, never running but taking giant strides and his head used to jerk backwards and forwards like a sand-dancer. Every ten seconds he would cry in his own distinctive way: "LINCOLNSHIRE EC...ho" and the "ho" would drift away, almost inaudible.

On completion of his rounds he would stand on the pavement in front of Fish Hill and sell his papers, until there were no more prospective customers.

He reached his zenith every Saturday evening, when he sold copies of the Football Echo as fast as the lads could bring them from the office in High Street. He was in competition with sellers of the Nottingham Evening News and the Grimsby Telegraph, but he covered the pavement between Harvey Gill's and the Benefit shoe shop like an electric eel, and he must have sold more than the other two put together.

On Sundays Fish Hill became a meeting place for the Salvation Army: they marched from the Citadel and formed a circle in front of the Assembly Rooms to sing their hymns and address the crowd.

For many years one of their stalwarts was Fan Taylor, who lived with her married sister down Pulvertoft Lane. Today anyone born with a hare-lip has an operation while still young, and there is little sign of their misfortune as they grow older, but, when Fan Taylor was born, there was no option but to live your life and carry on regardless.

This Fan certainly did, and her experience with the Salvation Army no doubt stiffened her fortitude, for she never hung back from selling "The Young Soldier" in the pubs and her voice could be heard above the band on a Sunday.

Innocent cruelty, peculiar to children, gave her the sobriquet "Icky Oy" but she never bore them any malice and seemed to enjoy their proximity, as she sang her hymns with gusto.

One of the regular hymns was responsible for her nick-name: "It be joy, joy, joy; it be joy to their young ears sounded like "Icky Oy, oy, oy; icky oy".

When I left the Boston Grammar School in 1950 to work at the Boston Guardian, I was told by Mr. Skepper, the editor, that I was replacing Peter Denman, who had gone to do his National Service in the R.A.F.

It was another 45 years before I actually met Peter, when he visited me with a mutual friend. I was saddened to hear recently that he had died at the age of 65.

I wonder if his neighbours in Laceys Lane, Leverton, realise what a full and varied life he lived in those 45 years.

He told me he was born in Brothertoft, where his father had a drag-line, but he was educated at Horncastle Grammar School because he lived with his grandparents.

He did his R.A.F. training at Wilmslow and was then posted to Spittalgate as a chef. After completing his National Service, he went to Grimsby and joined the Merchant Navy and enjoyed 19 glamorous, adventurous years serving with liners, travelling between Australia, Bermuda and the Pitcairn Islands.

His experiences during those years would fill a book, but he was only 39 when he left the Merchant Navy and began his life as a salesman.

His first job was selling double glazing for an American company and he proved to be a naturally gifted salesman: in fact he was the company's salesman of the year and he had to fly to Los Angeles to receive an award of £10,000.

Over the next ten years his jobs varied between selling chippers to fish and chip shops, selling mincing machinery to butchers, and he even landed the contract to supply all the ice cream to Butlins at Ingoldmells.

Peter had bought a bungalow in Punchbowl Lane and, when the value of property jumped so spectacularly, he took the chance to sell it and buy a semi-detached house in Langrick Road, and the £25,000 surplus enabled him to retire.

After a fall down the stairs, Peter sold his house and moved to the bungalow in Laceys Lane, Leverton, where he spent his last years happy in his garden.

What did Boston have fifty-one years ago that it has not got today? The answer is a Repertory Theatre. It was run by Dennis Franks and Phyllis Myerson, and gave performances at the Assembly Rooms Monday, Tuesday and Wednesday from 7.15 p.m. with a matinee on Wednesday at 2.30 p.m.

The plays were usually produced by Kenneth Monk and the stage management was usually in the hands of Kathleen Love. The regular company consisted of Dennis Franks, Kenneth Monk and Kathleen Love, already mentioned, plus Anne Summers, Ronald Bailey and Dawn Charatan. If the plays had more than six characters, local amateur actors or actresses were recruited.

The variety of the weekly programme can be illustrated by detailing the fare offered over five weeks in 1950. On week commencing 16th January the play was "The Two Mrs. Carrolls" by Martin Vale, which had been filmed in 1947 with Humphrey Bogart, Barbara Stanwyck and Alexis Smith. In the story an artist meets a new love while holidaying in Scotland, then returns to London and poisons his wife. He marries his new flame but soon meets another attractive girl.

In a complete change of genre, for the week commencing 6th February they put on a farce, "Is Your Honeymoon Really Necessary?" by E. V. Tidmarsh. "Dangerous Corner", the famous play by J. B. Priestley was the programme for 20th February, in which a group of friends gather for a party and discuss how different their lives would have been, if they had all told the truth years ago about a theft and suicide.

Beryl Pope, a Boston girl, who worked at the County Hall, appeared in all three of these productions. Local firms advertised in the programme every week but only the Trustee Savings Bank remains. The others were: A. Walker Ltd., the High Street ironmonger, Harvey Gill, the Tudor Restaurant, Ron Diggins, Herring's Taxis, J. W. Pearson & Son, the hairdressers and E. M. Valentine, the West Street fruiterer.

In the programme for 20th February Keightleys announced that there would be a Mannequin Parade held in the Assembly Rooms on March 20th, 21st and 22nd.

Until 1946 all boys and girls, who did not pass to go the High School or Grammar School, stayed at their primary schools until they were fifteen. The boys then from the age of ten or eleven went to St. John's School, but the girls continued their education at the various primary schools.

St. John's School was by no means ideal, as some of the boys were in classrooms on the third floor, and it overlooked the workhouse and the temptation to watch the inmates must have interfered with lessons.

On Saturday, 10th February, 1951 Kitwood Girls' School was opened by George Tomlinson, the Minister of Education, so girls had a brand new secondary school to attend apart from the High School.

Mr. Tomlinson was introduced by Alderman E. Wrisdale, the Chairman of the Holland County Education Committee, and the School Governors were present together with A. W. Newsom, B.A., the County Education Officer. The first Headmistress was Miss. E. Scorer.

The boys finally left St. John's School, when Kitwood Boys' School was opened on the 18th March, 1954. Kitwood Girls' School was in Marion Road, but Kitwood Boys' School was in Mill Road on the Woad Farm Estate.

The dedication and opening were performed this time by Alderman O. B. Giles, D.L., Chairman of the Holland County Council, but Alderman E. Wrisdale was again present as Chairman of the School Governors, accompanied by A. W. Newsom B.A., the County Education Officer.

The Service for Prayer for the new school was conducted by the Rev. A. H. Howard, Rector of Skirbeck and the Rev. V. C. Ibbotson, Minister of the Zion Methodist Church. Two appropriate hymns were sung: "He who would valiant be" and "I vow to thee, my country".

Others present included Coun. J. Henry Mountain, Vice-Chairman of the School Governors; Coun. E. H. Porcher J.P. the Mayor of Boston; Coun. T. S. Meir, a School Governor and Leonard Smith, the first Headmaster of Kitwood Boys' School.

For twenty-five years, from 1926 to 1951, no teacher struck more fear into the hearts of boys at Boston Grammar School than Frank Ronald Gilbert Bastick, known to them all as 'Bill'. He had gained his B.A. at London University, after attending Grammar Schools at Crewkerne, Sherborne and Southampton and, before coming to Boston, he had taught at Uttoxeter, Sedburgh and on Anglesey.

He was a first class teacher of English Language and English Literature, as the examination results over the years of his pupils will testify. He was also organist and choirmaster at Kirton Parish Church from 1926 to 1947. After leaving Boston under a cloud in 1951, he taught at Grammar Schools at Frechville (Sheffield), Knighton and Bishop's Castle in Shropshire, where he had been born.

A few years ago John Porcher and his wife, Janet, took the opportunity while visiting the Shrewsbury Flower Show, to go to Bishop's Castle and look for 'Bill' Bastick's resting place, for they had received a newspaper cutting from a friend telling of a memorial service for F. R. Bastick, who had been the organist at the parish church.

They could find no headstone in the churchyard, but the charming lady vicar checked the records and found that he had been cremated and no memorial existed at the church. They made enquiries in the local pub, 'The Six Bells' however, and were introduced to a Dave Richards, who told them that 'Bill' had taught him music in his schooldays up to professional standards.

He informed them that a Dr. Penny had bought 'Bill's house and converted it into flats, and he actually lived in one. He explained that 'Bill' Bastick was locally held in high esteem as both a teacher and musician, and in his memory Dr. Penny had named his flats, BASTICK HOUSE.

Later they met a charming lady of 94 sitting on a seat in the square in the middle of the small market town, and she told them that Ronald Bastick had taught her daughter music and she, herself, had been taught by his father, who had been even more strict than 'Bill'. She and her husband had attended many a civic function, at which 'Bill' had been playing.

Janet and John followed her directions and found the house and actually spoke to Dr. Penny's father, who confirmed the high regard 'Bill' had earned in his own home town. Janet took John's photograph standing next to the plaque, proclaiming No. 1 BASTICK HOUSE. There was a memorial for 'Bill' after all.

Peter Luff was one of six boys, who left Staniland School in 1944 to go to Boston Grammar School. The others were Victor Emery, Peter Day, Noel Holgate, myself and Gordon Butcher, who unfortunately was killed in an accident with a coal lorry at the top of Frampton Place in 1945.

Peter lived down Woodville Road and his father was an engine driver. At that time their house was one of the last, before fields separated the Forty Foot banks from the buildings, but since then the whole area has been developed and it is now difficult to imagine how it used to be. Peter ran the Meccano Club from his house and his mother allowed her home to be overrun regularly by a horde of enthusiastic schoolboys.

When Peter left the Grammar School in 1952, he served his National Service in the R.A.F., and spent four years at Cambridge University then joined the Colonial Service and became a District Officer in Northern Rhodesia.

His first post was at Kalomo, a town seventy miles north-east of Livingstone and the Victoria Falls. The administrative district was roughly the size of Wales and was divided into six native chief's areas, each with about a hundred villages, so Peter was kept busy, because government policy was that every village in each chief's area should be toured once a year by a member of the administration, and there were only three of them.

Peter would set out from District Headquarters with sixteen native carriers and a posse of tribal policemen. He always took a flagpole and a Union Jack, which was erected in front of his tent each day. Each tour lasted from two to three weeks and he generally covered from ten to fifteen miles a day, depending on whether the rough, narrow, sandy bush tracks could be negotiated by bicycles or on foot. At each village Peter had to collect taxes, keep an up-to-date census, review the work of the Native Court and help people with their grievances and complaints.

The temperature in the shade was 100 degrees Fahrenheit or above, and the romantic picture conjured up of scenes from such films as "Sanders Of The River" were far from the truth. The constant dust that Peter had to endure made him happy to reach camp at the end of each day and soak in a welcoming bath.

Since I was born the only Christmas I have not spent in Boston was in 1952. I travelled to R.A.F. Padgate on the 28th April that year with Charles Wright from Old Leake to start my National Service and, after square-bashing at R.A.F. Hednesford, I was posted to Kirton-in-Lindsey and spent the rest of my two years coming home most weekends. That Christmas however, I was on Fire Picket.

Being on camp at Christmas had its compensations; especially as there was a tradition that the officers served the lads with their Christmas Day dinner. I still have the menu today, signed on the back by ten others, who were on various duties and sat at the same table. The food was a definite improvement on that served most days: cream of tomato soup was followed by fried fillets of fish and game chips, then roast turkey and Yorkshire ham with roast and creamed potatoes, brussel sprouts and garden peas; Christmas pudding and brandy sauce, mince pies, cheese and biscuits, fruit and nuts. The last line of the menu read: beer, minerals and cigarettes.

I forget how many cigarettes we received each but I gave mine to Alan Marshall from Leeds, who was demobbed the following Easter and died two months later. During his short life he must have smoked thousands of cigarettes, so the two or three I gave him that day would hardly have contributed to his fate.

He was a brilliant footballer and was good enough to play for a League team, but the only lad on the camp who actually played for a club was Alec Orr, who had regularly played for Queens Park, the Scottish amateur club who played their games at Hampden Park. Most of the airmen on duty that Christmas were Scots, as they preferred to go home for Hogmanay.

By the time Christmas 1953 came round, I had been in the R.A.F. long enough to make sure I was not on duty. In fact I came to Boston with Flight Lieutenant Gunnell and his wife, who had relations in our area and were kind enough to give me a lift, and even bought a Christmas cake off my father. He was the officer in charge of the Progress Section, where I worked, and he and his wife did not live in the Officers Married Quarters but in a caravan on the airfield perimeter.

When did two ex-pupils of Boston Grammar School play football against each other at Wembley? The answer is December, 1953 in the Inter-Varsity match. From 1952 to 1987 all the matches been Cambridge University and Oxford University were played at Wembley.

Mike Pinner played in goal for Cambridge and J. W. (Johnny) Smith played outside left for Oxford. The following year, 1954, Mike Pinner was still in goal for Cambridge and he captained the team, but Johnny Smith now played left back for Oxford. As a matter of interest the centre half, playing alongside Johnny for Oxford University in 1954 was Frank Bough, the former television presenter.

It is probable that Mike Pinner had also played in the first Inter-Varsity match at Wembley for Cambridge University in 1952. He also played in goal for England's amateur team and was playing for Aston Villa at the time of the Munich Air crash but he transferred to Manchester United to help them, after the tragedy.

Johnny Smith lived down Westfield Avenue when he attended Boston Grammar School, and was a close friend of Dick Parkinson, who lived near the top of Woodville Road. They were both members of the Grammar School football and cricket teams, with Dick being a deadly fast bowler and Johnny a slow left-arm spin bowler. Dick Parkinson joined William H. Brown, the estate agents and auctioneers, eventually moving from Boston to Wisbech, and Johnny Smith stayed on at the Grammar School and then was accepted at St. Edmund Hall College at Oxford. After graduation he studied geology.

Michael Pinner gained a B.A. degree at Emmanuel College, Cambridge and went on to have a successful career in the law.

I received confirmation of the Inter-Varsity matches from Laurie Veale, who was himself at Queen's College, Oxford and played for the University football team. Laurie came to Boston Grammar School in 1952 and was appointed deputy headmaster in 1967. When Philip Johnston resigned as headmaster in 1977, Laurie was the acting headmaster, until Arthur Shrimpton was appointed in 1978. Laurie retired from Boston Grammar School in 1988.

Compared with fifty years ago, what is missing from the roads on a Friday and Saturday especially in Lincolnshire? The answer is hitch-hikers. When National Service existed thousands of servicemen, mainly airmen in this area, flooded the road verges and pavements, trying to get home as quickly as possible to spend as much of the weekend as they could with family and friends.

At the time two years out of your life seemed a pointless waste, but in retrospect it was time well spent and the experience was invaluable. It certainly widened your circle of friends; not that many life-long friendships were forged but you always remember those who shared your triumphs and tribulations, while you were being transformed from a faint-hearted sprog into a self-confident dodger of duties, taking advantage of every available skive.

When given the choice most local boys tried to join the R.A.F., because there were so many camps in Lincolnshire you stood a good chance of being posted near home, as it saved money on travel warrants. After square-bashing, when you were posted to a permanent camp, you found that most National Servicemen lived within a radius of fifty to sixty miles, except for a handful of Scots, who were unlucky as there were very few camps in Scotland. They always stayed on camp at Christmas and went home for the New Year, and they usually obliged if you were on duty at the weekend: they could not go home, so they were willing to do you a turn for an appropriate fee.

There was a certain art in hitch-hiking. You solicited more sympathy from the motorist, if you were actually walking instead of just standing, exercising your thumb. The exception to this was in a town; it made sense to position yourself a little way from a road junction, so that a driver had not picked up speed and it was less trouble for him to brake. Many a time, especially if it were raining and a car not only did not stop but splashed you as it sped past, the urge to shout "I hope your back wheels fall off" proved irresistible, but all was forgotten as soon as some kind soul took pity on you.

Your troubles were not always over, after you had been picked up. My friend, Roy Barton, while reminiscing with me recently, recalled the time when he was heading for Boston from his camp near Norwich, and a vicar picked him up. He said he could take him as far as King's Lynn and Roy sat in front with him, thankful that he would soon be half-way home. There were two children in the back however, and every time they came up behind another car they beseeched their father to pass it and go faster, which he did. Roy had not taken any notice before but the vicar was wearing glasses with extra thick lens, and he was leaning over his steering wheel with his face just an inch or two from the windscreen, peering through the glass. Roy said that was the worst journey he ever had and when they arrived in King's Lynn, he shot out of the car as fast as he could.

31st January, 1953: If you were alive and living on the east coast of England, you will remember exactly what you were doing. It was one of those days. It was one of the worst floods since the major flood in 1571, which was indelibly impressed into local history by Jean Ingelow's "High Tide On The Coast Of Lincolnshire".

Many lives were lost and much damage was done all along the east coast that day. Thousands of caravans and mobile homes were destroyed, and Mablethorpe was especially badly affected. Homes alongside the river in Boston were flooded, and the water at the Sluice Bridge poured into Norfolk Street and caused confusion.

I was in the Royal Air Force at the time, stationed at Kirton-in-Lindsey and all weekend leave was cancelled. The personnel from the numerous R.A.F. camps in Lincolnshire were all called out to the coast to repair the damage already done, and to try and prevent further damage. We were allotted the stretch of the North Lincolnshire coast between Great Coates and North Coates. Our lorry pulled up almost opposite Scibbans-Kemp biscuit factory.

The road did not run right up to the sea bank, so the lorry had to make its way along the headland of a field then turn at right angles into another field, which led to the bank. The floods had been caused by a record high tide coinciding with a period of very heavy rain, so the fields were very muddy and, if a vehicle strayed off the headland, it was a difficult job to retrieve the situation.

The criminal destructions of the hedges separating fields and giving shelter to birds and small animals had not been thought of in those days, so it was impossible for a vehicle going towards the sea bank to see another coming away, until it was too late and, as there was no room for them to pass each other, there was a huge delay, while one of the drivers had to reverse very carefully.

As a rule it does not pay to volunteer in the forces but, when the sergeant asked for a volunteer, I stepped forward immediately, anticipating his needs. The result was that, instead of spending the next two days and nights filling sand bags at the sea bank, I stood with a red flag at the L-junction of the two fields, making sure that there were no delays due to two vehicles meeting in the muddy fields.

When we finally arrived back at camp, all my mates fell onto their beds exhausted with aching backs, and I could find no-one who would have a game of table tennis.

Freddie Trueman celebrated his seventieth birthday recently, and a large proportion of his treasured possessions were sold by auction, including the cricket ball he used to take his record-breaking three hundredth test wicket. Watching him being interviewed on Yorkshire Television reminded me of the day I watched him playing....football, not cricket.

He was in the R.A.F. and was stationed at R.A.F. Hemswell, when I was posted to R.A.F. Kirton-in-Lindsey, about ten miles up the road. The two stations played each other one Wednesday and Fred played centre forward for Hemswell and scored a hat-trick. He was an old-fashioned centre forward; the kind who head straight for goal every time they receive the ball, and woe betide anyone who tried to stop him. As you might expect, he was very popular with his team-mates and was just one of the lads: you would not have thought that he was already considered to be one of the best fast bowlers of all time. While at R.A.F. Hemswell he played centre forward for Lincoln City Reserves.

R.A.F. Kirton-in-Lindsey was an Initial Training Station for pilots and navigators, and the cadets used Tiger Moths while on their course. I was Documentation Clerk, so every three months when a new flight came in, I had the job of helping them complete numerous forms. Many of the cadets had come from universities and several were sons of Sultans or Heads of States, but most of them hated filling in forms and some of the answers caused amusement back in the Progress office. Our office collated details of each cadet's progress during their three months, and if they passed their course I had to send their documents to their next station, so I became familiar with the names of most R.A.F. stations in the country. I often wonder how many have survived.

If a cadet failed narrowly, he was re-flighted and spent another three months at Kirton-in-Lindsey but, if he failed for a second time, his career as a pilot or navigator was over, and he had to settle for something less glamorous. Some interesting people passed through during the time I was there, but the cadets were kept separate form the camp personnel, so there was little chance to talk with them. The son of Sir Frank Whittle, the inventor of the jet engine was a member of one flight, and as you might expect, he did quite well. Only one Bostonian did his initial training while I was in control of the documents, and that was Gerald Hopper.

My earliest memory of local dramatics was going to Blenkin Memorial Hall to see Oliver Goldsmith's "She Stoops To Conquer". It must have been soon after the war, because I was still at the Grammar School. Our headmaster was a member of the Boston Playgoers' Society and, although I did not see "The Man Who Came To Dinner", I remember reading in the local papers glowing accounts of Leslie Waddams superb performance.

My sister was a member of St. James's Drama Society, so I was forced to see all their productions. They were lucky to be directed by A. J. Willard, who had professional experience and I knew most of the members: Jack Cole, Lesley Sutcliffe, Fred Welbourne, Ken Sharman, Martin Varcoe, Peter Day, Dick Leafe, Sidney Burgess, Terry West, and the ladies Doreen Bycroft, Lavinia Whalley, Madge Smith, Kate Luck, Valerie Kinsey and Margaret Ingram, whose performance as the Queen in "A Mirror To Elizabeth" is one of my lasting memories. St. James's Hall was a fine venue for their plays and I have never understood why such a hall and a church like St. James's were ever demolished.

Since 1964 my main interest has been in the productions of the Boston Operatic Society, which for the first six years were exclusively Gilbert and Sullivan, before "Merry England" broke the sequence. In the 36 years to 2000 they have performed "The Mikado" and "The Pirates Of Penzance" four times, "H. M. S. Pinafore", "The Gondoliers", "Patience", "The Yeoman Of The Guard" and "Iolanthe" twice, and "Ruddigore", "Utopia Ltd." and "Trial By Jury" once. "Trial By Jury" was actually their first operetta in 1964 but it is really too short to make a programme by itself.

My personal preference is for West End shows or film musicals, and over the years they have performed many of these: "Oklahoma!", "Fiddler On The Roof" and "South Pacific" twice, and "Carousel", "The Boyfriend", "Hello Dolly", "My Fair Lady", "Kiss Me Kate", "Show Boat", "Brigadoon", "The King And I", "Charlie Girl", "Anything Goes", "The Pajama Game", "West Side Story", "Cabaret", "Annie Get Your Gun", "Oliver" and "The Sound Of Music". Their repertoire has also included old favourites: "White Horse Inn" twice, "The Merry Widow", "Lilac Time", "Perchance to Dream and "Bless the Bride". Last year "Scrooge was very successful.

There are still many musicals they have not attempted and some probably present too many difficulties. For example "The Music Man" would require finding 76 trombone players and an extra strong stage. More seriously here are a few that would probably attract big audiences: "Gigi", "Kismet", "The Band Wagon", "Guys And Dolls", "Camelot", "Flower Drum Song", "Rose Marie", "The Student Prince", "The Vagabond King", "The Desert Song" and "King's Rhapsody".

There is little wonder that the recent mess of the month featured two properties in High Street. Fifty years ago that stretch of High Street between Fydell Crescent and the Goods Yard had three bakers, two butchers, three grocers, three barbers, three cobblers, two potato merchants, two builders, a glazier, a newsagents, a monumental mason, two fish and chip shops and four pubs.

If at that time the proposed by-pass with a bridge over the river between the dock and what is now the London Road pumping station had been built, High Street could have remained the busiest street in the town instead of the run-down area it became.

The inner-relief road with the Haven Bridge dissecting High Street completed the deed, but the die was cast in 1965 when it was decided to put yellow lines along High Street. They were then the vogue and were respected and feared for several years not largely ignored as they are today.

My father had moved to Boston from Kettering with his parents in 1904, and over the following fifty years they built up their bakery business to include a café in West Street and three delivery vans, which served 60% of the houses in Wyberton and a good proportion of those in Boston.

Soon after I came out of the R.A.F. in 1954 my father was persuaded by Cyril Valentine to stand for the town council as a Liberal, and he represented the South Ward until 1969. In those days councillors did not receive a penny, not even expenses, but my father enjoyed it and was a good councillor, in so far as he was always accessible not only to anyone with a problem, but also to Mr. Coley if he needed a councillor to countersign a document or letter.

His feeling of betrayal and despair was understandable, when the proposal to place yellow lines down both sides of High Street was made by none other than Cyril Valentine. One by one the formerly successful businesses had to close: our shop closed in March, 1969; my mother died in May and my father's health forced him to resign from the council.

It will soon be time again for the Academy Awards Ceremony to present this year's Oscars; a date which in the past has sometimes brought excitement to local families.

On March the 25th 1985 at the Dorothy Chandler Pavilion in Los Angeles County Music Centre, Jim Clark won the Film Editing Oscar for the 1984 film THE KILLING FIELDS.

At the same venue on April 9th 1979 Barry Spikings won an Oscar as one of the producers of the Best Film for 1978, THE DEER HUNTER.

Both these achievements were well recorded at the time, but another local man who has never received the accolades he deserved, was closely concerned with the film that won four Oscars at the Santa Monica Civic Auditorium on April 13th 1964. TOM JONES was named as Best Film for 1963, and also won the awards for Best Script, Best Score and a Best Director Oscar for Tony Richardson, whose Assistant Director was Gerry O'Hara.

The experience inspired Gerry and in 1965 he wrote and directed THE PLEASURE GIRLS with Ian McShane and Francesca Annis, which was successful enough to lead to him directing Gene Barry and Cyd Charisse in MAROC 7 in 1967, and then in 1968 he directed AMSTERDAM AFFAIR, a film about the Dutch detective Van Der Valk.

He returned to writing in 1969, and received good reviews when he filmed his own script for ALL THE RIGHT NOISES, which featured Tom Bell and Judy Carne.

Apart from the cinema Gerry was very busy writing and directing episodes of THE AVENGERS, MAN IN A SUITCASE and THE PROFESSIONALS for television.

In 1977 Gerry went to Canada to direct the film of Anne Mather's novel LEOPARD IN THE SNOW with Susan Penhaligon, Kenneth More and Billie Whitelaw.

When Joan Collins revitalised her career by filming her sister, Jackie's books, it was Gerry, who in 1979 wrote the script for and directed THE BITCH.

He received widespread recognition for writing and directing the very popular television series, CATS' EYES.

When the book, FANNY HILL, was made famous or infamous by a trial in 1965, the director, Russ Meyer, made a film version in Germany, but it was Gerry O'Hara who made the more successful version in 1983, starring Oliver Reed and Shelley Winters.

His long career as a writer and director speaks for itself, but perhaps an even greater measure of his worth is the list of famous directors, who have chosen him as their assistant, including Otto Preminger and the doyen of them all, David Lean.

Scriptwriter and Film Director Gerry O'Hara was not the only member of his family with a talent for writing. His brother Geoff, has brought pleasure to many people throughout the British Isles but, strange as it seems, his literary ability would never have blossomed but for an epidemic of foot and mouth disease.

In 1965 horse racing was curtailed and finally cancelled, because the epidemic prevented horses being moved around the country. Apart from half the male population walking around with a glazed look on their face and nothing to talk about, another serious consequence of this disaster was that The Sporting Life had nothing with which to fill their pages.

There was a limit to how far they could stretch the cards and selections for the greyhound race meetings, and they were desperate to find something to persuade regular readers to keep buying their daily copy.

Cometh the hour;   cometh the man: Geoff O'Hara submitted a story to The Sporting Life about a fictitious punter, who with his friends shared adventures which were crazy enough to be very entertaining, but were also feasible enough for the reader to imagine himself involved in similar escapades.

He called his hero Brogan. The Sporting Life welcomed Brogan with open arms and asked Geoff to provide them with regular stories. At the time he ran a betting shop at the rear of Shodfriars Hall, but with no horse racing his wife, Mary, could manage with their staff, so, while the emergency lasted, he wrote daily episodes and soon punters were turning to Brogan's page before they checked the dogs.

By time the restrictions on the movement of horses were lifted, Brogan had become so popular that The Sporting Life made room once or twice a week for their readers to keep abreast of his adventures.

In fact Geoff kept writing about Brogan for fifteen years and, when he finally finished in 1980, the Brogan story was still a popular feature of the Saturday edition of The Sporting Life.

About this time Geoff became busy helping his brother, Jim O'Hara, to run the Snax Club, which later became the Pump Square Snooker Club.

The foundation stone of Boston Parish Church was laid in 1309, and in 1969 a Festival Fortnight was organised to celebrate the 660th anniversary of Boston Stump.

The Festival was opened with a civic service at St. Botolph's Church with an address by the Bishop of Lincoln, then on Tuesday the 17th June, which was St. Botolph's Day, there was a special Children's Festival Service.

A programme of events was planned to interest people of all age groups, centred mainly in and around Boston Stump. There were various recitals and concerts in the Parish Church, featuring amongst others the Salvation Army Band, the R.A.F. College Cranwell Band and the Lincoln Cathedral Choir.

A Historical Association lecture entitled "Boston in the 14th Century" was given by Dr. Carus Wilson. A Choral Society Concert included Haydn's "Nelson Mass" and Purcell's "Te Deum" and there was also a Flower Festival.

A highlight of the fortnight was a procession through the Market Place on Wednesday the 18th June, of the cast in full costume of Benjamin Britten's "Noye's Fludde", including Owen Brannigan, Sheila Rex and a large number of children from local schools. Two performances of the work were given the following day in Boston Stump.

On Sunday the 22nd June the Southwold Jazz Band gave a jazz recital, and on Thursday the 26th June there was a Rotary and Police Gala Dance at the Starlight Room.

The whole town seemed to be involved; the Boston and District Chamber of Commerce organised a Shopping Fortnight with over 60 shops arranging demonstrations and shows, and there was a window display competition; the Witham Sailing Club put on a special course for beginners; students of Boston College produced a concert; local scouts had a camp fire at West Skirbeck house; several cricket and hockey matches were arranged, and the Lawn Tennis Club had an Open Tournament, while there was a Swimming Gala at the Boston Pool.

The Rev. David Scott was the Vicar of Boston at the time of these celebrations, and the Mayor was Coun. George Whitehead, who two years previously had been elected people's warden at St. Botolph's.

Jim Fossitt, who was in the same class as my brother at Boston Grammar School, starting there in the middle of the war, 1942, has been connected with Kirton Town Football Club for over fifty years, first as a player and then secretary. He has also been Chairman of Graves Park Social Club for over twenty-five years, and is clerk to Kirton Parish Council.

One foggy afternoon in the early 1970s he had a grim but memorable experience. He was waiting at the level crossing at Drainside South in Kirton and the lady controlling the gates explained that she could not open them, as she had an indicator telling her there was a train approaching her section.

It became obvious something was wrong, so Jim, who had trained as a journalist when he first left the Grammar School in 1947, went to the next crossing up the line, which was at Sutterton Dowdyke.

The sight awaiting him through the fog was horrendous. Again it was a lady gatekeeper and she had opened the gates to let the 'dilly' cart through just as the train had reached her crossing. The 'dilly' cart and its contents had been thrown onto the gatehouse and the train had dragged a body quite a way up the track.

The driver of the cart was at the side of the track with a head injury, so the body was that of his mate. Jim saw a boot near the crossing but, when he was about to pick it up, he realised a man's foot was in it.

He walked across the track to see if there was anything he could do, but met a doctor coming from the train and he said he had declared the unfortunate mate dead, and nothing could be done. The memories of that tragic foggy afternoon are still vivid in Jim's mind to this day.

If there were a controversial incident in a televised football match today, instant play-backs can be shown from all angles, to decide if the referee has made a mistake. In 1971 such an incident occurred in the league match between Leeds United and West Bromwich Albion, and it was seen by millions on 'Match Of The Day' that Saturday evening.

Near the end of the match a W.B.A. player broke clear of the Leeds defence and passed for Geoff Astle to score the winning goal. The whole Leed's team, most of the crowd and, I believe, the commentator all thought the player was off-side, but the referee gave a goal.

That referee was Bostonian, Ray Tinkler, and he is still adamant today, that the winger was in his own half when the ball was passed to him, so he was definitely on-side. With no play-backs at that time, his decision could not be verified immediately, and it was a talking point for many weeks.

Ray was on the Football Association Referees List from 1960 to 1976. He was a linesman at Wembley for the 1962 cup final between Spurs and Burnley, and refereed the amateur cup final in 1971. He refereed matches abroad at Prague, Ajax in Holland, Kaiserlauten, Barcelona, Milan, Genoa (Sampdoria), Florence (Florentina) and Rome (Lazio).

Ray has been on the Lincolnshire F.A. committee for thirty years, and has been Vice-Chairman. He has also been the Lincolnshire representative on the F.A. Council since 1993. He received a gold medal from the F.A. in1998 for fifty years service.

Ray entered Boston Grammar School from Staniland School in 1940 and left in 1945 to work for E. W. Bowser, where he was company secretary for over forty years.

During the war and for several years after the war, there used to be an annual one mile swimming race up the River Witham from approximately Upsall's boat-house towards Hall Hills. A crowd of people used to watch from both banks of the river and between ten and twenty swimmers used to compete.

The first time I witnessed the race from a popular position near Dr. Shaw's Ken Johnson from the Silver Spray fish shop in Liquorpond Street was the winner, but the next year my friend, Victor Emery, entered and won comfortably. I think he was fifteen then and he won the race subsequently every time he entered.

He was a regular member of the very successful water polo team, that at the time went several seasons unbeaten. When he left Boston Grammar School, he went to Hull University and gained a B.Sc. in mathematics in 1954. Later in 1957 he earned a PhD in theoretical physics from the University of Manchester.

He was a research associate in the Cavendish Laboratory in Cambridge from 1957-59, then went to the University of California at Berkeley. He returned to England in 1960 and was a lecturer at the University of Birmingham until 1963. In 1964 he took a post as an associate physicist at Brookhaven Institute in New York, receiving tenure in 1967. He was promoted to senior physicist in 1972 and from 1981-85 he was the Chairman of the Laboratory's Physics Department.

In March this year at a meeting in Seattle, Washington, Victor was presented together with Alan H. Luther from Copenhagen, with the Oliver E. Buckley prize for 2001 from the American Physical Society. Victor Emery and Alan Luther, who share the prize of 5,000 dollars, did the work twenty-five years ago, and today it is considered to be of crucial importance for understanding high-temperature superconductors, about which Victor is a world authority.

I was sorry to hear from Graham Smith, whose father Colin lives in Swineshead, and who also holds tenure at Brookhaven, that Victor Emery is suffering from an illness that necessitates him working in a ground floor office, and I am sure his many friends in Boston will wish him well.

On the last Sunday in September, 1921 the War Memorial on Bargate Green was unveiled by the Earl of Yarborough, dressed in a khaki uniform with scarlet-banded hat and ivory-hilted sword.

In his speech he paid a warm tribute to the fallen, and the great sacrifice they made for the liberty and freedom not only of Great Britain and the Empire but of the whole world.

The work had been carried out by Messrs. S. Sherwin & Son of Boston at a cost of £2,000, which had been raised by public subscription. It was built of Portland stone, raised upon a platform with canted angles four steps above the ground level, the bottom step being brought forward with seats at each of the four angles. It was a worthy monument to the 300 local heroes, who gave up their lives in the Great War.

A military parade was preceded from the Market Place by the band of the 4th Lincolnshire Territorials, playing a funeral march, and the bandsman later stood near the monument and accompanied the hymns.

A large number of ex-servicemen assembled on the Green with the relatives of the fallen assembling near the tank. The elementary schoolchildren were assembled in Bargate. A guard was formed of the local Territorials and two sailors stood as sentinels, with arms reversed at the corners of the memorial, the panels of which were screened by the Union flag.

Three vollies were fired and the band played the Dead March in Saul, then the National Anthem. The Mayor on behalf of the Corporation placed a large laurel wreath at the foot of the memorial, and numerous floral emblems were laid there by other public bodies and by relatives and friends of the fallen.

In 1859 to be qualified to register to vote a man had to own property and have at least £10 to his name. Each vote was recorded publicly and the newspapers printed the names of everyone who voted and which candidate they chose. The papers also printed the names of those, who did not use their vote and the reason they did not do so.

At that time Boston had two Members of Parliament, and the successful candidates were Herbert Ingram and Meaburn Staniland, both Liberals, with J. H. Hollway, a Conservative unsuccessful. The next year however, when Herbert Ingram tragically died in America, John Wingfield Malcolm, a Conservative, won the by-election from G. P. Tuxford, a Liberal.

The Conservative Lord Derby remained as Prime Minister, but lost a vote of confidence and Lord Palmerston returned to the post and formed a Liberal government.

At the General Election of 1865 John Wingfield Malcolm headed the poll at Boston, and Thomas Parry just beat fellow-Liberal, Meaburn Staniland into second place. Mr. Staniland, however, petitioned the result, alleging that many voters had been bribed by Mr. Parry. Eleven votes for Mr. Parry were scrutinised and disallowed, so he was unseated and Meaburn Staniland was reinstated as Member for Boston.

Lord Palmerston had remained as Prime Minister but three days before his 81st birthday in October he died, and was succeeded by Earl Russell with William Gladstone as leader of the Commons. The Reform Bill of 1866 would have enlarged the electorate by giving the vote to many working men, but the Liberal government was defeated and Earl Russell resigned. Lord Derby returned as a Conservative Prime Minister but he retired in 1868 and Benjamin Disraeli was named as his successor.

In March, 1867 Meaburn Staniland surprised everyone by accepting the Chiltern Hundreds and in the resulting by-election Thomas Parry was returned unopposed.

A General Election was called in November, 1868 and, whereas only approximately 1,600 voted in Boston in 1865, this time about 4,300 voted. For the first time two Conservatives were elected; John Wingfield Malcolm and Thomas Collins Junior, beating two Liberals; Meaburn Staniland and Mason Jones.

In the country as a whole, however, the Liberals scored an overwhelming victory and William Gladstone was asked by Queen Victoria to form his first government.

The first election to be held by secret ballot in this country was the General Election of February, 1874. The Liberal government of William Gladstone was defeated and the Conservatives with a majority of 83, their first majority since 1841, were returned to power, led by Benjamin Disraeli.

Once again Boston voted contrary to the country on the whole, and elected W. James Ingram and Thomas Parry, who defeated the two Conservatives, J. Wingfield Malcolm and Thomas Collins Jnr.

William Gladstone became Prime Minister for the second time, when the Liberals won the General Election in April, 1880. At that time the natural life of a Parliament was six years.

Thomas Garfitt, who had been elected unopposed at a by-election in August, 1878, headed the poll in Boston. He was a Conservative and the Liberal, W. James Ingram was the other successful candidate. G. F. Rowley (Con) and S. Buxton (Lib) were unsuccessful.

In the budget in 1885 the Liberal government proposed to increase the tax on beer and spirits, and nationwide petitions including one from Glasgow with 700,000 signatures, led to their downfall, and Lord Salisbury formed a Conservative government and called a November election.

A Redistribution Bill had been passed and both Lincoln and Boston had been reduced to one member. Boston's population was recorded as 18, 863 and the registered electors numbered 2,787. Liberal candidate, W. James Ingram won with 1,295 votes against 966 for the Conservative, N. Learoyd, so 526 electors did not use their vote.

Neither Lord Salisbury nor Gladstone held a majority, and in January, 1886 Lord Salisbury's minority government was defeated on an amendment to an Irish Bill. William Gladstone formed his third government but, when his Irish Home Rule Bill was defeated in June, it split the Liberal party with 93 voting against the government.

In the resultant General Election in July, 1886 the breakaway MPs stood as Unionists, and there was a coalition government with the Conservative, Lord Salisbury as Prime Minister and Lord Hartington leading the Unionists. In Boston a Conservative, H. J. Atkinson defeated the former Liberal member, W. James Ingram.

In July, 1905 the Conservative Government proposed a redistribution of Parliamentary seats: each municipal borough or urban district with a population over 65,000, would become a separate constituency but the number of seats would remain at 670. Before the Bill was passed, however, Arthur Balfour resigned his Government.

He had become Prime Minister in 1902, succeeding his uncle, Lord Salisbury, who had led the coalition Government of Conservatives and Liberal Unionists since 1886, winning the General Election of 1895 with an increased majority. Sir W. James Ingram, who had been knighted since the last election, again stood for the Liberals in Boston, but he again lost to the Conservative candidate; this time W. Garfitt.

Lord Salisbury again slightly increased his majority at the General Election in 1900. The country was in the middle of fighting the war against the Boers in South Africa, and Winston Churchill, who had been a war correspondent was elected to represent Oldham for the Conservatives. In Boston, Conservative, W. Garfitt was returned and the Liberals were represented by W. T. Simmonds.

Three years after Lord Salisbury retired, his nephew, Arthur Balfour struggled to stay in power, when the Conservatives split over Free Trade. He finally resigned his Government in December, 1905, and Sir Henry Campbell-Bannerman opted to call an election. In January, 1906 he won the General Election for the Liberals and became Prime Minister but, advised by his doctors, he resigned on April the 5th, and died on April the 21st., still living at Downing Street.

The King sent for Herbert Asquith and he was appointed Prime Minister, and he promoted David Lloyd George to Chancellor of the Exchequer and Winston Churchill, who had joined the Liberals, to President of the Board of Trade. In the resultant by-election Churchill lost his seat in Oldham (now North West Manchester) but he was returned to Parliament, after winning another by-election in Dundee in May.

1910 was an unusual year in that it saw two General Elections. In January, Herbert Asquith had problems with the House of Lords, when they threw out his Government's budget. This had occurred in the previous October and, after adjourning the House for a month, he announced a General Election, seeking a mandate to reform the House of Lords. He lost his overall majority but with the support of 40 Labour members he struggled on for eleven months, before calling another General Election in December.

W. Garfitt had lost his seat in Boston to the Liberal candidate, G. H. Faber in 1906, but the Conservatives regained it in January, 1910, when C. H. Dixon won against the Liberal, H. S. Lunn.

The Suffragettes were a major problem for Herbert Asquith, after the General Election in December, 1910 and the question of Irish Home Rule was tearing the north and south of Ireland apart. He only remained in power with the aid of the Irish Nationalists. Before another General Election could be called war was declared in 1914, and the main parties formed a Coalition Government with Asquith still Prime Minister.

In 1916, however, after a much-publicised disagreement with David Lloyd George, Asquith resigned his Premiership but remained leader of the Liberals. After the war an Election was quickly arranged for December the 14th, 1918, and for the first time women had the right to vote, and the whole country voted on the same day. The ballot boxes however, remained sealed until December the 28th, to allow members of the armed forces returning home to vote.

The local constituency was now called Holland with Boston and there was a sensation, when William Stapleton Royce, a JP from Pinchbeck, who was President of the Unionist Association (Conservatives), was adopted as the Labour candidate and won the seat by over 1,000 votes from Major E. Belcher, Conservative. He was Boston's first and only Labour Member of Parliament and held the seat for six years.

Sixteen women were candidates at this General Election and Countess Markieviez became the first women to be elected, but she was the Sinn Fein member for St. Patrick's Dublin, and like the other 72 Sinn Fein members she did not take her seat, so Lady Astor, who won the seat at Plymouth, became the first woman to actually sit in a British Parliament.

David Lloyd George thought the Coalition should continue until the country was back on its feet, but Asquith wanted the Liberals to return to being a separate party. In the event Lloyd George became Prime Minister of a Coalition Government and Asquith lost his seat at East Fife. Ramsay MacDonald, who as Labour leader said that Great Britain should not have gone to war, also lost his seat.

The Coalition Government finally collapsed in 1922 and a General Election was called for November the 15th. Although there were 335 Conservatives and only 133 Coalition Liberals in the Government, Lloyd George, a Liberal, had been Prime Minister and at a meeting of the Conservative M.P.s a resolution was passed to dissolve the Coalition.

William Stapleton Royce held Holland with Boston for Labour but with a reduced majority from Sir H. Fairfax-Lucy (Conservative), and E. S. Agnew (Liberal). Out of a local electorate of 41,700, there were 15,500 women.

When David Lloyd George resigned as Prime Minister of the Coalition Government in 1922, King George V sent for Mr. Bonar Law and asked him to form an administration, but first he had to be elected leader of the Conservative Party.

There were three separate Liberal parties, so it was no surprise when the Labour party emerged as the official opposition. Prime Minister Bonar Law died on October the 30th, 1923, and Mr. Stanley Baldwin was elected leader of the Conservative Party and became Prime Minister. He called a General Election on November the 17th, because his policies differed from those of Bonar Law and he wanted a mandate.

The Conservatives remained in power but with a minority government. William Stapleton Royce won the local seat for the third time but he died the following year, and at the by-election held on July 31st 1924 Mr. A. Wellesley Dean won for the Conservatives beating the Labour candidate, Dr. Hugh Dalton, later to achieve fame, by 800 votes with R. P. Winfrey, Liberal, a respectable third.

Earlier in January, 1924 Mr. Baldwin's government had been defeated in a vote of no-confidence, and for the first time in British history the leader of the Labour Party, Mr. Ramsay MacDonald, was asked to form a Government. It lasted only until October, when they lost the necessary support of the Liberals, and there was another General Election on October 29th, which resulted in a landslide victory for the Conservatives, and Stanley Baldwin was back as Prime Minister. A. Wellesley Dean increased his majority to nearly 5,000 over Labour, whose candidate this time was G. R. B. White with the Liberal, R. P. Winfrey again bottom of the poll.

In spite of the General Strike, Baldwin's Government survived until May 30th 1929, because of their large majority, but at the General Election they were beaten by Labour, who, however, needed the support of Lloyd George's Liberals to remain in office.

Mr. A. Wellesley Dean died on February 7th 1929, so there was a by-election in Holland with Boston two months before the General Election. As a result of the General Strike, the Conservative candidate, F. J. Van Den Berg, finished third, beaten by the successful Liberal, Jimmy Blindell, and G. R. Blanco-White, the Labour candidate. A fourth candidate, Frank W. Dennis of Frampton Hall, stood as an Independent Agriculturist and received 3,706 votes, just over a tenth of the poll.

Two months later at the General Election, Jimmy Blindell again was successful but this time the Conservative, F. J. Van Den Berg, was second and the Labour candidate, C. E. Snook, was third.

The General Election of October 27th 1931 was caused by the collapse of the world economy. The Labour Government of Ramsay MacDonald introduced a new Land Tax in their 1931 budget, and the Liberals under Lloyd George attempted to amend the tax and this led eventually to the resignation of the Government. A new all-party National Government was formed and Ramsay MacDonald remained as Prime Minister.

The TUC disagreed with the Government policy and this split the Labour Party, resulting in Ramsay MacDonald facing his own party on the opposition benches, led by Arthur Henderson. When the General Election was called, the candidates lined up as National Conservatives, National Liberals and National Labour against Labour and Liberals. The National Government won easily and, in spite of there being 470 National Conservatives and only 13 National Labour members, Ramsay MacDonald remained Prime Minister until June 7th 1935, when he exchanged jobs with Stanley Baldwin, who had been Lord President of the Council.

Jimmy Blindell stood as a National Liberal in Holland with Boston, and had a majority of 21,000 over his only opponent, H. J. Parker (Labour). At the next General Election however, again facing only a Labour candidate, E. E. Reynolds, his majority shrunk to 12,000. This election, held on November 14th 1935, resulted in Stanley Baldwin remaining as Prime Minister of a National Government, but it consisted of 387 Conservatives and just 33 National Liberals and 8 National Labour.

On May 10th 1937 Jimmy, (now Sir James) Blindell was killed in a motoring accident, and at the by-election on June 24th another National Liberal, Herbert V. Butcher, had a 7,000 majority over the Labour candidate, again E. E. Reynolds. On May 27th Stanley Baldwin had retired and Neville Chamberlain had replaced him as Prime Minister.

After war broke out the National Government became a Coalition Government, but the Labour Party still sat in opposition. Following the disastrous Norwegian campaign, the Labour Party on May 11th 1940 agreed to join the Coalition as long as Neville Chamberlain resigned. This he did and he was replaced by Winston Churchill, who thankfully remained as Prime Minister throughout the war. This Parliament had lasted ten years, when he resigned on May 23rd 1945, and had seen three Kings on the throne: George V, Edward VIII and George VI.

The General Election after the Second World War was held on July 5th 1945, but the votes were not counted until July 25th. An additional 25 seats were added to the new Parliament, making 640 in total and Labour won 393, giving Clement Attlee the opportunity to form the first-ever majority Labour Government.

By February 23rd 1950, the date of the next General Election, the country was disillusioned and disappointed, and Clement Attlee's large majority had shrunk to a wafer-thin six members. Herbert W. Butcher was elected for Holland with Boston at both these elections: first with a majority of 5,600 against A. E. Monks, the Labour candidate, then in 1950 with a majority of 8,000 against H. W. Lee, the Labour candidate, and Mr. Blankley for the Liberals. In 1945 Mr. Butcher stood as a National Liberal but by 1950 he stood as a National Liberal and Conservative.

After struggling for twenty months the Labour Government called another General Election on October 25th 1951, and a turnout of 82 per cent led to a victory for the Conservatives, and Winston Churchill returned as Prime Minister. Herbert W. Butcher again won Holland with Boston as a National Liberal and Conservative with an 8,500 majority over the Labour candidate, Janet Walters.

Winston Churchill retired as Prime Minister on April 5th 1955, so Sir Anthony Eden was Prime Minister when the General Election was held on May 28th 1955, and the Conservatives returned with an increased majority. Margaret Thatcher entered Parliament for the first time as the member for Finchley, and on December 7th Clement Attlee resigned as leader of the Labour party, after a record twenty years. In Holland with Boston newly-knighted Sir Herbert Butcher enjoyed a 9,000 majority over W. A. Rippon, the Labour candidate, and local businessman and councillor, Cyril Valentine, polled 5,581 votes for the Liberals.

Sir Anthony Eden retired as Prime Minister through ill health on January 9th 1957 to be replaced by Harold Macmillan, who, after a period of prosperity and Britain's best-ever balance of trade figures, increased the Conservative Government's overall majority to 100 at the General Election, held on October 8th 1959. Cyril Valentine again represented the Liberals at this election and this time polled 7,334 votes, but Sir Herbert Butcher was once again returned with a majority of 11,000 over J. D. Williamson, the Labour candidate.

Harold Macmillan decided to step down as Prime Minister, when he entered hospital on October 10th 1963, and Lord Home became the first peer to accept the Premiership for 61 years, but he could not sit in Parliament, so he renounced his peerage and won the Kinross by-election as Sir Alec Douglas-Home.

Harold Wilson became Prime Minister after Labour won the General Election, held on October 15th 1964 but with a tiny majority, so he called another General Election on March 31st 1966 and increased his majority to 98. Sir Herbert Butcher won the local contest in 1964 with a majority of 5,600 over the Labour candidate, W. Long, but he stood down in 1966 and Richard Body won the Holland with Boston seat as a Conservative, but his majority over R. H. Hickman, the Labour candidate, was only 316.

INDEX

	PAGE
R. J. ABBOTT	360
ABINGDON	320
"BAGGY" ABLARD	194
ABU KLES	293
ACADEMY AWARDS	391
ADAM	61
ADAM'S SCHOOL, FREISTON	275
W. H. ADAMS	291
J. W. ADDELSEE	126
ADEN	293
H. H. ADKINS	195
ADULT SCHOOL	123
THE ADVENTURE	152
A. E. C. BUSES	338
E. S. AGNEW	407
AIR TRAINING CORPS	366
AJAX	399
MRS. AKEHURST	88
ALDERSHOT	172
GRAHAM ALEXANDER	93
ALFORD	47, 230, 252, 341
ALFORD GRAMMAR SCHOOL	231, 278
ALFRED THE GREAT	246
ALGARKIRK	331
ALLAM & PERKINS	62
ALLAN HOUSE	124, 125, 341, 342, 343
BOB ALLEN	52, 353
JOHN ALLEN & COMPANY	295

NANCY ALLEN	*51, 353*
RUBY ALLEWELL	*186*
MARGARET ALLGOOD	*84*
ALLIED DUNBAR	*39*
ALPINE CLUB	*305*
BILLY ALTOFT	*194*
AMBER HILL SCHOOL	*40, 122*
AMBERGATE	*301, 302*
CHARLES AMCOTTS	*270*
AMPLEFORTH	*328*
AMSTERDAM	*225*
LORD ANCASTER	*321*
ANCHOR HOTEL (MARINE)	*294*
CHARLES ANDERSON	*285*
CHARLES FRANCIS ANDERSON	*285*
E. B. ANDERSON & CO.	*285*
F. S. ANDERSON & CO.	*307*
TIMOTHY ANDERSON	*284*
ANDERSON HOTEL	*305*
ANDERSON SHELTER	*305*
ANDERTON'S HOTEL	*320*
EWAN ANDREW	*335*
MARJORIE ANDREWS	*67*
MICK ANDREWS	*67*
ANGEL INN, SUTTERTON	*192*
ANGLESEY	*378*
FRANCESCA ANNIS	*392*
ANNE	*227*
ANTON'S GOWT	*214*
ANWICK PLACE	*108*
A. P. CRANE HIRE	*299*
TAYE APPLEBY	*51, 353*
ARABIA	*310*

ARCHAEOLOGY SOCIETY	*200*
HMS ARK ROYAL	*13*
ARGYLE STREET	*107, 178*
ERIC ARNOLD	*98*
MRS. ARNOLD	*98*
SIR WILLIAM ARMINE	*261*
ARSENAL	*183*
HMS ARTHUR (BUTLINS)	*182*
ARTILLERY ROW	*332*
ASDA	*345*
MR. ASH	*161*
ASHBOURNE	*286*
BERYL ASHLEY	*51, 353*
ALAN ASHTON	*236*
BENNY ASHTON	*181*
VIOLET ASHTON	*41, 51, 353*
ASHTON'S CARPET SHOP	*64*
ARTHUR ASKEY	*10*
HERBERT ASQUITH	*405, 406, 407*
ASSEMBLY ROOMS	*62, 63, 120, 326, 372, 373, 376*
GEOFF ASTLE	*398*
ASTON VILLA	*183, 198, 199, 383*
LADY ASTOR	*406*
ARTHUR ATKIN	*40, 201, 370, 372*
MRS. ATKIN	*370*
MR. ATKINSON	*118*

	PAGE
H. J. ATKINSON	*404*
RAY ATKINSON	*118*
ATHERTON	*231*
ATLANTIC	*163, 225, 256, 257, 276*
A.T.S.	*168, 170*
CLARENCE ATTERBY	*132*
CLEMENT ATTLEE	*335, 362, 410, 411*
AUGUSTA	*292*
BERYL AUPIN	*120*
SKIP AUSTIN	*16*
AUSTRALIA	*235, 236, 265, 283, 374*
JOHN AYRE	*273*
LEW AYRES	*126*
SIR EDWARD AYSCOUGH	*259*
BACUP	*153*
BADAJOS	*310*
GEORGE BAGLEY	*54, 59, 72, 81*
EDWARD ARTHUR BAILEY	*319*
RONALD BAILEY	*375*
TOM BALDERSTON	*57, 322*
BALDING COURT	*81*
ARTHUR BALFOUR	*404, 405*
STANLEY BALDWIN	*408, 409, 410*
JIMMY BAKER	*6*
BATTLE OF BALACLAVA	*310*

BANK STREET	*323*
A. BANKS	*126*
JOHN BANKS	*268*
JOSEPH BANKS	*235, 236*
BAPTIST CHURCH	*73, 76,*
	147
BARCELONA	*398*
BARCLAYS BANK	*41, 147*
J. BARDERSON	*309*
BARDITCH	*271*
BARDNEY	*224*
BARGATE BRIDGE	*101, 166,*
	361
BARGATE END	*101, 126*
BARGATE GREEN	*50, 101,*
	400
BARGE INN	*271*
BARHAM HOUSE OF BROKEN CROSS	*283*
GORDON BARKER	*82*
MR. BARKHAM	*108*
MICK BARNFIELD	*67*
BARNSLEY	*152*
GENE BARRY	*392*
TOM BARRAND	*178*
BARBARA BARTON	*354*
BARRY BARTON	*66*
CHARLES BARTON	*354*
GEORGE BARTON	*31, 354*
ROY BARTON	*65, 106,*
	354, 355,
	385
TED BARTON	*354*
BARTON-ON-HUMBER	*299*

	PAGE
MISS. BARWICK	79
BASEBALL GROUND	49
BASS STRAIGHTS	236
GEORGE BASS	236
BASTICK HOUSE	378
FRANK RONALD GILBERT (BILL) BASTICK	27, 378
THOMAS BATEMAN	268
BATH GARDENS	96, 327
HORACE BATTRAM	212
BATTLE OF BRITAIN MEMORIAL FLIGHT	357
FREEMAN BAXTER	159, 160, 328
JOCK BAYNE	48
BAY OF NAPLES	275
BAYUNDA DESERT	293
BEAST MART	321
BEDFORD	136
BEDFORD'S MILL	14
WILLIAM BEDFORD	341
DR. BEE	22, 36
BEAULAHS	165
GERALD BEAULAH	58
JOHN BEAULAH	87
BEAULAH INSTITUTE	372
BEATRICE	303
THOMAS BECKET	264
BEDFORD PLACE	166
JOHN BEDRYJCHUK	120
JUNE BEECHAM	182
RON BEECHAM	181, 182
BELCHFORD	196
EILEEN BELL	119
GEORGE BELL	42, 49
PETER BELL	42

STAN BELL	*178*
TOM BELL	*392*
BELL INN	*249*
MAJOR ERNEST ARTHUR BELCHER	*334, 335, 406*
RICHARD BELLINGHAM	*232, 233, 256*
BELVOIR CASTLE	*260*
MR. BEMBRIDGE	*187*
BERBERA	*293*
BENEFIT SHOE SHOP	*373*
LORD CHARLES BERESFORD	*293*
BERGEN OP ZOOM	*47, 355*
BERKELEY	*399*
LAWRENCE BERKELEY NATIONAL LABORATORY	*217*
BERMUDA	*357, 374*
MONTAGUE BERTIE	*260*
ANNIE BESANT	*278*
BESCO CLUB	*298, 370*
BEVERLEY	*213*
BICKER	*204*
BIMBO	*91*
BIRMINGHAM STOCK EXCHANGE	*·286, 307*
BIRMINGHAM UNIVERSITY	*217, 399*
BIRMINGHAM	*8, 138*
BISHOP OF LINCOLN	*73, 201, 274, 289, 395*
BISHOP'S STORTFORD	*236*
BISHOP'S CASTLE	*378*
BARBARA BLACKWELL	*89*
THE BLACK BULL	*23*

PAGE

RAY BLACKBURN	69
MURIEL BLACKBURN	132
BLACKFRIARS LONDON	279
BLACKFRIARS THEATRE	212
BLACK PRINCE	248
BLACK SLUICE	270, 304
AGNES BLACKAMORE	157
AMABILIA BLACKAMORE	157
BARBARA BLACKAMORE	157
BASIL BLACKAMORE	264
BILL BLACKAMORE	190
CHARLES BLACKAMORE	190
ERNEST BLACKAMORE	186, 346
ELLEN BLACKAMORE	190
IAN BLACKAMORE	158
IRENE BLACKAMORE	9, 364
JAMES BLACKAMORE	157
JOHN BLACKAMORE	157
LOUISA BLACKAMORE	84, 121, 122, 156, 345
MATTHEW BLACKAMORE	157
NELLY BLACKAMORE	188
NELLY BLACKAMORE JNR.	186
MARY BLACKAMORE	346
OLGA BLACKAMORE	158
OWEN BLACKAMORE	158
RICHARD BLACKAMORE	158
ROBERT BLACKAMORE	84, 157, 189, 344, 345
WILFRED BLACKAMORE	346
WILLIAM BLACKAMORE	157

WENDY BLADES	*41, 370*
BLACKBURN ROVERS	*154*
WILLIAM BLACKSTONE	*229, 230,*
	257
BILL BLAKE	*212*
CLAUDE BLAKEY	*217*
PETER BLANCHARD	*35*
MRS. BLAND	*107*
HAROLD BLAND	*214*
MR. BLANKLEY	*411*
GEORGE BEATSON BLENKIN	*276, 307*
BLENKIN MEMORIAL HALL	*60, 364,*
	388
JIMMY BLINDELL	*409, 410*
BLINDELL'S SHOE SHOP	*200*
DR. BLEWETT	*235*
THE BLUE LION	*181*
BLUE STREET	*107*
BLYTH	*227*
BOADICEA	*239, 240*
BOAR WAR	*319, 404*
B.O.C.M.	*96*
RICHARD BODY	*412*
HUMPHREY BOGART	*376*
BARBARA BOGGS	*54*
FRED BOHN	*188*
BOLINGBROKE CASTLE	*248, 262*
SIR GEORGE BOLLES	*254*
BONAR LAW	*407, 408*
SIR THOMAS BOOR CROSBY	*254*
PETER BOND	*218*
FANNY SUSANNAH BONTOFT	*285*
WILLIAM BONTOFT	*285*

BOND STREET	*10, 101*
CATHERINE BOOTH	*286, 287*
WILLIAM BOOTH	*287*
BOOTS	*36, 68*
WALTER SYDNEY BOOTH	*277*
"BINKY" BORDER	*25*
CHARLEY BORRILL	*178*
FRANK BORRILL	*194*
FRED BORRILL	*177*
FRANK BORZAGE	*127*
BOSTON	*325*
BOSTON AMATEUR DRAMATIC COMPANY	*282*
BOSTON & SKIRBECK IRONWORKS	*282*
BOSTON AUTOCAR COMPANY	*305*
BOSTON BOYS	*197*
BOSTON COLLEGE	*288, 396*
BOSTON CRICKET CLUB	*53, 107, 214*
BOSTON BRASS BAND	*302*
BOSTON & DISTRICT CHAMBER OF COMMERCE	*396*
BOSTON DEEP SEA FISHING COMPANY	*188, 361*
BOSTON EAST INFANTS SCHOOL	*313*
BOSTON GUARDIAN	*54, 291, 308, 343, 374*
BOSTON HEALTH SERVICES CLUB	*371*
BOSTONIAN HOSPITAL	*188, 189*
BOSTON LIBRARY	*328*
BOSTON LONG FENNE-END	*283*
BOSTON & DISTRICT MOTOR CYCLE & LIGHT CAR CLUB	*371*
BOSTON MOTORS	*43, 73*

BOSTON, MASSACHUSETTS	*208, 239*
BOSTON OPERATIC SOCIETY	*389*
BOSTON UNITED	*47, 48,*
	82, 107,
	131, 154,
	198, 202,
	355
BOSTON WEST INFANTS SCHOOL	*313*
EVE BOSWELL	*203*
BOSTON PLAYGOERS SOCIETY	*60, 282,*
	388
BOTANY BAY	*235*
BOTOLPHSTOWNE	*242*
FRANK BOUGH	*382*
THE BOUNTY	*289*
BOURNE	*84*
BOURNEMOUTH	*308*
E. W. BOWSER	*398*
BOWSER'S PARK	*246*
BOY	*179*
BOZEATS	*185*
BOSTON GRAMMAR SCHOOL	*14, 24,*
	25, 37,
	59, 62,
	64, 65,
	66, 81,
	87, 93,
	123, 136,
	160, 179,
	192, 193,
	194, 197,
	200, 203
	209, 210

	PAGE
	213, 214,
	217, 219,
	256, 268,
	275, 276,
	278, 290,
	306, 316,
	320, 342,
	353, 358,
	360, 364,
	366, 374,
	276, 378,
	379, 380,
	382, 383,
	388, 396,
	397, 398,
	399
FRED BRACKENBURY	*166*
JACK BRACKENBURY	*166*
MR. BRADLEY	*55, 363*
ANNE BRADSTREET	*234*
SIMON BRADSTREET	*234*
ARTHUR BRAIME	*71, 92*
LOUIS BRAIME	*71*
MAVIS BRAIME	*132*
BRADFORD ROAD	*113*
WILLIAM BRADFORD	*225, 227,*
	228
ANNIE BRAND	*321, 322*
LOTTIE BRAND	*321, 322*
OWEN BRANNIGAN	*395*
CLIFF BRANT	*204*
CECIL BRANT	*84*
EILEEN BRANT	*84*

NORMAN BRAY	*142, 146, 154*
TED BRAY	*54*
"WHIPPET" BRAY	*31*
BRASENOSE COLLEGE, OXFORD	*250*
FLIGHT SERGEANT "HAPPY" BREED	*140, 144, 145*
WILLIAM BREWSTER	*223, 224, 225, 227*
BRIDGE FOOT	*106, 108, 295*
BRIDGE STREET	*202, 215, 249, 284, 365*
BRIDGE STREET, LINCOLN	*330*
JACK BRIGHTWELL	*99*
MRS. BRIGHTWELL	*99*
STELLA BRIGHTWELL	*99*
SHIRLEY BRINKLEY	*119*
BRITANNIA INN	*21, 239*
BRITISH LEGION	*372*
BRITISH RAIL	*179*
BRITISH RESTAURANT	*86, 223, 332*
BRITISH RAIL CLUB	*41, 201, 298, 370*
BRISTOL	*142, 213, 300, 338*
W. BRITTAIN	*309*
BENJAMIN BRITTEN	*395*
JOHNNY BRITTON	*42*
BRIXTON	*287*

BROADFIELD LANE	*113, 297, 371*
BROADFIELD STREET	*5, 107, 113, 117, 182, 183*
ELIZABETH BROCKLESBY	*157*
GEORGE BROCKLESBY	*53*
BROADSTONE, DORSET	*213*
JAMES BROOKS BROOK	*310*
RUPERT BROOKE	*357*
BROOKHAVEN NATIONAL LABORATORY	*218, 399 400*
BRIAN BROOKS	*205*
GEOFF BROOKS	*57, 322, 366, 367*
BROGAN	*394, 395*
BROTHERTOFT	*270, 277, 374*
BROTHERTOFT ROAD	*67*
MRS. BROUGH	*24*
BROUGHS	*41, 201, 372*
MR. BROOMFIELD	*47*
LAURENCE BROWN	*351*
WILLIAM H. BROWN	*92, 383*
ROSEMARY BROWN	*42*
LORD BROWNLOW	*255*
BROWN'S BARBERS SHOP	*77*
PAMELA BROWN	*5*
TONY BROWN	*67*
BROWN'S GROCERY SHOP	*354*
BROWN'S YARD	*101*
BRYANT & MAY (MATCHGIRLS STRIKE)	*278*

LIEUTENANT BRUCE	*310*
DORA BRYAN	*351*
HYACINTH BUCKET	*9*
BUCKNALL	*214*
BRUMBY	*233*
THE BULL, PINCHBECK	*255*
JAMES BUCK	*295, 296*
OLIVER E. BUCKLEY	*399*
J. L. BURCHNALL	*306*
R.A.F. BULAWAYO	*144*
BULLIVANTS	*64*
HARRY BULLOUGH	*80*
HUGH BURDEN	*5*
MRS. BURGESS	*73*
SIDNEY BURGESS	*60, 389*
FRED BURGESS	*77*
BURGESS PIT	*101*
BURGH-LE-MARSH	*252*
LORD BURGHLEY	*254*
BURMA	*358*
BURMESE EMPIRE	*310*
JOAN BURNS	*369*
BURNLEY	*47, 195, 398*
JOHN BUNYON	*249*
G. BURR, FLORIST	*346*
BUOY YARD	*101*
BURRELL CUP	*198*
JIM BURROWS	*77*
BURROWS & MARSHALLS	*76, 77*
FRANK BURT	*216*
BURT BROTHERS	*41*
BURTON CORNER	*214*

BURTON ALTONS — 117
BURTON HALL — 283
MR. BURTON — 25, 91, 191
CHARLES BUTLER — 53
BUTLER-BREWSTER — 165
HERBERT V. BUTCHER — 410, 411, 412
BURTON HOUSE — 51, 52, 352
BUTLINS — 374
BUTTERWICK — 177, 182, 194, 195, 196, 248, 263, 264, 274, 341, 361
CHARLES BUTTERY — 62
CHARLEY BUTTRUM — 120
GORDON BUTCHER — 14, 67, 87, 379
S. BUXTON — 403
DOREEN BYCROFT — 42, 43, 61, 389
SPRING BYINGTON — 83
JOHN BYNG — 242

SERGEANT CADWALLADER — 135
CAISTOR — 359
SIR RICHARD CALDER — 280
CALIFORNIA PLACE — 86
UNIVERSITY OF CALIFORNIA — 399
ALF CALLOW — 63

MISS. CALTHROP	*18*
JOHN GEORGE CALTHROP	*275*
CAMBRIDGE	*171, 176,*
	199, 301,
	336, 399
CAMBRIDGE, MASSACHUSETTS	*232*
CAMBRIDGE EXAM	*59, 160,*
	210
CAMBRIDGE UNIVERSITY	*256, 380,*
	382, 383
CAMMACK AND SONS	*337, 338*
ELSIE CAMMACK	*337*
FRANCIS ALFRED CAMMACK	*337*
FRANK CAMMACK	*337*
RICHARD CAMMACK	*338*
ROGER CAMMACK	*337*
SIDNEY CAMMACK	*337*
TONY CAMMACK	*338*
JOHN CAMMACK	*67, 235,*
	236, 337
JUDY CAMMACK	*239*
CAMMACKS	*97*
PETER CAMMACK	*210*
SIR HENRY CAMPBELL-BANNERMAN	*405*
AMY CAMUS	*369*
CANADA	*7, 122,*
	162, 163,
	311
CAMEO HAIRDRESSERS	*64, 352*
CANNOCK CHASE	*137*
CAPE COD	*227*
MRS. CAPPS	*177, 341*
CAPUA	*275*

R.A.F. CARDINGTON	121
JANET CARESS	237
CARLTON ROAD	101, 124, 178, 341
CARLTON ROAD SCHOOL	30
RONNIE CARROLL	203
CARRS	115
E. P. CARTER	100, 125
REV. DAVID CARTWRIGHT	42
MAJOR JOHN CARTWRIGHT	277
CARTWRIGHT'S SHOP	107, 117
MRS. CARVER	227
CARVER ROAD	113
JUDY CARNE	392
JOHN THOMAS CATER	166
THE CASE IS ALTERED	270
W. E. CAURINGTON	22
CAVENDISH LABORATORY	399
ALBERT HAROLD CAWOOD	305
CAWOOD HALL	254
CELERITY	279
CENTENARY METHODIST CHURCH	209, 289, 290
CENTRAL PARK	9, 39, 53, 126, 322, 332
CETEWAYO	293
MRS. L. K. CHAMBERS	328
CHAPEL HILL	270
CHAPEL OF EASE	72
CHAPEL PASSAGE	188
CHAPEL ROW	178
JOHN CHAPPELL	213, 236

DAWN CHARATAN	*375*
CYD CHARISSE	*392*
MR. CHAPMAN	*177*
NEVILLE CHAMBERLAIN	
410	
CHANCELLOR OF THE EXCHEQUER	*335*
MAGGIE CHECKLEY	*76*
MR. CHECKLEY	*76*
CHARLES RIVER	*229, 232*
CHELSEA	*211*
CHERRY WILLINGHAM	*142*
CAROL CHESMAN	*42*
ALAN CHESTER	*205, 355*
ALFRED CHESTER	*319*
CHEERS	*90*
CHESS LEAGUE	*200*
CHEPSTOW	*249*
CHERRY CORNER	*365, 368*
CHEYNEY STREET	*65*
CHICAGO	*292*
CHIGWELL	*156*
CHILTERN HUNDREDS	*402*
CHINDITS	*358*
MAURICE CHOAT	*69*
R. J. CHRISTIAN	*272*
CHRISTIAN MISSION	*287*
CHRISTIAN REFORMED CHURCH	*225, 226*
CHRISTMAS ISLAND	*252*
WINSTON CHURCHILL	*4, 128, 404, 405, 410, 411*
CHURCH LANE	*372*
CHURCH ROAD	*191*

CHURCH STREET	*185, 201*
CHURCH OF ENGLAND	*229*
CHURCH OF SCOTLAND	*168*
CIEPLINSKI	*49*
THE CITADEL	*372*
CIVIL DEFENCE CLUB	*41, 201, 372*
CIVIL SERVICE	*160*
CIVIL WAR	*226, 232, 258, 260*
HUGH CLANCY	*52, 54, 353*
BASIL CLARK	*221*
BOB CLARK	*41, 370*
CHARLES CLARK	*221*
GEORGE CLARK	*220*
GEORGE CLARK, BARBER	*77*
ERNEST CLARK	*221*
JIM CLARK	*392*
JOHN CLARK	*39, 41, 370*
STEWART CLARK	*221*
TOM CLARK	*221*
VERNON CLARK	*221*
MRS. CLARK	*220*
MR. CLARK	*60*
CLARKE'S SHOP	*107*
MR. & MRS. CLARKE	*98*
JOSEPH CLARKE	*87*
PETULA CLARK	*136*
CLARKE COURT	*179*
JEAN CLAY	*119*
JOHNNY CLAES	*211*

HILDA CLAYTON	*77, 79*
MICK CLAYTON	*149, 217*
RAY CLEMENCE	*197*
SIR HENRY CLINTON	*254*
JIMMY CLITHEROE	*131*
BRIAN CLOUGH	*50*
COACH AND HORSES (PLUMMERS)	*293*
WILLIAM COBBETT	*242*
G. G. COCKRILL	*125*
BARBARA CODD	*35*
BERNARD CODD	*35*
ENA CODD	*35*
WILLIAM CODDINGTON	*234, 256*
CLAUDETTE COLBERT	*129*
COLCHESTER	*193*
JACK COLE	*61, 389*
JOHNNY COLAM	*42*
MR. COLEY	*58*
J. & J. COLMAN	*155*
JACKIE COLLINS	*393*
JOAN COLLINS	*393*
THOMAS COLLINS JNR.	*402*
EVE COLES	*41, 51, 52, 353*
MISS. COLLINS	*24*
"TITCH" COLLINS	*29*
COLLETT AND COMPANY	*283*
BILL COLLISHAW	*194*
THOMAS COLLIS	*291*
LORD COMBERMERE	*310*
COMBINED CADET FORCE	*136, 193*
PERRY COMO	*368*
CONGREGATIONAL CHURCH	*307*

CONGREGATIONAL SCHOOLROOM 123
CONGRESS HALL, LONDON 286
CONINGSBY 8, 11, 143, 250, 340, 356, 357
R.A.F. CONINGSBY 357
CONEY'S CAFÉ 365
CONWAY SCHOOL 342
CONSERVATIVE CLUB 41, 132, 201, 372
BILL CONROY 115
RENE CONROY 115, 132
RITA CONROY 115, 132
STAN CONROY 115
CANON A. M. COOK 209, 223, 235
CAPTAIN JAMES COOK 235, 236, 252
JOSEPH COOK 87, 308
C. V. COOK 320
LES COOK 181
ALASTAIR COOKE 167
FRANCIS COOKE 227
MAJOR JOSEPH COOKE 324
GEORGE COOK 253
CO-OP 90, 159, 351
GARY COOPER 127
KEN COOPER 188
PHILIP COOPER 67
COPENHAGEN 399
BATTLE OF COPENHAGEN 280

ALICE CORCORAN — *119*

CORN EXCHANGE YARD — *220*

CORNWELL UNIVERSITY — *217*

CORNWALL — *170, 175, 176, 253*

CORPUS CHRISTI GUILD — *251*

CORNHILL LANE — *285*

CORUNNA — *310*

COUNTESS OF LINCOLN — *226*

COUNTY HALL — *44, 167, 376, 87*

COURT OF SEWERS — *316*

HARRY COWAN — *53*

NOEL COWARD — *127, 145*

JOSEPH COTTEN — *129*

COTTINGHAM — *154*

JOHN COTTON — *208, 229, 231, 232, 233, 234, 256, 257, 266, 276*

SEABORN COTTON — *208*

COTTON HALL — *266*

COTTON CHAPEL — *201, 266, 276, 359*

COWES — *229*

SIR THOMAS COWLEY — *266*

"CURIOUS" MR. COX — *27*

MARGARET COX — *96, 97, 99*

MARY COX — *97*

MILES COX — *97*

MRS. COX — *97*

CO-OP, WYBERTON	*371*
WILLIAM COWPER	*240*
COWBRIDGE	*52, 295*
COWBRIDGE FOOTBRIDGE	*330*
COVENTRY	*8, 250, 340*
JOHN CRABB	*123*
H. W. (HARRY) CRAMPTON	*126, 162*
R.A.F. CRANWELL	*53, 139*
R.A.F. CRANWELL COLLEGE BAND	*395*
MERANY CRAVEN	*85*
THE CRAZY GANG	*95*
BOB CREASEY	*3*
ROBERT E. CREASEY	*295*
MRS. CREEK	*187*
CRESSY HALL	*255, 259*
MR. CRASHLEY	*73*
C. CRICK	*125*
WILLIAM CRICK	*312*
CREWKERNE	*378*
RON CROFT	*41, 370*
J. CROFT	*126*
OLIVER CROMWELL	*232, 261, 262*
THOMAS CROMWELL	*251*
CROPLEY'S BLUE GLIDER BUSES	*341*
CROOKS FERRY INN	*38, 202*
ERIC CROSS	*213*
GEOFF CROSS	*69, 213*
KEN CROSS	*69*
CROWLAND	*261, 263*
CROWN INN	*263*

CROWN AND ANCHOR TAVERN	279
CROSS KEYS HOTEL	307
LESLIE CROWTHER	9
FREDDY CRUMP	212
CROYDON	336
JOE CUPPER	57, 322
CURRYS	98
ALAN CURTIS	67
CUT END	165
DAGLAN	367
DAIMLER	340
DAILY HERALD	363
DAISY DALE	76
HUGH DALTON	335, 336, 408
DALTONS	77
DAMASCUS	157
s.s. DANAE	308
MRS. DAMMS	90
DARBYS	78
GEORGE DARWEN	48
ELAINE DAVEY	85
AUSTIN DAVIES	13, 294, 295
ETHEL DAVIES	295
"TINY" DAVIES	98
STEVE DAVIS	6
GEORGE DAWSON	324, 325
MARINA DAWSON	119
MAURICE DAWSON	42
SHIRLEY DAWSON	119
DORIS DAY	132

LEN DAY	*199*
PETER DAY	*37, 39,*
	68, 89,
	379, 389
DAY'S CASH STORES	*10*
DANIEL DAY LEWIS	*6*
ARTHUR LESLIE DEAL	*284*
ERNEST JAMES DEAL	*215, 284*
ARTHUR WELLESLEY DEAN	*335, 336,*
	408, 409
DEAN OF ST. PAUL'S	*250*
DEAN AND CHAPTER OF LINCOLN	*359*
DANIEL DEFOE	*242*
PETER DENMAN	*374*
JONATHAN DENT	*253*
"SNODDY" DEIGHTON	*26*
De HAVILLANDS	*37, 68*
KARL DENVER	*369*
FRANK DENNIS	*17, 266,*
	409
WILLIAM DENNIS	*269, 333*
DENNIS'S BUSES	*339*
ROLAND DEPEAR	*49*
DERBY	*288, 299*
DERBY COUNTY	*49, 149*
LORD DERBY	*401, 402*
DEVON	*170*
DETROIT	*339*
DIAMOND TAG COMPANY	*221*
PROF. GEOFFREY DICKENS	*210*
DICKINSON'S SHOP	*2, 107*
DIDSBURY COLLEGE, BRISTOL	*211*
DIGBY	*253*

	PAGE
R.A.F. DIGBY	139
RON DIGGINS	376
C. H. DIXON	405
BENJAMIN DISRAELI	402
DOCK	100, 124, 158, 314, 315, 344, 346
DONCASTER	151, 297, 299
DONINGTON	236, 243, 261, 265, 371
DONINGTON CHURCH	265
LORD DONOUGHMORE	310
DOLPHIN LANE	101, 178, 195
DOOMSDAY SURVEY	246, 254, 264
DOWNING STREET	405
DOWLMAN'S	178
AGGIE DOUGHTY	119
DOUGHTY QUAY	73, 117, 118, 271
ALMA DOUSE	85
MRS. DOWLING	154
CAPTAIN DOWSON	193
DORCHESTER HOTEL	95, 96
D'OYLE CARTE OPERA COMPANY	138
SIR ALEC DOUGLAS-HOME	412
DRAINSIDE SOUTH, KIRTON	396
FRANCIS DRAKE	236

DRILL HALL	*136, 307,*
DRILL HALL (NEW)	*332*
DRING'S FACTORY	*188*
BRIAN DRINKALL	*193*
CHARLES DRURY	*131*
DUBLIN	*406*
THOMAS DUDLEY	*229, 232,*
	233, 256
EARL OF DUDLEY	*229*
DUDLEY CLOSE	*108*
DUKE OF CAMBRIDGE	*220*
DUKE OF WELLINGTON	*286*
DUKE OF YORK	*159, 180,*
	344
DUKE OF NORFOLK	*250*
SIR JAMES DUKE	*298, 302*
DUKE STREET	*107, 108,*
	117, 178,
	298, 364
DUKE'S HEAD	*117*
GEOFF DUNHAM	*68*
DUNKIRK	*114, 171,*
	232
BATTLE OF DUNBAR	*232*
DUNDEE	*405*
DURHAM UNIVERSITY	*219*
ARTHUR DURRANT	*56*
HARRY DWYER	*33*
JACK DUTHOIT	*48*
JOHN DYER	*370*
EARL OF SURREY	*250*
EARL OF CONINGSBY	*356*

FIRST EARL OF LINCOLN (CLINTON)   254
SECOND EARL OF LINCOLN
(SIR HENRY CLINTON)   254
THIRD EARL OF LINCOLN (THOMAS)   229
FOURTH EARL OF LINCOLN
(THEOPHILUS)   229
EARL OF MANCHESTER   262, 263
EARL OF NEWCASTLE   260, 261,
                                     262
EARL OF YARBOROUGH   297, 400
BARRY EASTICK   202
LT. COL. G. EAST-KING   333
EAST FEN   241
EAST FIFE   407
EAST KEAL   177
EAST KIRKBY   8, 21,
                                     176
EAST LINCOLNSHIRE RAILWAY   296, 301
EAST LANCASHIRE REGIMENT   171, 172
EAST YORKSHIRE REGIMENT   333
EAST STOKE   157
EASTVILLE   22, 35,
                                     177
DR. ECKFORD   125
BATTLE OF EDGEHILL   260
SIR ANTHONY EDEN   411, 412
EDINBURGH   174, 175,
                                     236, 363
EDMUND HALL COLLEGE, OXFORD   383
EDWIN STREET   12, 35,
                                     66, 118,
                                     120, 187,
                                     207, 354

LANGLEY EDWARDS	*270*
EGYPT	*293*
RIVER ELBE	*325*
GRAHAM ELKINGTON	*193*
BILLY ELLIOTT	*50*
CANNON ELLIS	*321*
LYN ELLIS	*319*
CHUCK ELSAM	*82, 107*
JACK ELSAM	*107*
ELSAM'S SEEDS	*114*
ELSAM'S SHOP	*107*
ELSTON	*157*
ELVEDON, SUFFOLK	*305*
HARRY ELY	*176*
VICTOR EMERY	*27, 37, 53, 67, 89, 154, 187, 217, 218, 361, 379, 399, 400*
EMMANUEL COLLEGE, CAMBRIDGE	*230, 231, 233, 383*
H. M. ENDEAVOUR	*235*
MR. ENDICOTT	*233*
ENGLAND FOOTBALL TEAM	*197*
ETHEL	*313, 314, 315*
CORPORAL EVANS	*135*
EVE	*61*
EDWARD EVERETT	*276*
MAVIS EVERETT	*82*
ROBIN EVERETT	*69, 81,*

EXMOOR 192
HMS EXMOUTH 13

G. H. FABER 405
F.A. COUNCIL 398
SIR HENRY FAIRFAX-LUCY BT 335, 407
FAMILY HISTORY 200
ANN FARMER 106
FARNBOROUGH 59, 160
FARNHAM 213
TONY FARROW 39
FARROW'S CANNERY 155
JOE FARUM 205
CHARLES FAULKNER 54
RON FAULKNER 69
BILL FAUNT 205
J. FAUNT 126
FEDERAL BUSES 339
JIM FELLOWS 236
FEN ROAD 216
FENSIDE 116, 162
FENSIDE ROAD 124, 360
MR. FERGUSON 26
GEOFF FERGUSON 371
FIELD STREET 5, 39, 180, 212
FIELD STREET MISSION 321, 322
LADY ARBELLA CLINTON FIENNES 230
LADY FRANCES CLINTON FIENNES 230
LADY SUSANNAH CLINTON FIENNES 230
FIGHTING SERVICES CANTEEN 364
ROY FINCH 154

FINCHLEY	*411*
FINGERINGHOE	*193, 194*
GODFREY FINN	*358*
THOMAS FINN	*309, 324,*
	325
R.A.F. FINNINGLEY	*151*
FIRE STATION	*180*
FIRSBY	*301*
THE FIRST AND THE LAST	*152*
FISHER CLARK & CO.	*100, 220,*
	222
FISHTOFT	*202, 231,*
	264, 361,
	371
FISHTOFT DROVE	*295*
FISHTOFT MANOR	*304*
FISHTOFT ROAD	*288*
FISHTOFT SCHOOL	*35*
FISH HILL	*372, 373*
THE FIVE BELLS, GOSBERTON	*255*
FIVES COURT	*194*
THE FIVE LAMPS	*274*
JOHN FISHER	*220*
FIORENTINO	*398*
FLANDERS	*338*
FLEET PRISON	*234*
FLEET STREET	*213, 320*
FLEETWOOD	*188*
C. B. (BERT) FLEET	*308*
DEREK FLETCHER	*205*
KATE FLETCHER	*111*
MICHAEL FLETCHER	*111*
MATTHEW FLINDERS	*236, 265*

SAMUEL FLINDERS 236
FLORENCE 398
DR. R. C. FLOWER 125
FLYING FORTRESS 364
ERROL FLYNN 19, 127, 128
E. FOGARTY & CO. 68, 123, 286
EDWARD MICHAEL FOGARTY 286, 307
FLORA FOGARTY 286, 397
JAMES FOLLOWS 181
HENRY FONDA 128
FOLYPADS 245
FOOTBALL ECHO 373
GEORGE FORMBY 10, 131
FORD MODEL T 340
FORTUNE 227
FORTY FOOT BANK 113, 270, 301, 380
FORTY FOOT DRAIN 332
FOSDYKE 316
FOSDYKE BRIDGE 325, 332
JIM FOSSITT 396, 397
ROBERT FOWLER 236
FOUNTAIN LANE 42
HARRY FOUNTAIN, PILOT 81
HARRY FOUNTAIN 116
FORCES' FAVOURITES 358
AGNES FOX 159, 163
AUBREY FOX 178
CATHERINE MARY FOX 159
DEREK FOX 68, 199,

GEOFF FOX	*199*
KEN FOX	*199*
P. M. FOX	*197*
SYLVIA FOX	*85*
JOHN FOXE	*208, 236, 249*
FOSTER BROTHERS	*38*
FRAMPTON	*69, 92, 116, 162, 267, 268*
FRAMPTON MARSH	*267, 364*
FRAMPTON PLACE	*14, 178, 379*
FRAMPTON HALL	*17, 266, 267, 409*
FRAMPTON HOUSE	*267*
MELVYN FRANKLIN	*5, 212*
FRANCES BERNARD CLOSE	*113*
JOHN FRANKLIN	*236*
FRANCE	*355, 358*
DENNIS FRANKS	*375*
FRECHVILLE	*378*
FREDERICK III OF GERMANY	*303*
FREE LATIN SCHOOL	*256*
TONY FREEMAN	*49*
FREISTON	*194, 247, 248, 264, 274, 361*
FREISTON LOW ROAD	*324*
FREISTON ROAD	*162, 178*
FREISTON SHORE	*21, 248, 293, 294, 304, 325*

F. H. FRITH	*309*
FRISKNEY	*317*
JOHNNY FROST	*41, 141, 179*
ROBIN FROST	*67*
PAUL FULTON	*44*
THOMAS FYDELL	*249, 271, 272, 274*
FYDELL CRESCENT	*69, 87, 101, 126, 390*
FYDELL HOUSE	*15, 101, 234, 235, 249, 271, 274*
FYDELL STREET ANTIQUES	*371*
GAINSBOROUGH	*143, 223, 233, 240, 260, 261, 262, 263, 280*
GEORGE GALE	*64, 326, 347, 352*
GALE'S HONEY	*155*
WILLIAM GANNOCKE	*359*
GANNOCKS	*316, 358, 361*
GARDNER'S SHOP	*108*
THOMAS GARFIT	*403*
WILLIAM GARFIT	*289, 404, 405*

GARFIT & CLAYPON BANK 275
GARIBALDI 275
WILLIAM GARNER 325
GREER GARSON 128
JOHNNIE GARVIE 154
GAS COMPANY CLUB 372
PAUL GASGOINE 149
BRIAN GEDNEY 205
DR. A. C. GEE 125
MRS. GEE 13, 354
GENERAL HOSPITAL 53, 101, 124
GENOA 398
GEORGE HOTEL, SWAFFHAM 347
GEORGE STREET 2, 18, 60, 107, 178, 179, 183, 332, 347, 364, 372
GARY GERSON 82
RACHEL GIDDINGS 211
JOSEPH GILBERT 236, 252
GILBERT & ELLIS ISLANDS 236, 252
GILBERT & SULLIVAN 138, 253
"GINNY BOTTLES" (LOUIE THORP) 94
HARVEY GILL'S 373, 376
WILLIAM GLADSTONE 402, 403
GLASGOW 266, 403
JOE GLEDHILL 26, 91
GLIDERDROME 21, 62, 202, 203, 211, 322

ALDERMAN J. W. GLEED
(later SIR JOHN)   *343*
GOEBELS   *8*
GOERING   *8*
GOLD BEACH, OREGON   *44, 167*
THE GOLDEN LION   *33, 59,*
    203
OLIVER GOLDSMITH   *388*
MR. GOODACRE   *54, 178*
DEREK GOODALL   *152*
GOLDSMITH   *60*
H. M. GOODLIFF   *125*
GOODS YARD   *33, 34,*
    69, 76,
    110, 113,
    390
GOODS YARD SHED   *298*
ALFRED ADOLF GOODSON   *56*
GONVILLE AND CAIUS COLLEGE,
CAMBRIDGE   *320*
FLASH GORDON   *19*
SIR FERDINANDO GORGES   *230*
JOHN GORGES   *230*
GOSBERTON (formerly GOSBERKIRK)   *254, 255,*
    371
GOSBERTON BELNIE   *254*
GOSBERTON CHEAL   *254*
GOSBERTON CLOUGH   *254*
GOSBERTON EAUDYKE   *254*
GOSBERTON MONKS HALL   *255*
GOSBERTON RIGBOLT   *254, 255*
GOSBERTON RISEGATE   *254*
GOSBERTON SNOWHILL   *255*

GOSBERTON WESTHORPE	*254*
DERRICK GOSLING	*69*
GOSLING'S ORCHARD	*113*
GOSTELOW'S SLIP	*12, 165, 354*
EDMUND GOULDING	*127*
GRAMMAR GAZETTE	*360*
GRAND SLUICE	*240, 270, 279, 307*
GRAND SLUICE BRIDGE	*300*
GRANGER PUBLIC HOUSE	*165*
GRANTHAM	*48, 84, 99, 195, 202, 209, 260, 280, 301, 360*
GRATTONS	*372*
GRATTON'S YARD	*101*
ANDY GRAVER	*154*
STAN GRAVES	*67*
GRAVES & HOBSTERS	*41, 73, 137, 147*
GRAVES PARK SOCIAL CLUB	*396*
MR. GRAY	*178*
SHANE GRAY	*371*
LARRY GRAYSON	*9*
GREAT GONERBY	*195*
GREAT EASTERN RAILWAY	*299, 301*
GREAT HALE	*270*
GREAT NORTHERN PUB	*84*
GREAT YARMOUTH	*55, 76, 171, 173, 175, 347*

GREATER BOSTON 313

MR. GREEN 167

PHILLIP GREEN 193

GREEN LANE 113

GREENWICH 356

GREENWICH MERIDIAN 267

GREAT EXHIBITION 1851 282

BRIAN GREENWOOD 153

POP GREENWOOD 40, 370

MISS. GREY 275

EDDY GRIMOLDBY 204, 205

GRIMSBY 55, 150, 151, 165, 240, 296, 297, 303, 314, 365, 374

GREAT COATES 150, 386

GRIMESTHORPE 152

THE GREYHOUND 285

GRESLEY COACH 299

GREAT NORTHERN RAILWAY 296, 297, 298, 304

GRIMSBY TELEGRAPH 373

GROVE STREET 125, 220

GRIFFIN 231, 257

GUERNSEY 289

GUILD HALL 223, 224, 261, 297, 316, 319, 332

GUILDHALL STREET, PINCHBECK 255

ALEC GUINNESS 136

COXSWAIN GUNBY	*280*
KATE GUNBY	*187*
FLIGHT LIEUTENANT GUNNELL	*143, 144, 382*
MRS. GUNNELL	*143, 144*
GYPSY BRIDGE	*143*
JOHN GYSOR, MAYOR OF LONDON	*248*
GYSOR'S HALL	*248*
DICK GRESSWELL	*35, 53*
PILOT HACK	*313, 314*
WILLIAM HACKNEY	*294*
HALF CROWN HILL	*273*
HALL HILLS	*298, 398*
E. HALL	*126*
GEORGE "CODGER" HALL	*74*
HAVEN HALL	*248*
MALCOLM HALL	*5, 212, 322, 368*
MAUREEN HALL	*13, 354*
HALLMEY'S	*317*
HAMBURG	*314*
HAMPTON, NEW HAMPSHIRE	*208*
HAMPDEN PARK	*149*
MRS. HALL	*73*
W. HAMER	*126*
PERCY HANDLEY	*59, 74, 95, 160*
LUKE HANSARD	*59, 268*
SID HANSON	*177*
s.s. HARALD	*324*
HARBOUR MASTER	*314*

MR. HARDY	*79*
OLIVER HARDY	*83*
HARDY & COLLINS	*37, 62, 68, 77, 79*
WILLIAM HARE	*294*
GORDON HARKER	*11*
RAY HARLEY	*41*
JACK HARMON	*53*
SID HARMON	*41*
MRS. HARDWICK	*97*
HARMONY MUSIC	*351*
FRANK HARNESS	*92*
PRIVATE HARNESS	*14*
MRS. HARRIS	*12, 354*
"DADA" HARRISON	*178*
FRANK HARRISON	*332*
JOHN HARRISON	*68*
RAY HARRISON	*195*
TONY HARRISON	*68*
SYD & MAX HARRISON	*350*
LORD HARTINGTON	*404*
DAGFINN HAUGLAND	*170*
NILS HAUGLAND	*170*
JOHN HARVARD	*233*
HARVARD UNIVERSITY	*232, 256*
"COCKER" HARVEY	*31*
HARROGATE	*54*
GEOFF HASTED	*67*
CAPT. HASLAM	*136*
MISS. HAWLING	*80, 207*
MARGARET HAWORTH	*319*
HAVEN BRIDGE	*317, 390*

NATHANIEL HAWTHORNE	*243*
HAYDN	*395*
HELEN HAYE	*127*
JOHN HAYHURST	*252*
DON HAZELDINE	*49, 50, 52*
GEOFF HAZELDINE	*49*
HEALING	*55, 365*
HEANOR	*300*
BASIL HEATH	*61*
TED HEATH	*62, 203*
HECKINGTON	*252, 283*
HECKINGTON WINDMILL	*283*
R.A.F. HEDNESFORD	*134, 136, 139, 381*
ROBERT HELPMAN	*5*
R.A.F. HEMSWELL	*144, 387*
HENDERSONS	*194*
HENRY OF NAVARRE	*229*
HENRY, PRINCE OF WALES	*231*
ETHEL STRACHAN HENRY	*342, 343*
GEORGE HEPPENSTALL	*130*
R.A.F. HEREFORD	*153*
HERITAGE RAILWAY MAGAZINE	*300*
SIR EDWARD HERON	*259*
HERRING'S TAXIS	*376*
FRED HERRING	*43, 75, 76*
SID HERRING	*76*
W. J. HESSION	*22, 24*
HESSLE DRIVE	*113*
R. H. HICKMAN	*412*
EDWARD LEE HICKS	*289*

HIGH BRIDGE, LINCOLN	*224*
HIGHLANDS	*168, 171*
HIGH SCHOOL	*32, 87,*
	89, 97,
	99, 167,
	237, 341,
	343, 376
HIGH STREET	*1, 33,*
	41, 43,
	59, 69,
	73, 77
	81, 86,
	92, 117,
	118, 133,
	147, 161,
	178, 203,
	280, 285,
	295, 296,
	328, 354,
	356, 365,
	372, 373,
	390, 391
HILDREDS	*368*
ARTHUR "COCKLES" HILL	*320*
JACK HILL	*147, 153,*
	156
YVONNE HIMSWORTH	*91*
HITLER	*8, 115,*
	135
ERNIE HOBART	*11*
HOB HOLE DRAIN	*241*
HOGG'S BUSES	*294*
CYRIL LOUIS HOFFROCK GRIFFITHS	*319, 321*

HOLBEACH	*242, 359*
HOLBEACH MARSH	*326*
CLIFF HOLGATE	*187*
IVY HOLGATE	*187*
NOEL HOLGATE	*37, 62, 68, 78, 89, 138, 187, 205, 379*
HOLLAND	*5, 223, 225, 259, 355, 398*
HOLLAND FEN	*240*
STANLEY HOLLOWAY	*128*
HOLLAND-WITH-BOSTON	*334, 335, 408, 409, 410, 411*
REG HOLLINGSWORTH	*351*
J. H. HOLLWAY	*401*
HOLME'S CREAMERY	*181*
DEREK HOLDSWORTH	*42*
HOLLAND BROTHERS	*13*
RON HOLMES	*67*
HOLY TRINITY CHURCH	*287, 288*
HOLY TRINITY SCHOOL	*313*
MRS. HOMEWOOD	*73*
SKIP HOMEIER	*129*
LORD HOME	*412*
DR. A. HOPEWELL-SMITH	*320*
BRIAN HOOKER	*41, 141, 355*
GERALD HOPPER	*141, 388*
S. T. HOPPER & SON	*369*

HOOKER	*231*
TOMMY HORN	*39, 371*
RED HORN	*44*
HOP POLE	*181*
HORN REEF	*308*
HORNCASTLE	*196, 243,*
	257, 334
HORNCASTLE GRAMMAR SCHOOL	*374*
HORNCASTLE ROAD	*126, 177,*
	181, 222,
	324, 371
HOSPITAL LANE FOOTBRIDGE	*101, 330*
HOUGH	*231, 234*
ERIC HOUGHTON	*198*
ROY HOUGHTON	*48, 198*
HOULDER	*194*
REV. A. H. HOWARD	*377*
"CHELSEA" HOWARD	*41, 370*
REG HOWARD	*212, 322*
THOMAS HOWARD	*250*
WILLIAM HOWDEN	*279*
HOUSE OF COMMONS	*268*
HOWES AND DAVIES	*93*
DICK HOWES	*38*
"FROGGY" HOWES	*25*
JIM HOWES	*319*
PETER HOWES	*38, 39,*
	67, 202
GEORGE HOWSAM	*177*
GARTH HUBBERT	*115*
HAROLD HUBBERT	*115*
MR. HUDSON	*24, 30,*
	87

MR. HUGHES	108
HULL	8, 155, 181, 236, 260, 262, 308, 309, 329, 351
HULL UNIVERSITY	154, 210, 217, 253, 360, 399
RIVER HUMBER	225
JOHN HUMPHREY	230, 232, 256
CHARLES NEWHAM HUNN	87
N. J. HUNT	22, 24
HUNTINGDON	4
HUNTINGFIELD MANOR	264
HUNTS OF ALFORD	341
HURST'S FACTORY	187
HURST'S WAREHOUSE	248
LIEUTENANT HUTCHINSON	310
BRIAN HUTSON	371
REV. V. C. IBBOTSON	377
IBSTOCK	213
"ICKY OY" (FAN TAYLOR)	373
ICANHOE	237
ICELAND STORE	13
RIVER IDLE	225
ILLUSTRATED LONDON NEWS	291, 302
IMMINGHAM	225
INDIA	287, 305, 310, 365
INGELOW AVENUE	126, 319

INGELOW MANOR   *319*
m.v. JEAN INGELOW   *319*
INGELOW PRIVATE SCHOOL   *342*
ELIZA INGELOW   *317*
GEORGE INGELOW   *317*
JEAN INGELOW   *315, 317,*
318, 319,
385

JEAN (REBECCA) INGELOW   *317*
HENRY INGELOW   *317*
SOPHIE INGELOW   *317*
SUSANNA INGELOW   *317*
WILLIAM INGELOW   *317*
INDOOR BOWLING CLUB   *41, 201,*
371, 372

RED INGLE   *369*
INGOLDMELLS   *374*
INGRAM'S SEEDS   *114*
HERBERT INGRAM   *291, 292,*
302, 401

HERBERT INGRAM JNR.   *292*
WALTER INGRAM   *292, 293*
W. JAMES INGRAM   *402, 403,*
404

MARGARET INGRAM   *61, 389*
INVERNESS   *170, 173,*
174

IPSWICH   *317*
SIR ANTHONY IRBY   *259, 260*
IRBY STREET   *298*
ISLE OF AXHOLME   *262*
ISLE OF WIGHT   *229*
JUDAS ISCARIOT   *60*

ISOLATION HOSPITAL 124
RAY ISSITT 15
ITALY 275

DR. BERNARD JACKSON 28
JACK JACKSON 148
SERGEANT HAROLD JACKSON 332, 333
L. A. JACKSON 22
PERCY JACKSON 69
RICHARD JACKSON 224
MRS. JAKES 24
TONY JAKES 68, 213
JAMES STREET 12, 84,
120, 123,
157, 178,
344, 354
HARRY JAMES 368
JIMMY JAMES 350
PERCY JAMES 76
REV. THOMAS JAMES 256
JAMESTOWN 228
JAPAN 128
JAZZ CLUB 200, 202
MAJOR GEORGE JEBB 289
JERMYN STREET, LONDON 320
ELVIN JESSOP 253
G. JESSOP 125
GEORGE JESSOP 204
JOHNNY JESSOP 141
IVAN JESSOP 202
PERCY JESSOP 177
JEWS' HILL, LINCOLN 4
ALF JOHNSON, BAKER 178

ALFRED JOHNSON	*215*
ALFRED DE BOUYS JOHNSON	*215, 283*
BRYN JOHNSON	*39, 69*
C. W. JOHNSON	*67*
ISAAC JOHNSON	*230*
JOHNSON'S FISH SHOP	*107, 265, 399*
JOHNSON'S, LEVERTON	*194*
KEN JOHNSON	*15, 62, 113, 191, 361, 399*
LEONARD JOHNSON	*100*
RICHARD WADE JOHNSON	*284*
WILLIAM JOHNSON	*283*
WILLIAM WADE JOHNSON	*214, 216, 283*
W. & W. JOHNSON'S	*68, 114, 283, 284*
PHILIP JOHNSTON	*383*
JOHN OF GAUNT	*248*
JOSEPH JOHNSON	*23*
AL JOLSON	*13*
EMRYS JONES	*5*
JENNIFER JONES	*129*
MASON JONES	*402*
SPIKE JONES	*368*
REV. JOHNNY JORDAN	*18*
PETER JORDAN	*193*
J. S. G. SNOOKER CLUB	*371*
MRS. JUDD	*73*
JUKE BOX	*368*
MRS. JULIAN	*107*
TOM JULIAN	*107*

BOB JULIEN   *117*
GWEN JULIEN   *117*
JUNGFRAU   *305*
JUTLAND   *308*

KAISER WILHELM   *303*
KAISERLAUTEN   *398*
KALOMO   *380*
HJALMAR KARL   *168*
DANNY KAYE   *142, 368*
KEAL COATES   *371*
MR. KEAL, HEADMASTER   *59, 160, 161, 269*
MR. & MRS. KEAL, MILKMAN   *98*
EDMUND KEAN   *281*
KEIGHTLEY'S   *376*
CYRIL KEIGHTLEY   *192*
KELSEY BRIDGE   *60*
HAROLD KEMP   *50, 97*
DAME MADGE KENDALL   *281*
JOSEPH KENNEDY   *234*
BUXTON KENRICK   *275*
KENT COLLEGE, CANTERBURY   *210*
KENTISH TOWN   *342*
STAN KENTON   *368*
KENYA   *360*
KETTERING   *159, 329, 391*
KHARTOUM   *293*
KIDSTACKS   *8, 20*
CAPTAIN KIDD   *253*
KIDDERMINSTER   *300*

DEREK KILLICK — *40, 181,*

MADGE KILLICK — *92, 246*

REG KILLICK — *92, 246*

KING HAAKON VII, NORWAY — *170*

KING CHARLES 1 — *229, 231, 258, 263, 288*

KING CHARLES II — *258*

KING EDWARD VII — *269, 324*

KING EDWARD VIII — *410*

KING GEORGE III — *214*

KING GEORGE V — *407, 410*

KING GEORGE VI — *4, 17, 30, 410*

KING JAMES I — *226, 254*

KING HENRY IV — *248*

KING HENRY VIII — *250, 251, 316*

KING RICHARD III — *281*

MR. KING, BAKER — *178*

BILL KING — *74*

MR. & MRS. KING — *74*

KING STREET — *106, 107, 187, 298, 363, 364*

BISHOP EDWARD KING — *211*

KING'S CAFÉ — *365*

KING'S CROSS — *173*

KING'S CYCLE SHOP — *181*

KING'S LYNN — *228, 259, 261, 270, 314, 385*

KINGSWAY — *179, 353*

KINROSS — *412*

PAMELA KINSEY — *85, 89*

VALERIE KINSEY — *42, 389*

KIRIBITI — *252*

DORIS KIRK — *125*

FRED KIRK — *41*

MICHAEL KIRK — *193, 210*

LAVINIA KIRKBY — *54*

KIRTON — *16, 17, 69, 177, 179, 269, 331, 332, 333, 364, 396*

KIRTON BRASS BAND — *269*

KIRTON CHURCH — *332, 378*

KIRTON LEISURE CENTRE — *371*

KIRTON GRAMMAR SCHOOL — *59, 160, 203, 268, 269*

KIRTON GRAMMAR SCHOOL FIELD — *333*

KIRTON PARISH COUNCIL — *396*

KIRTON SCHOOL — *30*

KIRTON TOWN FOOTBALL CLUB — *396*

KIRTON HOLME — *67*

KIRTON SKELDYKE — *269*

R.A.F. KIRTON-IN-LINDSEY — *52, 139, 141, 143, 144, 145, 150, 151, 154, 381, 386, 387, 388*

BOB KITCHEN	*5, 62, 78, 212, 322*
ERIC KITCHEN	*78*
PETER KITCHEN	*192, 354*
LORD KITCHENER	*189*
ALDERMAN THOMAS KITWOOD	*312, 319, 343*
KITWOOD BOYS' SCHOOL	*377*
KITWOOD GIRLS' SCHOOL	*377*
DON KNIGHT	*121*
PILOT OFFICER KNIGHT	*145*
KNIGHT STREET, PINCHBECK	*255*
KNIGHTON	*378*
FRANCES MARY KNIPE	*341*
KWICK DRY CLEANERS	*369*
ANTHONY KYME	*254*
LABOUR CLUB	*101*
LABOUR EXCHANGE	*120, 192*
MARGARET LACY	*85, 89*
JIM LACEY	*136, 138*
LACEY'S LANE, LEVERTON	*374, 375*
PAT LADDS	*85, 89*
WALT LADDS	*78, 79, 92*
MRS. LADDS	*10, 178, 354*
LADY ELGIN	*292*
JEAN LAFITTE	*253*
J. LAIGHT	*125*
LAKE SUPERIOR	*292*
MR. LAMMIE	*178*

LANCASTER	*364, 367*
LAND ARMY	*168*
LAND'S END	*227*
LANGRICK ROAD	*374*
SAM LATHWELL	*79*
MR. LAUD, WELLINGTON	*55*
WILLIAM LAUD,	
ARCHBISHOP OF CANTERBURY	
231	
LAUGHTONS	*316, 358,*
	361
JOHN LAUGHTON	*359*
LAUGHTON'S CHARITY SCHOOL	*359*
LAVAL	*47, 355*
MARQUIS LAVELETTE	*310*
LA WARRE FAMILY	*255*
LAWN TENNIS CLUB	*396*
LAWRENCE LANE	*285*
TOMMY LAWTON	*197*
LAZIO	*398*
LEA GATE INN	*357*
ARTHUR LEAFE	*59, 160,*
	203
DICK LEAFE	*61, 203,*
	205, 237,
	389
JOAN LEAFE	*237*
IVY LEAFE	*203*
W. F. LEAFE & SON	*178, 347*
W. REYNOLDS LEAK	*296*
ARTHUR LEALAND	*319*
DAVID LEAN	*127, 393*
N. LEAROYD	*403*

DRILL SERGEANT LEATHERS	*9*
ALF LEE	*92*
DAVID LEE	*217*
GORDON T. LEE	*272*
H. W. LEE	*411*
MARGARET LEE	*96*
PETER LEEBETTER	*117*
LEEDS	*151, 153, 242, 347, 381*
LEEDS UNITED	*397, 398*
RICHARD LE HUNT	*260*
LEICESTER	*152, 154*
LEIGH-ON-SEA	*213, 236*
SIMON LE FEVRE	*239*
JOHN LeLAND	*242*
MARK LEMON	*291*
MOLLY LENTON	*132*
LENTON'S FISH SHOP	*132*
LENTON WAY	*92*
LEOPOLD	*303*
MATTHEW LE TISSIER	*50*
LEON LEUTY	*198*
SIR JOHN LEVERETT	*231*
ALDERMAN THOMAS LEVERETT	*234*
LEVERETT LANE	*257*
LEVERETT ROAD	*257*
LEVERINGTON	*192*
LEVERTON	*194, 317, 361, 374, 375*
BOB LEWIS	*19, 77*
DINX LEWIS	*187*

HARRY LEWIS	*19*
ABLE SEAMAN JOHN LEWIS	*280*
SID LEWIS	*52*
LLOYD LEWIS	*43*
LEYDEN	*225, 226, 227*
LEYLAND BUSES	*339*
LINCOLN	*4, 16, 82, 240, 259, 261, 262, 279, 280, 281, 296, 301, 330, 403*
LINCOLN CASTLE	*147*
LINCOLN CATHEDRAL	*223, 265*
LINCOLN CATHEDRAL CHOIR	*395*
LINCOLN CITY FOOTBALL CLUB	*144, 154, 387*
LORD LINCOLN	*262*
DICK LINCOLN	*15, 249, 271*
J. H. LINCOLN & SONS	*272*
LINCOLN'S WAREHOUSE	*12, 204*
LINCOLN LANE,	*159, 180, 181, 298, 344*
LINCOLN ROAD, SKEGNESS	*39*
LINCOLNSHIRE COUNTY COUNCIL	*300*
LINCOLNSHIRE ECHO	*372*
LINCOLNSHIRE FOOTBALL ASSOCIATION	*398*
LINCOLNSHIRE REGIMENT	*357, 358, 365*

LINCOLNSHIRE ROAD CAR CO.   *339*
LINCOLNSHIRE INDEPENDENT   *291*
LINCOLNSHIRE STANDARD   *38, 42,*
54, 84,
178, 181,
213, 234,
334
LINCOLNSHIRE TERRITORIALS   *400*
LINDIS TEA ROOMS   *187, 365*
RIVER LINDIS   *242*
LINDSEY   *278*
LINDSEY   *188, 189*
LIMARU, KENYA   *211, 360*
LIPTON'S   *40, 141,*
201, 206,
369
LIQUORPOND STREET   *1, 8,*
13, 70,
81, 107,
113, 121,
122, 123,
166, 178,
183, 209
265, 286,
290, 354,
399
LINGARDS   *368*
LINK TRAINER   *367*
LITTLE PET   *285*
THE LITTLE WONDER   *107*
LIVINGSTONE, RHODESIA   *380*
J. R. LIVOCK   *100*
LIZZIE AND ANNIE   *96*

	PAGE
LLANDUDNO	*55*
LLOYD'S BANK	*41, 101, 199*
DAVID LLOYD GEORGE	*405, 406, 407, 408, 409*
LNER	*372*
LOCK	*48*
NEIL LOCKWOOD	*108*
s.s. LOCKWOOD	*189*
LOCOMOTIVE STREET	*108, 298*
ALBERT LOMBARDINI	*289*
LONDON	*4, 142, 143, 145, 146, 156, 211, 220, 226, 243, 250, 255, 259, 269, 278, 286, 289, 295, 296, 299, 301, 303, 308, 320, 328, 276*
LONDON & CONTINENTAL FEATHER COMPANY	*285*
LONDON GENERAL OMNIBUS COMPANY	*338*
LONDON ROAD	*85, 100, 118, 124, 137, 178, 193, 215, 216, 245,*

471

	279, 284,
	296, 301,
	361, 390
LONDON UNIVERSITY	*335, 378*
W. LONG	*412*
LONG BENNINGTON	*152, 154*
LONG SUTTON	*135*
H. W. LONGFELLOW	*208*
J. W. LONGSTAFF	*325*
LORD LINDSEY	*260*
LORD NELSON INN	*43, 74,*
	80, 280
LORD OF BOURNE	*246*
LOS ANGELES	*374*
LORD NELSON FIELD	*8, 19,*
	30, 108,
	166
DENNIS LOTIS	*62, 203*
LOUISE ROOMS	*187*
LOUTH	*228, 240,*
	259, 296
MRS. LOUTH	*207*
JOE LOVELACE	*66*
LOVELACE'S	*165*
KATHLEEN LOVE	*375*
EDDIE LOVELEY	*10, 178,*
	354
JOHN LOVELEY	*178*
MARGARET LOVELEY	*41, 42,*
	51, 52,
	353
RAY LOVELEY	*194*
TOMMY LOWDER	*49*

WILF LOWE	*204, 205*
ERIC LUBBOCK	*355*
ARTHUR LUCAN	*10, 350, 351*
DONALD LUCAN	*351*
SKIP LUCAS	*3, 266, 289*
KATE LUCK	*389*
PETER LUFF	*36, 37, 68, 89, 379, 380, 381*
LUFTWAFFE	*356*
BELA LUGOSI	*351*
H. S. LUNN	*405*
LÜNEBERG HEATH	*3*
LUNN'S PICTURE GALLERY	*81*
MRS. LUNNINGTON	*161*
ALAN H. LUTHER	*399*
LYONS	*275*
BERTHA MABLESON	*187*
TED MABLESON	*53*
MACCLESFIELD	*222*
MABLETHORPE	*196, 386*
MACHO	*310*
WILLIAM CHARLES MACREADY	*282*
MRS. MADDRELL	*84*
GEORGE MADISON	*77*
MADRAS	*287*
HAROLD MACMILLAN	*412*
DR. T. MACTAGGART	*125*
MAGDALEN COLLEGE	*250*

MAHARAJA DULEEP SINGH	305
MAINE	230
MAIN RIDGE	307, 332
JOHN WINGFIELD MALCOLM	401, 402
BERNARD MALLETT	116
J. MALTBY	312
RAY MALTBY	166
MALTHOUSE	101
UNIVERSITY OF MANCHESTER	217, 399
MANCHESTER UNITED	383
MANHATTAN	225
MANITOBA	163
BRIAN MANNING	52, 147, 353
RUTH MANNING	187
REV. P. E. MANN	16
MANTON	233
FREDRIC MARCH	129
MARINE HOTEL	21, 248, 294
MARINERS ROW	1, 166, 354
MISS. MARINUS	281
MARION ROAD	377
MARKET PLACE	4, 15, 16, 101, 114, 178, 200, 220, 292, 305, 337, 346, 365, 395, 400

COUNTESS MARKIEVIEZ	406
MARKS & SPENCERS	220
R.A.F. MARHAM	21, 23
BOB MARRIOTT	66
H. C. MARRIS	100
MARSH LANE	206
ALAN MARSHALL	151, 153, 381
DEREK MARSHALL	67
JIM MARSHALL	77, 80
MARSHALL'S SHOP	107
MARTIAL ARTS	200
MARTHA'S VINEYARD	208, 249
BATTLE OF MARSTON MOOR	263
MARTIN'S, BAKERS	194
RALPH MASHFORD	67
TOM MASHFORD	62
THE MASON'S ARMS	21
ADA MASSINGHAM	187
DICK MASSINGHAM	204
ERNIE MASSINGHAM	62
MASSACHUSETTS	229, 233
MASSACHUSETTS BAY COMPANY	229
MASON'S SHOE SHOP	369
ANNE MATHER	393
ALEXANDER MATHER	209
MATTHEW FLINDERS WAY	113
MATTHEW FLINDERS	265
MATTERHORN	305
MATCH OF THE DAY	397
MAUD FOSTER DRAIN	243, 252, 330

MAUD FOSTER BRIDGE	301
MAUD FOSTER WINDMILL	155, 252
MAURICES GOWN SHOP	166
MAURITIUS	265
MRS. MAUVERLEY	88
MAY MAWER	112
MAYFLOWER	226, 227
JOCK McCARTNEY	48
JOHN McCRAE	357, 358
HEATHER McCRINDLE	175, 176
SAUNDRA McCRINDLE	175
JIM McDONALD	358
D. L. McEWAN	22
DOROTHY McGUIRE	129
TIM McKEEN	69
W. L. McKINZIE	22
HATTIE McDANIEL	63
DAVE McNAUGHTON	84
HECTOR McNEIL	29
IAN McSHANE	392
KITTY McSHANE	350, 351
MECCA	305
MEDAL OF GALLANTRY	309, 325
LEN MEDLOCK	316, 360
BERT MEEDS	178
T. S. MEIR	378
VICTOR MELDREW	9
RICHARD MELTON	250
MELTON MOWBRAY	49, 203
GEORGE MELLY	62
MELVILLE STREET, LINCOLN	330

MENS' OWN CLUB	*40, 41,*
	140, 141,
	201, 206,
	369
MERCHANT/IVORY	*275*
MERCHANT NAVY	*374*
THE MERCHANT OF VENICE	*282*
PAUL MERSON	*78*
METAMMEH	*293*
MELODY MAKER	*368*
JEAN METCALFE	*358*
MEXICO	*44*
RUSS MEYER	*393*
METAL BOX	*155*
J. C. MIDDLEBROOK	*210*
SIR THOMAS MIDDLECOTT	*269, 288*
RAY MIDDLETON	*50*
MIDDLESEX YEOMANRY CAVALRY	*293*
ROBIN MIDGELEY	*42, 52,*
	353
W. A. (BILL) MIDGELEY	*52, 55,*
	321
MIDGELEY'S SHOP	*6, 321*
JANET MIDGELOW	*89*
MIDLAND BANK	*187, 365*
BERNARD MILES	*5*
LEWIS MILESTONE	*126, 129*
MILL INN	*124*
MILL HILL	*281*
MILLENNIUM ISLAND	*252*
MILLER, BAKER	*194*
GLEN MILLER	*18*
MILAN	*398*

H. M. MILSOM, BUSES	*340*
MILLWALL	*198*
TONY MILLS	*78*
MILL ROAD	*377*
MINEHEAD	*192*
MINISTER OF EDUCATION	*377*
MINISTRY OF DEFENCE	*222*
MISSION TO SEAMEN	*63*
GORDON MITCHELL	*16*
GERRY "BUSTER" MITCHELL	*16*
JACK MITCHELL	*16*
MARY MITCHELL	*9*
MICHAEL MITCHELL	*193*
OSWALD MITCHELL	*350*
TERRY MITCHELL	*16*
THOMAS MITCHELL	*128, 209*
TONY MITCHELL	*16*
ROBERT MITCHUM	*129*
TOMMY MITCHUM	*48, 188*
MODENS	*177*
JAN MOLBY	*149*
KENNETH MONK	*375*
A. E. MONKS	*411*
MONTSERRAT	*82*
FIELD MARSHALL MONTGOMERY	*3*
DICK MOORE	*79*
PAUL MORAN	*125*
R.A.F. MORETON HALL	*148*
SIR HENRY MORGAN	*253*
SALLY MORLANDS	*61*
KEN MORLEY	*351*
KENNETH MORE	*393*
MORRIS'S CELLAR	*101*

CAPT. HERBERT HAYCROFT MORRIS   *25, 29, 84, 126*

MORRISON SHELTERS *356*
MOSCOW *4*
MOTHER'S PRIDE *177*
MOTOR CYCLE CLUB *81, 161*
JOHN MOTSON *115*
STAN MOTSON *115*
ANNIE MOULD *162, 163*
AUDREY MOULD *42, 60, 87*
CISSY MOULD *130, 143, 163, 348*
FRED MOULD *114, 137, 143, 163, 178, 322, 348, 356*
GEORGE MOULD *159, 163, 328, 329*
JAMES WILLIAM MOULD *159, 161, 329*
JIM MOULD *87, 342, 349, 396*
JEAN MOULD *163*
JOHN MOULD *159, 162*
THOMAS MOULD *162, 163*
MOULD AVENUE, TORONTO *162*
GEOFF MOULDER *53*
MOULDER'S *101*
MOUNT BRIDGE *76, 162, 178, 282*
MOUNT LEBANON *305*
JOHN HENRY MOUNTAIN *319, 378*

MOUNTAIN'S	*180*
MOUNTAIN'S PASSAGE	*131*
LORD LOUIS MOUNTBATTEN	*127*
MICK MULLIGAN	*38, 62, 203*
JOHN MUMFORD	*286*
MUNDESLEY-ON-SEA	*299*
MUNICH	*383*
AUSTIN MUNKS	*67*
MUNICIPAL BUILDINGS	*100, 124, 125, 323, 324, 329*
DOMINIC MURPHY	*206*
JOHN MURRAY	*49*
REV. WILLIAM MURRELL	*257*
MUSIC HALL	*350*
LEN MUSSON	*210*
MUSTONS	*316, 358, 361*
ROBERT OF MUSTON	*359*
FREDDY MYATT	*57, 322*
ALBERT MYERS	*73*
LILY MYERS	*73*
PHYLLIS MYERSON	*375*
NAIROBI UNIVERSITY	*360*
ERNIE NAPIER	*58*
NAPOLEONIC WARS	*309, 317*
NARRAGANSET INDIANS	*258*
BATTLE OF NASEBY	*263*
NATIONAL ASSOCIATION OF MASTER BAKERS	*363*
NATIONWIDE BUILDING SOCIETY	*200*

LYN NAYLOR	179
RICHARD NAYLOR	284
OLGA NEEDHAM	32
LORD NELSON	147, 280, 281
NEPTUNE INN	288
MR. NESBITT	178
NEWARK	113, 202, 240, 261, 262, 386
NEWARK EGG PACKERS	79
NEWCASTLE	199, 347
RODNEY NEWELL	68
NEW ENGLAND	288, 229, 230, 232, 257
NEW INN, FOSDYKE	325
NEW INN, SUTTERTON,	159, 163, 329
NEW PARK RANGERS	355
NEW STREET	366
NEW THEATRE	10, 41, 101, 201, 220, 372
ALAN NEWTON	204
"BUNGY" NEWTON	178, 369
SAM NEWSON	15, 272, 377
G. NEWTON	126
DR. JOHN NEWTON	209, 210, 316, 360
PETER NEWTON	204
NEWTON'S CORNER	178

NEWPORT COUNTY	49
NEW YORK	13, 399
NEW YORK, ENGLAND	196
ROY NICHOLS	118
RAY NICHOLSON	156
NIGG	174
RIVER NILE	293
NINE ROW	180
DAVID NIVEN	127, 128
NICHOLSON'S TOBACCONISTS	109
SYDNEY HERBERT NOBBS	289
MAYOR NOBLE	297
NORCROSS LIMITED	222
NORFOLK	261
NORFOLK PLACE	132, 166, 178, 278
NORFOLK STREET	100, 101, 188, 221, 222, 386
POP NORMAN	5, 322
MR. NORMAN, CYCLES	70, 166
NORMAN & SMITHSON	252
SIR JOHN NORRIS	260
NORPRINT SOCIAL CLUB	371
NORTH AFRICA	356
NORTHAMPTON	199, 213, 229
NORTH COATES	151, 386
NORTH SEA	308
NORTH SHIELDS	308, 309
NORTH VIRGINIA	228
NORTH WEST WATER BOARD	93
NORTHERN RHODESIA	380

NORWEGIAN ARMY	*168*
NORWICH	*155, 171,*
	172, 223,
	385
NOTTINGHAM	*118, 131,*
	137, 155,
	198, 259,
	287, 301,
	333
NOTTS. COUNTY	*198*
NOTTINGHAM EVENING NEWS	*373*
ALEXANDER NOWELL	*250*
OBEROMERGAU	*60*
ODEON	*10, 11,*
	19, 82,
	214
FATHER P. J. O'DONOGHUE	*87*
OGLE FAMILY	*255*
CROWN PRINCE OLAF	*170*
GEOFF O'HARA	*393, 394,*
	395
GERRY O'HARA	*392, 393*
JIM O'HARA	*395*
MARY O'HARA	*394*
OLDHAM	*153, 404,*
	405
JOSEPH OLDHAM	*325*
OLD BOLINGBROKE	*176*
F. L. OLDHAM	*126*
OLD BOSTONIAN ASSOCIATION	*306, 320,*
	321
OLD BOSTONIAN FOOTBALL TEAM	*204*

OLD CHURCH HOUSE	*359*
OLDRID'S PARK	*332*
OLD MOTHER RILEY	*10, 278, 350, 351*
OLD LEAKE	*117, 133, 177, 278, 361, 371, 381*
OLD LEAKE COMMONSIDE	*122, 177*
"BINGY" OLIVER	*181, 190*
FRED OLIVER	*181*
LAURENCE OLIVIER	*281*
OLIVETTE	*325*
OLYMPIA	*286*
OPERATIC SOCIETY	*200*
ORMSBY ST. MARY	*171, 173*
ORPINGTON	*355, 356*
ALEC ORR	*149, 151, 382*
ORSET	*310*
ORTON LONGUEVILLE	*163*
OSGODBY	*261*
DOUGLAS OSHEROFF	*217*
M. OSMENT	*22*
ALFRED OSTLER	*253*
OSTRICH INN	*273*
OTTO	*217*
REG OUGHTON	*53*
OUNDLE	*163*
R.A.F. OUTSTATION	*367*
WILFRED OWEN	*357*
O.W.L.S.	*168, 173*
OXFORD	*251*

	PAGE
OXFORD STREET	6, 97, 98, 161, 182, 207
OXFORD UNIVERSITY	382, 383
PACKHOUSE QUAY	249, 271, 304
R.A.F. PADGATE	133, 139, 381
JOHN PADLEY	202
PALACE THEATRE, HULL	148
HARRY PALMER	320
LORD PALMERSTON	401, 402
PETER PAN	204
BILL PANNELL	55, 90, 178, 278
HAROLD PANTON	178
PANTON BROTHERS, EAST KIRKBY	176
SERGEANT PANTON	145, 146
MRS. PANTON	145
ARTHUR PAPE	178, 195
PARIS	305, 310
PARIS EXHIBITION 1834	282
PARK SCHOOL	30, 89, 313
DICK PARKER	67
PARK ROAD	131
FRED PARKER	12, 188, 316, 360
H. J. PARKER	410
MISS. RUBY PARKER	14, 88
PILOT W. PARKER	325
MR. PARKER, ST. JOHNS	206

DICK PARKINSON	*91, 191, 383*
MARK PARKINSON	*13*
PARKINSON'S	*78*
JOHN PARRISH	*273*
MRS. PARROTT	*196*
PARRY GOLD MEDAL	*360*
PARRY SCHOLARSHIP	*360*
THOMAS PARRY	*65, 360, 401, 402*
PARRYS	*316, 358, 361*
MR. PARSONS	*112*
JENNY PARVIN	*188*
PATE	*48*
R.A.F. PATRINGHAM	*148*
PATRIOTIC BANK OF WASHINGTON	*275*
ROGER PAYNE	*152*
"PUD" PAYTON	*15*
PEACOCK'S	*180*
THE PEACOCK AND ROYAL	*21, 212*
MR. PEARCE	*83, 214*
PEARL HARBOUR	*127*
BOB PEARSON	*204*
PETER PEARSON	*204*
J. W. PEARSON & SON	*376*
ALAN PECK	*205*
GREGORY PECK	*4*
PECK AVENUE	*87*
ARTHUR GEORGE VILLIERS PEEL	*335*
DONALD PEERS	*366*
ELIZABETH PELHAM	*230*
HERBERT PELHAM	*233, 256*

PELHAM'S LAND	*230*
PEN STREET	*284*
SUSAN PENHALIGON	*393*
PENINSULAR WAR	*310, 317*
DR. PENNY	*379*
PENOBSCOT	*258*
MICHAEL PENSON	*69*
J. D. PERIAM	*210*
LINDIS PERKINS	*68*
PERMANENT WAY DEPARTMENT	*299*
W. H. PESTELL	*125*
PETERBOROUGH	*84, 106, 173, 202, 261, 296, 301*
PETTICOAT LANE	*285*
PHOENIX IRONWORKS	*279*
HARRY PIERREPONT	*179*
DR. PILCHER	*163, 167, 348*
DR. RICHARD PILCHER	*163, 348*
PILGRIM FATHERS	*91, 223*
PILGRIM HOSPITAL	*106, 195, 371*
PILLEYS LANE	*60, 108*
PINCHBECK	*255, 408*
PINCHBECK HALL	*335*
ANTHONY PINCHBECK	*263*
CHRISTOPHER PINCHBECK	*255*
PINFOLD LANE	*181*
MICHAEL PINNER	*199, 382, 383*
REV. PIPER	*73*

PITMINSTER, SOMERSET	*237*
PITCAIRN ISLANDS	*374*
THE PLOUGH	*80, 92*
THE PLOUGH, SWINESHEAD BRIDGE	*299, 300*
PLUMMERS HOTEL	*248, 293,*
	294
PLYMOUTH	*223, 227,*
	228, 233,
	406
POCAHONTAS	*228*
JOHN POCKLINGTON	*283*
POET LAUREATE	*318*
POETRY GROUP	*200*
QUEENIE POGSON	*11*
JAMES PICKER	*177*
POLICE STATION	*184*
MRS. POLKINGHORN	*84*
POOLE	*279*
BERYL POPE	*376*
POP SHOP	*366*
E. H. PORCHER	*378*
JANET PORCHER	*378*
JOHN "SCORCHER" PORCHER	*5, 212,*
	322, 378
PORTLAND	*400*
PORTLAND STREET, LINCOLN	*4*
ERIC PORTMAN	*5*
MAY POWELL	*199*
MICHAEL POWELL	*5*
TYRONE POWER	*19*
POSTMASTER-GENERAL	*221*
PRASUTAGUS	*240*
PRESERVATION TRUST	*235*

PRESERVATION TRUST BLUE PLAGUE	351
OTTO PREMINGER	393
PRESIDENT OF THE METHODIST CONFERENCE	360
PRAGUE	398
EMERIC PRESSBURGER	5
J. B. PRIESTLEY	244, 376
MICHAEL PRIESTLEY	67
REG PRIESTLEY	64, 352
PRINCE ALBERT	270, 303
PRINCE OF WALES	220, 303
PRINCE RUPERT OF THE RHINE	259
PRIVATEER	325
PROGRESSIVE BUS COMPANY	338, 339
JED PROUTY	83
MR. PULFORD	1
PULVERTOFT LANE	46, 65, 66, 96, 101, 110, 113, 116, 118, 119, 130, 144, 160, 207 296, 354, 356, 373
PUMP SQUARE	67, 101, 178, 195, 291
PUMP SQUARE SNOOKER CLUB	371, 395
PUNCH	335
PUNCHBOWL LANE	374
PUNJAB	305
PUPIL TEACHER'S CENTRE	341

PURCELL	*395*
PURITANS	*223, 231*
PUTNEY	*341, 342*
QUADRING FEN	*349*
ROGER QUAINT	*238*
QUATRE BRAS	*310*
QUEEN ELIZABETH 1	*61, 229*
QUEEN ELIZABETH II	*251*
QUEEN MARY	*208*
QUEEN MARY (QUEEN MOTHER)	*153*
QUEEN MARY	*215*
QUEEN VICTORIA	*220, 269,*
	303, 305,
	318, 402
QUEEN STREET	*107, 205*
QUEEN'S COLLEGE, OXFORD	*383*
QUEEN'S PARK FOOTBALL CLUB	*149, 266,*
	382
EDMUND QUINCEY	*231*
OSCAR RABIN	*62, 203*
VELJKO RADEKA	*219*
RAILWAY STATION	*126*
COL. RAINSBURROW	*257*
SIR WALTER RALEIGH	*228*
RALPH	*90*
RALPH'S LANE	*267*
RAMBLERS	*200*
RAMSAY MacDONALD	*407, 408,*
	409
ARTHUR MICHAEL RAMSEY,	
ARCHBISHOP OF CANTERBURY	*209*

AGNES RANDALL	*250*
FREDDY RANDALL	*38, 62, 203*
RANGOON	*310*
JIM RANSOM	*67*
RANSOME & MARLES	*48, 202*
RANSOME PLACE	*85*
BART RASTALL	*180*
BERYL RASTALL	*122, 186, 344*
BRUCE RASTALL	*179*
LEILA RASTALL	*43, 97, 167, 168, 169, 170, 171, 172, 173, 174, 175, 176*
RUBY RASTALL	*179, 181, 186*
THORA RASTALL	*122*
GWEN RAWSON	*120*
JOHN RAWSON	*302*
G. RAYNER	*92*
RONALD REAGAN	*128*
ALF READ	*204*
READING	*284*
READING UNIVERSITY	*215*
ISAAC RECKITT	*155, 252*
RECKITT & COLMAN	*155*
THOMAS RECKITT	*155, 252*
RED LION INN	*267, 281, 340, 369*

	PAGE
RED LION STREET	101, 123, 194, 202, 268, 281, 289, 297
RED LION INN, SPILSBY	47
RED CROSS HOSPITALS	269
RED SEA	305, 310
BRIAN REDMAN	68
JOYCE REDMAN	5
TOM REDMAN	199
REDSTONE GOWT	301
ALAN "CHUCKY" REED	181
BERNARD REED	41, 52, 147, 353
DOREEN REED	85
CAROL REED	128
OLIVER REED	393
THELMA REED	85
REED'S POINT	159, 328
JACKY REDMILE	16
REESON & BORRILL	177
AMBER REEVES	336
REGAL	10, 18, 19, 351
ERICK MARIA REMARQUE	126
DR. S. RENDALL	125
JOHN RENNIE	241, 272, 279, 316, 330
R. M. RENNOLDSON	272
HAROLD RENSHAW	41
REPERTORY THEATRE	375
THE RESOLUTION	252

ALEC REVELL 167
EDIE REVELL 166
GEORGE "GROWDY" REVELL 165
MARJORIE REVELL 85
"WOKKA" REVELL 31
REVESBY AVENUE 162, 235
SHEILA REX 395
E. E. REYNOLDS 410
REYNOLD'S CELLAR 101
RICE, WAITE & MARRIS 68
DAVE RICHARDS 379
GEORGE RICHARDS 296
ROBERT RICHARDSON 217
DENNIS RICKARD 32
T. H. RICKARD 126
W. J. RICKETTS 321
RICHMOND 210
H. RIDER HAGGARD 243
TONY RICHARDSON 392
ETHEL MARY RIDLEY 342
JOHN RIDLEY 208
HAZEL RIMINGTON 35
RIMINGTON-WELLS 93
RIO GRANDE 44
RIPPINGALE 84
W. A. RIPPON 411
SIDNEY RITSON 94
RITZ CINEMA, LINCOLN 4
RIVERSIDE 206
JIMMY RIVETT 355
THE ROBIN HOOD 33, 80
DENNIS ROBINS 46, 89
HEATH ROBINSON 143

ROBINSON'S, CHEMIST	201, 372
NICHOLAS ROBERTSON	315, 359
WILLIAM ROBERTSON	267
THOMAS SHAFTO ROBERTSON	268, 281
JOHN ROBINSON	225, 227
JOSEPH ROBINSON	308
REV. E. S. ROBERTS	320
MARJORIE ROBERTS	99
MARY ROBINSON	85
ROBINSON'S BARLEY WATER	155
ROCHFORD TOWER	60
P. R. ROETZEL	22
C. W. ROGERS	126
HENRY ROGERS	274
ROBERT ROLLETT	236
ROMANS	240
SIGMUND ROMBERG	346
ROME	398
BRIAN ROOKE	192
MR. ROOKE	192
ROPE WALK ROAD	298
LITA ROSA	62, 203
ROSEBERRY AVENUE	371
ROSEGARTH STREET	181, 182
ROSS FOODS	79
ROSSALL	306
PRESIDENT ROOSEVELT	234
CHRISTINA ROSSETTI	318
BERTHA ROWE	55
JAMES PARKIN ROWE	319
JAMES ROWELL	323
ROWELL ROW	10
G. F. ROWLEY	403

THE ROYAL GEORGE	*12*
THE ROYAL OAK	*43, 80*
ROYAL FLYING CORPS	*160*
ROYAL BOSTON YACHT CLUB	*285*
ROYAL NAVAL AIR SERVICE	*337*
ROYAL ENGINEERS	*358*
ROYAL TRAIN	*303*
ROBERT EVELYN ROY	*288*
WILLIAM ROY	*287, 288*
WILLIAM STAPLETON ROYCE	*332, 334, 335, 336, 406, 407, 408*
HARRY RUCK	*120*
THE RUGBY ROOM	*212*
THE RUM PUNCHEON	*21, 208, 249*
RURAL DISTRICT COUNCIL	*331*
DAVE RUSHTON	*41*
DOREEN RUSHTON	*35, 144, 147*
JACK RUSHTON	*144, 145, 153*
JOHN RUSKIN	*318*
LEN RUSKIN	*82, 107*
RON RUSKIN	*82*
EARL RUSSELL	*402*
RUSSELL SQUARE	*101, 341, 352*
MRS. RYALL	*333*
DICK RYAN	*42*
P. RYSDALE	*126*

SAARBRUCKEN	*21*
SALISBURY	*213*
LORD SALISBURY	*403, 404, 405*
SALVATION ARMY	*73, 193, 286, 287, 373*
SALVATION ARMY BAND	*395*
SALEM	*229, 233*
SAINT PAUL	*156*
SANDERSTEAD	*371*
PIP SANDS	*364*
TED SANDS	*177, 195, 341*
TOM SANDS	*107, 178*
TONY SANDS	*107*
SAMPDORIA	*398*
SANTA CLAUS	*98*
FRANK SARGEANT	*39, 92, 93, 205, 237*
JIM SARGENT	*67*
SAUL OF TARSUS	*157*
LORD SAYE AND SELE	*229*
REUBEN SALTER	*319*
SCALA RESTAURANT	*365*
STAN SCALES	*182, 184*
R.A.F. SCAMPTON	*139*
SCHOOL BOARDS	*312*
SCHOOL OF COOKERY	*177*
SCOTLAND	*376*
ALAN SCOTNEY	*53*
REV. DAVID SCOTT	*396*

RONNIE SCOTT	*202, 211, 322*
SCOTT'S FISH SHOP	*120*
MISS. SCORER	*377*
SCRIBBANS-KEMP	*150, 386*
SCROOBY	*223, 224, 225, 227, 228*
SCROXTONS	*81*
SEA BANK	*20*
SEAMAN'S INSTITUTE	*372*
SEDBURGH	*378*
GENERAL SEDGWICK	*258*
SEATTLE	*399*
STAN SELLERS	*206*
DAVID O. SELZNECK	*129*
SEPARATISTS	*223*
SEMPRINGHAM	*229, 231*
SEMPRINGHAM ABBEY	*229*
DENISE SENIOR	*51, 52, 353*
SESSIONS HOUSE	*350*
ANDREW SESSLER	*216*
MISS. SETH	*108*
SEVERN VALLEY RAILWAY	*300*
MR. SEWELL	*40*
DOROTHY SEWELL	*130*
LEN SHACKLETON	*50*
SHADY NOOK	*365, 366*
BRYAN "CURLY" SHARP	*39*
HARRY SHARP	*48*
RON SHARP	*180, 181, 182*

SHARP'S BUSES	294
JASPER SHARPE	62, 68
HELEN SHARMAN	61
JOHN SHARMAN	61
KEN SHARMAN	61, 389
SHAWMUTT PENINSULAR	257
SHEATH'S BANK	275
DR. M. J. SHEEHAN	125
SHEFFIELD	49, 156, 163, 179, 378
THOMAS SHEPHERD	324, 326
SHEPHARD'S, BAKERS	178
SHERIDAN	60
SHERIFF OF LINCOLN	246
SHERBORNE	378
SAMUEL SHERWIN	307
S. SHERWIN & SON	323, 400
SHERWOOD AVENUE	331
SHERWOOD BOYS CLUB	5, 39, 212, 322
SHERWOOD FORESTERS	171, 172
SHIP INN	137
SHIPWRECKED MARINERS' SOCIETY	309
SHODFRIARS HALL	101, 283, 295, 326, 350, 351, 394
SHODFRIARS LANE	204
SHODFRIARS SCHOOL	30
ARTHUR SHRIMPTON	383
SHYLOCK	281
DINAH SHORE	368

	PAGE
SIBSEY	*14, 177, 278, 341, 350, 359*
SIBSEY NORTHLANDS	*243*
SIBSEY ROAD	*214*
SIDNEY STREET	*115*
BILL SILMAN	*370*
SILVER STREET	*101*
ALASTAIR SIM	*11*
COLIN SIMMONDS	*205*
DERRICK SIMMONDS	*82, 123, 213*
GEORGE SIMMONDS	*48, 82*
JOHN CABORN SIMMONDS	*304*
WILLIAM TURNER SIMMONDS	*303, 305, 323, 326, 404*
SIMMONDS & CO.	*305*
SIMMONDS MILL	*308*
HORACE SIMPSON	*106*
LEN SIMPSON	*77*
RUTH SIMPSON	*106*
VIOLET SIMPSON	*85*
SIMPSON'S, STRAIT BARGATE	*337*
WILLIAM SINCLAIR & CO.	*113, 199*
SINCLAIRS' WAREHOUSE	*364*
SINN FEIN	*406*
THE SIX BELLS, BISHOP'S CASTLE	*379*
JIM SIZER, BAKER	*178*

	PAGE
SKEGNESS	*39, 54, 160, 177, 182, 197, 213, 259, 338, 339*
SKEGNESS ADVERTISER	*291*
MR. SKEPPER	*54, 374*
ALEXANDER SKINNER	*254*
GORDON SKINNER	*41, 141*
SKINNER, BAKERS	*194*
SKIRBECK	*125, 220, 244, 256, 284, 287, 288, 296, 277, 304, 312, 313, 377*
SKIRBECK CHURCH	*315*
SKIRBECK QUARTER	*5, 20, 33, 92, 97, 246, 279, 288, 289, 304, 313, 332, 359*
SKIRBECK ROAD	*96, 126, 160, 194*
SLEAFORD	*53, 137, 243, 261*
SLEAFORD ROAD	*101, 126, 131, 286, 298, 307, 361*

	PAGE
JACK SLEIGHT	67
ERIC SLINGER	62, 68
SLUICE BRIDGE	386
T. SMALL	238
SMALL'S EMPORIUM	307, 337
SMALLERS	77
GUS SMALLEY	62
MAY SMALLEY	131
CHARLES SMARTH	329
SMILING MORN	308, 309
ALEXIS SMITH	376
BARRY SMITH	93
BARRY TREVOR (BEATTY) SMITH	38, 39, 68
COLIN SMITH	219, 400
DON SMITH	68
GRAHAM SMITH	218, 219, 400
J. B. SMITH	38
J. G. SMITH	38
J. W. (JOHNNY) SMITH	38, 191, 382, 383
LEONARD SMITH	378
LAURENCE SMITH	339
MADGE SMITH	42, 61, 389
MARGARET SMITH	51, 353
NORMAN SMITH	219
PETER SMITH	41, 51, 52, 147, 353
PHIL SMITH	110
RALPH SMITH	267

JOHN SMITH	*228*
WINSOME SMITH	*42, 61,*
	389
W. H. SMITH, COAL MERCHANT	*76, 78*
SMITH'S BUSES	*339*
SMITH'S CLEANING & DRYING	*369*
SMITH & NEPHEW	*155*
SMITH & PEACOCK	*194*
CECIL SMITH, BAKER	*177*
LEN SMITH, BAKER	*177*
SNAX CLUB	*395*
C. E. SNOOK	*409*
SOHO	*211*
SOMERVILLE COLLEGE, OXFORD	*99*
REV. LORD DONALD SOPER	*209*
SOULBY'S CELLAR	*101*
SOUTH AFRICA	*215, 335*
SOUTH KELSEY	*259*
SOUTH SQUARE	*216, 248*
SOUTH STREET	*15, 271,*
	364
SOUTH TERRACE	*327*
SOUTHAMPTON	*197, 226,*
	227, 378
SOUTHERN RHODESIA	*144*
ARTHUR SOUTHON	*116*
SOUTHWOLD JAZZ BANK	*396*
s.s. SOUTHWOOD	*325*
SPAIN LANE	*274*
SPALDING	*33, 133,*
	261, 316,
	334, 338,
	339

SPALDING HIGH SCHOOL	*342*
SPANISH MAIN	*253*
SPAYNE ROAD	*187*
INSPECTOR SPARROW	*84*
SPALDING HOSPITAL	*124*
SPEEDWELL	*227*
SPICK AND SPAN	*366*
BARRY SPIKINGS	*316*
SPILLERS	*155, 196*
SPILSBY	*47, 54,*
	176, 177,
	287
SPILSBY ROAD	*32, 100,*
	124, 213,
	283, 342,
	343
R.A.F. SPITTALGATE	*138, 139,*
	374
THE SPORTING LIFE	*394, 395*
GEORGE SPURR	*253*
ST. AIDAN'S CHURCH	*72*
ST. ANDREW'S CHURCH, BUTTERWICK	*264*
ST. BOTOLPH'S CHURCH (THE STUMP)	*16, 28,*
	61, 67,
	72, 97,
	121, 188,
	201, 203,
	208, 209,
	211, 224,
	229, 230,
	237, 239,
	242, 244,
	251, 262,

	PAGE
	266, 273,
	302, 317,
	321, 346,
	358, 359,
	369, 395,
	396
ST. BOTOLPH'S DAY (17th JUNE)	*395*
ST. BOTOLPH'S SCHOOL	*30, 181, 359*
ST. BOTOLPH'S CLUB	*372*
ST. CHRISTOPHER'S CHURCH	*201, 202*
ST. DUNSTAN'S	*179*
ST. GEORGE'S CHAPEL, WINDSOR	*336*
ST. GEORGE'S HALL	*9, 181*
ST. GUTHLAC'S CHURCH, FISHTOFT	*264*
ST. JAMES'S CHURCH	*18, 60, 61, 364*
ST. JAMES'S BOYS SCHOOL	*313*
ST. JAMES'S CLUB	*41, 61, 201, 372*
ST. JAMES'S DRAMA SOCIETY	*389*
ST. JAMES'S HALL	*332*
ST. JOHN'S AMBULANCE	*206*
ST. JOHN'S SCHOOL	*376, 377*
ST. LEODEGAR'S, WYBERTON	*246*
ST. JAMES'S CHURCH, FREISTON	*248*
ST. MARGARET'S CHURCH, SIBSEY	*278*
ST. MARY'S CHURCH, FRAMPTON	*266*
ST. MICHAEL'S CHURCH (FENNE CHAPEL)	*264, 267*
ST. MICHAEL'S CHURCH, CONINGSBY	*356*
ST. HELENA	*311*
ST. PATRICK'S, DUBLIN	*406*
ST. NICHOLAS'S SCHOOL	*30, 288*
ELIZABETH ST. PAUL	*156*

504

PAGE

WILLIAM ST. PAUL	156, 189
ST. NICHOLAS'S CHURCH	98, 287, 288, 289
ST. PETER AND ST. PAUL'S CHURCH, KIRTON	255, 269
ST. THOMAS THE MARTYR	264
ST. THOMAS'S CHORAL SOCIETY	326
ST. THOMAS'S CHURCH	126
ST. THOMAS'S SCHOOL	85, 288
STAFFORD	136
STAG AND PHEASANT	181
STAGENHOE PARK	274
STAMFORD	230, 240, 261
STANBOW LANE	9, 40, 181, 189
STANFORD UNIVERSITY	216
STANDARD YEAST	341
DAVE STANILAND	53
GEORGE STANILAND	53
MEABURN STANILAND	320, 360, 401, 402
ROBERT WILLIAM STANILAND	86, 313, 319, 320
GEOFFREY STANILAND	320
STANILAND ROAD	113
STANILAND SCHOOL	14, 18, 24, 30, 35, 61, 64, 65, 75, 84, 86, 87, 88, 181,

	182, 183,
	199, 245,
	307, 313,
	364, 379,
	398
STANWELL'S	*64*
J. R. STANWELL	*126*
BARBARA STANWYCK	*376*
STAR AND GARTER	*298*
STATION HOTEL	*49*
STATION PAD	*85,101*
STATION STREET	*84, 157,*
	159, 178,
	182, 187,
	298, 344,
	371
STATIONMASTER SMITH	*14*
RIVER STEEPING	*241*
STELLS LANE	*298*
JANET STEPHENS	*131*
REV. J. STEPHENSON	*87*
PERCY STEVENS	*95, 96*
MRS. STEVENS	*73, 188*
JAMES STEWART	*127*
SIR HERBERT STEWART	*293*
STICKFORD	*262*
STICKNEY	*262, 371*
RENE STIER	*119*
STINSON'S GARAGE	*100, 124*
STOCKTON-ON-TEES	*211*
STOKE NEWINGTON CEMETERY	*286*
ALF STONES	*204, 205*
STONEBRIDGE DRAIN	*278*

BAS STOPPER   *41, 140, 141*

JACK STONE   *49*

ROCKY STONE   *142*

STONEYFORD LODGE HOTEL   *300*

MESSRS. STORR, SINCLAIR & HUGGINS   *302*

GEORGE "BUNTY" STOW   *31*

JOHNNY STOW   *107*

STRAIT BARGATE   *40, 141, 178, 201, 206, 295, 337, 340, 365, 369*

STRATHPEFFER   *168, 170, 173*

ERIC STRAY   *358*

STRINGERS   *165*

A. STROUD   *309*

SUFFRAGETTES   *406*

SUGAR BEET FACTORY   *339*

MARGARET SULLAVAN   *127*

YMA SUMAC   *369*

ANNE SUMMERS   *375*

SUNBEAM   *340*

SUNNINGDALE DRIVE   *202*

SURFLEET   *259*

SUTTERTON   *55, 108, 159, 163, 177, 226, 328, 371*

SUTTERTON DOWDYKE   *397*

LESLIE SUTCLIFFE   *61, 389*

SUTCLIFFE & CO.   *204*

GENTLE SUTTON	*267*
SUTTONS OF READING	*215*
INSPECTOR SWABY	*330*
STRAKER-SQUIRES BUSES	*338*
R.A.F. SWINDERBY	*153*
SWINESHEAD	*177, 180,*
	219, 230,
	270, 400
SWINESHEAD BRIDGE	*299*
SWINESHEAD RAMPER	*197*
SWING BRIDGE	*5, 96*
SWINN'S BREWERY	*80*
DAME SARAH SWIFT	*269*
SWAFFHAM	*347*
SWIMMING BATHS	*327, 396*
SWITZERLAND	*305*
SYRIA	*305*
TASMANIA	*236, 335*
TATTERSHALL	*254, 329,*
	357
TATTERSHALL CASTLE	*224, 229,*
	262
TATTERSHALL'S COLLEGE	*251*
TATTERSHALL ROAD	*77, 112,*
	124, 162,
	178, 187,
	298
JOHN TAVENER	*251*
JOHN TAVERNER	*251*
TAWNEY STREET	*13, 101*
BARBARA TAYLOR	*51, 353*
FAN TAYLOR	*373*

JOCELYN TAYLOR	*51, 353*
JOHN (JIT) TAYLOR	*123, 192,*
	210
KEN TAYLOR	*182*
MARGARET TAYLOR	*51, 353*
PETER TAYLOR	*68*
RICHARD "QUACK" TAYLOR	*68*
GODFREY TEARLE	*5*
BRIAN TEBBS	*186, 191*
HILDA TEBBS	*186, 189,*
	191
JACK TEBBS	*66*
MR. TEBBS	*113*
TEBBUTT'S SHOP	*369*
BAS TEFT	*355*
SHIRLEY TEMPLE	*129*
ALFRED, LORD TENNYSON	*240, 318*
TERRITORIALS	*400*
RIVER THAMES	*228*
MARGARET THATCHER	*411*
THAXTED	*349*
C. R. THEOBALD	*125*
THIEPVAL	*333*
FRANCIS THIRKILL	*274*
THIRKILL, SON & ROGERS	*274*
REV. STEPHEN S. THISTLEWOOD	*322, 326*
BILLY THOMAS	*80*
MISS. THOMAS	*79*
MISS. ESME THOMAS	*343*
G. W. THOMAS	*275, 341*
MRS. THOMAS	*292*
FRANK THOMPSON	*167*

PISHEY THOMPSON	240, 252, 267, 268, 275, 276
RONNIE THOMPSON	66
ORD. SEAMAN WILLIAM THOMPSON	280
THOMPSON'S MILL	100
MRS. THOMPSON	46
MAYOR J. THORNS	312
THORN'S CIGAR FACTORY	307
THOROLD STREET	101
THORPE	157
THORPE BRIDGE	143
LOUIE THORPE (GINNY BOTTLES)	108
THREADNEEDLE STREET	338, 372
THREEKINGHAM	246
THREE TUNS INN	262
JEFF THURLBY	69
THOMAS THURLOW	274
E. V. TIDMARSH	376
TIGER MOTHS	388
JOHN TILLING	39, 193
BILLY TIMBY	189
ROSE TIMBY	189
TICKOPRESS LIMITED	222
THE TIMES	319
TIN TABERNACLE	289
TILSON	234
BASIL TINKLER	237
RAY TINKLER	364, 398
TIVOLI THEATRE, HULL	351
TODMORDEN	153
GEORGE TOMLINSON	377
ROY TOMLINSON	205

TOMMY	*180*
E. TONGE	*282*
"TUSKER" TONKS	*27*
HARRY TOOLEY	*33*
TORONTO	*162*
TORQUAY	*192*
VISCOUNT TORRINGTON	*242*
TOTTENHAM HOTSPUR	*398*
BATTLE OF TOULOUSE	*310*
TOWER OF LONDON	*259*
TOWER ROAD	*126*
TOWER ROAD SCHOOL	*30, 313*
TOWER STREET	*178, 192, 371*
ARTHUR TOWLE	*278, 350*
DONALD TOWLE	*351*
MARYLYN TOWLE	*351*
SUZANNE TOWLE	*351*
KATHERINE TOWLE	*351*
ALISON TOWLE	*351*
MARGARET TOWLE	*351*
KATHERINE CHARLOTTE (KATIE)	*351*
TOBY TOWLE	*10*
TOWN BRIDGE	*165*
TOWN CLERK	*274*
BATTLE OF TRAFALGAR	*279, 280*
TRAFALGAR PLACE	*120*
TRADER DRAIN	*278*
TRADER MILL	*278*
TRADES FAIR	*338*
LORD TRENT	*99*
TRENT BRIDGE	*137*
SARAH ANN TREDENICK	*158*

RIVER TRENT	225
TRIMOUNTAIN HILLS	229
TRINITY COLLEGE, CAMBRIDGE	231
TRINITY STREET	12, 285, 286, 307, 308
TOMMY TRINDER	10
TROCADERO	54, 363
TROOPS	154
JANET TROOPS	89, 199
JOE TROUGH	48
FRED TRUEMAN	144, 387
GEORGE TRUEMAN	55, 177
TRUSTEE SAVINGS BANK	376
ROGER TUDDENHAM	167
CONEY TUNNARD	266
JOHN TUNNARD	267
THOMAS TUNNARD	267
TUNNARD BROTHERS	333
TUNNARD STREET	324
T.U.C.	409
JOHN TURNER	312
TEDDY TURNER	92
TUDOR RESTAURANT	365, 376
"TILLY" TURPIN	26, 290
TUVALU	251
G. P. TUXFORD	401
WEDD TUXFORD	283
WESTON TUXFORD	273
WILLIAM TUXFORD	283
WILLIAM WED TUXFORD	282, 283
GEORGE TWIDDY	16, 57, 322

A. TWIDDY	*126*
TYTTON	*246*
TYTTON HALL	*246*
TYTTON LANE EAST	*27*
RON UNDERWOOD	*149*
W. T. UNDERWOOD LIMITED	*339*
UNICORN FOOTBALL CLUB	*355*
UNICORN INN	*124, 247*
UNION JACK CLUB	*156*
UNIONIST ASSOCIATION	*334, 408*
UNITED BUS COMPANY	*339*
UNITED SOCIAL CLUB	*41, 201, 371, 372*
UNIVERSITY OF CALIFORNIA	*37*
BILLY UPSALL	*187*
GORDON UPSALL	*187, 198*
UPSALL'S BOAT HOUSE	*398*
U.S.A.	*44, 215, 318*
J. W. C. USHER	*210*
PETER USTINOV	*5*
DR. G. R. USMAR	*125, 179*
UTTOXETER	*378*
MARTIN VALE	*376*
CYRIL VALENTINE	*55, 56, 322, 391, 411, 412*
EMILY VALENTINE	*56, 322*
E. M. VALENTINE, FRUITERER	*376*
DICKIE VALENTINE	*62*
F. J. VAN DEN BERG	*409*

VAN SMIRREN'S FACTORY	*116, 119, 120, 132*
JAN VAN SMIRREN	*118*
ROBERT VAN SMIRREN	*118*
MR. VARCOE	*202*
MARTIN VARCOE	*389*
VAUXHALL FOOTBRIDGE	*330*
BRUCE VEAL	*57, 322*
LAURIE VEALE	*205, 383*
V. E. DAY	*4*
NELLIE VENTERS	*130*
TERRY VENTERS	*41, 370*
MR. VERE	*178*
PHYLLIS VICKERS	*10, 72*
REG VICKERS	*72*
VICTORIA CROSS	*309, 332, 333, 334*
VICTORIA FALLS	*380*
VICTORIA PALACE	*95*
VICTORIA INN	*181*
VICTORIA, PRINCESS ROYAL	*303*
HMS VICTORY	*280*
THE VINE INN	*4*
MRS. B. A. VINTER	*195, 196*
REG VINTER	*177, 195, 197*
VIRGINIA	*225, 228*
VIRGINIAN COMPANY	*226*
WILLIAM VOLLANS	*287*
V1 FLYING BOMBS	*355*
V2 ROCKETS	*355*

LESLIE WADDAMS	*25, 388*
ANN WAGSTAFF	*202*
WAINFLEET	*241, 262,*
	316
WAINFLEET ROAD	*283*
WAINFLEET ST. MARYS	*177*
NIGEL WAINWRIGHT	*361*
WAKEFIELD	*301*
REG WAKEFIELD	*31*
ANTON WALBROOK	*11*
WALES	*380*
WALDEN'S SWEET SHOP	*181*
A. ANDERSON WALKER	*125*
A. WALKER	*126, 376*
BERNARD EYRE WALKER	*342*
FREDDY WALKER	*69, 166*
JOHNNY WALKER	*217*
ROBERT WALKER	*129*
WALKER'S IRONMONGERS	*130*
WALMSLEY'S SHOP	*107*
WALNUT TREE WALK	*209, 290*
MRS. WALLACE	*63*
JANET WALTERS	*411*
WALSALL	*137*
WALTON-ON-THAMES	*117*
WALTHAMSTOW	*338*
WANTAGE	*121*
RAOUL WALSH	*129*
WAR MEMORIAL	*400*
FRANK WARD	*236, 363,*
	364
GEORGE WARD	*271*
JIMMY WARD	*90, 322,*

SARA WARD	117
"DONKEY" WARREN	15
MRS WARRENER	117
ABLE SEAMAN JOHN WARRUNDALE	280
DOREEN WARSAP	119
IRENE WARSAP	119
MARGARET WARSAP	119
WARSAP'S YARD	161
WASHINGTON	4, 275
JAMES WATERFIELD	253
BATTLE OF WATERLOO	214, 310
WATERSIDE NORTH, LINCOLN	330
TONY WATSON	132
JESSIE WATLING	61
EILEEN WATTS	85
MARLEEN WATTS	85
REV. THOMAS WAUGH	290
WAVERLEY CLUB	41, 201, 372
WAVERLEY STATION	174
WAVENEY CLUB	371
JOHN WAYNE	19, 83
WEAVER TO WEARER	369
MISS, MARY WEBB	343
COL. ARCHIBALD G. WEIGALL	334
FRANK WELBERRY	12
KEN WELBERRY	57
FRED WELBOURNE	389
THOMAS WELBY	260
WELBY	213
WELLINGTON	55, 365
ELIZABETH BROWN WELLS	285
H. G. WELLS	336

W. WELLS & SON — *123*
WELLS, BAKERS — *177, 341*
WEMBLEY — *382, 383, 398*
JOHN WESLEY — *209, 211, 242, 290*
SUSANNA WESLEY — *211*
WESLEY HOUSE, CAMBRIDGE — *210*
WESLEYAN CHURCH — *101*
WESLEYAN SCHOOL — *311, 313*
WEST BROMPTON CEMETERY — *319*
WEST BROMWICH ALBION — *397, 399*
WEST FEN — *241*
WEST END — *349, 390*
WEST SKIRBECK HOUSE — *396*
WEST INDIES — *230, 253, 283*
WEST STREET — *10, 54, 63, 93, 100, 120, 130, 178, 186, 192, 284, 296, 307, 323, 329, 340, 347, 351, 366, 391*
AUBREY WEST — *67*
JACK WEST — *118*
TERRY WEST — *9, 389*
MR. WEST OF SURBITON — *320*
MR. WEST, BAKER — *177*
WESTFIELD AVENUE — *331, 383*

	PAGE
BILL WESTKIN	15
DICK WESTLAND	42,. 51, 52, 353
MR. WESTLAND	234
WESTON, IRONMONGER	226
WESTON-SUPER-MARE	192
WESTMINSTER	334
MAE WEST	352
LAVINIA WHALLEY	42, 389
WHEATLEY	96
"FRITZ" WHEELER	26
MR. WHEELER	314
ALBERT WHELAN	350
DEREK WHELBOURN	40, 68, 123, 216
WHITE BRIDGES	118, 162
WHITE HORSE INN	64, 347, 352
WHITE HORSE LANE	77, 96, 118, 165, 166, 167, 340
THE WHITE HART	55, 181, 187, 249
WHITE HOUSE CLUB	371
WHITE LOAF HALL	247
WHITE TOMPKINS	187
COLONEL WHITE	172
FRANCIS THIRKILL WHITE	275
GEORGE WHITE	181
GEORGE RIVERS BLANCO WHITE	336, 408, 409
HENRY WHITE	279

KATHLEEN WHITE	92
PERCY WHITE	71, 92
WILLIAM WHITE (WHITE'S DIRECTORY)	278, 293, 320
EDWARD WHITE'S GARAGE	162
GEORGE WHITEHEAD	396
BILLIE WHITELAW	393
JIM WHITEMAN	68, 84, 213
MAYOR WHITING	234
JOHN WHITING	256
REV. SAMUEL WHITING	233, 256
WHITECHAPEL	287
WHITEHALL	362
SIR FRANK WHITTLE	141, 388
WHITTLE	154
WHITTLESEY	173
WHITTLE'S SHOE LACE FACTORY	181
BEN WHYERS	81, 92
IVY WHYERS	81, 216
PETER WHYERS	216
WALTER WHYERS	81, 91, 92, 223, 224
WIDE BARGATE	13, 77, 124, 125, 162, 178, 194, 281, 337, 341, 365, 400
REG WILCOCK	119
HORACE WILDEE	286
JOE WILDMAN	177

WILDMORE FEN	241
EDWARD WILFORD	272
H. C. WILKINSON	22
MRS. WILKINSON	24
MARY WILKINSON	130
JOHN WILKS	282
WILK'S MILL	282
WILLIAM WILKINSON	279
WILLER & RILEY	31, 187
A. J. WILLARD	389
WILLIAM THE CONQUEROR	246
HUGH WILLIAMS	5
MR. WILLIAMS	125
BOBBY WILLIAMSON	182
RALPH WILLIAM'S SHOP	74
J. D. WILLIAMSON	412
WILLIAMSON'S SHOP	180
WILLOUGHBY	228
WILLOUGHBY OF PARHAM	259, 261, 262
WILLOUGHBY ROAD	155
DR. CARUS WILSON	395
SIR CHARLES WILSON	293
HAROLD WILSON	412
SIR ROBERT WILSON	310
E. WILSON, SWAFFHAM	347
GEORGE WILSON	199
ROBB WILTON	6, 350
WIMELEUX	358
JOHN WINCOB	226
WINDSOR	336
RICHARD PATTINSON WINFREY	336
SIR RICHARD WINFREY	336, 408

LADY WINFREY	*336*
BATTLE OF WINCEBY	*262*
TONY WINN	*205*
WINTHORPE OLYMPIC	*39*
JOHN WINTHROP	*229, 230, 232, 233, 256*
CHARLES HENRY WING	*319*
SHELLY WINTERS	*393*
COLONEL ORDE WINGATE	*358*
WISBECH	*91, 192, 202, 383*
RIVER WITHAM	*223, 224, 240, 243, 279, 296, 313, 329, 398*
WITHAM BANK	*100, 303*
WITHAM MARSH SCHOOL	*343*
WITHAM SAILING CLUB	*396*
WITHAM TAVERN	*270*
WITHAM TOWN	*187, 270*
WITHERNSEA	*148*
GOOGIE WITHERS	*5*
WOAD FARM	*277, 353, 377*
WOOD GREEN	*333*
WOODHALL SPA	*143*
WOODLANDS	*179*
LES WOODMAN	*120*
CHRIS WOODS	*197*
RAY WOODS	*35, 106*

	PAGE
ALAN WOODTHORPE	40, 68, 123
KEN WOODTHORPE	62, 78, 205
ROY WOODTHORPE	62, 78, 199, 205, 364
WOODVILLE ROAD	36, 76, 80, 100, 113, 116, 162, 191, 265, 280, 380, 383
REV. WOOLL	231
MONTY WOOLLEY	129
WOOLWORTHS	267, 366, 369
LORD WOLSELEY	293
CARDINAL WOLSEY	251
WORMGATE	42, 194, 359
GLADYS WORTLEY	187, 188
H.A.S. WORTLEY	100
WRAGBY	275
WRANGLE	22, 35, 98, 177, 243, 252, 361
JOHN HENRY WRAY	311, 312
SAM WRAY	25
CAPTAIN WRIGHT	310
CHARLES (CHUCK) WRIGHT	67, 133, 136, 381
CHARLES WRIGHT	133, 177